A Celebration of Poets

Great Lakes
Grades 4-12
Spring 2011

A CELEBRATION OF POETS
GREAT LAKES
GRADES 4-12
SPRING 2011

AN ANTHOLOGY COMPILED BY CREATIVE COMMUNICATION, INC.

Published by:

PO BOX 303 • SMITHFIELD, UTAH 84335
TEL. 435-713-4411 • WWW.POETICPOWER.COM

Authors are responsible for the originality of the writing submitted.

All rights reserved. No part of this book may be reproduced or transmitted in any form or by any means, electronic or mechanical without written permission of the author and publisher.

Copyright © 2011 by Creative Communication, Inc.
Printed in the United States of America

ISBN: 978-1-60050-446-4

FOREWORD

Dear Reader:

Hope. In today's negatively laced headlines, hope seems to be lost to the back pages. Amid the struggles of the world with the economy, civil unrest, and just everyday living, hope seems to be waning. However, our youth provide a bright spark. They are not weighed down with the world on their shoulders. In reading the writing of today's youth, there is an optimistic light that shines through. A light that tells the story of love for friends and family. The story of spring emerging and creating a new green world. A story that does have the trials of a student's life, but also the joys of learning and moving past them. These students are aware of the problems of the world, but are not consumed with them. They still take the time to enjoy and write about the simple pleasures in life.

Each year as we publish the best student writing, I am amazed at the stories that are told, the feelings that are felt, and the lives that are shared with us through the safety of words. We are pleased to again offer this book as a testament of the hope these students have.

We have been working with student writers for over 18 years. Each year, we have students and teachers who take the time to write to us telling us of the hope that we share in providing our contests and books. We are glad that we are here to provide a creative outlet and give these students a spark to motivate their writing.

These students have taken the time to give a bit of themselves. We invite you to read what they have shared.

Sincerely,

Thomas Worthen, Ph.D.
Editor
Creative Communication

WRITING CONTESTS!

Enter our next POETRY contest!

Enter our next ESSAY contest!

Why should I enter?
Win prizes and get published! Each year thousands of dollars in prizes are awarded throughout North America. The top writers in each division receive a monetary award and a free book that includes their published poem or essay. Entries of merit are also selected to be published in our anthology.

Who may enter?
There are four divisions in the poetry contest. The poetry divisions are grades K-3, 4-6, 7-9, and 10-12. There are three divisions in the essay contest. The essay divisions are grades 3-6, 7-9, and 10-12.

What is needed to enter the contest?
To enter the poetry contest send in one original poem, 21 lines or less. To enter the essay contest send in one original non-fiction essay, 250 words or less, on any topic. Please submit each poem and essay with a title, and the following information clearly printed: the writer's name, current grade, home address (optional), school name, school address, teacher's name and teacher's email address (optional). Contact information will only be used to provide information about the contest. For complete contest information go to www.poeticpower.com.

How do I enter?

Enter a poem online at:
www.poeticpower.com
or
Mail your poem to:
   Poetry Contest
   PO Box 303
   Smithfield UT 84335

Enter an essay online at:
www.poeticpower.com
or
Mail your essay to:
   Essay Contest
   PO Box 303
   Smithfield UT 84335

When is the deadline?
Poetry contest deadlines are December 6th, April 12th and August 15th. Essay contest deadlines are October 18th, February 15th, and July 18th. Students can enter one poem and one essay for each spring, summer, and fall contest deadline.

Are there benefits for my school?
Yes. We award $12,500 each year in grants to help with Language Arts programs. Schools qualify to apply for a grant by having 15 or more accepted entries.

Are there benefits for my teacher?
Yes. Teachers with five or more students published receive a free anthology that includes their students' writing.

For more information please go to our website at **www.poeticpower.com**, email us at editor@poeticpower.com or call 435-713-4411.

TABLE OF CONTENTS

POETIC ACHIEVEMENT HONOR SCHOOLS   1

LANGUAGE ARTS GRANT RECIPIENTS   7

GRADES 10-11-12 HIGH MERIT POEMS   9

GRADES 7-8-9 HIGH MERIT POEMS 59

GRADES 4-5-6 HIGH MERIT POEMS 157

INDEX 251

STATES INCLUDED IN THIS EDITION:

INDIANA
MICHIGAN

Spring 2011 Poetic Achievement Honor Schools

Teachers who had fifteen or more poets accepted to be published

The following schools are recognized as receiving a "Poetic Achievement Award." This award is given to schools who have a large number of entries of which over fifty percent are accepted for publication. With hundreds of schools entering our contest, only a small percent of these schools are honored with this award. The purpose of this award is to recognize schools with excellent Language Arts programs. This award qualifies these schools to receive a complimentary copy of this anthology. In addition, these schools are eligible to apply for a Creative Communication Language Arts Grant. Grants of two hundred and fifty dollars each are awarded to further develop writing in our schools.

Allegan High School
Allegan, MI
Sarah Cooper
Nancy Hascall*
Jane Kiel

Assumption School
Belmont, MI
Hazel Bolin*
Katie Leeder

Bailey School
Hillsdale, MI
Mary Hamaty*

Benton Central Jr/Sr High School
Oxford, IN
Sandy Herre*

Clarkston High School
Clarkston, MI
Nancy Brown*
Ryan Eisele
Kathy Kuehn*
Laura Mahler
Richard Porritt

Covington Middle School
Covington, IN
Fawn Cox*

Crestwood Elementary School
Rockford, MI
Tracy Babcock*
Jennifer Bakita*

Culver Community Middle School
Culver, IN
Saundra Bailey*

DeKalb High School
Waterloo, IN
Gay Kirkton*

Detroit Academy of Arts & Sciences - Medbury Campus
Detroit, MI
Johnathan L. Carter*
Ms. L. Kinchloe

Detroit Country Day Middle School
Beverly Hills, MI
Carla Chennault

A Celebration of Poets – Great Lakes Grades 4-12 Spring 2011

Detroit Country Day Middle School (cont.)
Beverly Hills, MI
    Victoria Chiakmakis
    Charles Duggan
    Cheryl Duggan*
    Christina Salamon
    Stephanie Trautman

Dibble Elementary School
Jackson, MI
    Pat Elsey*

Dodson Elementary School
Canton, MI
    Karen Christensen*
    Leslie Corgan*
    Jill Dean*
    Bonnie Goodrich*
    Ms. Grahl
    Carol Greene
    Kimberly Groh
    Terri Kay*
    Mary Koltunchik*
    Shelley Lloyd
    Paula Mallia*
    Kris McLaughlin*
    Julie Smith*
    Kim Sparks
    Cathy Tyler*

Eagle Creek Academy
Oakland, MI
    Jean Ciotti
    Lindy Cubba
    Amie Gamache
    Michelle Trenta

East Jay Middle School
Portland, IN
    Deborah Kilander*

Floyd Ebeling Elementary School
Macomb, MI
    Jacquelyn Barker
    Lisa Bruce*
    Michele Fernandes

Floyd Ebeling Elementary School (cont.)
Macomb, MI
    Miss Nekoogar
    Robin Pizzo

Fowlerville Jr High School
Fowlerville, MI
    Katie Bowling*

Green Acres School
Montgomery, IN
    Leah Ruth Wagler*

Hally Magnet Middle School
Detroit, MI
    Karen Careathers*

Hampton Elementary School
Rochester Hills, MI
    Todd Doughty
    Jill Freels*
    Monica McCauley
    Jennifer Veach*

Hendry Park Elementary School
Angola, IN
    Mrs. Hulting
    Megan McDermid
    Tamara Steffel

Holy Name School
Escanaba, MI
    Cheryl Proksch*

James R Watson Elementary School
Auburn, IN
    Diane Dean*
    Denise Hall*
    Candace Post*
    Lisa Pyck*
    Susie Samuelson
    Pam Warner*

Joan Martin Elementary School
Hobart, IN
    Carrie Galka*

Poetic Achievement Honor Schools

Kingsway Christian School
    Avon, IN
        Heidi Conger*

Knox Community Middle School
    Knox, IN
        Kathleen Jerrell*

Lenawee Christian School
    Adrian, MI
        Angela Smelser*

Linton-Stockton Elementary School
    Linton, IN
        Kelly Lannan*
        Pam Puckett*

Manistee Middle School
    Manistee, MI
        Linda Coyle*
        Mary Hunter*

Mentone Elementary School
    Mentone, IN
        LeeAnn Rock
        Pam Sellers*
        Janie Shriver

Mercy High School
    Farmington Hills, MI
        Jan Mordenski*

Morgan Elementary School
    Palmyra, IN
        Laurie M. Grubb*

North Muskegon Elementary School
    North Muskegon, MI
        Jennifer Bouman
        Thomas Delong
        Ronda Pek

Northern Heights Elementary School
    Columbia City, IN
        Mr. Ferrell*
        Todd Geiger*
        Michelle Simmons*

Northview High School
    Grand Rapids, MI
        Sheridan Steelman*
        Audra Whetstone*

Oak Hill Jr High School
    Converse, IN
        Sherry Furnish*

Old Redford Academy - Elementary
    Detroit, MI
        Kendra Catanzarite
        Mrs. McFadden
        Ms. McPherson
        Ms. Perrigan
        Sabrina Ponder
        Mrs. Veitch
        Ms. Webb

Onsted High School
    Onsted, MI
        Michelle A. McLemore*

Pendleton Elementary/Intermediate School
    Pendleton, IN
        Margo Bill*

Perry Central Elementary School
    Leopold, IN
        Carmen Fischer*
        Rebecca Hubert*
        Angela Shelby

Perry Middle School
    Perry, MI
        Mrs. Hewitt*
        Sharon Johnson*

Posen Consolidated High School
    Posen, MI
        Mary Misiak*

Royal Oak Middle School
    Royal Oak, MI
        Mr. Cusenza
        Ms. Peters
        Tina Weathers*

Ruth Murdoch Elementary School
Berrien Springs, MI
Philip E. Giddings*

Sashabaw Middle School
Clarkston, MI
Anne Ortel*

South Bogard School
Montgomery, IN
Ruth Ann Graber
Justin Lewis Knepp*

South Spencer Middle School
Rockport, IN
Pam Lindsey*

St Barnabas School
Indianapolis, IN
Connie Schmidt*

St Bartholomew School
Columbus, IN
Susan McCormick*
Shannon Proctor

St Hugo of the Hills School
Bloomfield Hills, MI
Nancy Slifka*

St John Lutheran School
Fraser, MI
Susan Machemer*

St John the Evangelist School
Saint John, IN
Connie Hass*

St Mary Catholic Central High School
Monroe, MI
Amy Blanchette*

St Simon the Apostle School
Indianapolis, IN
Marie Povlinski*

Stanley Clark School
South Bend, IN
Doris E. Smith*
Gayla Vukcevich

Star International Academy
Dearborn Heights, MI
Mr. Abdullah
Amy Gullekson
Kimberly Miller
Ms. Smith
Lisa Stranyak*

Staunton Elementary School
Brazil, IN
Denise Brush*

Troy High School
Troy, MI
Meagan Foster
Elizabeth Gumbis
Jan Weil

Wayne Gray Elementary School
Addison, MI
Kathy McClure*

West Hills Middle School
West Bloomfield, MI
Mark Honeyman*

West Middle School
Plymouth, MI
Nicole Lerg*

West Side Middle School
Elkhart, IN
Mike Cebra
Mr. Gravender
Shanna Lamberton*
Mrs. Torres

Whitehall Middle School
Whitehall, MI
Craig Christensen
Mary Dykstra*

Wylie E Groves High School
Beverly Hills, MI
John Rutherford*

Language Arts Grant Recipients 2010-2011

After receiving a "Poetic Achievement Award" schools are encouraged to apply for a Creative Communication Language Arts Grant. The following is a list of schools who received a two hundred and fifty dollar grant for the 2010-2011 school year.

Adolph Schreiber Hebrew Academy, Monsey, NY
August Boeger Middle School, San Jose, CA
Bedford Road School, Pleasantville, NY
Benton Central Jr/Sr High School, Oxford, IN
Birchwood School, Cleveland, OH
Blue Ball Elementary School, Blue Ball, PA
Bonneville High School, Idaho Falls, ID
Cedar Ridge High School, Newark, AR
Corpus Christi School, San Francisco, CA
Crestwood Elementary School, Rockford, MI
Dodson Elementary School, Canton, MI
Dr Howard K Conley Elementary School, Chandler, AZ
Eastport Elementary School, Eastport, ME
Emmanuel-St Michael Lutheran School, Fort Wayne, IN
Fannin County Middle School, Blue Ridge, GA
Fort Recovery Elementary School, Fort Recovery, OH
Frank Ohl Intermediate School, Youngstown, OH
Frenship Middle School, Wolfforth, TX
Gateway Pointe Elementary School, Gilbert, AZ
Greencastle-Antrim Middle School, Greencastle, PA
Greenville High School, Greenville, AL
Hancock County High School, Sneedville, TN
Holy Child Academy, Drexel Hill, PA
Holy Cross High School, Delran, NJ
Holy Family Catholic School, Granite City, IL
Interboro GATE Program, Prospect Park, PA
John E Riley Elementary School, South Plainfield, NJ
Joseph M Simas Elementary School, Hanford, CA
Lee A Tolbert Community Academy, Kansas City, MO
Malvern Middle School, Malvern, OH
Merritt Central Elementary School, Merritt, BC
Metcalf School, Exeter, RI
Norfolk Christian Middle School, Norfolk, VA

Language Arts Grant Winners cont.

Pioneer Career & Technology Center, Shelby, OH
Providence Hall, Herriman, UT
Ramsay School, Ramsay, MT
Reuben Johnson Elementary School, McKinney, TX
Round Lake High School, Round Lake, MN
Sacred Heart School, Oxford, PA
Selwyn College Preparatory School, Denton, TX
Shadowlawn Elementary School, Green Cove Springs, FL
St Elizabeth Catholic School, Rockville, MD
St Lorenz Lutheran School, Frankenmuth, MI
The Oakridge School, Arlington, TX
Tomlin Middle School, Plant City, FL
Vista Fundamental School, Simi Valley, CA
Walsh Elementary School, Walsh, CO
Washington County Union School, Roper, NC
Woodland Intermediate School, Gurnee, IL
Woodward Granger High School, Woodward, IA

Grades 10-11-12 Top Ten Winners

List of Top Ten Winners for Grades 10-12; listed alphabetically

Sarah Bauer, Grade 10
Valley Christian High School, CA

Katie Borne, Grade 10
Commonwealth Connections Academy, PA

Jake Fortner, Grade 10
Jennings County High School, IN

Linda Kou, Grade 11
Collège catholique Franco-Ouest, ON

Kiki Lawson, Grade 12
Crosstimbers Academy, TX

Nolan Mackey, Grade 11
Rock Hill High School, SC

Alison Malee, Grade 11
Loyalsock Township High School, PA

Rachel McDaniel, Grade 12
Evangelistic Temple School, OK

Lauren Wingenroth, Grade 12
First Flight High School, NC

Maggie Zhang, Grade 11
Fayetteville-Manlius High School, NY

All Top Ten Poems can be read at www.poeticpower.com

Note: The Top Ten poems were finalized through an online voting system. Creative Communication's judges first picked out the top poems. These poems were then posted online. The final step involved thousands of students and teachers who registered as the online judges and voted for the Top Ten poems. We hope you enjoy these selections.

A Classic Love Story

Writing a story, now that's my thing.
Four sentences on paper is just plain boring.
The rhyming's not clever, the words make no sense.
I like my stories with a twist in the end.

People may love this, but I certainly do not.
I'm out of my element without any characters or plot.
A classic love story, with a happy ending.
I want that much more than this poem I'm sending.

With poetry I struggle to find what to say
With my book the words flow endlessly all day.
And essay or poem, that's surely unfair,
Add a writing contest to the list if you dare.

Celeste Crowell, Grade 10
John Adams High School, IN

What Is Love?

Love's true meaning is lost in modern day.
The word is so commonly tossed around,
And the lack of meaning brings some to say
That love is something that cannot be found.
Is love the cold emptiness here tonight,
When she is not with me, here by my side?
Or is it the warmth when I hold her tight,
And I feel her breath and heartbeat inside?
No, none of these can describe what love is.
Far too complex, but simple in nature.
You know when it's there. 'Tis the warming kiss
Of the sun over a brand new future.
    I pray that all may feel this warming bliss.
    For life 'thout love is the sun 'thout its kiss.

Erik Donarski, Grade 11
St Joseph High School, MI

Loving You

If loving you is so wrong
Then why does kissing you feel so right

I find my self wishing I was with you
Here I sit all alone again

Everyone telling me it's so wrong
I'm watching my back tryin' not to get burnt

I have run away hidden inside my feelings
Lost forever more no more shying away no more

Tear down my walls come inside
make me whole show me how to live

Adam Mangold, Grade 12
Concord Montessori & Community School, MI

Forgive Me

I acknowledge that I have made mistakes
I pray that I haven't caused you any pain
If you'd forgive me, I'd do what it takes
To end your pain; make it all go away
I'd go the distance and I'd find a way
To make it all better; make it all right
If you'd forgive me, we could be okay
I'd move from the dark and toward the light
I am sorry for the mistakes I've made
But now I am changing myself for good
Your forgiveness sets me free every day
And I thank you, as I forever should
These eyes were once blind, but now they can see
Thank you for this peace you have given to me

Sarah Styma, Grade 12
Posen Consolidated High School, MI

Graduation

A bright new beginning is soon to come
The months fly by in a blink of an eye
Mixed emotions and excitement for some
Graduation will run your money dry
Parties are fun and friends will come and go
Memories made and always remembered
It's time to go out to the world and show
That I grew up and I should be honored
I'll miss my teachers and friends from high school
Not the homework and projects that took time
Walking around school and thinking we're cool
This is it and it is our time to shine
I'm going to miss the times I had here
But I'm taking on the world without fear

Lindsay Ponik, Grade 12
Posen Consolidated High School, MI

Bitter Cold

The bitter cold against your skin
Hits you right when you walk in
People watch from the glass
But on the ice you've got to think fast
A guy in the net and five on five
Blades so sharp they cut light knives
With a drop of the puck, and time counting down
They're off to the win before the buzzer sounds
Slap shots, hat tricks, and assisting too
Are idealistic ways to make each move
Back and forth, the players glide
Skating around as ice shards fly
Baseball, soccer, or climbing the Rockies,
I don't know about you, but my sport is hockey.

Devan Rucker, Grade 12
St Mary Catholic Central High School, MI

High Merit Poems – Grades 10, 11, and 12

Tides of Time

The gentle tide halts,
As the child plucks gems
Nestled in the shore.

Her eyes
Like droplets of fresh dew ripe with promise.
Reflecting wonders of the Earth —
An ocean soaked in radiance,
Golden streaks weaved into the innocent sky,
As a gentle breeze
Cradles her laughter to all depths.

Now those eyes
Are no longer brilliant
But tainted by time.

But the resounding laughter echoes
As the tide recedes,
Exposing the treasures for one second,
Before renewing the shore
Once more.

Aoxue Tang, Grade 11
Pioneer High School, MI

A Memory Painted on a Porcelain Skyline

On a brightly colored Sunday morning,
A voice wakes the dreams of a silent coast
Under the constellation's under lacing;
Across the clouds is the sound of a ghost.

Hiding underneath the waves of cold sheets,
Trapped inside a melody that she sings.
Even if the stars beckoned, would you leave?
Sing me to sleep as we fall in the sea.

But even if you were sick, I'd still stay
Under the broken bones falling down
And your eyes, still shining to this day,
Would wake me up to hear your melodic sound.

Sleeping, only waiting for the choice
To awaken to the sound of your voice.

Scott Wiley, Grade 11
Stoney Creek High School, MI

The Image of a Crystal Tear

When I look at the rain I think of my tears
The tears I see when I wake up from this dream
The tears I shed because this dream is not real
The tears that show the cracking of my heart
   Dodging left and right repeatingly
The tears that can show, but cannot explain
   That I would wait my whole life for you
   Even if my heart ended up with a stain.

Savannah Anderson, Grade 10
Pennfield Sr High School, MI

The Love of a Mother

Young baby lost and confused as a
Floating cloud lost in the sky.
Relying only on her
Mother,
Caretaker,
Parent,
Feeding her baby delicious moist apple sauce.
Hopeless father never doing anything right,
Feeling of abandonment as he walks away ignoring the
Cries of the baby, doing nothing but lazing
Around drinking beer,
Eating chips,
Watching football.
Young baby taken away from her
Helpless and useless father,
Leaving with her mother never
Relying on no one, working hard in
Order for her and her baby
To survive, thrive,
Succeed.

Chelsie Blevins, Grade 12
Clarkston High School, MI

A Soldier's Wish

   Wave after wave the enemies poured in.
Knowing they were out numbered the soldiers fought to the end.
   A miracle was far from their minds.
Only to turn and see the last wave moving in from behind.
   Each one came together ready to die fighting.
With the raise of their weapons they began striking.
   All of the soldiers knew the battle was done.
But none of the soldiers would drop their guns.
   Every soldier was praying to God even though it was hopeless.
They would be talking to him in just a few moments.
   There's only one thing on their minds that they can't shift.
It's something that every last soldier has ever wished.
   As the enemies raised their guns and shot at their prey.
Every last soldier had gotten blown away.
   What was this wish that they left alone?
This wish is simple they just want to come home.

John Bastin, Grade 10
Thomas A Edison Jr/Sr High School, IN

Camera

She is a camera, capturing the moment
in a blink of an eye.
Every image is remembered until it gets lost in thought.
Shoved in empty boxes in the attic of her mind,
the once brilliant pictures fade, darken, blur;
fragments of some seem to have gone missing.
Still, the most vivid memories remain.
But where once the glossy lens saw only youthful happiness,
it has lost its sharp focus. Now, in old age,
it sees only a dusty loneliness, a forgotten memoir.

Dana Fouchia, Grade 12
Mercy High School, MI

Ode to Basketball

Ode to basketball, and all of its amazement.
From the ground shaking dunks,
To the jaw dropping blocked shots,
Basketball never fails to amaze.
Ode to basketball, and its shocking moments.
From the Cinderella teams winning it all,
To the powerhouses that suddenly fall,
Basketball will reveal it all.
Ode to basketball, and the heartbreak it can bring.
From the close games you might lose,
To the blowouts you are on the losing end of,
This game can bring disappointment.
Ode to basketball, and the happiness it brings.
When you win that final game,
There is no such thing as pain.
It works as a pain killer for the night.
A wise man once said before,
Basketball is the game that makes you soar.
I love this game we call basketball.
It is the game I long for.
Ode to basketball

Seth Gonyea, Grade 12
St Mary Catholic Central High School, MI

Excuses, Excuses

I sit in class,
trying not to hear,
the sounds all around me.
I need to listen to the teacher.
It does not matter,
there's nothing I can do,
they will not stop.
I need to hear the teacher.
But it's all I can hear —
The clock ticks.
The fly buzzes.
The pen clicks.
Teacher?!?!
The foot taps.
The watch beeps.
The water splashes.
Teacher?!?!
The book bangs.
The elbow bonks.
The students chomp, moan, murmur, hiccup, whine, blab…
…No wonder I'm failing this class.

Carlee Zimmerman, Grade 11
Northview High School, MI

Favorite Places to Go

My Tree Stand
up in my tree stand shooting big bucks;
Houghton Lake
catching big pike, bass, and walleye;
Bowling Ally
throwing the ball, hitting the pocket, watching the pins fall;
Baseball Field
swinging for the fences, diving, giving it all;
Lake Summerset
jet skiing, swimming, and playing with friends;
My Home
sitting with family watching TV;
At My Sister's House
playing with nieces and nephews;
My Room
sleeping with my kitty cat;
Lunch At School
sitting with friends talking about what's going on;
Joe Louis Arena
beating on the glass rooting for the wings.
Depends on the mood, they are all really fun to do.

Aaron Kane, Grade 10
Onsted High School, MI

I Love You

It's hard to explain how I feel about you
Everything you do is just so cute
No matter what you do
It's hard to tell you what is deep inside my soul
There are so many ways to say it
That I just can't choose
But what I can say about you is this
You keep me warm when I'm cold
How I have you all to myself
So many ways that my feelings could be told
You hold me when I cry
You make me feel like I'm soaring through the sky
You lift me up when I'm down
You're by my side all year round
There are so many ways of what I need to say
Something I need to say today
I just hope you won't turn away
You are my earth and sky
You are always by my side
I love you from dusk to dawn
I always loved you all along

Brittney Cowell, Grade 10
Pansophia Academy, MI

I Want To

I want to be different,
to leave an everlasting imprint.
I don't want to fight the power —
I want to destroy it.
I want to toss my identity
like a cigarette out a car window.
To become no one at all
or everyone at once.

I want to take a hammer to all of the expectations
and a sword to the norm;
shatter them both into a billion pieces,
then take those pieces
and paint them bright colors and toss them to the waves.
I want to grow older and have others
point and whisper in hushed voices
behind the back of their hands.

I want to be simple and intricate, selfish and generous,
creative and derivative, affluent and destitute, one of a kind and mass produced.
I want to swim with Poseidon and to fly with Hermes, to arm wrestle Hercules.
I want to prove EVERYONE wrong; to live like Fitzgerald, to write like Poe and to become immortal like Shakespeare.

Taylor Ricca, Grade 12
Clarkston High School, MI

Ode to Eyes

You do not know someone until you have looked deep into their eyes.
It shows you something that nothing else will reveal.
To understand the depth, feeling, emotion, and wonder behind them is to see beyond the night skies.
Actions done, words spoken, gifts given, the kindness in eyes is what helps you heal.
Eyes that burn like fire can send your soul into a world of torment.
Eyes that are deep pools of water bring peace of mind.
Eyes greener than an evergreen bring adventure and spirit to a tired soul.
When you find the eyes you have been looking for, it's like an angel has been sent.
Eyes so enticing, they beg for you to search and see what you can find.
You learn about the person behind these beautiful eyes, the person who makes you whole.
Eyes like a beacon, which can be seen for miles.
To be seen by you forever and always,
through pain, sorrow, laughter and smiles.
Eyes so serious and so content they strike you and make you feel so many different ways.
Ode to these eyes; these eyes belong to the special one.
These eyes are the door to what really matters.
These eyes have lead me to what has become my being, my cost.
These eyes cut to my core and can seem to weigh a ton.
These eyes can be soft, kind, and loving until my heart shatters.
When looking in her eyes, I've never been more okay with being lost.
Ode to the eyes I will enjoy the rest of my life.

Bryan Applin, Grade 12
St. Mary Catholic Central School, MI

Morning

For the day to begin the sun must rise, when it hits the brink you open your eyes. Color blasts through that starry sky, shades of you shine high with pride. Casting upon an amazing sight, looking on the days of your life. Reflecting off giving light, a ray of warmth says every thing's all right. The smell of freedom with a hint of might, for this moment I share peace to the night.

Nathan Gubanche Jr., Grade 12
Sault Area High School, MI

I Think of You

When all is dark,
And the world is cold,
I think of you.
When all is still,
Not stirs a soul,
I think of you.
When all is lost,
And I feel so alone,
I think of you.
When the sky is gray,
As dark as stone,
I think of you.

When I feel small,
Like a tiny child,
I think of you.
When I lose myself,
And need to smile,
I think of you.
Natasha Kitchen, Grade 10
Mackinaw City K 12 School, MI

Ode to Chuck Taylors

To the Converse sitting on the shelf
in the Foot Locker store:
with every glance I steal your way
I want you more and more.

Your perfect fit phantoms my foot,
your leather shines like gold.
I thank the gentle, steady hand
with which your stars were sewed.

I long for you!
I pine for you!
I need you on my foot!

I'll save for you;
you will be mine,
lest I go kaput.

Until that day, here you stay
perched upon that shelf.
I know someday, I'll find the cash
and have you for myself.
Caryn Snuske, Grade 12
Lapeer West Sr High School, MI

Perfection

The little girl watched
The dolls march in rows
Each perfectly dressed
In ribbons and bows

She couldn't help but be jealous
Of their perfect parade
But when she tried to join in
The dolls each started to say

"You're different from us
So full of imperfection
You little black sheep
You've lost your direction

To join our parade
Cast off your humanity
Trade skin for plastic
Trade passion for sanity"

The little girl thought
But quickly turned away
"I like who I am
And that's who I'll stay."
Sophia Li, Grade 10
International Academy East, MI

My Dear, Black History

You are strong and resilient
Wise and spiritual
Original yet diverse
And much more than simple

You are much more than jungles,
Huts, and "kinky" hair
So how can a month describe you?
More than unfair!

You overcame a hardship
With all your glory and might
Centuries worth of agony,
But you sure put up a fight!

You also created music,
Monuments, literature and art
And still, now you go to college
Express your soul and heart!

Bliss and pride — African power
Pure, brown beauty
This is what you mean
My dear, Black History.
Donovan Dennis, Grade 11
University High School Academy, MI

Fantasy

Out of all
The billions of people
In the world,
You chose me to love.
What if I were to say
I was beyond your
Imagination?

That I wasn't real,
And you made me up
With all the
Imperfections and
Flawlessness
You could ever think of?

What if this
Was one's dream?
Would you still want me
To be real?
Would you
Actually choose me,
As your Fantasy?
Christina Nguyen, Grade 10
St Joseph's High School, IN

Existence

Existence is despair beneath the eye,
The dark room of life that doesn't lie.
The shuttered space that's in the corner,
The picture shakes then I mourn her.

The dark room of life that doesn't lie,
The children speak only with a cry.
The picture shakes then I mourn her,
The tears are out down in the corner.

The children speak only with a cry,
Standing on the ground waving bye.
The tears are out down in the corner,
Only if I could've warned her.

Theirs not a time from day to day,
I just didn't know what to say.
I wish I didn't break the tie,
Existence is despair beneath the eye.
Chris Tellis, Grade 12
Wylie E Groves High School, MI

She Whom He Will Guard

An angel looked down to earth's sinful people.
To look upon she whom, he will guard, as she sits in the chapel's steeple.
Beyond Heaven's pearly gates,
A beautiful girl beheld his gaze.
He watched carefully as she grew tall,
And as her character showed, it was for her he would slowly fall.
His patience grew thin,
He could not wait, for until death would win.
Through her dreams he came and went,
But from heaven or hell, she could not figure, from which he was sent.
Yet still foolishly she fell.
She cared not if he came from heaven or hell.
She still loved him all the more,
Though she could never remember, from the dreams what for.
Then he revealed from where he came.
He showed his true form and she saw his beautiful, yet chilling, appearance and knew of his fame.
He was the angel of death, he who took lives.
Yet still she loved him and for this she paid a price.
She was locked inside a padded room, until the day
Her true love came and took her away.

Katelyn Rayl, Grade 10
Western High School, IN

Thing I'd Like to Try Someday

Going scuba diving
To see the different colored fish;
Going sky diving
Getting a high adrenaline rush as my eyes get dry from the air;
Going bungee jumping
Feeling that thick spit in the back of my throat as I step on the edge of a bridge, wondering if I should bite my tongue and know I accomplished something or chicken out;
Travel to Australia
Being able to tell people I've been somewhere new and exciting and not just around the United States. Being able to know how they live their lifestyles and what their cultures are;
Trying sushi
Feeling the squishy texture in my mouth as my face expression explains it all;
Running a marathon
Sweating with a dry throat, smelling of glory, knowing I CAN do WHAT EVER I put my mind to;
Going to the Grand Canyon
Feeling so little as I'm standing next to it;
Meeting someone famous
Being able to ask them questions I feel are important to know and being scared and nervous;
As I add more activities that I would like to do in life I notice that life is full of amazing things. Accomplish your goals and know that you will succeed in life if you put your mind to it.

Erinn Tiede, Grade 10
Onsted High School, MI

No Name

It may seem like you're here, but in reality, you're not. You have a name, but you don't exist; you're nothing. Your mind falls deep in the pits of unknown-ness, while your name lies softly, softly it lies sleeping. Dreaming a name, with no time to spare, your name is a temple, doesn't exist because it's rare. I know your spirit, that you have a name, that you are alive, but you are dead. No signature, no style, no character, no credits, your name has a reputation untold because it's inactive. Crying silently inside: vanished, extinct, departed, screaming so loud, but it will all change when hell freezes over.

De'Qjuan Taylor, Grade 11
Detroit High School for the Fine and Performing Arts, MI

Hidden Away
I am two people,
One locked away for no one to see,
For fear they will not notice me,
I lock away my shyness,
Far away in solitary confinement,
Where I don't have anything to fear,
Accepted and not bullied.

The other me,
The me, you and everyone sees,
I am free to mingle and make friends,
I'm bold and loud,
Not afraid of expressing myself,
Outgoing,
Athletic,
There is nothing this me can't accomplish,
That's why I show it,

This is me.
Mason Swartz, Grade 10
Allegan High School, MI

Separate But One
We all come separately.
By different cars
from different towns
and different lifestyles.
But when we're at the studio, we're one.
Just one.
We breathe together
laugh together
dance together.
And then we get back into our different cars
and drive home to different towns
and different lifestyles
where we live as thirteen separate girls
…until next time.
Alexa White, Grade 10
Paw Paw High School, MI

Geese
They fly in the sky
With the most perfect V formation.
I stand in AWE of them.
Watching them take turns
In the front,
Helping carry the pressure of leading.
The song that they sing
Is like a chant
To help encourage
The one that is leading.
Their formation
Stays as perfect
As it started.
Stephanie Vierkant, Grade 11
Allegan High School, MI

Living
I am from dusty, dirt back roads and hundred year old pine trees,
From an old farm house and a big red, run-down barn.
I am from mud wrestling and late night karaoke,
To day-long fishing trips and frog hunting.
I am from a huge family of step sisters and half brothers.
From "she stole my makeup!" to "I know I can always talk to you."
I am from Sunday morning church and communion.
I am from a loving family, from big hugs to even bigger laughs.
I am from overcooked hamburgers on the grill to sun tea in a jelly jar.
I am from every day a new adventure, to memories I'll never forget.
I am from butterfly catchin' and tree climbin' to county fairs and car shows.
I am from "why don't you think before you speak?"
To "I may be old but I can still catch you with my whippin' hand!"
I am from four-wheelin' and bike rides, to swimming and mile long jogs.
I am from fun, from adventure.
From smiling, from laughing.
From happiness, from memories.
From loving,
From LIVING.
Kayla Yarbrough, Grade 10
Allegan High School, MI

Favorite Places to Go
I go to football games to watch the head-splitting hits;
basketball games to see the last second buzzer beater shots;
baseball games to catch the home run hits;

concerts to be blown away by the breathtaking artists;
movies to spend some relaxing free time;
friends house because they involve me and make me feel like I belong;

camping to spend some quiet time alone in the woods;
out to eat to enjoy the mouth watering food;
fishing to catch that one that got away;

hunting to see the monster typical white tail buck;
so as you can see I like to go many different places;
and which thing I do depends on how I feel and how much time I have.
Randy Schneider, Grade 10
Onsted High School, MI

Life Talk
I've got something to tell you
But you're not going to like what I have to say
But you need to know that you don't have to live your life this way
You can do your own thing
And not follow the lead of society
I want you to live your life to the fullest but this is not the way
Your problems may come and go but I am here to stay
I'll still be standing here waiting for you to come back around some day
I love you more then you will ever know
But you have gone lower then any one could go
That is what I had to tell you
And I'm glad you listened to what I had to say.
Shelbi Baker, Grade 12
Northview High School, MI

Experience

Though it's been long the pain still remains because I remember that very same day
when you left our world, but in my heart you remain I will never forget that one tragic day.
When I lost your love it was sad and true but never again will I cry over you, I know why you left
though it was sad I've been through this day many times in the past.
Do you believe my pain? Is it sad and true? This experience I had while I cried over you,
as you laid in that casket chill crossed your face I can't believe how they feel this pain.
I still get sad I still may cry every time I remember that day that you died, but just
looking back I remember the days where all we did was play and play.
I was young and never did understand why you left why your life did end.
At that time I could not comprehend what happened to you, where was my best friend?
But just looking back on those times we had I can't believe it's all in the past. I miss
your heart but your soul lives on in the bodies of those who you loved.

Nicole Furgerson, Grade 11
Allen Park High School, MI

Baby I Promise to Stay with You!

"Baby I promise to stay with you no matter what happens in our life!" When you look back, I'll always be there with you? I want you to know, that hearts are like glass. So please don't break them into many pieces because they can break very easy. If I had to choose between breathing and loving you, I'll save my breath. To say I love you very much. Did you know that I loved you once, love you still, always have and always will love you. So it really is not worth it to argue and fight because that can cause us to stress and depress. I don't ask for much because with you; I need you to know without you [tomorrow] wouldn't be worth the wail and [yesterday] wouldn't be worth something. I love you with all kind of things. "There are only two times I want to be with you; now and forever." When I first met you, you stole my heart? When I first saw you, I was scared to talk to you? When I first talked to you, I was scared to kiss you? When I first kissed you, I was scared to love you? And now that I love you, I'm scared to lose you. If I lose you, my entire life will be tearing apart; but I'm so glad you are in my life. Did you know that every time I see you, you always smile at me and that makes me know you really do love me. Then after you smile at me, I always respond to your beautiful smile then I look into eyes and smile right back at you, afterward we start kissing and we both say "I LOVE YOU VERY MUCH WITH ALL OUR HEART," then we hug and kiss; after that I SAID, BABY I PROMISE TO STAY WITH YOU!

Marquise Pope, Grade 10
Detroit Academy of Arts & Sciences - Medbury Campus, MI

The Girl

I sit on a bench outside, and watch the kids play on the slide.
I look into their eyes, and pry for what is a secret, a mystery from their history.
All I see is happiness through their eyes. No mystery, no secret, and no pain that is identified. I fear, that no one else has a past like me, I scream in my head and say "why me?" I put my face in my hands I draw myself away from the sounds, and let my tears overflow away in my hands. I look up and a girl catches my gaze, with a look on her face, why so much pain, why so much misery? I avert from her gaze, and stare into a daze. I turn around where she lied, and for saw such happiness, that is so scarce to pry into someone's eyes. I wish to talk to her, to be friends with her, but I see that she's not interested with a girl who conceals pain and misery in her life. I arise from my seat, and walk towards east, and find the answer to my question I seek "why me?"

Maryam Lafi, Grade 10
Central Academy, MI

Dragon

Waking up in a forest, I walked to a clearing and there he was. The majestic dragon towered over me, his scales a deep red. His great veined wings able to reach great soaring heights. I walked up to him and touched his scales. I could feel the heat emanating from them. His great head turned toward me. I looked into his eyes and saw wisdom and understanding there. He put out his claw. I climbed in and he put me on his back. I could feel his muscles bunching up. Then he sprang aloft and we were flying through the air. It was thrilling to fly through the sky, to look down and be able to see the ground rushing past us. I knew he wouldn't let me fall. I could hear his massive wings beating. He breathed golden fire and it was beautiful. I could smell the smoke. It was so strong, I could taste it, but I wasn't bothered by it, and I realized that this was where I belonged. As he touched down in the clearing, I knew he had become something others had not. He became a partner. An ally. A friend.

Russell Childress, Grade 10
Jennings County High School, IN

grass imprints

the satellites and stars
we lay under them tonight
connecting them together
with whispered dreams;
prayers of pretend

(this memory)
the air holds our breath
all the timeless nights
we can call mine
yours
and ours.
"unforgettable"
you swear it is.
you are the beautiful color that dies.
(i'll never keep.)

let the grass keep the imprints
of me
you
ours.

Cory Jensen, Grade 12
Reed City High School, MI

The Robotham Collection

Nutcracker
    That plays a lovely melody;
Metal pencil sharpener figurines
    Are very interesting;
Michigan State objects
    Have the best college team's logo;
Model cars
    That I have built by hand;
American Chopper Series model bikes
    Are unique in their own aspect;
Hooters' wet naps
    Produce loud laughter;
State quarters
    Are collected by everyone;
Hats
    Allow me to express myself;
Taz memorabilia
    Show off the best Looney Tunes character;
Car/Part advertisements
    Have physically appealing women.
The things I collect reflect in me, the fact that I tend to be a pack rat.

Ellis Robotham, Grade 10
Onsted High School, MI

My Love

The amount of water that's in the sea.
The number of stars there are in the sky.
My love can't be measured
And it cannot be asked "why?"
How many trees in the rain forests?
How many rocks along the shore?
However many there are,
I'll always love you more.
Don't ask me why.
Don't ask me how.
I just know that I love you
And you're all I want right now.
Count the fireflies
And count the lady bugs.
Count the animals upon the earth
And count the number of our hugs.
Added all together
It's still not enough.
I'd need more than this world
To show you my love.

Olivia Tam, Grade 12
Columbus North High School, IN

How I Spend a Summer Day

Sleep in…
    Open my eyes only to close them again as if night only began;
Lay out in the sun…
    Feel the warmth of the sun on my skin yet at the same time wishing for a breeze;
Play beach volleyball…
    Seeing the ball come my way, I prepare myself to get it back over the net;
Go for a swim…
    Cool off in the refreshing water;
Have a barbecue…
    Satisfying my hunger with a juicy burger;
Baby-sit my niece and nephew…
    Make sure they stay outta trouble;
Take the dog for a walk…
    Pulling at the leash as she drags me down the road;
Spend time with friends…
    Summer just isn't the same without them;
Listen to music…
    Sing along to my favorite song;
Sit by the fire…
    Watching the vibrant fire as it dances in the wind.

Sydney Jenkins, Grade 10
Onsted High School, MI

Wishes

Wishes are things that come from the heart, going no place at all.
You can wish in a fountain, or even to God, but your wishes won't be heard.
Laying on the freshly cut grass, angry and alone.
I gazed upon a diamond black sky, one that seemed to devour all light.
I feel like it's my soul.
Speckled with golden falling stars, I wonder what life would be like, making wishes here and there.
I close my eyes and do a silly little thing, I make a wish upon a falling star, knowing that my wishes will never be heard, answered, or even acknowledged.
It's that little bit of feeling of happiness that will keep me going.
I see darkness behind my eyelids, clenching onto my locket, and wishing with all my might. World peace or happiness would be nice, maybe for everyone to get along. I never cared for bullets much, and the blood of innocent ones.
Everyone should walk this world together, holding hands and laughing, with no care in the world. Sounds like heaven up above.
All these people that are power hungry should live on an island, away from us all. The war has lasted far too long; it needs to end real soon.
I smiled and laughed at how silly this sounds, wishing upon shooting stars.
With my locket still in hand, I open it to see my loved one, a soldier, one of the best. Please bring him back home to me. Alone but feeling at peace.
Gazing upon that diamond black sky, wishing to be heard.

Rachel DeWald, Grade 11
Clarkston High School, MI

Summer 2010

Swimming:
Ice cold water biting at your legs.
Laying around freely:
Napping like a cat, not a worry in mind.
Laying in the sun:
Feeling the beating bright rays soaking.
Camping at Yogi Bear:
The aroma of burning campfire wood and the relaxation of being away from home.
Bundy Hill Off-road Park:
The rush; the dust covers your entire body.
At the cabin:
It is like an escape getaway; the trees surround you.
Movies:
The aroma of buttery popcorn floating around.
Cedar Point:
The thrill of the roller coasters; the fear that you overcome; the gratitude you feel when you get off a ride.
Hanging out with friends:
Laying around and just talking about everything; being silly!

Jaycie Flynn, Grade 10
Onsted High School, MI

Number 1

The worst thing is holding onto someone who doesn't want to be held onto. Don't fall for someone unless they're willing to be caught. The thing about falling in love is that if you do it right you will never hit the ground. Life is too short to be anything but happy, *so kiss slowly, love deeply, forgive quickly*, take chances and never have regrets, forget the past but remember what it taught you. Sometimes you have to smile and pretend everything's okay holding back the tears and walking away. If you want to see the rainbow you must go through the rain if you want to see TRUE LOVE you must go through the pain. Women were made from man's rib, not from his head to be superior, not from his feet to be walked on, but from his side to be equal. Not from under his arm to be pretended but from next to the heart to be loved. Your true love will realize how much they want to be with you and he/she will call you
 Second to no 1.

Tre'Veona Hamilton, Grade 10
Detroit Academy of Arts & Sciences - Medbury Campus, MI

Discovery

Sitting at this rattled piano,
I plunk out a single note;
It resounds deeply off the thick walls.
No longer wanted,
It craves for company and eagerly waits to sing.
I listen to my fingers and gently tickle the ivories —
The sound takes me by surprise.

We hit it off.
It tells me its story and I tell it mine.
It creaks and moans with age.
Yet as the tips of my fingers glide over the keys,
A mellifluous sound resonates across the room.

The black and white ivories are suddenly a blank canvas,
And I am the artist.
The notes dance and twirl in the air,
A musician's ballerina.

My ears take delight in our interaction,
As if we were made for each other.
I no longer notice its broken hinges, its chipped black paint,
The blanket of gentle dust encrusting its surface.

After striking the last chord in place, I proclaim, "I'll take it."

Lucy Guo, Grade 11
Columbus North High School, IN

Feeling Back In

Consider the closet
Appealing and alluring and easy
To hide inside its iron walls and lock
Out maybe and possibly hate

Take your father, push him away
Seek shelter from his disapproval
In that space where secrets reside
And where courage dies

Take your mother
Give a truth, gift her knowledge
Wish that you could take it back sometimes

Hope that you find solace
In that hole in the wall
Where they are not allowed to judge
And where the world believes
You are not vile

Hide inside those padded walls which deceive
Feel straight jacket calm
And then see from that ground
That life could maybe be
Possibly worth living free

Cameron Martin, Grade 11
Harrison High School, MI

Melody

Words uttered many times before,
I am compelled to do so once more.
It is a part of my living soul,
Who I am — makes me whole.
Some have a flower inside,
That blooms and opens to confide.
Others have a glimpse of a season,
Or a passion giving their life reason.
But I have a little song,
That has kept me joyful for so long.
Drums keep tune with my heart,
My vocal chords do their part.
A tune's mere pattern makes my soul move,
To a peaceful harmony or a dancing groove.
Songs of passion make me yell and scream…
Or make me cry over a lost little dream.
Onto my arms goose bumps it brings,
Reminds me of old memories as it sings.
What will the new notes help me see,
What will the old melody say to me?

Holly Thieman, Grade 10
Reitz Memorial High School, IN

Sisters

When we were little
We played Barbies
I was always Ken
You were always Barbie.

As I grew older
You were always there for me,
You taught me how to tie my shoe
You taught me how to ride my bike too!
Remembering the good old times
Bring back a lot of great
Memories that I share with you.
I just wonder if you miss me as much as I miss you.
Now we're older and time has passed, but our childhood
Memories will forever last.

Christie Nelson, Grade 10
Pine River High School, MI

Wasteland

I just want to waste.
Waste away with you under the rays.
Melt together as our minds die.
Die from pollution and the power.
Forget the power.
I don't have any.
You leave me powerless.
A simple sentence and
my mind turns to mush I can't think clearly can only
sink down further down into the wasteland of my dreams.
I lie awake dreaming of us in hopes that your whisper eats my ear.

Lindsay Borkin, Grade 11
Trillium Academy, MI

High Merit Poems – Grades 10, 11, and 12

Creamy Delightfulness

A black tide pool sits at rest. Waiting patiently. Two little white cubes sitting at standby, looking like ice, but tasting sugary. Playfully bumping into each other, slowly dissolving away. Covered by a wave of off-white tinted creaminess. And then covered by another wave, this one a rich light brown color. The cubes are slowly being dissolved because of this long dark pole that is turning the black tide pool a light tan color. The smells coming off of this tide pool are of the French Vanilla and Hazelnut persuasion. Slowly, slowly, the cubes go into the whirlpool that has been made, saying goodbye to where they loved to be. Now, they are one with the pool. The long dark pole is slowly removed, but not before the whole tide pool is covered in what appears to be massive amounts of snow. The pole returns, and the once black tide pool is now a tan color. The flavor? French Vanilla Hazelnut with sugar and creamer. My favorite type of coffee.

Hannah Hormann, Grade 12
Northview High School, MI

My Big Brother Brady

My big brother Brady is mindful and kind
You should see he's like that all the time

Brady is a big brother to me instead of being against me
I go to church and learn about heaven
Because that's where we want to be

Brother, you saved my life
Realize that, because I was about to die
But then you entered my life

On the day everything was going so bad
You made me glad instead of being mad

Happy you made me
Each and every day you put me to see
Realize that heaven is where we want to be?
Because you are like a big brother to me

Realize that every day we want to succeed
On the day I was going to die
You had saved my life

Did you see that?
You should see that I left you alone
Now you have given me a brand new home

Kenneth Causey, Grade 12
Hillier Educational Center, MI

Twilight Moon

The pretty summer nights
Beautiful nights in may
When the shadows show at twilight
To say goodnight to the day.

In the sky the creeping moon
Sends out its brilliant glow,
For the heavens to see
A beauty that seems almost unreal.

On a little murmuring stream
Its light gently throws,
A cast where lazy water flows.

The sun cannot take the place
For the beauty of the moon is too great.
Nor take the smile from it's face.

Through clouds above the moon shines bright
Lighting a path for the lost.
As it gently cast a glow upon the earth.

On and on in heaven's high
The moon it winds it's way
Until the dark streaks in the sky
Give way to the new day.

Cayla Wells, Grade 12
Northview High School, MI

Life Is Not Fair

Life is not fair.
Life is closer than a sliver,
Blades and flesh.
An inch matters.
The reek of sewers is over us.
A muss cloud elevated.
The blind of an eyelid,
We hurried home.
To food and worship,
Thrives us to go on.
From going crazy is to clutch an empty stare,
And a silence half-breathing dream.

Tyler DeWald, Grade 12
Wylie E Groves High School, MI

Life Moves On

No matter what happens, life moves on
So no matter what happens you have to stay strong
When you walk away you never look back
But sometimes later on you wish you could change the past
But like life you just have to move on.

Life moves on but nothing lasts forever
So you should cherish the things you love more than ever
Live life to the fullest, make every day worth it
So you can know that your life had purpose
So cherish every moment before life moves on.

Jaelan McDonald, Grade 10
Detroit Academy of Arts & Sciences - Medbury Campus, MI

Sports

The serve ricochets off her arms
The set floats off her hands
The hit kills the ground
The block misses
Volleyball, fall

Dribbling up the floor
Someone tries to steal the ball
Looking up to score
Someone tries to block it all
Basketball, winter

The smell of track
The air against your back
The hair out of your face
The start of the race
Track, spring

Amanda Lovell, Grade 10
Mendon Middle/High School, MI

Untitled

I am ten point New Roman scribe
I am hushed whorls of smoke
ghosts of bittered wax
weeping, always weeping.

We are captives.
Held inside can shaped jellies
and dried meat husks.

We are whisked away,
only to be snatched brutally
by buttered golden fluffs of dough.

And you.
You are the worst of us all.
You are the bitter rhubarb scars,
clanging aftertastes of badly cooked crusts.

Elizabeth Roberts, Grade 11
Riverview Community High School, MI

Morning Time

The first glimpse of the sun
Awakes the earth for a new day.
The flowers perk up
Stretching their long green arms,
Towards the sky.
Baby animals cry out,
Full of mysterious energy
Asking to play.
Running up and down the damp trees,
Their parents call to them,
To stay close by.
The world comes alive again.

Marissa Buskard, Grade 11
Northview High School, MI

Heart's Victory

love is not a heart's victory, it is a cold and broken state of mind
how can love be true if no one around is ever kind
sadness falls down in the form of sadistic pain
falling in droplets of raging rivulets of rain
this pain I speak of hurts like a burning fire
brought on by the onset of a heart's burning desire
I walk down the streets every single day
and when I see intimacy more pain is brought my way
I try to see things clearly but my tears blur my vision
it seems every choice I make about love turns out to be a bad decision
I wanted you to know, and wanted you to care
all I ever really wanted was for someone to be there
so I sit quietly in the confinement of my lair
and do nothing at all but wallow in my despair
I remember the cold things you said and it makes me want to shiver
so I let my feelings show by the flowing of a red river
my mood is always shifty and changes like the weather
the memories seem to fade but the emotional scars last forever
this is not the life I chose, I didn't want it to be this way
but I guess this is how God wanted me to live so what more can I say

Kennith Kucera, Grade 11
Lakeview High School, MI

Love Is Painful

All the love that history knows
is said to be in every rose
Yet love has broken my every bone
That is while I'll always be alone

I look at my life and now I see
That no one will never love me
I go left love goes right
That is why I cry myself to sleep at night

I wrote this poem to say good-bye to my sorrow
But it will still be there when I wake up tomorrow
Whoever is reading this poem may think I'm insane
Truth is I wrote this poem to ease my pain
When you know love's scorn like I know it
Then you shall truly know the pain and sorrow of me because I am the poet

Kharii Love, Grade 11
Warren Central High School, IN

Pray

As I read the pages of *A Boy Called It*, I wonder how one person could be so cruel.
As I read through my teary eyes, I prayed.
I prayed that somehow, someway God would make a way for those millions of kids
Who are stuck in a home full of abuse sexually, mentally, physically, emotionally
I prayed that sooner rather than later they know they are not alone
I prayed one way or another God helps them escape the grasp of that one terrible monster
I prayed that they know the power of their beauty and that no one can take that away
I prayed that they pray and that they know their prayers are never going unanswered
But mostly, I prayed they never give up on life, God, and most importantly themselves.
I want you to know there is someone who loves you…*me*!

Riaunah Washington, Grade 11
Ben Davis University High School, IN

High Merit Poems – Grades 10, 11, and 12

Come Back to Me
I pray to see you
My children cry for you
Wife of mine
Come back to me
I watch over you
Making sure you're safe
The mother of my children
Come back to me
Every day I think of you
Your love stays with me
My love
Come back to me
I talk to you every day
I see you every day
My best friend
Come back to me
I fight for you when you're not around
I save you from getting hurt
My sister
Come back to me
Angelic Houston, Grade 11
Northview High School, MI

Loved One
You gave your love,
As if it was endless.
We always knew no matter what,
You'd give us forgiveness.
To us you meant the world,
For nothing could compare.
But when you left,
You separated a perfect pair.
From this day on,
We will truly miss you.
Without you here,
We don't know what to do.
Right now we'll cry,
For it seems right.
But we know you'll be safe,
For you have made it to the light.
So now we leave you,
In the arms of our father.
To live happily in heaven,
Without a single bother.
Danielle Breen, Grade 12
Engadine High School, MI

Please Don't Grow Up
He wraps his little hand around my finger
His radiant blue eyes dancing with life
His expression reads of childhood elation and innocence
His smile never ceasing, only spreading further across his lips
His laughter so pure and vivacious one can't help but smile at its sound
There is so much he has yet to discover
So many truths he has yet to unravel
He is so full of hope for he knows not of the horrors of this world
I'd give everything for him to stay this little
To never know of all the dark deeds and wickedness that fill the world
To never be abandoned or disappointed
Drew, please don't ever grow up
Rachael Miner, Grade 11
Waterford Kettering High School, MI

The Perfect Ones
Spirits high, clearest sky
Golden fields
Breath, bounty, wholeness
When we imagine a world
Where God is real
And stars reveal the future truth
Did we ever know it in our youth?
Mystical, Whimsical
More than just a phrase
Old values, New values
Wisdom, and faith
Honor, Song, Honesty
Friendship, and charity
Loyalty that never ends
When we are more than what we are
We are who we want to be
Lovely, ethereal dreams
Strong, and self-possessed
That is when we will do
What we know is best
Caitlin Osment, Grade 12
St. Mary Catholic Central High School, MI

Seek and Find
Seek and find
Find and fall
The world keeps on spinning
Even when you're on top
You've got to keep moving
You'll slip if you stop
You don't have to change
If you have the right step
But, you must keep it up
Never rest 'til you're dead
Leap over the cannons
Weather the winds
Stick to the truth
That's how it wins
Donielle Owens, Grade 11
Rockford High School, MI

Yin-Yang
In the darkest shadows
There is a speck of light
In the brightest of lights
There is a speck of dark

For every evil
There is an equal good
For every hero
There is a villain

In every villain
There is some good
In every hero
There is some evil

Yin is light
Yang is dark
It is like this
To keep balance
Westley Coy, Grade 10
Jennings County High School, IN

Memory
I'm trying to move on,
Letting go of you.
Gone are the days of
Our laughter and dreams.
But you, your memory
Haunts my thoughts
Why can't I just forget?
Memories of golden days,
Smiling together, innocent hearts.
Now I look back but you,
You're not who I thought,
The girl I remembered.
I don't want to see you
In that way anymore.
Not with the truth in front of me.
Maia Sutter, Grade 10
John Adams High School, IN

Christmas

My mind is clouded with thoughts
of pestilence and vulgarity.
There is no easy fix for something
long broken
as I learned once.
It has been some length of time
since I could think
happy thoughts.
Where I truly could wake up
and marvel in a day's presence
as opposed to
dreading it.
Each day is a present
Neatly wrapped
the item inside always different.
I'm not the one who
receives coal.
Put on your face
Unwrap the present
keep a smile,
and live.

Joyce Squillante, Grade 10
Forest Hills Central High School, MI

Night

Dreams: running, falling, confused
They haunt us, these dreams we return to.
Dark dreams.
Dreams where
Sweat pours
Eyes dart
Fingers clench
Teeth chatter
Heart constricts
Legs tremble
Arms reach
But there is nothing.
Dreams where
We can't find it.
Dreams where
We can't escape it.
They haunt us, these dreams we return to.
Dark, endless, mysterious.
Running, falling, confused.
They haunt us,
Dreams.

Nadia Torres, Grade 11
Clarkston High School, MI

Brown Eyes Blues

A pair of breathtaking brown eyes, tainted with joy.
A pair of stormy sky blues, strangled but coy.

The past lays slaughtered behind,
the future mysteriously beams.
The present unfolds one day at a time,
all tenses are not as they seem.

Framing a scene to hold like a photograph,
a heart holds all moments dearly.
The aroma of lust leads down a path,
one follows so sincerely.

Deep in the forest under a sky of black,
three words waved a white flag "surrender."
Sprinted across the terrain, then around back.
A lust so strong, had only wanted to befriend her.

Brown eyes so true, played like an immature fiddle.
Dark browns proved the fool, as sky blues teetered in the middle.

Drawn in like a moth to the light, as unbelieved as an old folklore.
A smile once so bright, now as washed up as driftwood on the shore.

The brown eyes are lost in the stormy sky blues.
You don't know how much I wanted to hear you say, "It's not me, it's you."

Morgan Hanks, Grade 12
Northview High School, MI

Down the Tree

I will call my wife Sunlight
For she will illuminate all doubts and darkness
And she will nourish our seeds
Who will look up to her
And they will grow under her solar gaze

I will name my daughter Genre
So that she will have many tastes
And be able to eat steamed rice with the people of the Far East
And hold conversations in Latin when she rides down gondolas in Venice

And for my son, I will name him Specs
So that he can enhance what people see
And what they see will be through him
And he will make little lenses
Who will be Bifocals and Trifocals

And with my mistress I will have my last child
And we will name her Secret
And tell no one

They will all be part of my family
And we will call ourselves Daydream

Nicholas Herd, Grade 12
Saginaw Arts and Science Academy, MI

Things That Scare Me

Snakes
   They slither through the grass undetected.
Cancer
   Can attack at any moment without warning.
Clowns
   Pop out of nowhere and scare the "bejesus" out of me.
Dark
   Unpredictable.
Mountain Lions
   Lurk in the dark stalking their prey.
Boogie man
   Is in the closet waiting for me to enter the room.
Sasquatch
   Stronger than the average man, he can rip a man limb by limb.
Drowning
   The dreaded feeling of water filling my lungs.
Cemeteries
   Harmless by day, scary by night.

Cory Hunt, Grade 10
Onsted High School, MI

A Rainy Day

Sometimes our love feels like a rainy day;
it's dark and damp on a young woman's heart.
The long day puts everyone in dismay;
the sky's tears reflect deep pain, rain like darts.
Thine eyes are as gray as the stormy sky;
lightning is just like your sudden temper.
It's on these days that the birds just won't fly.
Sometimes, you merely stay in a slumber.
It washes away the yesterday's hurt,
and when the sun comes out the air is clean.
The sky's tears satisfy our growing thirst,
and the world shines bright with a newfound gleam.
I'm just thinking of the love that we share;
you've revived me from death, I do declare.

Nora Slavin, Grade 11
St Joseph High School, MI

Fly on the Windowsill

Fly on the windowsill
Blinded by the light that the room conceals

Unhappy with life as he knows it
But too small and unremarkable to show it

Unhappy and seen as a stain
To be aware of in the rain

The fly dies on its back
Too small and unremarkable to make a crack

The fly dies trapped on the windowsill
Blinded by the light the room conceals.

Desean Jones, Grade 10
Detroit Academy of Arts & Sciences - Medbury Campus, MI

Ode to Swag

It is something neither destroyed nor produced;
It is more than fitted caps and Timberland boots;
It is more than white tees hanging down my knees;
It is more than dressing and acting how I please;

A lifestyle it is, but not limited to;
It is not just clothes from Hollister or Limited Too;
I wonder if it's an identity or proper disguise;
As I wear my NBA brand socks to my thighs;

False, commercialized swag is an expression of wealth;
In its true form swag is an expression of self;
It's neither tangible nor abstract;
It is more than wearing chains until you have a bad back;

It is natural yet it is manufactured;
It is old news but it is a brand new chapter;
I ponder this as I lace up my Nike sneakers;
I am a student and swag is my true teacher.

Nikhil Chaturvedi, Grade 11
Detroit Country Day Upper School, MI

Love is…

What is love, you may tenderly look to,
But a soft voice that whispers in your ear,
Telling you that your heart knows what to do.
Or that unselfish thought for who is dear.
Love is the secret look in someone's eyes.
It affirms truth and makes it crystal clear.
Not of pride or conceit, yet meek and wise.
When you know they need be held very dear.
What more is love but living now, not then?
When we've a reason to live tomorrow.
Then you know this person must ne'r be far.
Slowly, it grasps you, forgets all sorrow.
   Sooner or later it all disappears,
   Leaving your life with so many more fears.

Chelsea VanderZwaag, Grade 11
St Joseph High School, MI

Burned Out

You've been my one and only love for so long,
You hurt me more than once, when I did nothing wrong.
I kept your love inside of me,
It was wrong, but my heart had to disagree.
I took on too much; it was more than I could handle,
The symbol of our love, was the fire from a candle.
You left me, but the heat from the fire raged on
Too bad it has to end, as soon as I move on.
It felt weird and strange each time you arrived,
We've been through so many problems, but our candle survived.
Trust doesn't exist, I won't believe you, no matter what it's about
Our candle survived so much, but when you returned you found it
Burned out.

Cortney Smalley, Grade 11
Old Redford Academy Preparatory High School, MI

Ode to Summer

Ode to summer.
Warm weather surrounds me.
The sun beams down on my skin.
I feel extremely happy.
Ode to no worries.
Thoughts run through my head.
Day by day I create memories.
I am always trying to get ahead.
Ode to a new beginning.
I will be given my own key.
Next year will be eye opening.
I will strive to create a new me.
Ode to being on my own.
I will have new responsibilities.
They will be shown.
They will know my abilities.
Ode to summer life.
Life is calm in the summer,
Not full of strife.
I make my own beat to life, like a drummer.
Oh I wish it was summer, ode to summer.
Brittany Dazel, Grade 12
St. Mary Catholic Central High School, MI

Comatose

Life's just a dream,
I can't figure out what it means;
everything in this so called reality,
will never make perfect sense.

The meaning of life,
will never be right;
too many ways it could go,
nothing more, nothing less wrong.

Why can't I find my way,
through this time of sheer misery,
where everything I want is just inches away;
and I'm just that much closer to falling off the edge to get what I want?

Why does it all seem impossible?
Just wanting to be with you is so hard;
confusion comes into play,
and never again do I want to wake up from
my fantasies, for life is nothing but pain.

I stay asleep; only in my dreams,
for everything I want I can have here, unlike reality; it's so easy.
I wake up, never again going back, for now it all makes sense;
I have to wait for everything good, that's just out of reach.
Jennifer Tokarz, Grade 10
Lowell Sr High School, IN

Conformity

In a world full of circles
I'll be bold and contradict
The accepted Social Norms
That my heart conflicts
Before the world, my content
Is first concern
My comfort comes first
That is all for I yearn
To fit the mold of the expected
Depletes my soul
Of all its flowering seeds
Rejecting my role…
Demands of a certain way
Orates commonality
I am in discord
For what of morality
Break away from the bounds
Gripping tightly all of us
Grimace no longer — be stronger
Hear freedom's gust
Individual against conformity
Tammy Duyen Do, Grade 10
Homestead High School, IN

Outside the Box*

I am from passion,
From peace and love of God's living things.
I am from the warm white hospital bed,
The clean smell burning my nose.
I am from poverty to prosperity,
From residents to gypsies.
I am from the little two bedroom house, a room shared with my older sister,
The quiet giggles hushed by our mom when we should have been sleeping,
And the many camping trips with my dad.
I am from the act-like-a-lady,
And take-it-like-a-man.
From the don't talk about it,
To let it all out.
I am from the quiet prayers with hands held,
And warm dinner rolls shared around the table on a Sunday after church.
From the witty wisecracks that erupt into laughter,
And family movie nights on the weekends.
I am from the "perfect" family with no problems at all,
And every thing's a fairy tale.
I am from old pictures kept in small shoe boxes,
Holding hostage the many memories and stories waiting to be told.
Kimberly Miller, Grade 12
St Joseph High School, MI
Modeled after "Where I'm From" by George Ella Lyon

High Merit Poems – Grades 10, 11, and 12

Finding Mars

The cold night air enfolds us in
Its icy tendrils.
We are both embraced by its loving grip
Looking up to the clear sky above.
The stars twinkle and shine
Causing the curiosity of our minds to search in vain.
We look for a lone star in the galaxy above
Searching for a cherry hue, different, yet familiar.
The color is distinctive, reminding you of better days,
Reminding me of you.
As the cold overtakes my body,
The shivering racks my frame, teeth chattering.
Now I'm enveloped in another grip,
No longer cold.
We stand, tangled up in each other's warmth
Marvelously content with our own company.
That memory will last forever
Tucked into the recesses of my mind.
Because, as Einstein said,
Some seconds last longer than others.

Emma Van Nostrand, Grade 11
Allegan High School, MI

Those Eyes

What gets me up in the morning is the sight of those pools
They're dark and mysterious, like two polished jewels
To gaze in them is to abandon all reality
And want only to be lost in them for all of eternity,
Oh how I get lost in those eyes.

They shine when she smiles and shimmer with love
When I'm happy or sad they're all I can think of.
My cheeks burn with a fire that's like a thousand suns
And when we are together it feels like we're the only ones
Oh how I get lost in those eyes.

I get goosebumps and act silly whenever she is around
And love to keep her smiling and never see her frown.
At the end of the day when I think of those pools in the light
I can fall asleep smiling all through the night.
Oh how I get lost in those eyes.

Peace sends me deep into sleep each night only when
I know that the next morning it all starts again.

Brandon Strantz, Grade 10
John Adams High School, IN

Death of a Loved One

   The death of a loved one is never easy
especially when I see her go
   The love inside me never fades
but the pain is there to stay
   With all the years of memories
stuck in my mind
   I wonder why it had to end
the way it did
   I held her hand as the life drained out
of her
   Trying to hold back the tears with what strength I
had left
   I keep thinking that she will be in a
better place
   But I want her to stay here
with me
   Late at night, with the image of her holding on
to me
   I think that she is in a better place with the rest of
her family

Sarah Green, Grade 10
Jennings County High School, IN

Six O'clock and Time to Read

Mystical mysteries holding my attention.
Words that take me to another dimension.
Love, despair and desire on every page.
Stories of life fitting for every age.
Six o'clock and the sun is slowly descending.
The world begins its slow transcending.
A book to explore the world.
A book to show life's mysteries unfurled.
Deep insight into the human conscience.
Books to take away the real world's nonsense.
Books to fill lonely evenings,
To allow fantasizing before sleeping.
Let everything slip away.
And leave your thoughts to play.
Books can transport you to any instance.
You can be caught in its novelty brilliance.
You can dance among the pages of your dreams,
And explore all its themes.
But books aren't real and their joys fade,
The only thing you need is the present day.

Teresa Lovejoy, Grade 11
Bishop Luers High School, IN

Intergalactic Festival of Wonders Unimaginable
Lanterns filled the sky like stars
Destined to leave from Pluto to Mars
While aliens watch from afar
The festival of Paremental is where we are

Townsfolk leave from indoors to the streets
These citizens are, for real, great beasts
The monsters jump, dance, and do great feats
While others watch and eat their meats

Attendees bring out their traditional clothes
That consists of gold jewels, tunics, and red pantyhose
With flamboyant pointy hats that they chose
The bells jingle-jangle as the time goes

Alas, the time has gone by so fast
The music came, and then passed
All the vicious beasts have had a blast
When the final lantern leaves the sky at last

Ariel Milinsky, Grade 12
Wylie E Groves High School, MI

Lost
Darkness falls and happiness drowns.
I follow deeper into the forgotten abyss worn like a gown.
Have I reached the bottom where I can be found?
No, I have not. Not for now.

The pressure keeps building pushing me to drown.
There's no sense of hope, I'm just going down.
Sometimes I dream someone's there to save me.
Then I wake up and darkness I still see.

Where is the sun? Why will it not shine.
If it shines then there is hope and all will be fine.
She will bring good news and happiness will be found.
The sun shines and I can finally touch ground.

Good-bye to the cold and being without lust
I am no longer tainted with no one's trust.
Hello life that I can survive.
I will accept my experienced life.

Brittney Irish, Grade 11
Northview High School, MI

I Believe in Love
I believe in love.
Between a man and a woman
A man and a man
A woman and a woman

I believe in loving someone so much
That no other person is a temptation
Because you already have perfection in the palm of your hands
And never doubting the love between the two of you

I believe in coming home to the same person every day
In having nonstop butterflies in your stomach
I believe that even when you've been hurt,
Even when the love of your life breaks your heart, it'll be all right

I believe in happiness.
I believe in faithfulness.
I believe in perfection.
I believe in love.

Elaina Gardner, Grade 12
Wylie E Groves High School, MI

Parking
Finally, finally,
we get there.
Silver Lake.
A state park surrounded by trees.
We drive along a winding path,
show our passes,
and continue down the natural boulevard.

Dorothea pulls to a stop in the shade
and says
"Am I all right? What's the sun going to do?"
I think about the sun.
I think about west.
I think about the glare
glancing off the lake
at the end of the day.

I say,
"I think you're okay."

Susan LaMoreaux, Grade 10
Community High School, MI

Smile

Eyes meet,
twinkle,
and greet.

She smiles.
Why did she smile?

It was one of those
rare
smiles
with a sense of reassurance in it
not of a feigned friendship
but of spontaneous emotion
extending freedom and fellowship
conveying solace and solidarity
without avarice or avail
for no apparent reason.
And that, made all the difference.

Kyle Burkardt, Grade 12
St Mary Catholic Central High School, MI

Wedding Dress

Batiste, charmeuse, chiffon
Crepe, damask, faille
Organza, pique, satin
Even taffeta
It could have been yours
Love
The Minotaur of your mind
Only it knows the way out
Kill it to escape
A blade
Once curiously colorless
Like a wedding dress
Now conspicuously crimson
The course once clear
Now serpentine
The end is near
Or is it?

Raagini Suresh, Grade 11
International Academy East, MI

Ambition

Make a wish
Take a chance
Laugh
Follow your dream
Be yourself
Close your eyes
Hope
Hang on tight
Listen to your heart
Make the difference
And most importantly, never give up

Megan Wabich, Grade 11
Northview High School, MI

Love and Sacrifice

You are all I need and all I lone for
So beautiful your smile I adore.
Everything about you in my heart is where I store it
I love your smile, your laugh, and who you are I adore it.
I can't name another girl that I would want to be with
I would give up anything to be with you
But all I know is these words are true.
I fell in love with you
My world my everything it isn't a thing I wouldn't do for you.
I care for you with a passion
You are my fire even when we go out you know we stay matching
I'll always be there no matter what happens,
You'll stay on my mind even when I'm napping.
I'll give up anything to hold you down
Because when I need somebody you can always be found
You're the thing I want the person I need where I want to be so I made you my noun
Sometimes I know I can be a clown I'm so happy because love I've found.

Demetrius Hudson, Grade 10
Detroit Academy of Arts & Sciences - Medbury Campus, MI

Girl

I find it hard to say farewell to the calm nights.
Girl always on my brain keeping me wide awake.
Finally dose off, yearning my dreams in the end will be right.
There is nothing to lose, there is nothing at the stake.

Girl's genuine beauty is something girl will in no way ever understand;
Girl believes she is told deceitful lies about her outer self.
Yet, I still keep driving myself wild as one of girl's fans.
Do not be fearful of what the future holds and come down from that girl's high shelve.

A loss of breath when our eyes rarely meet.
I die inside just a bit when girl shows me a gentle smile.
Time will only tell if our companionship will offer us anything to reap,
But for now all I can do is be myself and present to girl my style.

Girl would be the girl I would give my life for,
Girl is everything I strive for, making me melt down to my core.

Nathaniel Theobald, Grade 12
St Mary Catholic Central High School, MI

Talents I Have

Something I can do is sing and stay in tune,
Also is wheelchair racing, go fast and pass the others.
I love to do photography, take pictures of pretty things,
I can sew a little bit, I'm not the best though.
I love writing poems, I can tell you how I feel,
To go with that is story writing, love to make new worlds.
I am awesome at band, I have been in it for years and many to come.
I'm pretty flexible. I can bend my toes and legs.
I'm always baking sweets, my favorite is dark soft brownies.
Drama club is next, I like to sing and act.
The last thing is art, I like to paint and make new things.
These are some talents I have!

Kaitlin Gassert, Grade 10
Onsted High School, MI

Twitter

Growing up is hard to do
Come June we will all have to
Seasons come and seasons go
In the fall we'll be in the know
With new adventures helping us grow
Starting new lives, whatever that might be
It will be interesting for the rest of us to see
Those who stay and those who travel
Let's hope their lives don't unravel
Education never ceases
It comes and goes in many pieces
Some are big and some are small
Life's lessons learned by all
Always have fun when you can
Live like you're sticking it to the man
Take opportunities when they come around
Good fortune is rarely found
Unless your desire is like a blood hound
Love the people in your life
And always forgive those who cause strife
Life is short, life is sweet, you can read all about it in this tweet.

Danielle Gentner, Grade 12
St Mary Catholic Central High School, MI

Art Class

The smooth wood pencil in my hand,
Energy streaming out of me, on to the page.
The tension of the day melting away.

The paint swirls into different hues,
The colors in my mind collide with the page,
My eye travels up the canvas.

Take a deep breath in,
The scent of paint and pencil,
Forever haunt my days.

The smell of an art room the feel of an art room
The magic of an art room
This is what makes my day.

Samantha Sanders, Grade 11
Northview High School, MI

Snowy

The wintertime wind blows, snowy and cold
Flakes drift through the wind and fall to the ground
One lands softly upon my ice cold nose
They pile up without making a sound.
The sun shines, making the blanket glitter.
My breath creates a cloud in the cold air.
The wind gusts and the snow begins to stir,
Snow crystals blow 'round and land in my hair.
The snowy days are quite short and freezing.
They're, however, some of the most pleasing.

Lindsey Bartz, Grade 12
Posen Consolidated High School, MI

Full of Wonder

I stand atop the mountain looking down to the town
Wondering if what I'm seeing is real
I have to stop and take a minute to wonder what was.
Wishing I could have seen what original really looks like
Wondering why man has gone so far to make man happy
By taking advantage of the defenseless valley
Wondering where I could go to be alone with a valley like this
Again wishing I had seen what I missed
But still appreciating this wonderful sight for what it is
Realizing how small I really am
Looking down on people who think they are so big
Looking to the sky feeling somewhat lonely
As I gaze at the stars
I start thinking if we are the only ones
Offsetting my previous thought of how small I thought I was
Changing it to how microscopic I must be
Opening my mind to new adventures of what I wish I knew
Wondering if I will ever know

Nathan Cowan, Grade 12
Clarkston High School, MI

Love Is Like a Flower

During the romance, love is a flower,
Beautiful and new, growing every day.
The feelings withheld seem to empower.
Forever always seemed so real, never far away.

Things were perfection; life was on cloud nine,
Nothing could ever carry them back down.
Hearts were joined together which once did shine,
But soon darkness came; the shine became drown.

Why do we have such a feeling of love?
We only feel heartbreak and suffer dread.
Feeling depressed and worthless, deprived of
The heart, held together by a thread.

Kaylin Ziebarth, Grade 11
St. Joseph High School, MI

Sunrise

Love is a sunrise, or so I believe,
Providing a reason to start one's day.
A fresh beginning is what we most need,
Love and sun both heal one's dismay.
Much like light pours out over the town,
Greeting those who wish to start new,
Love enters the heart of one with a frown,
Forcing their smile to shine through.
As the goodness of love or light compiles,
The truth of these things will surely reveal,
That love, like the sun, does not stay awhile,
A realization as cold as steel.
Though sun will set, and darkness appear,
Remember, always, that new sunrises are near.

Forest Burczak, Grade 11
St Joseph High School, MI

Home

I am from the smell of burning firewood,
Coming from the fireplace of the milk house where my dad would go to get away for a bit.
I am from wide open fields,
    And the smell of fresh cut alfalfa waiting to be made into hay bales,
I am from trying to catch snowflakes on my tongue in the winter,
    And jumping into piles of colorful leaves in the fall.
I am from rainy days,
    And mud baths with friends.
I am from stormy nights in the living room of the old farm house,
    And telling ghost stories until mom would have to comfort us from nightmares.
I am from riding my first horse through the neighbor's yard as the sunshine fell upon the grass making it extra green,
I am from homemade tents hanging from clothes pins on the clothes line while the radio plays soft country music,
    And hide and go seek games out in the musty hay barn while my dad mows the lawn.
I am from the farm, where boundaries are endless.
I am from home.

Devon Fox, Grade 10
Allegan High School, MI

Hope, Faith and Waiting

I am sitting on the outside of these prison walls,
where you are always being guarded. As I watch your soul grow older.
I realize the more I wait for you, the more the life we had fades away.

When I was a little girl and believed you when you said "Fairy tales have a happy ending." I had faith in your words.
I had faith that you would someday walk out of these prison walls with me to our castle
where I was once going to be your little princess.

I am 15 now and without a crown. Still watching from the outside of your prison bars.
Waiting for the day you again walk with me to be the day the sun shines on my palace.
You slay the dragon that demolishes my body and mind from the inside out, the dragon that guards my tower.
Destroy the bed of thorns, because I am tired of lying down on all these wounds at night.
Tame my wild fires.
Help me have faith in you again. My faith in you is quickly fading but my love for you is
never ending.

Taylor Burk, Grade 11
North Putnam Sr High School, IN

Mistakes I've Made

I've held a grudge with a good friend that was over something stupid and immature;
I've given up when I couldn't hold on any longer;
I've let someone go when I needed their love, support, and presence more than ever;
I've said some heated words in times of anger and frustration;
I've pushed people away when I thought I needed space, when I really needed comfort;
I've done things I shouldn't have when I thought they were right and it was me against the world;
I've led people on when I didn't mean to;
I've let people use me when I thought we were more;
I've made stupid decisions that could've really hurt people in the end;
I've "cried over spilled milk" when I had nothing and no one left.
These are the mistakes I've made. Conscientiously and sub conscientiously, willingly and unwillingly. Some I did as vengeance, while others were mere accidents.

Brandi Hawkins, Grade 10
Onsted High School, MI

A Daughter's Memory

My father was a soldier; a great soldier he was
He fought for our country and risked his life
I watched as he left and said his last good bye
I watched as he boarded and got ready to fly
I waited and waited for letters to come
I waited for his phone calls as my body began feeling numb
I turned on the television to witness the sight
As I watched my throat began to feel tight
I felt queasy and saw a blurry vision of his body being carried off
I saw that vision and realized that I might not see him again
Tears down my check; I remembered our moments

Memories
When you taught me how to ride my bike; you took me slowly
When I fell, you ran to me and carried me home and healed my wounds
When you get hurt, Who will heal your wounds?

Memories
When I played soccer, you cheered me on
You stood there like a proud father, a father proud of his daughter
You always told me I was your light; I'm shinning my light for you to come home; I lit your path
I thought you would have found it, before that treacherous storm hit; it killed you just as I lit
I am so proud to say, that you were my father, my honor, and a brave soldier

Batoul Al-Ibrahimy, Grade 12
Star International Academy, MI

How I Spend a Summer Day…

Tanning: My skin is always glistening, and bronzed. I love the way the sun feels soaking through my skin.
Having movie days: I stay up all night and all day, bundled in a blanket watching movies.
Bonfires: At night, everyone sits around the fire, roasting marshmallows and telling stories.
Swim practice: I wake up early in the morning, and swim for hours on end.
Parties: I go to parties almost every night. Every party, I make new friends and fresh memories with them.
Swim meets: I go to swim meets that are hours away (every week) and the feeling of getting first place is outstanding.
Fireworks: Watching the tantalizing colors burst into the night sky with friends and families.
Working: Getting a job (as a lifeguard), and while having fun, I also was making money.
Hanging with friends: Almost every day, I go places with friends and make many new memories.
Hanging out on the lake: Staying out for hours a day in the middle of the lake with friends.

How I spend a summer day is unlike anything else. I cherish every moment of it. My best memories that I have made, come from summer. This summer is only a couple months away, and I'm already planning new things to do!

Autumn Prinz, Grade 10
Onsted High School, MI

A Woman's Broken Heart

Turned back by love's unwanted arms, women look towards men and blame it all on them, heartbroken tears run down her face from the late night, p.m., to the early morning of the a.m., eyes sore from the light that shines into her mind, into her soul, not wanting to leave the loneliness of her dark hole, to wallow and roll around, to frequently break down, only coming up once and a while for air so she doesn't drown, betrayed by her so called king, he took away her crown, chopped up her tree of self-esteem and it just fell down, this was more than just flesh, it was a mortal wound, to the psyche, because when you look at her, her face is never smiley, personality turned bitterly icy like the winter winds, feisty because she couldn't let any man have the key to her heart, so she held it ever so tightly, when men would try to have her, she poisoned their hearts like ivy, making them feel her heartbreak, she felt it was satisfying and justly, but is she blindly turning her heart off until she opens it up to the one that is knightly and regards women highly and his armor which shines brightly, enough so she can see a glimpse of true love slightly, maybe I'm the one that can show her the way she should be treated, which is rightly

Jordan Lyons, Grade 10
Lewis Cass Technical High School, MI

The Brownest Eye

What about the brownest eye?
What about the kinks atop my neck that compliments the silky strands that never grew (against my wishes).
What about my broadened hips that have spread because my only worth is birth.
What about the large epicenter of my face that is the butt of all jokes leaving me wanting to change it.
What about my tar-like skin that has endured slashes, bubbling blisters and bruises.
What about my large lips that are frowned upon, but many get injections to mimic them exactly.

"All the world had agreed that a blue-eyed, yellow-haired, pink-skinned doll was what every girl child treasured. This is beautiful, and if you are on this day 'worthy' you may have it."

But what if...
What if I didn't want that?
What if I am content with my brown-eyed, brown-haired, tanned-skinned doll?

And if you are on this day 'worthy' then you may be strong enough to endure the struggle that comes along with what she has, the beautiful blessing that comes along with being a part of such a rich heritage.

This is beautiful, and if you are on this day 'worthy', you may have it.

Brittany Wright, Grade 12
Saginaw Arts and Science Academy, MI

The Aspiration of a Tree

Those trees...

Sitting in the forest with years of growing beneath their belts,
the warm sun above their heads, and the wet soil at their feet.
Their leaves sway peacefully in the wind, while the aching and painful rumbling of chain saws sound below...
Watching, as their fellow foresters are chopped at the trunks,
the other trees mourn for now, just as everyone would.
But deep down they know that they'll be in a better place.
The ones leaving, know they will serve a purpose in the afterlife. So, they accept their long fall down, thinking, "Soon enough, I'll be all fancy in this world where those creatures called 'humans' will mark their feelings, creativity and their words of wisdom upon me."
There is a great chance that I'll become an essay that a child's teacher would admire.
And that A in Admiration would be placed upon my forehead in a fine and flashy, red ink.
I could be an important document, or a piece of art, or a story that will be passed down from generation to generation...
Hey, I can see it already.
Someone's deepest moments, toughest challenges, and best experiences will be shared with ME! Yeah, Me!
This is...The aspiration of a tree.

Anthony Grimmett III, Grade 12
Cody High School, MI

The Girl in the Mask

Today I walk with a mask glued to my porcelain face for I am not truly known for me.
I walk in the shadow of an expectation, not the truth.
I am the girl you see in the coffee shop but never ask about the weather.
The weather for me is rocky and full of pain and judgment.
You sit there and base your opinion of me in the first few minutes of my arrival.
You think that I am just a pretty broken face like any other teenager that comes in on Saturdays.
The truth is that behind the perfectly positioned mask I wear is a beautiful, powerful key link to your future.
The future I lead is one of love and awakening.
You see the girl in the coffee shop but do you ever truly think of the expectations that she is living up too.
You see the outcome but do you ever see the effort and process that comes with it.
So today I am the girl in the mask, tomorrow I am your future.

Angelica Stegehuis, Grade 10
Chesaning Union High School, MI

A Fallen Heart

Blackness etches deep within
A sorrow I can't contain
My soul unborn, so hurt it lies
Swallowed up in vein
Not always was there such as loss
A vacancy of heart
This bleak, abhorred, and desolate land
Was blissful in the start
A time now passed, once ruled with zeal
A phoenix fueled in flames
Then fell apart unto the rocks
Of lies and other shames
And now this broken being of mine
This shattered shard of self
Has become a small and helpless thing
Whose faith falls back in stealth
So now to life I've closed myself
For what more is to gain?
I've found this place to be only one
Of lies, of hurt, of pain
Mary Iott, Grade 12
St Mary Catholic Central High School, MI

Innocence

Rain drops
Cloudy skies

Thunder
Lightning, and frightened cries

Dark rooms
Cold air

Loneliness
A child, does anyone care

Musty smells
A fallen tear

Beaten
An innocent child, filled with fear
Kylie DeMink, Grade 10
Mendon Middle/High School, MI

Examiner of Earthworms

Higgledy piggledy
Charles Robert Darwin
He spent a whole five years
On the Beagle

Studying some finches
In the Galápagos
"Anti-creationist!"
The church did scold
Mitchell Vitez, Grade 10
Catholic Central High School, MI

A Far Away Friend

Back in the day
You were one of my first friends
From wrestling to football we were in it together
Like Butch and Sundance
Partners in crime
Doing what we wanted when we wanted
All we did was play some simple 64
Goldeneye, Turok, and Super Smash Bros. were the favorites
Summer all we did is play air soft, paintball, and football — tackle of course
Now all you want to do is
Smoke this, drink that
When we chill out it's like dang man don't you wanna slow down on that?
I can't count on you 'cause you're always buzzin'
I can't trust you 'cause your always trippin'
And you can't remember 'cause your always fuzzin'
So there you have it
I said…and I don't care
Maybe you will slow down
But most likely not
Anyway I said my word
Later

Matt Vandermeer, Grade 12
Clarkston High School, MI

Beginning to End and Back Again

Cold and nearly silent,
A long wispy breeze rustles fallen leaves in the moonless night,
Fresh dew is born on thick tufts of tousled grass.
Above, the air seems to lift,
Shades die away to reveal soft tints of blue,
Drizzling to the ground, warmth thaws the earth,
The world blinks its eyes open, coming to life.
The sweet notes of light colored song birds float above the naked oaks
Eagerly welcoming the sun and dawn:
So soft and gentle with its touch,
With delicate arms of glorious light
Stretching across the east.
The sun slowly climbs toward the top of the sky,
Where it reigns king for all to see.
How quickly his rule is over,
Moving the sky to mourn the sun's departure
With harmonious hues that descend
Into blankets of blue and black once again.
To the darkness, the dancing stars gleam
Hope in the numbing absence of the sun.
Araceli Garcia, Grade 10
Forest Park Jr/Sr High School, IN

High Merit Poems – Grades 10, 11, and 12

Moment
The lights are out, your eyes are dim.
It's time to sleep, to dream again.
Lost in thought of the day's events.
Thinking about how each moment was spent.

Did I make someone smile? Did I spread good news?
Help out a friend, or cure someone's blues?
Did I shine unto others with a gentle smile?
And love every moment like a newborn child?

Life will change. People, too.
But love is love, and you are you.
Share them both with arms to embrace
The beauty of each brightened face.

Time is out, your heart is dim.
It's time to sleep, you smile again.
Lost in thought of your life's events.
Thinking about how each moment was spent.
Jake Fortner, Grade 10
Jennings County High School, IN

Hidden Beneath
underneath, the truth lies buried way down —
hidden so no one ever will see me,
the real me, that never makes any sound…
locked tightly away and I keep the key
to never be revealed to anyone
except for me, hidden I will just stay
alone in the world 'til my time is done.
here I am! this is me! a lonely stray
away from the judging eyes in this place,
lost and at a distance I will remain —
no changing! I will continue this race
and I will just fight and endure this pain.
from this time forward, the truth will be sealed —
underneath the truth will stay unrevealed…
Haley Toliver, Grade 11
Norwell High School, IN

Running
Shoes going against the pavement   step after step.
Skin is burning   from the sun's hot rays.
Going to keep running   breath after breath.
Imagine people chasing me   to keep motivation.
When I reach the top of the hill,   I shall be victorious.
Slowly making my way up   feeling dehydrated.
Legs are aching,   running out of breath.
Closing my eyes   thinking about the end.
The finish is in sight   I am going to make it.
Taking the final steps   almost at then end,
Feeling like I'm going to faint   all hope feels lost.
I close my eyes and stop thinking.   I am on top of the hill,
Accomplishment,   I am victorious.
Travis Bentley, Grade 10
Allegan High School, MI

Through the Wake
Running across the water with the straps hugging your feet like
A bear shimmying up a tree
The board jumps the wake roughly and smacks the water
With its shiny blue bottom
Screams as it hits the water again
Gliding over the Miniature Mountains of blue

Pulling tight to relieve the tension
The rope whistles with every strand of string tied together
Passing through the wind behind the boat
Resting in the middle
The board stands on the his pedestal,
Between both white caps on the sides
Splashing through the frustrated waves

Letting go of the rope
As it sags like a tree branch without water
The board swallows the water until he disappears
Sinking into the giant blue abyss
The water rises to the top as he sinks to the bottom
And only to come up for a gasp of air
Emma Atwell, Grade 12
Clarkston High School, MI

Monster
Hurry…someone help me, please.
There's a monster in my mirror and it's trying to break free
I see anger in her eyes, her smile spells deceit
The voice that echoes from inside her bears a fiery heat
The monster in my mirror is trying to escape
I can't say that I blame her,
Doomed to this pitiful, helpless fate
My monster in the mirror, she looks a lot like me
I stare in wonder at her…what should I believe?
She is pleading for my aid…but is she leading me astray?
She reaches out toward me
Pleading for a change
Tears fall from her tormented eyes
As the mirror begins to break
I place my hand upon the glass
I give the monster what she asks
Complete control, unstoppable
This surely could end in disaster
Though one thing I know is true
I am safe here within my monster
But I'm not so sure about the rest of you.
Susan Downs, Grade 11
Benjamin Bosse High School, IN

Butterflies
There are always butterflies flying around in my stomach.
I'm climbing to the top of his heart.
That's so deep in our hearts.
I love my baby!
Gabrielle Jeffrey, Grade 12
Brandon High School, MI

Those Dreams of Yours

They say to us we can't reach the sky,
unlike birds above, we'll never fly.
"you fools," they say. "You crazy brothers!
You'll never fly just like us others!"

They say she'll never have any say.
They say "You women have your own place,
and in your place is where you will stay."

"He'll never be anything," they say.
"His vulgar music will never play."
They say Ragtime will soon be forgot,
that in the future it won't be sought.

"It's pure ambition! You're just a kid!"
They say "You'll fail, like the others did!"
They say age limits ability,
that youth deserves no equality.

They say I'll never do this, Ill never do that,
That I'll forever be where I'm at.
"Those dreams of yours... you'll never win.
Com'on girl just throw the towel in!"
But the Wrights, women, and Joplin did,
so let's you and I make our own bid.

Katherine Durkee, Grade 11
Washtenaw Technical Middle College, MI

A Stranger I Have Met

You are not a thing of the heart,
Nor an emotion of the mind.
But a chemical reaction,
That tells us 'you are mine.'

And possesses us completely,
And erases all logic and thought.
And compels and manipulates,
Till we act as we should not.

You come in various shapes,
And you come in countless sizes.
You make it very hard for us
With your numerous disguises.

Why did you show yourself to Romeo,
And to his Juliet?
Or scheming Scarlett O'Hara,
And her infamous dear Rhett?

I think I've passed you on the road,
Caught a glimpse a time or two.
But even if indeed we have met,
I wouldn't have known it was you.

Rebecca Barth, Grade 12
Northview High School, MI

How I Spend a Summer Day:

Swimming
    I splash around in the cool water with my friends;
Tanning
    The sweet smell of suntan oil slowly lulls me to sleep;
Water gun fights
    Everybody and everything is soaking wet;
Tubing
    I try to hold on to the slippery handles as the boat tries to shake me off;
Bonfires
    I watch the radiant stars as the smoke swirls into the night sky;
Car rides
    I cruise around with no place to really be going;
Hanging out with friends
    The gossip never stops and the fun never ends;
Reading
    I pick a nice shady spot underneath the willow tree to get lost in a new book;
Fishing
    I'm always trying to catch the biggest one, but I'm not sure on how to unhook it;
Going out on the boat
    The waves are crashing around in a rhythmic pattern against the boat;
Summer days come and go, but the memories of what I did last forever.

Michaela Clute, Grade 10
Onsted High School, MI

The Soul of Music

What is music?
Just notes on paper?
Random sounds that just happen to go together?
Or
Is it passion, anger, love, joy?
Is it a different interpretation of words that we could never say?
Feelings we never thought we could feel?
Does it make you feel powerful?
Like when the music gets loud, and you get that weird sensation up and down your arms?
When you just can't help but close your eyes and sway with the music?
Where you feel as if you are one with the music?
What do you call that?
The power of the music?
The sound?
Or the soul?
The Soul of Music.

Amber Roberts, Grade 10
IN

The Lone Wolf

The snowy Arctic is silent, all but for the foot steps of the lone Arctic wolf.
As he walks he lets out a mournful, almost dead howl, as if he is lonely.
He is searching for his mate, the beautiful, young, princess of the Arctic.
While he is walking he lets out another howl, this one is worse.
The moon is full, he looks up, gazing into the dimly lit, Arctic night.
When the sun begins to rise on the frozen tundra, he lets out one last mournful howl.
He is the prince of the Arctic, in search of his love.
This last howl is responded by another howl, he has found her.
They touch noses, and run away into the morning sun.

Troy Brittingham, Grade 11
Gibson Southern High School, IN

High Merit Poems – Grades 10, 11, and 12

Life Unexpected

The way it looks, life is always scary
Good times, bad times, you think it's all okay
One second you are happy and merry
The next it vanishes and goes away
You think you have it all, love, happiness
Once you're with someone you begin to trust
Hoping, praying, it will not be a mess
You hold back, but letting go is a must
You've seen others go through hurt of that kind
It closes you off and makes you afraid
It's not easy to leave those things behind
You've seen your best friend be loved then betrayed
Sometimes you have to let go and believe
If someone really loves you, they won't leave

April Miller, Grade 12
Posen Consolidated High School, MI

My Best Friend

During these times you have your ups and downs
Things all around you are getting tougher
Life at this age is harder than it sounds
But I know I can always count on her
She is there for you to share with
Knows all of my little secrets
We are such good friends, it's not a myth
Helps me take the risk I won't regret
We can sit and laugh the whole night through
A girl that I could tell anything to
She wouldn't take more than she needs from you
Not just her, but I got my whole crew too
Just couldn't see how anything could go wrong
When I have my best friend tagging along

Tracy Mulka, Grade 12
Posen Consolidated High School, MI

Warrior's Eye

The fight of a warrior was in his eye,
The elegance of an eagle was in his face
His thoughts, clear as the night sky
Is magnificence in any place.

And his voice, the horn of a car;
And all the kindness in his heart
His future, bright as a star
Has all the little things, like the quicky mart

There's nothing like it when he is here
Like a cheetah running though the field
Nothing in the world that he fears
Like a corpse his lips are sealed

Joe Levin, Grade 12
Wylie E Groves High School, MI

Sweet Getaway

She placed her hand upon the keys,
And her head glanced down at their position.
Her back slanted slightly and stiff locked knees,
Doubtful of her song's composition.
Lips, like a frog, puckered in resentment of offering,
As the piano sang her most remembered melody.
The audience might pretend to be caring,
But deep down they will never know her tragedy.
The sound of the piano's pound is her sweet getaway,
The black and white express the emotions she can't comprehend.
The heavy notes' pings create a steady pathway,
To lead her to her sweet sorry godsend.
But who would have known her talent was so bright,
For the eight hundred year old piano stole the spotlight.

Alexandra Mickey, Grade 11
Northview High School, MI

The Sky

The bright blue sky, I see it in my eye
The clouds swirling, the winds are a-whirling
The colors twinkle in the midnight sky
The days they come, the dusk lights a-twirling
The rise of sun, telling you day has come
Along with the sun, here comes the green leaves
When the moon rises up, the day is done

The colors glowing, the light a-snowing
The time is ticking, the light is lifting
Time drifting, night's sky swifting, moon glowing
The earth as it move, grooves and is shifting
Twinkling, the sky is so very bright
Sky is beautiful, forever tranquil

Leanne Buczkowski, Grade 12
Posen Consolidated High School, MI

Sonnet IV

They burned and glowed fires of deep red
and smoke smiling in gentle purples, blues
and all drifting, beguiling sweet of hues
sweeping the position of which we stand.
The fires dancing full of grace, they leapt
forth and from the fathomless face, they cried
lightning until they burnt the chase, they died
with a vigor not known to race, they kept.
An utterance broke from our lips with pain
as we watched the cinders glow and come gray,
our hearts groaned and sang of the mourning day
while the ashes dropped in colors of rain.
And sinking deep to reach the buried soul,
they fall unto us, thus nourishing whole.

Andrea DaViera, Grade 12
Valparaiso High School, IN

Ode to Summer

Ode to summer,
Which sets us free,
When the school bells are silenced.
Ode to summer,
Which makes us taste,
The wonderful heat and warmth on our lips.
Ode to summer,
Beautiful, hot,
Wonderful and free.
Ode to summer,
Outside all day long,
In the beautiful weather.
Ode to summer,
Freedom for you and for me,
From school and all of the insanity.
Ode to summer,
With wind, rain,
And the sun in all of our window panes.
Ode to summer,
Miles of roads left untraveled,
From summers past.

Andrew Lamour, Grade 12
St Mary Catholic Central High School, MI

My Journal

The things in my journal have nothing in common
random thoughts
parts of songs I like
lyrics I write myself
and pictures of celebs. I love

One thing that I can't keep my eyes off
is what you wrote
the last three words
"Love you babe"
makes my heart ache

I hear your voice
every time I read it
and that's when my stomach turns
one little tear runs down my face
I whisper
"I miss you"
what you wrote
keeps my journal
Alive…

Jenifer Silva, Grade 10
Beaverton High School, MI

R.I.P. Joe Aubuchon

One second you're there
The next you're not
You said prom wasn't your thing
But no one knew the truth

The pain is always there
I understand it is going nowhere
But life goes on
Time scabs wounds
But never fully covers

I never understood your pain
But you were like my little brother
I took my cue from you
I will always protect family,
And that includes you too.

Watch out for us from up there
You are always loved, from now until the end of eternity
R.I.P. Joe Aubuchon,
A beloved brother, son, friend and family member.

Rebecca McLachlan, Grade 12
St Thomas More Academy, MI

Footprints

Right foot, left foot, right foot, left foot
I try to walk perfectly in the footprints set before me
But I can't, there is a fault in my step
The prints are largely and strongly set
Mine will never take the same shape
The shoes you wear are too big to fill
Too big expectations that I will not fulfill
So don't bother leaving your shoes behind
Today, I walk in my own
Today, I don't walk in the prints of other people's lives
But instead I leave prints on theirs
Today, I'm becoming more like me
And less like you
I have my own great expectations
I set my own course
I set my own pace
Head held high, onward
No longer will I walk in the shadow of yours
I cast my own now
At the end of the day, when the sun is gone
I'm the one who's going to shine

Courtney Sebo, Grade 10
Zionsville Community High School, IN

Regrets of the Past

That day will always be burned in my memory.
Every time I face the mirror I see a reflection I despise.
Two years have gone by but it feels like yesterday.
Why must I live in misery repeatedly?

At a young age I remember laying in darkness,
Hearing bizarre noises that were near.
Knowing my brother might be gone forever.
Having a diagnosis that was terminal,
Or so we thought.

Fast forward eight years and fate called upon me yet again.
If you are truly the master of your destiny,
Why did I feel so powerless?
I heard the noises once again
But no one was there to guide me.
Suddenly I'm in a room,
A room full of toys to calm the kids.
A room full of tissues to dry the tears.
I reach for one as my eyes begin to swell,
When I realize my grandma is gone.

Kara Brinn, Grade 10
Allegan High School, MI

Seasons

Winter with its white snow,
Covering everything with its white blanket of snow.
The beautiful covering of the pine trees that make it seem
As if we lived in an icy wonderland.

Spring with its flowers that are ready to blossom,
With its bright beautiful colors
Filling the world that we live in with the
New life of the flowers.

Summer with its heat and sunrises on my skin,
The hotness of the sand in between my toes,
Children playing in the water and making slashy
Splash with the water.

Autumn with its cool crisp nights,
Children playing with its yellow, orangey, red
Warm colored leaves
Giggling as they blow away.

Knowing that winter is coming again.

Monserrat Escamilla, Grade 12
Clarkston High School, MI

Since the Beginning of Time

Call me the river
that flows to the sea.
Call me the tip of the sky
that looks down on Everest.
Call me the sand between your toes
when you walk on the beach.
Call me the wind
that bends and blows through the land.
Call me the sun
that illuminates the sky.
Call me the ocean
that's seen by all but, touched by few.
Call me the snigger from a child
that grumble of an elder.
Call me the seasons
that are forever changing.
Call me Mother Nature.
I can be excellent at times and dreadful the next.
I can be swift and humorous, but sluggish and tough.
I'm all that breathes, walks and flies
I am life.

Journey Root, Grade 10
Allegan High School, MI

The Man in the Mask

Who is the man in the mask?
He is a man challenged with two contrasting tasks:
when a friend is in need of help or is down,
it is him who comes and helps, picking them up off the ground.
Yet he hides behind that mask, prevent all from seeing,
his true feelings and problems that may come into being.
Running, hiding, always helping everyone first,
however it is helping himself that he thought was the worst.
He thought: no one needs to know what goes on in my life,
no matter how much of it is anger, sorrow, and me living in strife.
I am here for my friends, to help them in their hour of need,
if I only thought about me and my time and problems,
it would only show my greed.
Plagued by personal problems and sorrow,
this he doesn't want people to see,
so on with the mask tomorrow
so he'll continue to seem happy as far as the eye can see.
Masking all emotion so we do not see
the true person that lies beneath; just waiting to be set free.
So, who is the man in the mask you may ask?
He is a person that is contained within the mind of you and me.

Quinlan McWilliams, Grade 10
John Adams High School, IN

Waste

I'm sorry it had to end like this
I wish it could have ended in bliss
But fate is not my friend in life
Fate only brings me mortal strife

I wish I wasn't like this anymore
I wish my life wasn't such a whore
Love, I'm sorry, I couldn't make you happy
I was right all along; I'm just so sappy

Mother and father, please ignore the crowd
I just wish I could have made you proud
But I just wasted my life and time
Trying to find some stupid rhyme

But most of all, my darling love
I wanted you to know
That you deserve so much better than me
And I know it's something you'll never see

I'm not who you thought I was
I'm not as happy as I seem
Except to you love. I never lied
Not even in the end, on the night that I died
Dakota Taphouse, Grade 11
Onsted High School, MI

Baby's First Day at the Beach

Upon my arrival, the sand welcomes me,
takes me into his home.
Although this means removing my shoes,
he responds kindly, enthusiastically,
by kissing my toes.

His other guest, the shallow water,
greets me similarly
by flashing her sparkling eyes.
A dazzling smile ripples across her face
before she takes me in her grasp
to dearly embrace me.

Lastly, the sun, so brightly,
so happily, comes forth for introductions.
Full of warmth,
of life and hope,
he nearly glows as he approaches,
making me blush with delight.

Nearly unseen in this photo,
these will be my guardians for life,
my natural godparents,
the only I will ever need.
Katie Kemp, Grade 12
Mercy High School, MI

Changing, Rearranging

I'm looking at the pieces
Of the puzzle
That I used to be

I tried to put them back together
But their shapes
Have changed radically

They don't fit together anymore —
I just don't
Make sense anymore

The colors are all different
The picture has all changed

I can't be who I used to be
I'm being rearranged

I've got to look ahead
Embrace the future
Accept the change

But the past —
It's hard to let go of…
Christina Nicole Wilson, Grade 12
Riverton Parke Jr/Sr High School, IN

Untitled

Take the color green for example.
Green is a seemingly
forgotten
favorite color,
what with the masses
and their obsessions with deep blue,
how they write
entire serenades
about the sky on stormy horizons
and the taste of the cool, clear air
when the wind subsides…
They can have their fun,
I suppose.
After all, dullness is always an option.

Either way,
you can bet
that while everyone else
stares into the ocean,
that I'll be off
sitting in some tree
starting at them.
Travis Root, Grade 10
Grandville High School, MI

Exodus

Begging for forgiveness.
Facing the end.
A dance full of emotion.
It started a trend.

Dressed in all black,
From head to the toe.
What we're repenting
Only each of us knows.

Words sung in Latin.
Makeup smeared from our eyes.
The anger turns to sadness.
Making each of us cry.

Hand to the heavens.
Head hung down low.
Screaming in terror
As far as fear goes.

A piece full of darkness.
Our flaws, how they range.
So when Judgment Day comes,
What will you do to change?
Megan Yee, Grade 12
Harrison High School, MI

Investigating Love

Oft I've dreamed of being a sleuth
And unraveling sundry mysteries
From chaos to deduce the truth
As such, life has hereto been a tease

But you remain unsolvable
Sadly out of reach
Without as yet a name to recognize
My mind knows not your proper niche

Still I have no guarantee
That things will ever change
Even once you've met me
My task mayn't rearrange

It could be for life
That you my mind befuddle
Though married for years
I may remain in a muddle

Perhaps for years I'll play detective
In the very pleasantest of ways
With marriage as my last elective
I'll be learning all my days
Andrea Paul, Grade 12
Grand Ledge High School, MI

High Merit Poems – Grades 10, 11, and 12

Daddy's Little Girl

What can I do but let you go,
Do I even have a choice,
Why can I still see your face,
Why can I still hear your voice?
When you left me long ago,
Even after all these years,
Your memory still brings me tears.
Why did you leave me,
So far away,
I wish that I could hear you say,
"You are daddy's little girl,"
I thought that you would always stay.
I came to the visit,
Only to find,
That you had left us all behind,
I wish that I could hear you say,
"You'll always be my little girl,"
Before you decided,
To leave this world.
Catherine Hornick, Grade 11
Troy High School, MI

Harvest Moon

a light breeze ruffles my hair
I am in a field
staring at an orange moon
the darkness slowly envelops me
I listen to the sounds of the night
the chirp of the crickets
the swish of movement in the grass
the night orchestra
conducted by the moon
for the sole listener…

…me
Marissa Morgan, Grade 12
Portage Northern High School, MI

How Fast It Goes

It is terrifying
How fast time goes
First it rains
Then it snows
Winter comes
And cold wind blows
Then slowly blooming
Green grass grows
The world keeps turning
Under our nose
It is terrifying
How fast it goes
Brianna Lisak, Grade 11
Valparaiso High School, IN

Twisted Mind

She wasn't always this way
She was fond of reading and the water
Her friends all loved her
She found herself thinking, at the worse time
She swerved, found herself and her car in the ditch
She didn't like who she was
She loved the dark poems
All the dark words and pictures
You would have never guessed who she was on the inside
She never showed anyone
She didn't want people to know
At night she wrote those dark writings for hours
It soothed her, made her calm
One day she plans on coming out
She felt like a fake, they all knew her secret
They hated her, she was done for and they will never accept her again
Her mind was always twisting she never knew what was right
She hated herself, things never felt good enough
She doesn't know who to talk to
She feels alone
She knows no one will ever understand
Meghan Mary Crosby, Grade 12
St Mary Catholic Central High School, MI

Sun at Night

A cool summer night,
   In the middle of a field,
      I look up to the sky with anticipation.
Pinpricks of light burn endlessly, vast distances away.
Wind rushes through the trees, pine, spruce, birch, and oak.
The sweet, pungent smell of freshly cut grass,
   Wafts through the cool, summer night air.
The hushed whispers of the sleeping world are all that are,
All that wish to be known.
My dad, huddled in his spot under his fluffy sweatshirt, makes a sound,
   And lifts a finger skyward, over the line of trees.
And there like a second sun,
   The comet shows itself.
A dazzling orb of white and blue,
   A heavenly aura about a brilliant core,
      And a beautiful wispy tail stretching across the night.
Anthony Polito, Grade 12
Clarkston High School, MI

Another Chance

I would give
   my great grandma a day to talk to her husband,
      a chance to ask why.
I would give
   her the chance to take back all of her memory of this horrible thing,
      the chance to take the Alzheimer's away.
I would give
   her the knowledge of what was about to happen,
      a chance to stop her husband from taking his life.
Nate Fairbotham, Grade 10
Allegan High School, MI

Page 41

Life Is Not a Door

Life is not a door
That you keep running in and out
You can't keep leaving and returning
I'm sick of the games when will
You ever be serious
I'm tired of people walking in and out
When will there ever be that one that stays
This time I will not let you back to do the same
You will realize what you had
Then it will be too late
I'm done playing can't take it anymore
I'm starting to feel sick on this bumpy road
I will no longer accept this ride
So before you walk out
Just think about what I just said
Because you will no longer be accepted
In this life of mine…

Briana Koger, Grade 10
Detroit Academy of Arts & Sciences - Medbury Campus, MI

Fast Life

When you are young, you want to live life fast
You always want to be in the fast lane
Just slow down and try to make it blast
It goes by too quick, seems just too insane
Things will got by in the blink of an eye
You will make bad mistakes along the way
Always tell the truth and never a lie
Do this and life is more fun day by day
You life will change directions like the wind
Never a straight road, there's always a turn
To make the right choices, have a calm mind
Can't be lazy, work hard for what you earn
The early years in your life are the best
Go out with friends and never rest

Shane Hentkowski, Grade 12
Posen Consolidated High School, MI

Life

It is like a river
Slowly, changing its path through its course.
It is viewless and unseen
Take flight of a soft intricate dream.
It is a threadbare cycle
Who knows when the world around us will deplete it?
The wails of the newborns enter our world
And the sighs of the dying leave our world.
So many beings leave before they could try to understand
What it means, what it gives us, and what it is.
It gives us laughter and sorrow
Thought of feeling and soul and sense and love.
It makes the earth go round.
We hope its journey runs forever.
It is life…

Ankita Mangal, Grade 10
Troy High School, MI

Grandpa

A smiling face
With pearly-white dentures
A polo shirt,
And Khaki pants,
With American Flag suspenders:
His usual attire
Oh and his unforgettable
John Deere hat.
What do you see?
A typical Grandpa.
What do I see?
I see a man on his deathbed,
Slowly dying from a rare cancer.
His heart is filled
With a love for his family that is unfathomable.
Unable to talk,
He intricately mouths the words:
I love you
To my grandma.
Holding on until every last breath,
He peacefully passed in the arms of his sweetheart.

Eleni Sinigos, Grade 12
Northview High School, MI

Poison Pressure

You sat and watched standing tall and confident
As you fed him poison out of your palm
As he complained, yet did so slightly unwillingly.
You sat back and watched, eyeing him devilishly,
Not wanting to suffer alone.
The world was crumbling at his weary feet.
Placed all the heavy blame on his shoulders
For the wrecked man to bare alone.
Leaving you free of all worry and ache.

You stealthily convinced the world he was the terrible person
And fed the gossip-hungry media lies after he was sent away.
As he choked on years of substance.
I hope the smoke clears from your empty head.
I hope you see what great damage you have done.
I hope you see that we will no longer believe.
That you and your conceiving ways weren't always the one.

Lindsey Schenten, Grade 10
Clarkston High School, MI

Goodbye Yesterday

I wish I could go back, to the days when I could dream
Where I could walk into my closet and put on my favorite jeans
Without working until we died and eating a small meal a day
I had purpose to my life, and I liked it that way
When I could hang out with my friend, knowing she is still alive
I now can only hope there's greener grass on the other side
And I have dreams that I keep dreaming where they kill us anyway
Well, I guess we have tomorrow but goodbye to yesterday

Samantha Polonis, Grade 10
L'anse Creuse North School, MI

High Merit Poems – Grades 10, 11, and 12

Hello, Goodbye
The little brown dot on the skin in between your
Thumb and pointer finger, and
The way your eyes are never actually particularly
Green, or blue, or gray…
The way that I look at your skin and
Recognize it as my own.
The way I see you as mine, only mine, as I know,
You feel for me.
Watching your body movement and realizing
We're speaking the same language.
Staring at your fine hair and remembering
How soft it is, wishing it was in between my fingers.
Remembering your arms were the safest place
I use to ever feel…
Now knowing
That I can love you as much as I can,
You will say whatever you will,
You will leave whenever you want,
But I will never get you like I want you,
That you will never be
Here.

Sierra Baker, Grade 11
Clarkston High School, MI

The Unforgiving Nightmare
Anger. Anger consumes my mind.
My being. It's a demon clawing
at my soul, body, and psyche.
Ripping me limb for limb
to leave me with only my faith to dangle.
My raw wounds fester and burn,
constantly reminding me of this devil.

Mother Nature, won't you cease?
You send us disease
through waves and quakes.
Now there is permeating radiation
so we live further in trepidation.

The houses are gone and children and families weep.
The putrid smell of garbage makes my stomach growl.
When will I wake up from this nightmare?
I wish to run away — far away.

Alexis Wait, Grade 12
Allegan High School, MI

Everybody Dies, Not Everybody Lives
Everybody dies but not everybody lives
To be alive doesn't mean that you live.
When you come into this world with nothing to give.
When you live this life you could just not be living at all.
Because life isn't really living at all
Everything you thought and everything you saw
What if one day you woke up and had dreamed it all?

Jason Jackson, Jr., Grade 10
Lakeview Jr/Sr High School, IN

One Day
Through the seven seas I sail.
When all the seas so blue,
I dream of that one day, to tell you my tale,
On the day I'll spend with you.

As I ferry souls to the other side,
Just knowing you have my heart with you,
I wish you had come along for the ride.
As do my hardworking, loyal crew.

As I sit in my cabin looking out to sea,
I count down the days, months, and years.
Wishing you were here with me.
The day draws near, I hold no fear, until I hear,

The sound of a song sung so long ago,
I know you will never let me go.

Libby Devlin, Grade 11
Bishop Luers High School, IN

This Girl
Oh how I love you,
The only girl I could ever think of.
But I stop to question if you do too,
Feel the way I do, about this love.
I can never shake you from my mind
For you have left an imprint on my brain.
I tried to treat you with what I knew to be kind;
If you asked, I would do it, even kiss you in the rain.
I'm sorry I made a mistake,
I never meant to overreact.
I offer you my heart to take,
Please forgive me; I just did not know how to act.
So if time says we are not meant to be,
Remember, I will always be in love with thee.

Jason Dagger, Grade 12
St Mary Catholic Central High School, MI

Unicorns
Will we ever see unicorns again?
Oh, Father, warm my cold and dreary heart
For it is nothing but a murky den
Of lions; tearing love and joy apart
Will I hear hooves, impatient on the ground?
Or see a silhouette against the moon?
For to an unbelieving world I'm bound
So even if I do, it won't be soon
But if I look at life with child's eyes
I'll see that they were never lost at all —
They are the clouds that run through sunlit skies
The light their golden horns, the wind their calls
To heaven look — great kingdom in the air
And you will find the unicorns are there

Susan Lockwood, Grade 12
Northview High School, MI

Pains of Our Nation

written on this page are the pains of our great nation
we try to solve the issues and pains with arbitration
still, wars are started, and it only leads to bloodshed
so we express our sorrows and sadness by the mourning of the dead
they are heroes setting examples by the lives that they have lead
showing to us the path that we should tread
we support them and pray for them every night and day
as the people of our nation search for a better way
we do this so we can end the lives of soldiers being lost
because everyone knows that in war death is the cost
I don't know why they think that sending troops overseas
will bring stability to governments and bring tensions to an ease
all they do is cause more pain, strain and sorrow
hundreds were lost today how many will die tomorrow
violence breeds only violence, anger and lots of misery
we are fighting a war that is one of the worst in our history
I try to rid myself of the thoughts night and day
yet still I contemplate these things and I guess I'm trying to say
is that wars not only hurt families, but also destroy their foundation
so I say to god as I say to you, God help this U.S. nation
James Greenwood, Grade 11
Manistee Catholic Central School, MI

The Love of a Father

The man I've loved forever
One who is strong, caring and clever
Someone who I turn to when in trouble
That's there to pull me out of the rubble
Where would I be without this man
I honestly have became his number one fan
He has been hurt in different ways many times
From many people and actions of all kinds
I never understood why or even how
But my confusions are much clearer now
The devil is trying to knock him down
Trying to make this man look like a clown
But this man stays true to the Lord
Going to war with a very sharp sword
I would give my life for this man to be let go
Even though he will refuse and always say no
Who is this man that I really do love
He is my father who was sent from above
A father's love that I can keep
Who is in my heart very deep
Anita Regalado, Grade 12
Melvindale High School, MI

Fleeting Flora

So sweet the scent of flowers flee,
Such transient beings glow.
Wavering in the warm summer's breeze,
Their venerable beauty undeniable to all.

Can you hear them sing an aria in the dew?
Their voices soft as fresh cotton.
They wear the rain drops like diamonds;
They glissade in the wind, swans on a crystal lake.

Their smell as one of perfume,
They scent the earth with their favorite melody.
A fragrance known in India and Persia,
How wonderful and graceful they are.

Yet they are but evanescent beings,
Soon they fade and pass away.
Can you hear them sing an aria in the dew?
Their voices soft as fresh cotton.
Braden Sellers, Grade 12
Christian Academy of Indiana, IN

Don't Listen

Don't listen.
Don't listen to anyone that says you are not good enough.
Cool enough.
Small enough.
Smart enough.
Tall enough.
Strong enough.
Tough enough.
Don't listen.
Don't listen to anyone that says you don't have the right look.
Right body.
Right clothes.
Right shoes.
Right hair.
Right voice.
Right friends.
Don't listen.
Be you.
Because YOU are more than enough.
Alisha Le Mire, Grade 11
Northview High School, MI

Space

I often find myself lost in space
The vast darkness cools my face
I gaze at the moon, stars,
Sometimes even Mars
Meteor showers rarely appear
And zero UFOs, no fear
Planets, solar systems, galaxies galore
It's up to me to discover more and more.
Adam Wilmes, Grade 12
Mater Dei High School, IN

High Merit Poems – Grades 10, 11, and 12

Time Stands Still

Comforting warmth encircles me,
All the pain and rage dies away.
As the smiles spread over my face
I know we both know this is the way.
Still, as his breathing slows and deepens,
The tears once more start to fall;
Every good thing has been taken from me,
That's why I keep building walls.
The pressure builds and builds,
And my sobs are straining to be heard,
Until I sink my teeth into my hand;
I have to repress the wailing words.
In a whirling instant he's awake,
And pulling me closer to him;
My fears are crushed under his promises
And scattered at his very whim.
His lips gently caress mine,
His hands cupping my cheek;
Time stands still and my tears dry
And for a while, I'm no longer weak.
Raechel Lenz, Grade 11
Concord Montessori & Community School, MI

I Hate That I Love You

Lucky me, lucky you
Look at us, we are fools
I kiss him, I rebound
I kiss you, and I drown
He made me feel unbelievably real
But my heart was bare without a shield
In that moment, it was just a steal
In that moment, it was just a deal
They say second is best
But my heart chose you first
They say forget the rest
In contrast, you were the worst
I wanted you, I still do
I hate myself for loving you
After what you did, I still care
Immaturity still gets you nowhere
I am mad that I cannot get mad at you
I am mad that I am foolishly in love with you
Real or not, true or false, speak to me again
I miss you, so tell me, where do I begin?
Kyna Garrett, Grade 11
Portage Central High School, MI

We

   It is movement.
   It is capable.
   It is thought.
     It is life.

It is love.
Lucas Goedde, Grade 11
Mater Dei High School, IN

Journey

Life is a journey. Life can be swift.
Life was bestowed as a God-given gift.
As we make our way through the ups and the downs,
We must always remember to
Do away with our frowns.
Time is precious. Time flies too fast.
Time will never return once it's past.
As we look to our future, we await each new day.
We must always remember to
Not let memories decay.
Love is real. Love always survives.
Love is the key to success in our lives.
As people walk in and out of our hearts,
We must always remember that
Giving to others is where love starts.
Death is unpreventable. Death is a mystery.
Death places you somewhere new based on your history.
As we think about where our eternal home will be,
We must always remember to
Live a good life so God's face we may see.
Michelle DeMarco, Grade 12
St Mary Catholic Central High School, MI

College Bound

After twelve long years the time has come,
the next stage of life has now begun.
High school's done, classes taken and finished.
The time left as a kid is now diminished.
After endless homework, quizzes and tests,
always working to be the best.
Sculpted by the hands of school and life
a young man has risen above the strife
caused by stress, pressure and goals
and his mind and body have paid the tolls,
but all that work will serve him well
when on June 1st he hears that bell.
He'll leave his school, towards college he'll go,
where his new life will help him grow.
Reaching for the sky, shooting for the Moon,
all his efforts will pay off very soon.
Because of all his hard work and dedication
he will make a difference for himself and his nation.
He will be successful, happy and free
but above all else, he will be all that he can be.
John Williams, Grade 12
Clarkston High School, MI

The Place

Where I arise
The habitat where I flourished
My niche, my palace, my shelter, my home
The place
Where I became me.
Kenneth Medilo, Grade 12
Wylie E Groves High School, MI

The Prey

The cat crouches low
Tightening its leg muscles
Lowering its head
Squatting its broad shoulders
Now barely distinguishable in the undergrowth

His prey is scrambling now

Its breath is coming in short hard gasps
With desperate abandon
It crashes through the forest
Then stops to listen

The cat has become restless
It compensates by sinking lower
The pressure builds on its hind legs
Barely able to control the irresistible
Urge to leap forward

A twig snaps
And echoes through the forest

The spell has broken.
There will be no escape.

Alex Stickley, Grade 12
Allegan High School, MI

The Little Things

Sometimes I think it's the little things.
Like the way your mothers hands feel when you're sick,
Or the way your father tells a story.

The little things of relationships.
Like a goodnight kiss.
Or talking all night, barely touching at all.

The little things of songs.
When the music gets quiet,
Or loud, and you lose your breath.

The little things that make you you.
Your smile, laugh
How you get excited over things that may not matter

The little things of nature.
A warm sunset,
A cold snowfall as the moon glistens off the blanket of snow

I think it's all those little things, added up to make a big thing
Added up to make up your mind
To make life what it is, to make it worth living for
Or not living for at all.

Kortny Jewell, Grade 11
Northwestern Sr High School, IN

The Real Killer

The world's most vicious killer,
   Attacking the old and young,
That strikes without cause or warning,
   Is gossip's venomous tongue.

The poisonous snake is a sissy compared with this unruly knave,
For a heart has broken,
   And dug, for many, a grave.

Oh pity the misguided moron who goes about spewing his guile,
Believing his wiles are hidden behind a transparent smile.

God grant, on the day of judgment,
   Whatever my failings have been,
Of gossip I shall not be guilty,
   That murderous, home-wrecking sin.

Taylor Hildebrand, Grade 10
Allegan High School, MI

And Then There Were None...

With my name accost in red, Scarlet be dread
My sister's love is lost, for powers cost
Leering, peering through the bars of the cage
The mornings light here is forbade
While walls of cobble stone endure for sure,
My fledgling sanity is not procured
Day in, day out, monotony ensures
To dream a dreamless dream is the cure
With lightened feet I'd tread, living though dead
The singing dolls whom that I most adore
They soon shall cease their singing ever more
Then once again alone, bound by cages stone
Until my wayward dreamless life is done
And finally then there will be none...

Jared Page, Grade 12
Christian Academy of Indiana, IN

The Lord's Distraction

The houses on the building in my hand
show skyline signs that I have love to brew
but lack ability to comprehend
the disappointment in the girl too blue
that whimpers holding tightly to my palm.
The darling I once knew sleeps clutching fear
with muscle even gravity can't calm.
Rebellion is unsuccessful here.
I mustn't turn to duties till this goes
for sadly mending most malicious miles
will worsen woeful wounds that never close.
I wait till she shines, showing shimmered smiles.
The Lord does not have it so easy, friend.
Oh, when shall Mother Nature's crying end?

Kristie Robinson, Grade 11
Stoney Creek High School, MI

Love of My Life

Storms keep me from the love of my life,
They cover the streets
With rain, snow and ice,
Making for a dangerous trip
That at times is not worth the risk
This love is my medicine
That puts a smile on my face.
But when I am ill
And cannot receive the daily dose,
I become overwhelmed with heartache.
At times, I have a busy schedule
Filled with school, homework and chores.
I cannot find enough time to get out the door
For the love of my life.
But often they say —
What you love, you make time for
So I give up my sleep,
And begin the treacherous journey
Into the rain, snow and ice —
To run
For the love of my life.

Colleen Grassley, Grade 12
St Mary Catholic Central High School, MI

The Wind

The door opens
The wind gently blows through
Carrying the scents of spring
An orchestra of simple aromas

Lilacs, fresh cut grass, and last night's rain

The wind gently blows through
Swirling the pages of an open book
These scents mingle with the pages
In an intricate dance known only to them

The wind dies down
Leaving these scents behind
The only fragrance to prove he was ever there

Emily Wartella, Grade 12
Allegan High School, MI

Love

I fight, I scream, I cry
I'm trapped in love's lies
Bounded with madness suppressed with fear
The time is not now but it's almost near
Working my way through the pain
I have no regrets, no sorrow and no shame
Here I am by myself
Footsteps in the darkness with no one else
My life is drowned with all the silence
I just pray for a day without any violence

Aarionna Richardson, Grade 10
Jackson High School, MI

Ode to Spring

We saw you, but you went away
We want you to come back
To bring warmth and smile to our day
Your sun is so bright
To scare away frosty Jack
Please come back to show us how to live, just right!
We love to be warm and free
While we laugh on while playing hackey sack
Run, play ball, catch, climb up a tree
April showers bring May flowers
Let's go out and run in the rain
And maybe even build a tower.
We can imagine we are riding a train
With your friend summer.
But we have not met summer just yet!
We have to wait for June, July, and August, bummer!
While we wait we will enjoy making bets
On who will fall in the dirt and mud?
And see the faces with all the fun,
When they make a great thud.
Spring, let's grab the sun and go for a run!

Matthew Pulter, Grade 12
St Mary Catholic Central High School, MI

Oedipus Rex at His Best

The higher one is, the harder one falls,
Young Oedipus Rex knows best of them all.

With a mother a wife and a brother a son,
This tragic tale has only just begun.

A father a victim of fate gone wrong,
Left only with a blind prophet to sing the truth of this song.

When crossroads meet, blood is shed,
Turning a baby's crib into a mother's bed.

The truth is revealed and chaos ensues,
It is time for the culprits to pay their dues.

A suicide for one, exile for another,
This much can happen when a boy loves his mother.

Olivia Stenzel, Grade 12
Clawson High School, MI

Spring Break 2011

As the moon hugged me goodnight,
I laid myself into bed.
I had a million dreams rushing through my head.
Spring break is coming so fast, California here at last.
The dream of the sun kissing me during the day,
Not listening to what they all say.
The water that dances in the light,
All the famous stars that will be in my sight.

DeAnna Bond, Grade 12
Wylie E Groves High School, MI

Self-Confidence

What do you see when you gaze into a mirror?
Are you the person you want to be?
Are you just as you appear
Warm and bubbly like a hot cup of tea?

Are you the person you want to be?
Do you see yourself as unique?
Warm and bubbly like a hot cup of tea
Take a closer peek.

Do you see yourself as unique?
Does every flaw catch your eye?
Take a closer peek
Before you let out that sigh.

Does every flaw catch your eye?
Are you just as you appear?
Before you let out that sigh,
What do you see when you gaze into a mirror?

Claire Andrews, Grade 10
Bishop Luers High School, IN

Stand Back, and Watch Me Fade

Look at me now;
can you really say that you're proud.
it's that time, where I could run away;
and there would be nothing left to say.

I don't have anything on my mind;
it's what happens when I lay flat on the finish line.
You're the one who thought you should be the blame;
then I thought, I should do the same.

I know, I just gotta believe;
but not when you're the one who has been deceived.
So, you go watch me;
and ask yourself, "Is this what I want it to be?"

But really, can you say that you're proud;
if so, do me a favor and scream it out loud.
Do you feel it inside;
or feelin' yourself dying, but you're still alive.

Brianna Silva, Grade 10
Forest Park School, MI

Unique

The
tall
green
stem stands tall and proud
with
the colorful flowers and their leaves
surrounding it making it more unique
than the rest

EJ Lewis, Grade 12
Wylie E Groves High School, MI

The Winter Wind

Whispers of the algid wind are willfully sent,
Transpiring by inane trees' new descent.
Stop it now before it spreads all falsehoods
Within the ubiquitous, white-cloaked woods.

The prodigious trees of blush, rich-green
And the placid, blue lake once captured a scene,
Possessing a vitality that was truly adored,
But now form memories wistfully stored.

Crunches from grounded snow remain,
Along with cold hisses left as a stain.
It laughs at our faces in cruel apathy
And disposes us with inexorable misery.

The Winter wind ignores the true beauty
And focuses on its disdained, selfish duty.
Blinded by the need to cause lamentation,
The wind will halt from the sun's revelation.

Jonathon Parker, Grade 12
Fruitport High School, MI

Ocean Thief

Waves
Crashing gently into my legs
Washing shells
In creamy shades of pink and orange and blue
Onto the white sandy shores of Sanibel Island.
Salty water soaks through my shorts,
Cooling me from the setting sun,
Refreshing like a drink of water
As I run and laugh in the ocean.

Suddenly, a single shell scrapes across my foot
I cry out and grasp at the twisting water
But the angled bit of red hot sunlight
Alters the reflection
And my perfect white sand dollar washes away
Towards the sinking sun,
That appears to be drowning in the vast ocean waves,
Just like my hopes and dreams and smiles
Just like my sand dollar.

Kendra Mantz, Grade 10
Clarkston High School, MI

Things My Parents Tell Me Repeatedly

"Clean your room."
    "You don't exist in it," I prevailed;
"Stop texting."
    "I am talking to very important people," I snarled;
"Speak explanative."
    "Listen better," I said softly;
"Be respectful."
    I rolled my eyes in disgust;
"Don't say that."
    "Don't listen," I snapped;
"Get better grades."
    "Would you like to try this?" I questioned;
"Try harder."
    "I can only do so much," I pleaded;
"Go to bed."
    "I'm not sleepy," I said as I yawned;
"Speak more clearly."
    "Understand me," I mumbled;
"Get the phone."
    "You have legs," I answered.
I think of things I want to say, but know I never can.

Sydnee Hubbard, Grade 10
Onsted High School, MI

Perfectly Alone

I could see her at the end of the hall.
She walked elegantly,
Step after step,
And sway after sway.
She was my love,
And I wanted nothing more.

Her deep brown eyes
Glinted in the dimly lit hall.
Her magnificent black waves rolled down her back,
Hugging her shoulders tightly.
She was lovely,
And I never saw a woman so beautiful before.

She smiled — perfect teeth
Surrounded by luscious heart-shaped lips.
She waved and giggled lightly,
And kissed him. I turned around,
To the empty hall behind me,
And I walked away:
Alone.

John Redman, Grade 11
Clarkston Senior High School, MI

You're Always with Me

There are days when everything seems bright,
But days come when nothing goes right.
During the most desperate moments of my life
I know you're there walking by my side.
You never leave me,
You never abandon me.
When I cannot longer walk,
You hold my hand and pull me along.
When I need to scream and talk,
You stay quiet and listen to me until I stop.
When I trip and fall,
You cure my injuries and pick me up.
When I have no strength to take another step,
You carry me and take me in your arms.
I know you're always there watching after me;
Clearing the path so I can safely go through.
I'd be lost and lonely,
If it wasn't for you.
Thank you, to the One and Only,
My dear Lord.

Erika Espinoza, Grade 10
Columbus North High School, IN

Escape

You've found my escape through the darkest of nights.
The city turns, but the light still shines so bright.
I've waited my turn, but you've never called my number yet.
Could this be that you tried so hard to forget?

You've found my weakness, but I take the wave and ride it
Through the sandbars to the darkest of pits.
I've fallen to you, though I don't know why.
But shield me from the world, lead me to the sky.

Can I ever escape, one way or another?
Out of this mess, out of my head.
Oh girl, can you save me?
Out of this stress, out of my head.
Hopefully this time, but it's not over yet.

All the things I wanted to say, but I never did stay.
So you say it's over, we've been getting older.
Say it slower,
But it's not over.

Jerald Shi, Grade 12
Troy High School, MI

Mirror Image

The beautiful girl
Who stares back at me;
What does she think?
How does she feel?
Why does her world seem so perfect,
And mine but dashed dreams?

Amelia Reckelhoff, Grade 11
Mater Dei High School, IN

Home

Personality of colorful hot air balloons
A great open field with no place to hide
A gust of warm summer wind, a huge thunderstorm
Leaving me awake, alive, drenched anew.

Light gentle rain, spring drizzle, kissing my burnt skin
Then a bright hot sun, beautiful blue sky
Loyal trusting puppy, to defend me he will bite
A best friend, we take cover in the dark.

Giant teddy bear, always cuddles, listens, consoles
Rich brown sugar eyes with soft French silk skin
A patched wooly blanket, a big comfy old couch
He is my earth, my sea, he is my home.

Natalie Douma, Grade 12
Wylie E Groves High School, MI

Snow in April

I hate you. I really do.
I can't stand to look at you.
You're pale white, wet,
and disgusting.

You ruin any day,
even if it isn't a Monday.

You think you're beautiful,
but you're really not.

Whenever I see you,
I want to scream.

I can't stand you.
Who do you think you are?
I don't know why you think
people actually like you.

I don't mind you in the winter,
but it's spring now.
You need to go away.

C'mon snow, no one wants
you around in April.
Just go away.

Holly Nellis, Grade 10
Clarkston High School, MI

Why?

How unjust
Everything you've ever worked for…gone
Lost by the random wrath
Of just one little word, six letters long

It's simply not right
How could one day you have so much?
And the next wake up with so little
Why did it have to be you?

Why here, why now?
Without me there to help
I feel like all I can do is simply wait
And watch the seconds as they pass by

When will I see you again?
What if tomorrow's one day too late?
How do you say your last goodbye?
Where will I be when you're watching me?

Who will hold your hand?
This isn't my illness, not my ailment
So why do I feel like I'm dying inside?
Why is it I can't just accept this?

I'll love you, forever and always grandpa.

Trevor Sundelius, Grade 11
Northview High School, MI

Concrete Angel

Small and eloquent,
Dignified and graceful.
Full of life,
What an angel.

Never frowning,
Always smiling.
Living happy,
Heart full of love and warmth.

Just so perfect,
Child of light.
Must have been heaven-sent,
Truly someone to behold.

Once a beautiful child,
Now a concrete angel.
Her life ripped away,
Stolen by a thief in the night.

Purest light,
Shone like gold.
Now watching like a guardian,
Is a concrete angel.

Tina Foote, Grade 11
Sandusky High School, MI

Love

Love is horrid
Love is kind
Love is accepted
Love is declined

Love leaves you dumbstruck
Love leaves you blind
Love leaves you free
Love leaves you confined

Love shows no mercy
Love shows no heart
Love shows no point
Love shows no part

Love is powerful
Love is helpless
Love is eternal
Love is ageless

Ugne Paalksnyte, Grade 11
Northview High School, MI

Yin and Yang

I watch the darkness outside my window
When violently it is turned to light…
Revealing the world
Then back to dark…
Followed by a tremendous roar
That makes the house shudder with
Fear
I am mesmerized by the mix of
Beauty and power
Dark and light
Wind and rain
Yin
And
Yang

Kelci Snyder, Grade 11
Allegan High School, MI

Corn

Stalks in the field stand like soldiers,
maligned yet ready for battle,
or like the battered girls of the chorus
who strain to remain uniform.

They are inquisitive eavesdroppers—
girls craving drama,
nosy little brothers,
worried old mamas.

They are intricate structures
casting their dark empty shadows
over an unpopulated city.

Laura Williams, Grade 11
Mercy High School, MI

Things My Parents Say Over and Over

"No"
When I fling my shoes across the living room.

"I love you"
As I leave to go to my friend's house, to play cards.

"Whatever"
When I annoy them by asking if I can go out to dinner frequently.

"Shut up"
When I'm yelling around the house about to do something I do not want to do.

"Clean your room"
When my clothes are all over the floor, and my bed is not made.

"You want so much"
As I ask for the money that is lying in the center of the table.

"Be nice to your brother"
When we fight about him always getting away with everything, hence hitting me.

"Be safe"
When I leave to go shopping.

"Have fun"
When I'm getting ready to go to Florida with my Aunt Barb.

"Call me when you get there"
When I am walking out the door to go hangout with my friends.

Liz Cundiff, Grade 10
Onsted High School, MI

I Wish I Would Have Asked Katie Smith to Homecoming Freshman Year

Like a cage, I feel trapped
All alone, in the dark
My mind's almost snapped
Waiting to make my mark
Decisions form my road
The path I lay for my life
Stuck in the same mode
Wounds hurt like a knife
But as I sit and think
The wounds will heal
My ship won't sink
It's not a done deal
I look at who I really am
What I want, where I stand
Am I the lion or the lamb?
Do I extend a helping hand?
I am whom I choose
When I seem to do wrong
When I'm about to lose
Your smile, your song
Remind me why I live

Anthony Mercurio, Grade 12
St Mary Catholic Central High School, MI

The Old Spinning Wheel
Spinning wheel
Butter churn
Old Log Cabin
My heart does yearn
Mountains, valleys
Hills and dales
The countryside
Never fails
The peaceful nights
Under the stars
The lightning bugs
Trapped in jars
When morning comes
It's back to work
To plant some seeds
Out in the dirt
This is the life
I long to live
Until that time
Hard work I'll give
Jessica A. Wesley, Grade 10
Wapahani High School, IN

Believe Me I've Tried
I can't get away
I can't try to hide
I can't let you go
believe me I've tried
I can't walk away
I can't make you mine
I can't make this work
believe me I've tried
I can't live this way
I can't make it right
I can't continue on
believe me I've tried
I can't make it stop
I can't continue to cry
I can't begin to move on
when my feelings won't die
Karla Harman, Grade 10
Mount Pleasant Sr High School, MI

Suffocation
Suffocation, can't breathe
Don't you see? I need you,
Here with me?
You're my life, my oxygen.
My only hope, without you here
I can't seem to cope, so little by little,
I lose my breath, suffocation
You say it hurts to be watching and seeing
But it doesn't matter,
Because you're still breathing.
Danni Mason, Grade 11
Princeton Community High School, IN

A Writer Within
University letter after college offer, they pile up quick.
My future paths all laid out in front of me, before long I'll need to pick.
Friends and teachers ask, "What career are you going to take part in?"
"That's easy," I smile. "I'm a writer within."

I can visualize it now, a journalist with a piquant story to cover,
So many important facts, dates, and details that I would uncover.
My most formidable writing printed for society to read,
If I can do this, what I have done, is succeed.

I will have a stand set up for me and wait for the queue to form,
Where I will scribble my name on my book that's been born.
An author with a chronic need for writing,
This urge, this passion is there for my fighting.

My English teacher places my paper on top of my desk,
She smiles at me and says "This writing is very picturesque!"
I stare at my "A" paper and realize that for my interest I'm a contender,
So I say, "Mrs. Perrin I'm a writer within, remember?"
Victoria Azmanova, Grade 10
South Vermillion High School, IN

Paradise Found
Will you trust me if I take your hand and lead us on the search for ultimate bliss?
Abandon your daily doldrums for the unknown that awaits us on the horizon.
Winds whirl our worries off into an open sapphire sea, surrounding us in a salty kiss.
Feeling so alone, yet for once, so together, we embrace under the glow of the midnight sun.

Abandon your daily doldrums for the unknown that awaits us on the horizon.
As your wrinkles of tension begin to vanish, our destination comes ever closer.
Feeling so alone, yet for once, so together, we embrace under the glow of the midnight sun.
Gentle waves rhythmically lap at our shore, orchestrating the music of a great composer.

As your wrinkles of tension begin to vanish, our destination comes ever closer.
Pristine beaches of gold envelop us; is this our long-awaited Eden?
Gentle waves rhythmically lap at our shore, orchestrating the music of a great composer.
Summer forever illuminates our souls in this unchanging season.

Pristine beaches of gold envelop us; is this our long-awaited Eden?
Winds whirl our worries off into an open sapphire sea, surrounding us in a salty kiss.
Summer forever illuminates our souls in this unchanging season.
Will you trust me if I take your hand and lead us on the search for ultimate bliss?
Taylor Firestine, Grade 12
Bishop Luers High School, IN

High Merit Poems – Grades 10, 11, and 12

Unbreakable Heart
i feel like a bug on the windshield of your life
but not one that gets wiped away quick
i'm off to the side where the wipers don't reach
INVISIBLE, BROKEN, AND UNWANTED
because you were moving too fast
you never saw me right in front of you
so i sit here in an endless slumber
and wait to be woken
but this slumber is not meant to be broken
for i am not healed
so i warn you to be careful
for you may not like what i have become
because you broke my unbreakable heart
into pieces and although i try
it will take years to mend them back together
but once i'm better
i'll have learned two things
first, don't give your heart to someone
because they're bound to stab it
second, even the strongest of people
can be torn apart
Joná Begley, Grade 10
Jennings County High School, IN

Combined
Throughout my life I've seen many things
Faced many demons, shed many tears
I've never considered the joy love brings
I shut myself up in a shell for years.

Look at us now; what're we going to do?
I am in it for life, don't let me fall
I've realized life's nothing without you
I've given you my heart you have it all

Here I stand and look what you've done to me
Opened me up to things I've never known
I've taken flight, you have set me free
I'm showing you feelings I've never shown

You've given me your heart I have it all
We're in it for life, you won't let me fall
Sara Hunt, Grade 12
Posen Consolidated High School, MI

Let Go
When it rain it pours
and through that my feelings are sometimes hard to ignore.
Trying to dodge life's bullets to get to that door.
I have to let my feelings out I have to stand in the rain
and let go all my pain
then it will be easier to move forward.
Erika McCall, Grade 12
Romulus Community High School, MI

Pain That Can't Be Forgotten
You are so vivid in my mind
It was like you were just here I hate it
But I just did not care
Three years gone by since you died
You can never be erased from my mind
You lay there in that bed
That pale face, that silent look
But I knew you were dead

I've never been the same
It was like I just turned around
And went the wrong way
My heart that day in May

Was like an artist chiseling away
Piece by piece
My hope that came from you
But my love will always stay…that's OK

I feel the clouds watching me, I know there is a key
That can lead me to thee
I get halfway there, when my heart pulls me back in the chair
Grandpa I will never forget that day in May
When you just left me there…
Mikayla Quick, Grade 11
Lake City High School, MI

The Monster in You
It is waiting all the time
It lives in you always
It notices what you are doing
It waits for the right moment
To break out to destroy

The older people around you, help you
To try, to keep it inside of you
Lock it and never let it out
Hide it, so that no one can see
And learn how to control it

Not in truth…
Nobody can control it
Nobody can hide it
Nobody can keep it in chains
Nobody can prevent it, from breaking out

It is evil and it is in everyone of us
It wants to cause havoc during your whole life
You could never hold it back
Because it is, the nature of
The human
Hannes Rode, Grade 12
Grandville High School, MI

Struggle

Drugs is how they lose their mind,
think about it all the time.

Sex is how they lose control,
turning up into who knows.
Prostituting every day,
getting diseases on the way.

Money is what they think is going to
get them somewhere, but the truth is
that it's not it's just making them swear.

Money got spirits in it but most people don't
believe, they just use it to gamble and sell dope and weed.

A struggle is all the time,
drugs is just a deal,
sex is just prostituting and money ain't for real.

Uniqua Slaughter, Grade 12
Northwestern High School, MI

The Sun

The sun brightens my dark and dreary day
Its rays hit my body and make my face grin
Soon enough clouds begin to hide the rays
And quickly my whole world turns very dim
Without the sun my happy soul is black
The clouds are covering my everything
I can easily tell there is a lack
Without the sun's rays I will never sing
My shining sun is apparent no more
Its gorgeous rays are pointing elsewhere now
Why can't I just push the clouds out the door
They can get out of my life and take a bow
I really wish they would just go away
Then again I can have a happy day.

Kirby Klecha, Grade 12
Posen Consolidated High School, MI

The World's Tallest Building

Towering over everyone like a skyscraper
You teeter back and forth in the wind.
Your $300 Patent Leather
Pointed-toed stilts wringing your soles of blood
As you strut,
Nose up and arms akimbo,
Down Michigan Avenue.

Afraid of heights, you don't dare look down
And your needle-like heel gets stuck in the sidewalk.
You fall down to earth,
Crashing and tumbling,
To the pavement below as everyone watches
Just like the Twin Towers.

Chelsea Dehn, Grade 12
Allegan High School, MI

The Best of Us

It's hard for things to get worse,
When there is nothing of which you care.
You lay with the rest of us,
Far from the best of us,
Consumed in nothing and fully aware.
Loving is a gift and not something they'd need to hear.
Careful to be not so careful,
They're others but not alternates,
Colored in every colorless.
Out of sight but within conscience,
They're hidden in the trees
And swallowed by the shadows.
Swept with the wind and curled in the clouds.
It holds the best of us.
Beneath the bridge and
Above your great god's hands,
Is the difference of the best of us.

Marlena Schizas, Grade 12
Wylie E. Groves High School, MI

The Dream

The dream was like heaven
The date set back to 1447
Blue skies with a yellow sunset
Horses that are spread out beyond the horizon
A dark figure forms at the top of the hill
Dancing and swaying to the wind that fills
The air with a rhythm that sings so sweet
The moistness of green grass underneath its feet
Twirls and hurls itself to a seat
It closes its eyes and silently sleeps
The vision gets blurry and it's hard to see
The dark flowing shadow begins to sink
Back in the present a wooden stake appears
To kill the dream that was once so real

Alyssa Palazzolo, Grade 11
Dwight D Eisenhower High School, MI

The Struggle

I can feel the Angels guardfully watching me,
As the Demons try to morph me
Into what they want me to be.

I can see the Angels crying,
As they sense my willpower dying
And the Demons sighing.

I can hear the Angels willing me to be strong,
As I try to break free from the Demon's song
But I can't stop dancing within the throng.

I can smell the Angels' mystical flowers
As they embrace me, giving me the power
To rise above the Demons this fateful hour.

Meghan Hoskins, Grade 12
Mooresville High School, IN

Our Shoes

We all come from different walks of life,
So different, we often cause each other to strife.
We pass each person as if they were just another,
But in God's eyes we are all brothers.
Caught up with self-ambition,
It seems that it has become a tradition.
Each person has their very own story,
But we all live only life for self-glory.
We never care to ask,
As if we wear a mask.
We tend to believe that we are interesting,
And that everyone else is boring.
We have so much to learn,
But no one shows concern.
If we are all our brother's keeper,
Then why don't we go deeper?
When should we know where to go,
Why is it that we have to move on slow?
Everybody has different views,
So ask somebody if you can walk in their shoes.
Know that your shoes are yours though and don't trade them.

Brian LaFreniere Jr., Grade 12
St Mary Catholic Central High School, MI

Vanity

Is it hard living in a world of vanity?
Its walls closing telling you to conform
It is a shadow of insanity
Well tonight babe you're in rare form
Makeup and jewelry covering everything plain
In an outfit that makes all the men stare
Your mask is the air of confidence
All the jealous women pretend not to care
And the men lose all their sense
But babe I can see your emptiness
Tonight you target me straight from the start
Trying to capture me in your web
But I'd never let you near my heart
And now my patience for you is starting to ebb
All because I can see you're hollow

Dakota Mace, Grade 10
Jennings County High School, IN

Squash

Amid the thorny vines the squash remain intertwined.
Strung like bulbs on a Christmas tree,
they hang together
yet become tangled in each other's lives.

They cannot break off on their own.
They cannot rise or fall
without affecting the others.
Such are the joys and pains
of familiarity.

Michelle Alosachie, Grade 12
Mercy High School, MI

The Light

Dew that settles on the grass
that we touch as we watch the sun pass over our heads in the sky
isn't enough to make the blades touch Earth.

The heavy beads of water that form on the tips
aren't as bad as the rainfall not of the sky.
Moisture forms on my lips after a good cry.

The sigh of the world can be heard from here
where angels have already rescued from fear
the light that once lit up my life,
but now will never be again.

His words are so cold to freeze my heart.
Tears have never felt so warm.
It's almost a praise as they slide down my face.

Hearts that were previously drawn on the foggy window glass
have faded over time,
but will never completely go away.

The black curtains have been drawn for good
to block out this same light that I once loved,
but it will always find cracks to shine through
and it will haunt me the rest of my life.

Hannah Kay Jenkins, Grade 11
Castle High School, IN

A Thousand Ships

Over the high translucent waters they ride,
Whispering words of lust and desire through the night.
Embracing the dream the goddess had bestowed
In return for her golden prize of beauty.

Past lovers and histories now forgotten
As they lay under the moonlit sky,
Unaware to the growing feuds
And the conflict that will follow them
As a thousand ships are launched.

Entwined in her wild paradise,
Her heart filled with love for her destined lover
As her daughter and husband lay in the distance
Long forgotten.

Dazzled he remains,
Swept in by her perfume and
By the face of his brief future.

Now together they sleep,
Undaunted by the emergence of morning
And the destruction they will bring
To the approaching city
And their future.

Sara Knutson, Grade 12
Black River Public School, MI

The Perfect Rose
The delicate petals,
glistening with fresh dewdrops.
The pungent smell,
creeps into my senses.
There holding it,
my one true love,
seeking appreciation,
for this one perfect rose.
His light chocolate brown eyes,
melting into my soul,
seeking for pleasure,
seeking for love.
Once again I turn to the rose,
taking a breath,
filling in with the sweet pungent scent.
The needle sharp thorns,
dig deep into my skin.
Never once to look away,
from those searching eyes,
who so faithfully brought me,
the perfect rose.

Ashley Wilcox, Grade 12
Brandon High School, MI

A Frozen Love
Ice is a boundary between the cold air
And the cold water,

Cracks in the ice
Are openings where water and air say hello
Because in winter they are apart
For 4 months out of the year,

Almost forgotten,
A forgotten love

All because of a frozen sheet of water
Jealous because it doesn't get to feel
The kiss of the swift air

As the air across the ice searches for a crack
Water is waiting to burst out
And kiss the air but only to still be caught
Under the ice

A frozen love feels like forever

Sarah Hulsmeyer, Grade 12
Clarkston High School, MI

I Am From...
A busy mom and an absent dad.
From switching from house to house,
    Mom's one weekend, Dad's the next.
A household haunted by love turned to hate.
From violence and abuse.
    Physical, mental, chemical.
Fear and fighting,
    harsh words and harder punches.
From a family later divided by death.
    "I'm sorry for your loss," and "Be strong, he's in a better place now."
Sad, sympathetic looks,
    Very few laced with understanding.
From painful, haunting memories
    overshadowing the happier days I live today.
Now in a world where people don't judge me by my past,
    where I can be who I want to be.
Myself.

Mandy Huitt Wray, Grade 10
Allegan High School, MI

My Friend
I feel like I've known you forever, but I haven't known you long.
We are always doing things together whether it is bad or good.
You fill this place in my heart that I never knew or understood.
Since you have filled that spot I don't know anyone else that could.
You mean the world to me and I will always have your back.
We have been through a lot together, learned many lessons and learned them well.
You will always be my best friend, the one that's there when I need someone.
You are the one I can talk to about anything, anything at all.
And I know that I am close to your heart just as much as you are to mine.
We may get in some petty fights but they always fade away.
Because what is in the past is in the past, the future is yet to come.
I always see you being my best friend no matter how much I love and hate you.
I consider you to be a sister and I treat you like one too.

Kaitlin Norton, Grade 12
Brown City High School, MI

Come to My World
I live in a world you can't grasp
An astounding sapphire abyss
We inhabit the same planet yes, but our worlds could not be more different
I glide through silk
One slip into my world and you could discover things no one knows
An abundance of color and life
You visit my world, even though if you make one mistake you've sealed your fate
A beautiful brine welcomes you
You come like an ambassador to a foreign land
The freedom never ends in my home
So come and visit, if you must, but once you're here you'll never leave
Covered in scales I live
So let the sea take your heart, with its wonderful and deadly beauty

Victoria Howell, Grade 10
Jennings County High School, IN

High Merit Poems – Grades 10, 11, and 12

With All Your Heart
Though some don't understand
why people decide
to defend our country
or why they care
for everyone's freedom
and some decide not
to treat them as heroes
yes, war is a terrible thing
but so is not having freedom
the freedom men, women, and children
are deprived of every day
in the countries overseas
America is a caring place
they're fighting for freedom
over here and over there
so treat our heroes and heroines
with the respect they deserve
and support them
with all your heart.
Amber Lodewyk, Grade 12
Northview High School, MI

Deception
To look into the bright blue eyes
See lies, deception and agony.
Lures one in like a clear blue sea,
But destruction can exist
From something, so beautiful.

False hope, living a lie.
Rose, everything is perfect,
Thorn, but it is not.
Looks can be wonderful
But very deceiving.

Together forever
Together no more.
Gorgeous, illuminating.
Shadows creep in
Black and beautiful.
Kellee Olson, Grade 12
Harrison High School, MI

Pulchritude
We could have been so
pulchritudinous,

Together in
the sun.

But in the dark, crepuscular night,
You did
not believe
in us.
Katie Doyle, Grade 12
Stoney Creek High School, MI

Things Under My Bed
Blue sled
  Wading through the crisp air;
Big Scrapbook
  Made to divulge a tale;
Dirty Laundry
  That's been idle for a week;
My Cat
  That sleeps and purrs all day;
A Series of Books
  Lay scattered and wait to be opened;
Action Packed VHS Movies
  Eagerly waiting to be watched again;
Papers
  Crumpled, and jumbled, due today;
Action Figures
  With their parts strewn about;
Belts
  Frayed, and torn, faded and worn;
Maybe I should pick up this mess.
Tyler Peavey, Grade 10
Onsted High School, MI

Night Sky
I look at the sky
The stars so bright,
I've never seen,
So lovely a sight.

I give a big sigh
As the wind ruffles my hair.
All my worries gone,
I have not a care.

As time passes by
And the sky spins around,
I listen to the night,
The most peaceful of sounds.
Alyssa Yeager, Grade 12
Northview High School, MI

The Hallway
Too long.
An endless journey,
But with no intention.
Like going to the store
And not buying anything…
Pointless.
To go down it, torture.
To turn away, possibilities.
It can lead anywhere.
From your least favorite class,
To your most favorite person.
The choice is yours!
Harley Grimes, Grade 10
Mendon Middle/High School, MI

Fear
It lingers in the night
Like a shadow in the dark.
Its claws prepared to fight,
As sharp as the teeth of a shark.
It stalks unsuspecting fools,
That know but don't want to think
That fear itself follows no rules
And will attack before they can blink.
The heart starts to race,
Everything slows.
Fear and its evil chase
Delivers its blows.
Dorian Ash, Grade 11
Northview High School, MI

Sometimes
Sometimes I can't stand you
Sometimes you make me cry

Sometimes I wish I didn't have you
But then I know I would die

Sometimes I lie awake and wonder
Why was I given to you

But then I realize it doesn't matter
As long as I've got you
Ashley Bower, Grade 10
Pinckney High School, MI

Grades 7-8-9 Top Ten Winners

List of Top Ten Winners for Grades 7-9; listed alphabetically

Adela Baker, Grade 7
Clague Middle School, MI

Aimee-Lee Belzile, Grade 9
Ecole Secondaire Catholique Horizon, ON

Elizabeth Daley, Grade 7
St David Junior High School, AZ

Kendra Donahue, Grade 7
Sandwich Middle School, IL

Diana Harmata, Grade 9
West Jr High School, MO

Emily Murphy, Grade 9
Trinity High School, NH

Michael San Juan, Grade 8
Palmer Catholic Academy, FL

Brian Simonelli, Grade 8
Hanson Middle School, MA

Shaye Stalians, Grade 7
Glen Edwards Middle School, CA

Sarah Taylor, Grade 8
Our Lady of the Pillar School, MO

All Top Ten Poems can be read at www.poeticpower.com

Note: The Top Ten poems were finalized through an online voting system. Creative Communication's judges first picked out the top poems. These poems were then posted online. The final step involved thousands of students and teachers who registered as the online judges and voted for the Top Ten poems. We hope you enjoy these selections.

My Walk

As I walk the endless beach,
The sun shines upon my face,
It's like my guardian angel,
Following me wherever I go.

The waves continuously crash against the shore,
Whoosh, whoosh.
The sound — so soothing.

My hair blows in different directions,
Because of the chilly sea breeze.

With the sun, sand and sea,
Life on the beach is exactly where I want to be.

I don't want the day to end,
But the bright beautiful sun is gently fading away.

MacKenzie King, Grade 8
St Barnabas School, IN

Bubble

I'm in a bubble
that sways with smooth accuracy
(Yet, I'm tired of being trapped and lonely)
I'm a hazardous machine with no technique
my life, unique.

But something is not right.

I'm exceptionally fierce
I cannot fight that I'm peculiar
So I stay in the bubble

I should fight back
But I'm waiting to take the initiative
(Although waiting is a nuisance)
I'll choose to stay forever trapped
inside my glistening bubble

Alexis Robles, Grade 8
Culver Community Middle School, IN

An Express Highway

An express highway is like life
I want to go fast,
So I ignore the rules
Maybe I'll crash each car
I want to get a job, or make money faster
So I do cheat, and do bad think,
Maybe my life will crash and I'll feel awkward
So I go slowly, yet I still rule the highway
I never crash each car and I'm safe,
I study, and get job and make money slowly
But I do not cheat, and bad think,
I will never crash my life and I'll be happy.

Daehyun Lee, Grade 7
Ruth Murdoch Elementary School, MI

My Sport, My Passion

The ball hitting the bat
The feel of the ball in my hand
Running at full speed to the next white rubber
The thrill of sliding and knowing I'm safely home
The bright lights shining on my *Field of Dreams*

The sound of the crowd cheering is music to my ears
My teammates working as hard as I am
My parents supporting me again
My brother says he's proud

Another skinned knee, but I don't mind
Icing my shoulder, but it is worth working through the pain
Yes, I'm talking about baseball
Baseball,
The all American pastime
Baseball, my sport, my passion.

Jake Carpenter, Grade 8
East Jay Middle School, IN

What? Spring?

I wait and wait for Spring time to come
Around the corner I see snow melting
There are finally no faces that look glum
There are no snowballs which means no pelting

Time to stretch my legs again one more time
I go outside so many new flowers
Maybe I'll go to Paris and see a mime
I will go tour the Eiffel Tower

Just kidding I have no time nor money
I will take my time with a hop, skip, jump!
I am serious this is not funny!
Don't believe me, then I'll be in a slump

Dare me not I might just wear a bonnet
Do not worry this is just a sonnet…

Danielle Tatoris, Grade 8
St John Lutheran School, MI

Summer

Blue skies and butterflies
Sunshine and apple pies
Sleeping in 'til noon and hoping school won't come too soon
Having endless fun, hanging out with friends
Wishing summer fun will never come to end
Tubing down the lake or sipping a nice cool shake
You'll remember this forever
Even in the middle of September, when you're back at school
You'll remember all those times swimming in the pool
Losing track of time and getting unusual tanning lines
Beach days and orange haze
You watch the summer slowly fade away

Megan Allen, Grade 7
Ruth Murdoch Elementary School, MI

Understand

Call me that guy
I'm always there,
I am a blizzarding hail from South Dakota
I'm difficult to handle,
I'm a Venus fly trap
I snap about the smallest things,
I'm the spinal cord of a scorpion
I am a death trap of the Sahara,
I'm green and I'll put you in a haze
Like Oscar the Grouch,
I'm the three pointers in a basketball game on a Saturday night,
I am the flight hand in cards
I always get the job done,
I am a unique treasure
One of a kind,
I am a problem solver
I'm always dealing with everyone else's drama,
I'm a life changer,
I am the guy you want to hangout with.
Jared Pearce, Grade 9
Allegan High School, MI

What Did I Do Wrong God?

Dear God,
Oh God what have I done wrong?
You make me wake this morning
Only to go to dreadful school.
Each day it will take up my time,
There'll be new teachers,
Homework,
School books,
And don't forget pressure.
There'll be new people who'll become my friends,
And anticipation over who'll be on the sport teams.
God, I know you care,
Or you wouldn't have made those people,
People who thought up schools.
So God,
Make this year,
One to remember,
Especially those memories of 7th grade.
Whether good or bad.
Sarah Munsell, Grade 7
Oak Hill Jr High School, IN

Do You Remember When

Do you remember back when we were little kids.
The silly things we would laugh about not
knowing what the next day would bring.
Do you remember back when we played outside all day
or if it was a rainy day we would work on a puzzle
or watch a good movie our favorite *Sweet Home Alabama*
Do you remember back when we would
stay up all night and talk about that boy!
Do you remember back when there
seemed to be so many problems like when I didn't see you for a day?
But we still promised to be best friends forever.
Do you remember back when we were
right there for one another if we had troubles.
Do you remember back when we couldn't
wait till we got to the Middle School. So we could
see one another every day.
Do you remember back when we stopped talking
and we went are own ways with new friends.
What Happened?
MaKayla Rieke, Grade 9
DeKalb High School, IN

Truths

Love is for the ones who adore us
Although it always ends up in the hands of ones who ignore us.
Dreams are for our conscious minds;
They may be our only secret.
Family is our base
Even when they might be mistreated.
Respect is lost faster than it is earned.
Politics argues about lies.
Consumerism is wasteful,
But slavery is still sewn into our shoes.
Beauty always develops
Both internally and externally.
Responsibility is both forced and learned,
And mistakes are made to be fixed.
All the hate in the world:
Chaos is always conjured, then health becomes clichéd.
Addiction makes us frightened.
The power of faith, it moves people.
But who can tell the truth?
Kaylin Higgins, Grade 8
West Hills Middle School, MI

Spring

Spring
It looks like flowers blooming everywhere
It sounds like birds chirping in the early morning
It smells like wet dew drying in the sun
It tastes like cool, fresh water
It feels like the beginning of all great things
Spring
Maren Wisniewski, Grade 7
West Middle School, MI

Simple Tunes

Give me some blues, some jazz, some simple rhyme.
So I got a simple tune to pass the time.
Some rap, some country, some rock and roll.
Give me a rhyme so I'm ready to go.
Give me beat, a tap, a little clang.
Something to make me move my thing
So give me a simple tune.
Tony Rasmussen, Grade 9
Posen Consolidated High School, MI

The Hike of Your Life

Pack up your gear
And prepare yourself.
Remember to always keep going.

Set the pace for the group,
The stronger ones in the rear to push the weak.
Remember to always keep going.

Persevere through steep edges and
Jagged rocks like sharp angry knife blades.
Remember to always keep going.

Up the hill now, don't slow down
For it is downhill on your return.
Remember to always keep going.

You can see the top now and want to go
But you remember those who are struggling behind you.
With an outstretched arm you help them up
And gaze at the majesty of the landscape together.
Remember to always keep going.

Elliot Taylor, Grade 8
St Barnabas School, IN

Racing Experience

I love the drop of the gate
The roar of the 42 engines
blasting off the gas around the first turn.
The leader is thinking about going faster and faster.
The follower is thinking, "I hope he backs off just a little
so I can capitalize on his laziness."
The last place lapper is holding on with all his might
hoping just to cross the finish line in one piece.
But mostly the sound I love more than any other
is the sound of my bike
and my bike only.
Just knowing you're the leader
the one who has trained and waited for this moment
to be in the front of the pack.
Then, right before I cross the finish line
I take a deep breath of relief.
In that moment I realize
that out of 42 riders
I'm the one crossing the finish line first.
I was the one going faster.
I was the one being followed.

Josh Green, Grade 9
Lenawee Christian School, MI

Lincoln Memorial

30 feet tall and sitting in his chair,
Wearing a big, tall hat shaped like a square.
Looking straight ahead, sits Mr. Lincoln.
I would like to know, sir, what are you thinkin'?

Alex Dennis, Grade 7
Whitehall Middle School, MI

Summer Means

Summer means
Long warm nights spent out on the front yard
Laying, looking up at the stars
And thinking about what was going to happen next

Summer means
Sneaking out with your friends
To run around the streets
Arms linked, not having to pretend for once that everything is okay

Summer means
Splashing around in a pool
Floating around on a raft
Falling gently asleep while laying in the sun
Summer means
Waking up late to the smell of fresh cut grass
Going to the mall, And having a good time
Summer is a time for friends
A time that there is no need for guy trouble
Summer means living for the moment
And not having a worry in the world

Emilee Rhode, Grade 9
Brown City High School, MI

Our Rainbow Love...

Stars shine like the twinkle in your brown eyes,
They drive me crazy with your smile...
The blue sky in the morning,
And the gray sky at night,
The yellow sun beating down.
Your hand in mine...
My hand in yours...

Promise me you'll think of me every time you look up at the sky.
When the orange sunset comes I shall kiss your cheek
Then fade away in the green trees.
Summer passes and fall comes,
You see the leaves change to red and start to fall...
But then the white snowflakes fall and I must go.

Summer has come again
And I've thought of our pink love.
But when I find you,
You've found someone else, and my heart starts to break.
But when I see you happy,
It reminds me of the rainbow love we had...

Alexis Vargas, Grade 7
Saginaw Arts and Sciences Academy, MI

Ice Day

The sleek blanket shattered like glass when stepped upon
Salt pellets sprinkled down from the sky
As diamonds hung in little pouches from the branches
Tinsel drenched the trees wanting to remind everyone of Christmas

Kennedee Semans, Grade 7
Whitehall Middle School, MI

High Merit Poems – Grades 7, 8, and 9

3K Portage
Trudging on a narrow path in the middle of nowhere,
Carrying the weight of a 9 year old on my back
Laughing, singing songs, bonding with 2 best friends
Trying my hardest to stay on my feet
The smell of damp trees and wilderness surrounding me

Every corner turned
Is a hunt for the open sun and lake
It's never found but optimism is still here
The end is hopefully near

A halo of bugs above my head
Swatting them with frustration
Almost at my wits end
Wanting to sit on every log seen
But pushing myself a little further
One step at a time

The end of a tunnel is here!
Open land, open lake, sun shining bright
Turtled on my back, the best feeling ever
Finished before my counselors
My face is glowing pride and confidence overflowing my heart
Camp Tamakwa 10 day canoe trip 3k portage
Nicole Doctoroff, Grade 7
Detroit Country Day Middle School, MI

The Owl's Game
Wide imposing daggers
Penetrating deep into my soul.
Breath taken, infatuated,
At eyes disturbed by what they have witnessed
He turns away as though I were as inconspicuous as a leaf.

What has this beast witnessed?
The hunt
The chase
The thrill
The finishing swoop
The pride of survival

And for what?
Another breath…
Another day…
Another night?
To him it is all a game.

So I stand there in awe.
Why is it that I cannot play?
Perhaps it is all an illusion;
We all play a special part.
Just in a different version.
Alyssa Dail, Grade 9
Lenawee Christian School, MI

Nostalgia
I hear her voice,
Abnormal, not the way a grown woman's voice should sound.
   Our feelings
Aftermath of a hurricane memories hazy
   The thought
Abstract and persistent truly tragic

Some feel sympathy, possibly malicious guilt
   physically deficient

Exceptional, exquisite, sensible mentally
   She was unique
Her different techniques genuine
We all show our allegiance to Susan
   A fierce fighter
Tia Romig, Grade 8
Culver Community Middle School, IN

To My Papa and Dada
I miss you my papa
I miss you my dada

It's been a long time since we last talked
I miss all those times we would take long walks

There was a point in time when we all lived together
The bond our family had was like a fat man in leather

Sunday dinners is where we would meet
To me and my sisters this was the greatest treat

As time goes on and memories fade
I'll be old and with you one day…
Kendra Neff, Grade 8
West Side Middle School, IN

The Silent Pond
Down past the road, and out through the trees.
Hiding in the brushes, hidden by the leaves.
A quiet still pond, blue as the sky.
Silent as a hummingbird, where I go to cry.

To the clear cool waves, painted golden by the sun.
Where I go when days are gray, the place to where I run.
Sometimes on happier days, when I want to play.
The dragonflies around me land close to where I lay.

No matter how I'm feeling, no matter what the day.
My silent pond awaits me, never much to say.
With strong arms to wrap around me, to comfort me in sorrow.
To let me know that come what may, it will be here tomorrow.
Valerie Curtis, Grade 7
Ruth Murdoch Elementary School, MI

Summer
Let the school year end.
No more waiting for the weekend.
Let the fun times start.
They'll stay forever in our heart.
Crazy water fights.
Amazing endless nights.
None of this is a sin.
SO LET THE SUMMER BEGIN!
Ashley Meyers, Grade 9
Posen Consolidated High School, MI

One Week
7 days full of smiles and worry.
6 nights composed of laughter and tears.
168 hours of endless conversations,
that contained no voice.

For 10,080 minutes I thought I loved you
and in one second,
I knew that I'd lost you.
Billie Wrobleski, Grade 9
Allegan High School, MI

Promise
The rainbow won't be back.
So, Heaven, promise me
You'll let my body breathe
I promise, I'm persistent
My rollercoaster's empty
Fill it with sympathy
Heaven, promise me
Jasmine Potter, Grade 8
Culver Community Middle School, IN

Shoes
Shoes
Squeaky, protective
Running, jumping, sprinting
Protection from the ground
Walking, tiptoeing, sliding
Cozy, stinky
Footwear
Brian Chrzanowski, Grade 8
St John Lutheran School, MI

Football
The feel of grass under my cleats
The wind flying against my helmet
I know I'm running too fast to get caught
The feel of the oval is my motivation
I am a thief on the field
Football is not just a game
It's my way of life.
Bodhi Farquhar, Grade 8
Culver Community Middle School, IN

Love Is a Mystery
Love is a mystery
It's unusual
Love is a dark alley
You never know what's around the corner
Love is that feeling in your gut
When your stomach does twists and turns
Love is the reason you wake up earlier than usual to impress someone
Love can be a broken heart
A teardrop on your face
Or a smile that stretches a mile
Love is like a battlefield
Unsafe but sometimes rewarding in the end

Love is going to take you
Shake you
But it will make you

Yesterday is history
Love is a mystery
And today is a gift
That's why it's called the present
Megan Childs, Grade 7
Fowlerville Junior High School, MI

Perfectly Mismatched
What if I was perfectly mismatched?
Would you still love me?
If I woke up in the morning slightly frayed around the edges,
the tic-tac-toe black and white of life becoming the gray space of hard decisions in my eyes?
If I went to bed at night rested already, mind entranced by the sleepy peace of a river drifting,
shifting in dream catcher channels of my mind?
If I knew that socks should be juxtaposed, thoughts and actions, wealth and poverty,
grand descriptions and homely speak, purple with white stripes and white with purple dots?
Snap, snap, a union of opposites,
blended into one creamy violet action of starting a day with wonderful feet?
What if I forced a laugh to ease my misery,
the slippery burble wish-washing a woebegone fact pinned discreetly to my heart?
And what if I didn't smile when I was happy, if I just sat in a mental yoga position and
knew that I could be one with the world spinning in me?
If I just sat letting the symphony of a parallel universe run like a stream over my mind?
Crickets chirp, whoosh of a moon bird, crinkle of a smile, ringing note, clear and pure,
of a dancer, click-click of thoughts falling into place, pitter-patter of light feet as sunbeams
sidestep clouds, crescendo of a moment, bittersweet sigh suspended in memory…
What if I was perfectly mismatched? Would you still love me?
I think you would.
I hope so…
Katy Dyer, Grade 7
Stanley Clark School, IN

The Beach
Sunshine's on the water and the sand.
All around you hear kids running and laughing.
You see people run into the water for relief from the heat.
You'll see sand castles, abandoned by their makers, waiting to be ran over or washed away.
Alexandra Hart, Grade 8
West Side Middle School, IN

High Merit Poems – Grades 7, 8, and 9

Tipping Nature's Scale
Autumn weather fills the air,
as trees drop their color
one piece at a time.

Facing an unknown threat
that plows, cuts, and chops
anything in its path.
Breaking the steady
balance of life.
Breaking the constant
cycle of life.
Breaking the innocent
lives of many.

As autumn weather fills the air,
and trees drop their color
one piece at a time,
one would say,
"Why add more weight
to the scale
that has balanced
nature for so long?"
Jonathan Calso, Grade 7
Detroit Country Day Middle School, MI

Hate
Hate is…
The flames of fire in Hell
Hate is…
The devil drinking ice water
Hate is…
Being an outsider
Hate is…
Pitiful, ugly, and stupid
Hate is…
What takes away our family members
  or that embrace of loved ones
Hate is…
Something I can't feel for you.
Jillian Clair, Grade 8
West Side Middle School, IN

The Banana
One day I met a banana
Who had a bandana
I asked the banana
Where he got his bandana
He said that he got it from his nana
From cabana in Montana
I asked the banana
When he would see his nana
So he can get a bandana
And he said that he can't because
She moved to Havana
Jon Petrovich, Grade 7
Royal Oak Middle School, MI

Moving
Yes, I am a flower blooming in the Spring.
I'm growing up and moving away soon,
Taking everything with me.

Yes, moving to a new home, but not at all forgetting my past,
Taking all I have down the road that I have chosen,
Vowing not to forget what I have learned in my fourteen years.

Yes, I'm going to stay myself and not try to be a clone,
I'm going to keep my identity throughout everything;
Moving into a new home and staying who I am throughout my journey.

Yes, I will remember: my values, my family, my friends.
I will cherish everything I have been taught;
Remembering my mistakes and learning from them.

Yes, I will live my faith as I have thus far,
I will stay on God's side and walk in His footsteps,
Recalling all my days where I have been taught to live by His words.

Yes, I will be thankful for the blessings I've been granted,
Remembering that I can always count on those who love me, and
Showing pride in my God-given abilities.

Yes, I will be the best I can be.
I will love and care for all every step of the way —
Moving, but leaving nothing and no one behind.
Kayla Streicher, Grade 8
St. Barnabas School, IN

In Between My Fingers
Each hand has five fingers
All just as important as the rest
The itty, bitty pinky smallest of them all
The little bride or groom, who one day will wear a ring
The rude and ugly middle finger standing ignorant and tall
Pointer comes next, always showing the way
All that leaves is the thumb, the misfit of them all
My fingers are important, but something matters more
The spaces are where another's fit beautifully
No one should be alone, forced to face the world by themselves
Everyone has another half
Babe, open your eyes
Rip your blinders off
Why can't you see what is right in front of you?
I remember the first time we held hands
I thought that it was right
My fingers intertwined with yours, like a vine growing on a new branch
Holding on so tightly, afraid of letting go
Love this young never lasts, but it feels just as strong
But without you, those spaces would be empty
And why should I be alone?
Ella Merritt, Grade 8
St Barnabas School, IN

My Crazy Week!
This week has been strange,
This week has been crazy,
When I look back, everything is just hazy.

This week has been tiring,
This week has been fun,
Finally, everything has been said and done.

This week has been stressful,
This week has been fast,
I know for sure, that the memories will last.
Hailey Katulski, Grade 7
West Middle School, MI

Shadows of Darkness
The darkness lies within the dark,
and never comes to light.

It creeps around in the shadows,
and only lives in night.

The darkness hates life and love,
and tells a lot of lies.

One thing's for sure though,
and that is, that darkness never dies.
Lanae Hochstetler, Grade 9
Harlan Christian School, IN

Winter
Snow falls everywhere
Hats and gloves cover us up
Icicles dangle from trees
Candy canes make our hands sticky
The sharp chill nips our noses
Snowballs whiz through the air
Sleds slide down hills
Snowmen wave to everyone
Ice skaters glide along
Lights twinkle in the night
Keelin Kraemer, Grade 7
West Middle School, MI

Who Is the Sun?
The Sun peaks out
between the clouds of overcast.
The Sun only wants
someone to see its light.
Who is the Sun?
I am the Sun.
All I want is
for someone to see
my light and
talent.
Taylor LaBine, Grade 7
St Stephen School, MI

My God
I love God with all my heart, he died for me, that says a lot
He took the burdens of our sins, caring and loving, that's what he does

He died for me, that says a lot
Powerful and almighty over sin, caring and loving, that's what he does

The devil is afraid, and this is good if I were him I would
Powerful and almighty over sin, miracles and powers for which he does

The devil is afraid, and this is good If I were him I would
Son of God and full of might, miracles and powers for which he does

I repent and he forgives
Son of God full of might, the light of the world he fills us up

I repent and he forgives
Act the way he would want, the light of the world he fills up

Full of love for which he gives
Act the way he would want, hail to the king almighty

Full of love for which he gives
Died on the cross for you and I, hail to the king almighty

Treats everyone the way we should
Died on the cross for you and I, I love the lord with all my heart
Cameron Krzewski, Grade 7
St John Lutheran School, MI

How to Run Sweet Sixteens
Coach tells us to line up on the base line.
All of the sudden, worry flies through the air
and there is no doubt that the same question
is racing through all of our minds: "Will she make us run it?"

We watch Coach intently
to see if those two words escape her mouth,
those two little words that make us want to run and hide.
Her mouth opens as she says: "Sweet Sixteen."
And we're off.

The first down and back is effortless.
Two and three isn't as simple.
It's four down and backs that kill us.
Let's stay determined and don't give up!
Keep our breathing steady and run as fast as we can.
Try to ignore the pain, push through it.
It's the climax, the top of the mountain.
Remember, we're halfway done.
Finish so intensely on the last down and back that we're gasping for air.
Don't stop until we cross that line.

We're done. It's over.
We have accomplished a Sweet Sixteen…but there is more to come.
Halle Smith, Grade 8
Kingsway Christian School, IN

High Merit Poems – Grades 7, 8, and 9

Alone
Blackness
A gaping black hole
An endless tunnel
Emptiness

A lost piece of a puzzle
Forever gone
Never to return
Never to be found

For a world without love
Is not a world at all
Samantha Glaza, Grade 7
Royal Oak Middle School, MI

True Love
True love within my heart,
Handsome in my sight;
Who has a caring embrace,
Holds me in his arms;
Time to time I cherish,
For our time we spent;
Awing at our young love,
Your kiss as soft as snow,
For I wouldn't settle,
For anything more;
My dear love to be,
You're so sacred to me!
Allison Maurer, Grade 8
West Side Middle School, IN

Basketball
I run
I dribble
I jump
I fall
I block
I pass
I miss
I trip
I scrape
I shoot
I score
I win
Genevieve Parkey, Grade 7
West Middle School, MI

Wandering
Like a lost puppy
my mind is wandering away
now I don't know where it has gone
oh how will I find it
please oh please will you help me
Mason Jorgenson, Grade 8
West Side Middle School, IN

Fishing
Hearing your alarm clock going off at 5 am.
Putting on your Bass Fishing jersey with all of your sponsors on it.
Getting in the truck and driving to the lake.
Checking into the tournament.
Seeing the fog rising off the lake water.
Setting up the rods and reels.
Putting the boat in the water and turning on the sonar graph to find the fishing spot.
Putting the boat into drive and driving 60 mph to be the first to get to your fishing spot.
Getting to the fishing spot.
Casting to the stumps and reeling in and using the trolling motor to move around.
Finally setting the hook on the fish.
Reeling and fighting the fish.
Catching the fish and putting it into the live well.
Casting and reeling again and again.
Switching the lures.
Setting the hook.
Catching more fish.
Hoping to have enough fish to win the tournament.
Going to the weigh-in and the total weight was 30 lbs.
Winning the tournament and winning $100,000.
Bryce Popa, Grade 8
St Barnabas School, IN

The Struggle for Food
A ll I can think about is this
B ecause it fills me with so much bliss
C ausing me to think of its awesome flavor
D eciding whether to devour or savor
E nveloped in its orange, yellow, or white color
F or every time I enjoy it, it becomes smaller
G one it becomes with all its goodness
H olding my stomach as I feel it digest
I imagine when it was first here
J ust about to make me shed a tear
K nowing there is more of it and it is free
L aziness is the only huge obstacle that is stopping me
M any a time I have encountered this trouble
N ever having to have to hustle
O utstanding effort is not required
P ower is the thing I want to desire
Q uitting is not an option, I have to go all-out
R eaching out for it, I give a shout
S afe in my hands, I bring the food up close
T o finally have this food, the burrito, I accidentally drop it on my clothes…
Joel Paea, Grade 8
Ruth Murdoch Elementary School, MI

Be Not Afraid
I'm not afraid to die even though I may cry cause I know the Lord is by my side.
I'm in pain I hurt inside but I'm not afraid to die angels will come
I'll take my heavenly flight my spirit will rise my hurt will die
as I rise through the skies I'll meet my Savior all pain will be gone
I'll rest eternally never to die *always alive.*
Samantha Ammerman, Grade 7
Lincoln Middle School, IN

The Lake
The lake has an image
of
silver skies
green grass
tawny trees.
It reflects everything it sees,
but never shows what it is,
as though afraid
to open up
to people,
afraid to be
hurt again.
Sometimes I feel like
that lake
drowning in others
attempting to speak out
trying to break out
but never
succeeding.
Sydney Matthys, Grade 7
Stanley Clark School, IN

Mighty Roar
— Hear the mighty roar
Blowing through your ear,
Feel the breeze ripping your hair out.
One, by one, by one.

— Show no fear
Show mercy
Just listen
Listen to that mighty roar

— Shhh, can you hear it
I can, can you
Listen,
It's trying to tell you something.

— Open your eyes
Open them
And you'll find out
That it was just a dream.
Megan Stafford, Grade 8
Centreville Jr High School, MI

Lost
Upon losing something,
You must only regret,
What you have done,
Not what you must do,
For only in losing,
Must one learn to find,
That one thing that's special,
Yours, hers or mine.
Daniel Simmons, Grade 7
Assumption School, MI

Laughter
Laugher is like a germ,
easy to spread around.
Hard to get rid of.

It's also like medicine,
when your heads down,
a little dose of it
makes you feel better.

Laughter is also like love,
you don't know when it's
going to walk into your life.
And when it does you
can never get enough.

Laughter can jump around,
making each day brighter.
Laughter can make
your body stronger,
it can make you last
a lot longer.

Laughter is a prize,
that you cannot see
with your own eyes.
Abbey Suida, Grade 7
Fowlerville Jr High School, MI

Delicious Masterpiece
As I look into the cold, blue cup,
filled with creamy bliss,
I see how beautiful you truly are

Your chunks of fudge,
your pie crust pieces,
everything about you,
is absolutely
flawless

Made splendidly
with love,
your inventor
is a real genius

Putting the perfect portion
of toppings, it is certainly
not too overbearing

As my spoon dips
into that smooth ice cream
that Dairy Queen is known for,

I anticipate
every bite.
Julia Price, Grade 8
Kingsway Christian School, IN

So Much Depends Upon…*
so much depends
upon

that steady cool
breeze

that blows up my
sails

and drifts me
away

into the
sea

and far, far
away
Sylvan Benton, Grade 7
Whitehall Middle School, MI
*Inspired by William Carlos Williams

Tropical Twitch
The toucan tangoed to the tropical twist
Turning this way and that,
He started to twitch

The twitch started tiny
Then tripled in size
It started toward his toes
And stretched to his thighs

This terrible twitch
Then tickled his ears
Then started to fill
His eyes with tears

The toucan then tripped
And tumbled to the floor
"*Thank goodness*" he thought
"*That twitch is no more.*"
Morgan Benoit, Grade 7
Assumption School, MI

Grandma
from the time I walked in the door
I knew my heart would be sore.
when she told me my head went down
and a smile turned to a frown.
although you left without goodbye
I know someday we will say hi.
goodbye and wish you well
even though my heart fell.
I know now what I never did
life is a gamble I never win.
Breanna Nehls, Grade 8
West Side Middle School, IN

High Merit Poems – Grades 7, 8, and 9

The Arrow

'Round, 'round, and 'round it goes.
Where it will stop, not a soul knows.

Snaking through the end of time,
swirling 'round this poem of mine.

Circling endlessly on a numbered face,
indefinitely reaching into boundless space.

Taking the life of an unfortunate duck,
spinning to determine one's luck.

'Round, 'round, and 'round it goes.
Where it will stop, only you know.
Morgan Scott, Grade 7
Christ the King School, IN

Soldier

A soldier is fierce, persistent
He steadies his rifle as
He moves across the shadows…

Guns fire, bullets blaze
The soldier doesn't flinch, but lays
He waits for the perfect moment to shine,
Then fires his rifle towards the enemy line

This soldier stays alive
Yet some others don't survive
Their allegiance, all, remembered
While the enemy just surrendered
Paul Foersch, Grade 8
Culver Community Middle School, IN

Who Are You?

Who or what are you?
I never met you before.
But I sincerely thank you,
for giving me my lovely dad.
He gives me so so much!
Love and clothes,
makeup and such.
I know you're in a better place,
and we will all see you soon.
Marina Fernandez, Grade 8
West Side Middle School, IN

The Best Shopping

When would shopping be the best?
Cabelas would win that test.
Up and down all the aisles,
we could walk a lot of miles.
When it's time to call it quits,
all the guys throw their fits.
Travis Sharpe, Grade 7
Posen Consolidated High School, MI

Questions

Why am I here, I sometimes ask myself
Am I part of a cruel experiment, or perhaps something else?
Is there really someone watching, someone who cares?
Does it really matter, does He even care,
If I have these questions that leave me in despair.
Is anyone right? Is anyone wrong?
Should I believe what they say, should I go along?
Sometimes here on earth we have so many questions,
And we find there aren't quite as many answers
But one thing for sure, I believe and trust my Lord and Savior who is my all
And Who has got me through it all when I'm about to fall
And sometimes when I ponder I finally realize
That I'll never understand till I have recognized
And seen Him face to face with my own eyes
So I guess I'll just have to ponder, question and wait,
For a little while longer until I see His face.
Kaitlin McArthur, Grade 8
Ruth Murdoch Elementary School, MI

Saltwater Dreams

Gasping for a breath,
You can't make it to the surface,
As you stare at the blackness beneath your feet,
A light show begins,
Surrounding you in radiant blue and splashing green,
You drift up to the surface,
Glancing behind you,
A massive blue graceful giant,
Just like that it's gone,
You turn and something moves,
It clutches onto you and you try to shake it off,
A shower of ink is all that's left,
Surrounded by sharks,
Hungry and ready to attack,
Full of adrenaline and scared to death,
This is my dream and someday and somehow my dreams will come to life!
Caitlyn Reichstetter, Grade 7
Perry Middle School, MI

I See You

If only you could see what I see,
I'd show you your eyes and what they mean to me.
They mean love and kind gestures,
Warmth of an everlasting fire, the song of hope, and inspiration.
Overall, I see a person no different than the others,
With the will to be successful and the dream to be someone.
Someone who desires to be intelligent, important, and well-respected,
But that's not all I see…
I can see more, but my list would be too long.
So with my new mindset, I'm moving on.
Something more personal, more challenging,
More than what I see in you,
Which is…
Trying to find out what I see in me.
Leah Carter, Grade 7
Cedar Springs Middle School, MI

Time

Time ticks on,
And I'm drawn farther,
From the light,
I dream of the divine paradise,
I wish I lived in,
Drawn alone,
Darkness flows through,
Say goodbye to that,
Little girl you once knew.

Skylor Rushlow, Grade 8
West Side Middle School, IN

Summer Pleasures

I was walking through the woods
Looking for a ringtail coon,
We saw a long baby snake
And even saw a small loon.

I'm wishing I was fishing
Or swimming in the deep lake.
But mom says I don't get to
For there's still some leaves to rake.

Christopher Wagler, Grade 7
Green Acres School, IN

Twinkling Bright

I hop in the cab and say to the driver,
Can you take me to the Eiffel Tower?
The eye of the beholder can see its power,
and all the majesty of a flower.

The lights so sparkling bright,
They shine in the dark night.
It really makes me appreciate life,
for I will always remember this sight.

Chelsea Harrison, Grade 8
Bloomingdale Middle School, MI

Motorcycles

Motorcycles are awesome
Nobody doesn't want to ride
Outside riding
People love their sound
Quiet bikes are for the weak
Riding is awesome
Slow is boring
Time is nothing

Ben Wise, Grade 8
West Side Middle School, IN

Gorgeous Outside

The sun gazes down,
our shadows are casted out,
it's gorgeous outside.

Amanda McCormick, Grade 8
Delphi Community Middle School, IN

Stand Up

It's not over, just because one door closed
Doesn't mean the next one won't open, don't' give up

It's not over, never give up
Just try harder, don't give up

Have faith in yourself, never give up, just try harder
Your dreams matter, never think less

Have faith in yourself, don't let anyone stand in your way
Your dreams matter, never think less

Life is about taking risk, don't let anyone stand in your way
You might feel broken, but that will change

Life is about taking risk, everything happens for a reason
You might feel broken, but that will change

Stand up for what you believe in
Everything happens for a reason, one choice could change everything

Stand up for what you believe in
Sometimes you need to put others first, one choice could change everything

Live life to the fullest and never turn back
Sometimes you need to put others first, stand up.

Katie McAtee, Grade 7
St John Lutheran School, MI

Summer Fever

I wanna be out of school so freakin' bad, sitting here makes me really sad
I wanna be in the pool with my friends, laughing about old folk in Depends.

Oh every time I close my eyes
I wish it was summertime
up late every night, all right, take the dare,
you better prepare for summer fever.

I would have hair like Gaga, people talkin' blah blah
I'll give you my stylist but my look is priceless
I'll probably walk around town in my fly kicks
'cuz I'm so hot like a bomb goin' tick tick
give a few numbers like here hottie have this
leave for vacation, yeah, your gonna miss this
been a long time since I've seen the ocean
bring everything plus your tan lotion
I'd probably swim with the dolphin
swallow the water and get me a coughin'
you can't forget about me 'cuz everywhere I go my phone be like RANG.

Oh every time I close my eyes
I wish it was summertime
up late every night, all right, take the dare,
you better prepare for summer fever.

Madison Booe, Grade 8
Covington Middle School, IN

High Merit Poems – Grades 7, 8, and 9

Love Bloom
A flower as delicate as a feather,
Two hearts, connected by a tether.
Always in bloom, always in season
The two hearts declare, "Love is the reason!"

Cannot be bought, cannot be sold
For love has an iron-strong hold
Stronger than a cable of steel,
The love so visible, you have to believe it's real.

And if allowed to wither and wilt,
It will seem as though your world will tilt.
When let alone, a heart will weep
For the other heart it longs to keep.
It will sob, and mourn and cry
And the lonely heart will wonder, "Why? Oh, why?"

But when they finally reunite,
The fire of passion will ignite.
Consuming all that's within its way,
The passion's motives will not sway.

Love's delicate first bloom,
In my lonely heart has a room.
Rachael Stedman, Grade 8
TS Nurnberger School, MI

Where I Come From…
I'm from fresh snow falling from the trees,
from a small town,
and parents who will never let me leave.
I'm from late nights and sleepy days.
I'm from looking in the mirror,
and wishing I could change.

I'm from trust misplaced and mistakes made.
I'm from tears shed,
and best friends' aid.
I'm from new crushes,
and old flames.
I'm from a sharp blade,
that deepens old wounds and makes new.
I'm from bold faced lies,
and bitter truths.

I'm from good grades turned bad,
to working to keep them up.
I'm from some broken hearts,
and some unbearable pain.
I'm from regrets,
and the need to erase.
Deanna Luton, Grade 8
Kalkaska Middle School, MI

The Men with No Mask
This is how the world is seen
through the eyes of a brain so keen
Clever and witty until their demise
yet they cannot see through my disguise
I tried wearing a mask to make things better
it clouded my ego like darkened weather
I ripped it off yet nothing had changed
the world's always cold, that's nothing strange
To the people who let their light shine
masks will shade their brightest minds
And nothing's new, they just leave things out
this tactics used for children that pout
We make the world think nothing's wrong
but in the end, masks makes no one strong.
Jeffrey Anderson, Grade 9
Anderson Preparatory Academy, IN

How I Love Thy Carolines
How I love thy pretty Caroline C.
How I love thy pretty Caroline A.
She is very pretty, this I can see
The other one is also as pretty
What should I do, they both are very cool
Should I tell them I do love both of them
Or will I just look like a huge big fool
But I think one of them likes Daniel Clem
I will ask both of them out for tonight
It does not matter what they will both do
I just hope one of them will have a bite
My heart flies for them with love like my kite
How I love thy both pretty Carolines
My heart pounds for them like the organ chimes.
Jared Brush, Grade 8
Grosse Pointe Academy, MI

Summer
The summer is the perfect time to rest.
A three month time which makes one feel divine.
The summer is a bright green, leafy fest.
The taste of fruit, cool and sweet, lemon lime.
June is the time when school has lost its grit.
A fresh new month when you have a blast.
A time when the web is not tightly knit.
The trees are a blur as you run by fast.
July is the month when it gets quite hot.
The fresh smell of flowers drift through the air.
The kids go running and playing a lot.
This is a time that is fun and quite rare.
Then the birds fly up for the night to rest.
This is why summer is truly the best.
George Spica, Grade 8
Grosse Pointe Academy, MI

I Don't Want to Grow Up
I don't want to grow up
I miss getting rocked to sleep by my father
Holding my teddy bear and bankie
Getting tucked in by my mother

I don't want to grow up
I miss playing with my Barbie dolls
Dressing up
Playing all day long

I don't want to grow up
I miss swinging on my swing
Pretending to be a princess
Dreaming without any worry

I don't want to grow up
I miss how life used to be
Going back in time is impossible
Being a kid at heart isn't
Sarah Newton, Grade 8
East Jay Middle School, IN

Seasons
I love the feeling of a fresh breeze
on the hottest summer day,
these are the moments we need to seize
before they go away.

Next thing we know the leaves will change
and snow will fall from the sky,
our lives begin to rearrange
and the years seem to all fly by.

Now the school year is finally done
but its bittersweet indeed,
I know I've had a lot of fun
but there has been a growing need.

A need to never leave this place
I want to stay right here,
but sadly this isn't my case
the future is my biggest fear.
Zoe Melnyk, Grade 9
Tecumseh High School, MI

No Longer
You are no longer here with me,
I am no longer filled with glee.
I cried the day you went away,
I hate that you no longer live today.
I love the way we used to play,
I no longer live this way.
I can no longer see you tomorrow,
my life is only filled with sorrow.
Brock Crockom, Grade 8
West Side Middle School, IN

A Christmas Tree
Beautiful beyond belief
and decorated with color.
Neatly tied bows
and dressed up for occasion.

Such a joy to be around.
Standing in the crowded corner,
but staying in place.
While holding a star.

Comes to visit once a year
in the month of December.
Holding gifts for the family
with beauty and grace.
Kendall Hirschman, Grade 9
Posen Consolidated High School, MI

Dear Human
From the earliest of dawn
We wake up in your lawn
We don't groan nor stretch
But simply try our best
We gather your watermelons and cherries
But you guys think that we are scary
There is obviously a misconception
For we are nothing in the big green ocean
And when your canine disturbs our home
We have no choice but to make him moan
We do not have many complaints
Because we are nice little saints
So be careful where you leave your Oreo
We just might be eating it down below
David Woo, Grade 9
Troy High School, MI

Show
Show your pride,
Don't keep it inside.
Show your accomplishments,
You earned them.
Show your abilities,
They are gifts given to you.
Show your smile,
It is one of a kind.
Show your talents,
Everyone's are different.
Show your endeavors,
Others might join you.
By showing these actions,
You can make a difference.
Austin Esquivel, Grade 7
St John the Baptist Elementary School, IN

Chicken Suit
In his fluffy chicken suit
With his head sticking out the top

He has a big radiant smile
As if he was really happy about something

What was it?
A joke, a party,
Or could he be a mailman
With his big red mail bag
Excited to do his job

Or maybe he thinks he is a super hero
Getting ready to fight crime
But he doesn't feel intimidating
Because his costume is fluffy,
And he's missing his mask.

If you were to remove the costume
You would end up with a regular man:
Overly excited over something

Whatever it might be,
He could have just
Lost his mask
And his mind.
Luke Gelfius, Grade 8
Kingsway Christian School, IN

The Widow's Pain
I can do this.
I can lift my head way up high.
I can do this.
I won't let the public see me cry.

Here I go.
Walking next to his corpse.
Was I a good wife?
Why do I feel remorse?

I must be strong.
I must lead the nation.
I must say so long
I have people to wait on.

I don't feel complete.
I never will again.
Who is watching over ME,
Certainly not them!

I watch over Caroline.
I watch over John.
I keep the country in line.
This nation will go on.
Jacqueline Caserio, Grade 8
St Hugo of the Hills School, MI

High Merit Poems – Grades 7, 8, and 9

As Would the Wind
Like the wind, they come and go,
some fast others slow.
I feel a kinship,
for I flow with them.
Seems effortless as we sway,
like a wildflower, on a summer's day.
Until stand still,
when cold air comes,
whips your face, and steals your lungs.
Stops the heart,
shatters it through.
My only way out,
is by you.
I want your hand,
and I need your aid.
Until the gust,
sweeps me away.
Nothing to do now,
just move along.
As would the wind,
consistent and strong.
Kaylee Herr, Grade 8
West Side Middle School, IN

Here and There
There.
Where the sun kisses her cheeks
through finger like branches.
There.
Where the river flows
like life, full of meanders.
There.
Where her memories grow more vivid
as nature sings its rhapsody.
There.
Where she still feels him
holding her tightly.
There.
Where the trees whisper his words
'I love you.'
'Here.'
She sighs
sitting without him.
'There.'
she wishes she could be
miles away, beside him.
Kaitlin Park, Grade 9
Lenawee Christian School, MI

Football in My Hands
With a football
in my hands,
I will impress
all my fans.
Anthony Tirado, Grade 8
West Side Middle School, IN

As the Seasons Change
I look out the window as the seasons change
The rain slowly comes down as the seasons change
The breeze blows softly as the seasons change
The days become longer and I know summer is coming
The sun beats down as the seasons change
The shade of a tree provides comfort as the seasons change
The air becomes cooler and I know autumn is coming
The trees become vibrant with color as the seasons change
The leaves fall lightly as the seasons change
The wind becomes stronger and I know winter is coming
The snow falls lightly around me as the seasons change
The fire blazes as the seasons change
The snow starts to melt and I know spring is coming
So as I look out the window every day is different and I know the seasons are changing
Maya Turon, Grade 7
Ruth Murdoch Elementary School, MI

All of Us
The sun rises and falls behind the hills
The ducks sit in the pond flapping their bills
Deer run and leap with beauty and grace
The rabbits run like they're in a race
I'm so lucky to see all this beauty yet sadly my children may never see
When the seals slip and slide all over the ice
The polar bears enticing fur coats and how on those ice drifts they stay afloat
Clever as foxes are they never saw an ending so near yet safety so far
It is sad to think every time we leave the sink running
The natural beauty so stunning is crying please "save me!"
If only we could save one single tree
The Earth is theirs just as much as ours why do we make them live like they are behind bars
If we share the land between all of us maybe we can save ourselves from us
Spenser Baron, Grade 8
Mill Creek Middle School, MI

Tonight
She is truly loved.
Through every imperfection.
These tears hit the floor with a different meaning tonight.
This time, it's not because of a silly, little boy.
For once, it's not about how her family is crashing down.
Tonight, all of that doesn't matter.
Tonight, the overwhelming amount of God's love has consumed her heart.
Her sins are forgiven with His Son's blood.
She realized tonight that she is truly loved.
With every sin is forgiveness,
With every let down is hope,
And with every struggle is strength.
Tonight, she was shown the true sacrifice.
Logan Hensley, Grade 9
Southwood Jr/Sr High School, IN

Pool of Ripples

Clear as plastic,
Dry as the ocean.
No color, just nothingness.
As it sits on the tree,
Or the rooftop,
Or the forehead of the little old lady dressed in white.
It makes a quiet sound as it falls.
As it falls, the above world is not so blue.
Shades of grey appear, acting as a shield for the Earth.
Some cry out, others run.
When it takes its trip from the sky, it does not come alone;
Millions come along for the ride.
One falls on her head, then another in her hand.
She grieves for its heartless soul, nowhere to run, nowhere to hide.
She dashes for the river bank, intrigued to help her new friend.
She stands on the bridge, carefully extending her arm.
It falls.
It's closer to the water now.
It hits the surface! The surface ripples,
The ripples expand and so does her friend,
Away from her and the rest of the world.

Nia Hightower, Grade 8
University Preparatory Science & Math Middle School, MI

A Student's Prayer

Dear Lord,
   My alarm clock went off this morning
   I got up and got ready
   Today is the first day of school
   I have butterflies in my stomach
   Once I've gotten ready it's time to go to school
   But I feel like something's missing
   But I don't know what
   I get on the bus and head to school
   I get there
   The butterflies that were in my stomach
   Are now boulders pressing
   On my chest
   I know everything will be all right
   So God give me the strength for this day
   And guess what, everything is all right

Kilie Pond, Grade 7
Oak Hill Jr High School, IN

Beautiful Flowers

We walk through the woods and look around
We see tall flowers, small flowers, big flowers, and little flowers
But they are all still beautiful flowers.
You can pick them, smell them and put them in your house
You can give someone flowers who you love so much.
But no matter how you have them they are still beautiful flowers.
Flowers are a good way to brighten somebody's day
If they are sick or even upset people always love flowers
Flowers are so beautiful no matter how they are.

Austin Sharpe, Grade 9
Posen Consolidated High School, MI

Someone

Someone who was always there
Someone who was closer to me than
my own shadow.

Someone who was there
when no one else was.
Someone who never strayed
from my side.
Someone who supported me through and through

Someone who listened.
Someone who cared.
Someone close.
Someone there.

Someone who is missed.
Someone who was left behind.
Someone who will be seen again.
My friend.

Anna Kahle, Grade 7
St Bartholomew School, IN

It Burns Inside

It burns inside and out.
My parents don't know what it's about.
The black hole burns deeper into my soul.
Like a growing piece of smoldering coal.

They say things that aren't even true.
For ages to come as we all grew.
They find ways to make fun of me.
They don't know what it's really like to hear and see.

Crying barely helps the pain inside.
As the pain spreads from side to side.
Depression is a horrible disease.
So I'm begging, get me out of it please.

Tally Diaz, Grade 8
West Side Middle School, IN

Invisible

The red curtain is hung.
The curtain that had once hid young through old actors.
The silence the peacefulness.
The black leather seats that had once held promises of
Laughter, whispers, smiles.

You're standing there
All eyes on you.
The stage that had witnessed sadness, worries, joy.

Every time I walk on that stage
Everything goes away.
The audience, the stage, the crew.

Cristina Aguirre, Grade 7
St Bartholomew School, IN

He Left

June 22, 2010
I loved him dearly
He left for the
United States Air Force.
He was amazing.
Bright, strong, amazing
Big brother. I didn't want
Him to leave.
He left for San Antonio, Texas.
Lackland Air Force Base.
June 22, 2010
Madison Lanham, Grade 7
Oak Hill Jr High School, IN

That Special Person I Love

The sight of someone
You hold so dear.
It just shows how much you care.
He is tall
And he loves to play his guitar.
He loves to hunt
He shoots his gun.
Pow, Bang, and a thud.
You can tell how much
Someone cares when that
Special person is your crush.
Alena Deal, Grade 8
Covington Middle School, IN

Court Dreams

Squeaky shoes on hardwood floor
Sound of bouncing balls
Swoosh of the net
Communication amongst players
Sweat beads drip off bodies
Rebounds off the rims
Coaches from the sidelines
Stands of fans
Two teams on the floor
Trying hard to score
Winner wants it more
Tatum Schultz, Grade 8
Culver Community Middle School, IN

Washington D.C.*

So much depends
Upon
The white domed
Building
A place for
Heroes
The five sided
Building
Wyatt Sherman, Grade 7
Whitehall Middle School, MI
*Inspired by William Carlos Williams

Abortions

Think before having abortions, why should you
Smart or dumb, so it's all right to murder

Why should you, they're living people too
So it's all right to murder, imagine if you were that baby

They're living people too, think before doing
Imagine if you were that baby, step up as if you were that helpless child

Think before doing, is it really right
Step up as you were that helpless child, think do you really want to murder

Is it really right, think about it
Think do you really want to murder, it's a big decision

Think about it, why wouldn't you want a baby
It's a big decision, that baby could make a change

Why wouldn't you want a baby, make the right choice
That baby could make a change, think before having abortions
Benjamin Hagen, Grade 7
St John Lutheran School, MI

Free Throws

The whistle blows.
A foul is called.
I hear the other coach complaining to the ref.
I look at the clock, two seconds left, down by one.
To the free throw line I go.
As I go up my shoes squeak, the crowd murmurs.
I feel the bright lights on my skin, like the sun on a summer day.
"Two shots," says the ref.
I dribble twice, sweat dripping down my face, like I just ran a marathon.
I set, I shoot. It looks on target. The ball hits the back rim and bounces straight up.
Swoosh. It goes through.
Tie game.
I breathe a sigh of relief; I look around to see my teammates offering high-fives.
I slap their hands and get ready for the next shot.
"Relax," I say to myself.
Two dribbles again. I set, and shoot.
I close my eyes.
"Swoosh."
I open my eyes to my backyard as the ball bounces slowly back to me.
Game over.
Noah Scheer, Grade 8
St Barnabas School, IN

Hurt Me All Over Again

Every now and then I think about you, I lost the feeling but I'm scared.
I've become dependent on you all over again.
Then there are the nights I dream about you.
I can't get closer to closure, even though I finally know it's over.
Every time you make it into my head, whenever I see you,
I think you won't turn around and hurt me all over again.
Allison Sowle, Grade 9
DeKalb High School, IN

The King of Winter
Winter is cold, like a mean king's heart.
He makes the whole country cold.
His icicle crown is frozen.
He has a beautiful snow covered coat.
He's always cold and gets bigger and colder.

Nicholas Kanaski, Grade 8
Verona Mills School, MI

Drifting Carnival
Rescue
Hopeful, grateful
Crying, hugging, cheering
Limping back to shore
Safety

Leah Rynearson, Grade 8
Trinity Lutheran School, MI

Camping
Driving out into the dark
Catching fireflies in big jars
Roasting marshmallows
Cooking over big fires
Weeping when leaving

Christopher Hamilton, Grade 8
St John Lutheran School, MI

Book, Book*
Books, books shouting at my mind.
I would read them anytime.
To me they are very dear.
I will always keep one near.

Melani Gosselin, Grade 7
Whitehall Middle School, MI
*Inspired by William Blake

Summer Summer*
Summer summer fly a kite
Right now it feels so right
Such a graceful way to fly
Almost like a butterfly

Justin Warvszewski, Grade 7
Whitehall Middle School, MI
*Inspired by William Blake

Chuck
There once was a boy named Chuck.
He really wanted a hockey puck.
He like to play the sport.
So he went down to the court.
And there he had some good luck.

Kelsy Zimmerman, Grade 7
Whitehall Middle School, MI

Beauty of Simplicity
Salty air dances around me as I stand at the edge of the ravine.
I look around at what I call home.
Waves are crashing, the foam slipping back where it came from.
The gulls are screeching, trying to be heard over the waves.
I know this is where I belong.
I walk down the well worn path made by humans and creatures alike.
I know it like the back of my hand.
As I reach the beach, sand crunches around me.
I see a little turtle struggle around, looking around the huge world.
I pick up a rock and throw it.
I see it fall into the water, swallowed by the waves.
I wade into the water, and swim to my favorite rock.
As I sit on the rock, I gasp.
I see a dolphin, jumping and twirling just for me.
I hadn't had this happen for years.
Wishing I had a camera, I breathe in the moment, not wanting to forget.
As I go inside, I smile.
What a good thing the Lord has given me.

Molly Dashiell, Grade 7
By His Grace Learning Academy, IN

Life Is a Book
Life is a book
You can't judge it by its cover.
It has a beginning and an end
And many chapters in between
But in this book you can't read from the end to the beginning.
Life is a book
It has turning points in it
It may be happy, sad or romantic
Each page may be filled with laughter and excitement
Or, it might have pain and despair
Life is a book
You might go through challenges and problems
You might be put in sticky situations with other characters
Depending on the book, you might find danger or excitement
Or in your book it might be boring and dull
Life is a book
If your book is not sounding as you want it to be, you can rewrite your book on the way
Each book should be well treated and respected.

Peter Harris, Grade 7
Royal Oak Middle School, MI

Remember When
Remember when getting high meant swinging at the playground
Remember when pain was cause by a skinned knee
Remember when we danced in the rain
Remember when we played in the leaves
Do you remember?
Do you remember when we would dream about growing up
Remember when drama didn't exist
Remember when boys had *cooties*
Do you remember when we didn't know about the troubles of the world
And we couldn't wait to grow up!!!

Mikayla Rearden, Grade 7
South Spencer Middle School, IN

Robots

The major dream many people have.
Will they replace us?
Will they live beside us?
Time will tell.
If we can create them
They will do things
We don't want to.
Mowing the lawn.
Making our food,
And all the other little things.
When they get comfortable
Living like us
Will they replace us?

Jacob Hall, Grade 7
South Spencer Middle School, IN

David Lemieux

D ependable for everything
A ddictive to
V ideo games
I nteresting
D angerous

L ove music
E minem is my idol
M ORE SHOES
I ntelligent
E ternal shoe lover
U nique
X -treme

David Lemieux, Grade 8
West Side Middle School, IN

So Much Depends Upon

So much depends
Upon
The wind in my
Hair
My feet moving
Fast
The passing of
People
The yelling of the
Crowd
And me, winning the
Race

Serenity Menzock, Grade 7
Whitehall Middle School, MI

Simple

Simple is better.
This is undeniable.
Those who know are wise.

Kipton Hall, Grade 9
DeKalb High School, IN

The Little Leaf

A big green leaf high in the trees
Received the sun's brightest rays
And the fresh drops of rain

A little green leaf
From a simple sprout
Its roots weak in the ground
Received drops from the bigger leaves in the trees
And a thin ray of sunlight

The big leaf grew bigger blocking out sunlight
The little leaf lived on hearing the mocking cackle from the leaves above
I gave him many cool drinks from my flowing waters

The big leaf started wondering
How the little leaf was still alive
He called down to me
"Has little leaf died yet?"
I ignored him and flowed into the nearby pond

Fall came with its cold winds and diminishing sunlight
The big leaf fell from its tree brown and crumpled
Its true beauty finally showing
The little leaf lived on till the day I dried up
Growing bigger than ever

Whitney Davis, Grade 8
West Hills Middle School, MI

Not Always

it won't always be this way
little sisters won't always be running through the creek
little brothers won't always be bouncing on the mattresses

it won't always be this way
there won't always be children eager to dance and sing in the basement
there won't always be clamor to be tickled and hugged and adored

it won't always be this way
there won't always be whispering in the hallways,
bantering in the bathrooms,
giggling in the kitchen,

this house won't always be built of laughter.

so when he tiptoes up to you,
when she tugs at your sleeve,

instead of turning away in annoyance,
instead of ignoring their hopeful smiles,

grab his weathered mitt
crack open her favorite book

because it won't always be this way.

Adela Baker, Grade 7
Clague Middle School, MI

Wedding Day

Thick Rose Lips
Stripes of brown in her hair
Her eyes appear sorrowful
Is she having second thoughts?
On this long awaited day?

Bushes of green surround her
What is she doing here?

Is she walking down the aisle alone?
Will she go on with it anyway?

Deep pink surround her eyes
What is she trying to hide?
Does she know that she's beautiful?

Curly locks of blonde cover her face
Specks of pearly white on her ears
She is trying to appear older than she is

Is she afraid?
Afraid of what she might be giving up?
Or does she really love?
Love with all her heart
That she would leave this life to live another?

Haley Ransom, Grade 8
Kingsway Christian School, IN

Gotta Be Me

As we proceed on this journey
That we call life
Sometimes I seem to confuse myself
Between the wrong and the apparent right

Every day is a new test
Trying to look the best
Yes that is my quest
Trying to be better than the rest

But why do I crave this?
Do I get a cookie or will somebody tape it?
How will I prove it?
To all those who are still with it

An epiphany dawns on me
No need to get caught in the flow
Trying to prove things to those who don't really care to know

I gotta stay focused
Keep my mind firmly in control

I gotta get up and be me
Its my life
I have to write my destiny

Maharshi Nagda, Grade 9
Troy High School, MI

Totem Animal

Totem animal
If you were an animal what would you be?
A free spirit that belonged to you
A gentle wave that overtook your life
Something that mattered so much
This is your totem animal
A mocking jay with its brightly gray-blue wings
A snow leopard playing in the snow
A fox sneaking through the bushes
You can choose...
You feel like yourself, but you really want to hide
An animal that helps to bring out your real truth
That is your totem animal.
Think about a monkey swinging through the canopy
This is a jumpy person.
A small fawn cuddling toward the mother
This is a shy person.
It may sound weird, but to bring out your real self; think it is real
Feel it, breathe it, love it
This is you.

Ananya Ravi, Grade 7
Boulan Park Middle School, MI

The Holocaust

The Holocaust was a scary thing, no one ever expected
It started with Adolf Hitler, who said that Jews should be rejected
They were mistreated for most of World War II
They were forced from their homes, what were they to do?
They were sent to concentration camps, given small rations of food
This in turn left the Jews in a very depressed mood
At these camps the Jews were exterminated for no reason
And for what? They had committed no treason
They were told that they would take a shower
But in fact, they were gassed within the hour
The Nazis marched for them miles and miles
They were then killed and thrown into piles
But these people were brave and continued to cope
They had truly never lost their thought of hope
And then one day it was finally done
The Nazis had given up, they had gone on the run
Now that the allies were here
The Jews had absolutely nothing to fear
They had finally been set free
They now live amongst everyone, with you and with me.

Larry Jasper, Grade 8
St Hugo of the Hills School, MI

Stars

The night is so beautiful when filled with stars
you always wonder what they really are
shining so bright like the city lights
multiple stars next to the moonlight
up in the universe oh so high
so beautiful in the dark night sky

Shelby Berry, Grade 8
West Side Middle School, IN

High Merit Poems – Grades 7, 8, and 9

What Can I Say
I never thought
I would find someone
That understands me
Usually they would get confused
And say that I'm confusing
And would give up early
But him he's everything I never regretted
To be with
To me I'm a fireball waiting to go off
But he's the only one who
Can control what I do (not always)
But if I don't
Then he would get mad
And start an argument
I really didn't care about his attitude
It's just love
Who would have thought of that?
What can I say?
I'm hard to control
Tamika Gardner, Grade 7
Hally Magnet Middle School, MI

Summertime
I sit in school and watch the clock,
Watching so intensely, just like a hawk.
When the bell rings,
The whole class screams!

We run down the hall,
Every student will call,
"Summertime fun,
Is for everyone!"

The summer is a time waited for,
Something fun to explore.
Going to the beach, and having fun,
Lying on beach towels in the sun.

Having fun with all my friends!
The fun just never ends!
I'd just like to say,
I can't wait for the first summer day!
Talisa Gonzalez, Grade 8
Ruth Murdoch Elementary School, MI

Florida
White sand and blazing sun.
Florida is a dream.
Cyan skies and salty sea air.
Swarms of soaring seagulls.
Elaborate sandcastles and deep holes.
Sun burnt skin and sun screen.
Morning walks and amazing sunsets.
Almost impossible to say good-bye.
Joe Davey, Grade 8
St Barnabas School, IN

Princess Zippy
Zippy
You are my crowned princess
The love of my life
The sole reason my heart beats
Your mane blowing in the wind
So rich and thick
Your lively, loving eyes
Shining bright and beautiful like quartz
Your wandering whiskers
Searching for treats in my hand
Nudging my pockets
Your wonderful whinny
Sounding majestic and regal
The way you think everything's about you
Like a true princess
Mary Richter, Grade 8
St Charles Borromeo School, IN

Birds
Bird songs fill the air,
With their pleasant harmonies,
Singing without care

They fly through the trees,
And float gently to the ground,
Softly on a breeze

Seeking food to eat,
Looking under every twig,
Hoping for a treat

They fly to their nests,
And as the sun slips away,
Birds lay down to rest.
Zoey Caballero, Grade 7
Ruth Murdoch Elementary School, MI

What a Week
What a long week
What a crazy week
What a fun-filled week
What an up-late-every-night week…

What a long week
What a confusing week
What an exciting week
What an I-wish-I-could-sleep-in week…

What a long week
What a basketball kind of week
What a homework-filled week
What a test-every-day week…
What a long week!!
Drew Smiley, Grade 7
West Middle School, MI

Things That Describe Me!!!
D elightful Daughter
E xcellent Student
J oyful Girl
A wesome at Cheering
H ard headed at times

M otivated to excel in everything
O pen to everything
N ever been influenced by drugs
E ager to finish what I start
T ough cookie

I ntelligent beyond my years
R ely on my cellphone
V ibrant
I ndependent
N ever gives up
G reat at most things
Dejah Monet Irving, Grade 8
West Side Middle School, IN

Miracle
The sun and the moon
The stars in the sky
The shape of the trees
The warmth of the breeze
The sound of music
The taste of freeze
The gift of family
The gift of friends
The choice of good
The choice of bad
The sight of the oceans
The sight of the lakes
The ability to breathe
The ability to see
The gift of life
The gift to be free
And the gift to be
Plain old me.
Kayla Piljac, Grade 7
St John the Baptist Elementary School, IN

Cooper
I know you're gone
And it's been so long
But our love never leaves
And the pain can never ease
You loved to be outside
But always hated the tide
Loved to chase a soccer ball
That's what I missed most of all
The memories that we have shared
Will follow me through my despair
Tessa de Leon, Grade 8
West Side Middle School, IN

I Am Me
If you are you,
then...
Who am I?
Should I be who you want me to be?
or should I be me?
I have my own mind,
I don't need yours to think for me.
If you want to do it,
do it!
Don't force me,
because you are you,
I am only me.
Tyler Gorczewicz, Grade 8
L'anse Creuse Middle School East, MI

Misery
B ehind the gates of despair
C an you see my bleeding heart
D are to come closer
E verything is gone
F ollow from my life
G ive me hope
H elp me through this
I can't take it anymore
J ust end this suffering
K eep away from me
L eave me alone
Samantha Huser, Grade 8
West Side Middle School, IN

The End of Time
The time has come
the end is near

Prepare your sins
for him to hear

The Lord is coming finally
he will arrive in all his glory

He will judge upon his throne
he's come to call his children home
MaryKatherine Klaybor, Grade 7
Christ the King School, IN

Wrestling Never Takes a Break
Hitting moves hard and fast
Even if it means putting someone in a cast.
Just think of someone who makes you mad
But lack of intensity will do you bad.
If you don't fight like a wildcat
Then you will be pinned, flat on the mat.
You can try to fight out
If you don't, you will be down for the count.
Tony Vaughn, Grade 8
West Side Middle School, IN

I Am
I am a strong and courageous young man,
I wonder what life holds for me as I get older.
I hear hurtful rumors about different sorts of people.
I see stressed people every day that need to just relax,
I want to have good health throughout my life,
I am a strong and courageous young man.

I pretend that the world is perfect,
I feel love on my shoulders of people that love me.
I touch pig skin in the fall months and have the time of my life.
I worry for elderly men and women and hope they have good health,
I cry when I see death and when I get disappointed,
I am a strong and courageous young man.

I understand that life goes on no matter what.
I say that I am fine sometimes and that is not always true,
I dream that I will grow up and have done something helpful to the world.
I try to make peoples lives more beneficial throughout the day.
I hope to make the world a better place before I pass away,
I am a strong and courageous young man.
Nicholas Kelly, Grade 8
L'anse Creuse Middle School East, MI

The One from You
The one from you.
Every time I hold it in my hand, my heart lurches. I smile.
I start to think of the one who gave it to me.
It was on the choker necklace that I hated to remove.

The one from you.
The bead of which,
Bears my name,
Of long since passed,
'Annie,'
That which you still call me.

The small, yet long, creamy white bead,
With the smaller still black letters of A.N.N.I.E., the name that you still call me.

The one from you.
But now it is lost, forever hiding in an unknown place.
'I long for it so. Just as I long for you.
For you are absent from my life.'
The one from you.
Anne Skornicka, Grade 9
Lenawee Christian School, MI

Misleading
This place I speak of is where people live or die.
The smoke floats throughout the air.
Shrieks and screams emanate randomly with the constant sound of the machines.
Sobs of pain fill the air as some people lose it all.
Lights blink and flash as it seems as everything is spinning.
These are not the sounds of war but what sounds escape from the casino at the front door.
James Scott, Grade 8
Grosse Pointe Academy, MI

High Merit Poems – Grades 7, 8, and 9

Travel the World
I want to see the world
Blue as far as you can see
Turns to white when it crashes up on the shore

I want to taste the world
Pastries and cakes from France
Pasta and lasagna from Italy.

I want to feel the world
Rough, ragged terrain of the mountains
Even and smooth fields of green

I want to hear the world
War of the bees in the summer
Cold voice of frost in the winter

I want to smell the world
Colorful flowers dancing in the breeze
Green grass proud of its new haircut

I want to travel the world
Rachel Lindsey, Grade 7
South Spencer Middle School, IN

Ignorance Is Bliss
She put on her make-up
thick. dark. elegant.
She was secretly disgusted with it,
With the gunk that made her look fake.
but she knew it would impress him.
And oh, how she lived to impress him.
The doorbell rang,
and she felt
nervous. empty. but hopeful.
The door was opened cautiously,
after a single signature-red lipstick kiss
was planted on the mirror.

He stood still in the doorway —
gorgeous. expressionless. perfect.
Her arms wrapped around him in a cold embrace.
He smelled vaguely of a foreign perfume,
and purple lipstick
stained his white collar.
She convinced herself she was imagining it —
because she'd been taught ignorance is bliss.
Marisa Henrickson, Grade 9
Allegan High School, MI

Miracles in Life
A miracle is a baby being born,
Or a small piece of corn.
Another is rainfall wetting the grass,
Or a teacher teaching a class.

A miracle is a cure for cancer,
Or a blind person being able to see.
A life being saved,
Or an end of a war.
A miracle is no more hatred,
Or laughter in everyone.

A miracle is peace in the world,
Or no more diseases and sicknesses.
A miracle is a discovery of a new world,
That can be populated with animals and people.
Javier Correa, Grade 7
St John the Baptist Elementary School, IN

Life Is a River
Life is a river,
Sometimes fast flowing and rapid,
Sometimes slow and calm.
Life is a river,
It can't turn around,
Always flowing towards one single place.
Life is a river,
Touching and changing everything around it.
Life is a river,
Overcoming obstacles,
Always making it through.
Life is a river,
And though it never stops,
It may come to an abrupt end.
Filling out into the ocean with all the other rivers,
At rest.
Patrick O'Brien, Grade 7
Royal Oak Middle School, MI

How to Sew Your Heart Together
Your heart has been broken you say
It seems to me what you need is crochet
A stitch of family and friends should do the trick
A seam of God would be my pick
Embroider some great memories to fix that gap
Gather some more love for an extra scrap
All you need is things you adore to fix your heart
In the end you'll have a marvelous work of art
Erin Gabriel, Grade 8
Trinity Lutheran School, MI

My Dear Aunt
Death always occurs at the wrong time,
I remember everything you did and didn't pay you back a dime,
As I start to see you in my dreams,
I wake up and cry but try not to scream,
I wish you were here standing next to me,
Until you do I'll beg and plead,
Just so you know, hear me say,
That you're always in my heart, and here to say.
Destiny Williams, Grade 8
West Side Middle School, IN

September 11th

People today
imagine a better place.
Shattered hearts.
10 years have gone by.
An image no one wants to see.
Who's to blame?
We spooked like cattle
as this snuck upon us.
No prior knowledge.
There are lives lost
every day that we live,
though not a moment goes by
that we don't remember the breaking news that we heard.
It's sad,
It's not even funny.
Because of who cried.
You'd cry too,
if a statement was heard on the news
One you loved
died in the attack.
The famous tragedy.

Haley Patton, Grade 7
Sashabaw Middle School, MI

The Firefly Within

A firefly zips through the dark sky,
All lonely with one speck of light,
Nowhere to go in sight,
And by the thought,
The feeble firefly froze,
By the chill of the night,
Falling down second by second,
Its speck of light turns dim,
Darkness overpowers the sky with the moon hidden,
The firefly lands peacefully,
It's filled with dainty feelings inside,
But there is no longer any light outside,
The creatures of the night screech with fear,
Until the sun rises at dawn,
And the firefly is nowhere near,
Opening its swollen eyes, the firefly finds itself hidden,
Hidden from outside, hidden from the world,
The firefly sees the creatures surrounding,
But everyone stares right through one another,
The strangers' eyes glare and spark,
Finding nothing, but themselves.

Meghan Tudor, Grade 7
Heritage Jr High School, MI

Cool Kid

Mr. Popularity, so brave and tough
Only strong with a computer
Mr. Popularity, always with friends
Only strong with a computer
Let's get real, always with friends
It's time to stop
Let's get real, say that to their face
It's time to stop
Show us that you can talk, say that to their face
Get off the computer
Show us that you can talk, the computer is your truth
Get off the computer
Your popularity fades away, the computer is your truth
Beyond that screen is life
Your popularity fades away, when the power's out
Beyond that screen is life

Tyler Grazia, Grade 7
St John Lutheran School, MI

Embracing Age

Age.
What is age?
Nothing but a number?
Yet something over which we lose precious slumber.

Why hide your age?
Not embrace a new and wonderful life stage?
Why be ashamed to grow old?
It is better than the alternative, we are told.

As you age, age with grace,
Do not lose the sparkle in your face.
Age has many things to give,
Wisdom, family, one more day to live.
Aging is something of which to be proud,
Therefore, cherish your age and say it loud.

Courtney Chennault, Grade 9
Detroit Country Day Upper School, MI

Fall

The smell of fresh air,
beautiful colors everywhere.
A nice cool breeze wraps around
you body in a warm jacket, hat, and gloves.
Jumping in a pile of rakes leaves.
Laying on the ground watching the clouds roll by.
After you're done with imagining, you know what comes next.
Hot chocolate.

Paige Haske, Grade 7
Posen Consolidated High School, MI

Months of the Year

February is the month of love and cupids
Growling thunderstorms happen in April
Howling monsters prefer October
Icy roads and sidewalks form in December
January is when everyone celebrates New Year's
Kites flying in July
Lucky clovers in March
Making Thanksgiving feasts in November

Felicia Vega, Grade 8
West Side Middle School, IN

High Merit Poems – Grades 7, 8, and 9

To Be Happy
We are together, yet still apart.
We are the same, but so distant.
It's as if thy earth is separating us
Never letting us meet.
The same sun, and the same moon set on us
But we are isolated from one another
We were divided, but once the same
We see each other in our dreams
And pictures us uniting
Then we wake to meet our fate
Knowing that time is our barrier
We reach out for one another
So close yet still so, so, far
We will wait and wait becoming sad
Sometimes from our absence, but then we realize that
One day we are destined to meet again
To share, to listen
To enjoy our togetherness, and…
To be happy.
Jacob M. Osborne, Grade 8
Perry Middle School, MI

Remember the Day
Remember the day you told me you loved me
You took my hand
Kissed me
And said all my worries will go away
Remember you said
You can't love another
Your heart was mine
My heart was yours
There was no other
Well yeah sure that lasted a while
Remember the day you said
This is not working
I'm done with you
Yeah now do you remember, you thought you broke my heart
But do you remember the day I told you
You really didn't hurt me because I didn't give you my all
I bet you remember that day
Cause you thought you played me
But really you got played
Shanise Bivens, Grade 8
Hally Magnet Middle School, MI

To My Aunt
It was too soon when we said goodbye.
I was so shocked all I did was cry.
I think about you all the time.
When I think about it why did you have to die?
It makes me sad, but I'll be all right.
When I visit you it gives me fright.
That's why I pray every night.
Casey Weidner, Grade 8
West Side Middle School, IN

God's Novel
Life. There is no way to describe it.
Things happen without an explanation.
Why? Wonders.
Fill my head asking why does this happen?
Why is it happening to me? I don't know
No one will ever know these answers.
Questions will go through your head unanswered.
Everything that happens, God makes happen.
God creates life. God creates everything.
He creates the air we breathe, the land we live on.
Our lives are like God's novel.
You never know what's going to happen next.
As the pages turn, something new happens.
We read them as we go.
The pages turn,
And something gets added to the novel every day.
Things happen. People make mistakes.
You want to take them back?!
Sorry you aren't able to.
You can't erase them.
They are written in ink.
Alexandria Snyder, Grade 7
South Spencer Middle School, IN

My Heart Cries
Day and night my heart cries for you.
You left me unexpectedly
What was I supposed to do?
On the phone laughing and joking
Oh boy I adored you oh so much
Now you're gone we can't keep in touch
All the memories hit me like it was yesterday
Some were good, some were bad
During 10 months with you kid
It's been the best
You're not like other dudes
So I say forget the rest
You were the best I ever had like that drake song
Living without you felt like no lights on
Now that you're gone I have to accept it
But since you're gone forever I'll never regret it
Deanna Cornelius, Grade 8
West Side Middle School, IN

Salvatore Giunta — Tale of Valor
The Congressional Medal of Honor is only given to a few
Saving lives in Afghanistan is what he was born to do
Specialist Giunta moved swiftly to save three men
He will always be considered a U.S. Army gem
Running into heavy enemy fire to provide medical aid
While prepping and throwing some very important grenades
By acting so quickly and gallantly
He saved his comrades lives valiantly
Joseph Testa, Grade 8
St John the Evangelist School, IN

Lonely, Alone

The leaves dance
around in circles,
The grass sways
from side to side,
But I just stand there,
lonely, alone.
The moon glistens
in the night sky,
The sun rises
ever so high,
The birds fly away
and leave me to stand there,
lonely, alone.
White frost lays
on a field of green,
I'm the only one left,
with my branches outstretched
and my trunk held high,
I'm finally
proud to be standing
lonely, alone.

Adrienne Paton, Grade 7
West Middle School, MI

Now and Forever

As I am here lying right in bed,
I think about why,
Why I swim.
I've got the answer in my head.
I swim for the adrenaline,
Getting a new best time.
I swim for all the laughs,
All the people by my side.
I swim for out-touching,
Making podium by a tenth.
I swim for how it hurts,
No sport could be as intense.
I swim for the concentration,
Not wiggling on the block.
I swim for the competition,
No way it will ever stop.
As I am lying right in bed,
I think about why,
Why I swim.
I've got the answer in my head –
Now and forever.

Annie Patterson, Grade 7
West Middle School, MI

Chocolate Chip Cookies

Chocolate chip cookies, I love them a lot.
They fill my mouth all steamy and hot.
They are so sweet and very round.
I love to see their golden brown.

Rhianna Sheesley, Grade 7
Whitehall Middle School, MI

My Feet Write the Story

As my feet swiftly glide across the floor,
They act like a pencil brushing across the page.
All those twists and turns are the relevance of a story.
Making this beauty is not an instant process, it is simply improvisation.
It is more than just seeking; it is an art that is finding.
My feet are the needles that guide the thread to stitch a magnificent work.
When you are so deeply involved with the movement,
It is dreaming only your feet become the dreamer.
When you watch the story being told, your eyes dare not want to look away,
For you are hypnotized with its elegance and grace.
For when you see dancing so fragile as this,
You know the story is as wonderful as the feet.

Taylor Brich, Grade 8
St Barnabas School, IN

Dream Home

A lush lawn, a bountiful garden, and a glistening pool
Are just some of the features on the outside of my miraculous dream home.
On the inside,
A breathtaking entryway, lavish leather furniture, and splendid marble countertops.
But perhaps the most important feature of my phenomenal dream home
Are the people inside.
My heartwarming family and my appreciative guests
Will flourish within my home.
So many wonderful memories will occur on countless occasions.
Every moment I am blessed enough to live in my dream home,
In all of its incredible beauty and serenity,
Will be cherished by me until my last breath.

Mark Elinski, Grade 8
Boulan Park Middle School, MI

Blazing Lights

As the birds end their songs,
And the exhausted sun starts to set
Colors streak across the sky
Dancing in radiant reds, brilliant oranges, dazzling purples, and majestic pinks
The hues fill up the blue atmosphere,
Illuminating it as if someone
Were putting on a light show
But no one's there
In a flash they're gone disappearing into the night.

Lauren Steel, Grade 7
Perry Middle School, MI

True Friends

Friends are true
When you are blue
They're always there to help you through
No matter what you do

True friends are hard to find
Especially ones like mine
Even after time
They'll be friends of mine

Lyndsey Romel, Grade 7
Posen Consolidated High School, MI

Night

The night
   It initiates hazardous consequence
The night
   is malicious, but aesthetic
The night
   is intrigue with deceived dreams

My dreams are strange but exceptional in
The night

Jose Castaneda, Grade 8
Culver Community Middle School, IN

The Five Sense Buffet
Walking in the door I shook off the cold from outside,
The host saying in a friendly voice, "How are you today,"
Hearing the sounds of silverware chiming on the plates,
Hidden under the low groan of people talking and enjoying their meal,
As I walk to my table, I make no eye contact with anyone, everyone has their heads
Down focused only on their meals and conversations.
I stroll through the small tables and go immediately to the buffet,
There I grip a warm plate that felt like it just came out of the dishwasher.
I slide my plate along the counter creating a noise like someone sawing wood that
Seemed to drown out the voices of others.
The smell of the food seemed to reach out to me and grab me,
Taking control of my mind, making me see the piles of food as mountains of endless satisfaction.
I grow excited I grab the warm, metal spoon in my hand and begin
To scoop the different foods onto my plate.
The sizzling, steaming, strips of steak seem to melt between the tongs that are used to hold them.
I strolled through the rest of the buffet like a kid in a candy shop,
Taking my time before I make it back to my seat with a full plate.
There I took my time sampling everything and enjoying every taste sweet, spicy, or plain
Delicious. I was a satisfied critic, that enjoyed the meal on all levels and as much a I could
For all my five senses.

Nat Otley, Grade 8
St Barnabas School, IN

Who Is My Dad?
My dad is like a bed, he's soft and cuddly on the nights when I feel afraid
My dad is like a pressing comb, he straightens me out when times get rough or nappy
My dad builds the bricks that protect me from the things that try to harm me or put me in danger
My dad is like the lightning in my life, he comes when a dark sky is above my head
My dad is like a piece of plastic, I can see through him and what I see is my grandma
My dad is like a concert, he has a lot of people in the center of his heart
My dad is like a fortune teller, he knows what I am going to do even before I do
My dad is like a sheep herder, he knows what to do to keep the household in order
My dad is like a comedy movie, he knows how to light up a room and make anyone laugh
My dad is like a strainer, he separates the good things from the bad things
I could go on about my dad, but to sum everything up,
My dad is:

MY DAD

Naomi Nichols, Grade 7
Hally Magnet Middle School, MI

Night
The moon rises over the sun.
The sun sings its goodbye and kisses the Earth with a fire sky and leaves.
As the stars lift up they smile and shine in the cold, dark, emptiness of night. Each one telling their own story.
The moon grins with her work and the winds dance to the trees sweet lullaby.
As the stars leave, the moon bows to the sun and waits until its her time again.
As the wind blows my hair, my eyes focus on the beauty of God's gifts.
Ice crystals sparkle every inch of waters land.
White speckles of roaming, yet not lost sand.
Brave grass shift their way out of dunes and sway in the wind's whispering words.
Waves that call to the listeners and you lose yourself in the language of the tides.
The sun hugs my heart and my soul cries out with relief.
All in all, my smile is wide.

Breana Ristau, Grade 9
Plainwell High School, MI

Jerkin All Day
J erkin can't die
E xcited when winning
R eady to battle at all times
K ing of dougie
I n many jerk videos
N ever stop practicing

A lways jerkin with friends (crew)
L aughing when people think they can jerk
L oud and hyper

D on't stop battling till I lose
A lways being supportive of what I do best
Y ells when I'm in my zone
Tarez Baker, Grade 8
West Side Middle School, IN

Summer Time
Summer vacation soon will be
I will accept it happily
But then my school days will be past
Something that will just not last

Along with that also comes work
And throwing hay with a pitch fork
Mowing the yard and hoeing weeds
Growing vegetables for our needs.

Playtime comes when our work is done
Then it is really time for fun
We never tire of softball
Something we can play till fall.
Wilma Arlene Graber, Grade 8
South Bogard School, IN

The Poem
I am going to make a clever poem.
I am still not sure what to write about.
I could write about a small garden gnome.
that idea probably would not work out.
Or I could write about a baby bird.
Can you give me a really good idea?
Maybe a wild buffalo herd.
That was not my most creative idea.
Maybe I will write about thinking.
But that requires using my mind.
Maybe I will write about hunting.
But the fact is that, that would not be kind.
I am needing an interesting thought,
But an interesting thought I have naught.
R.J. McCarren, Grade 8
Grosse Pointe Academy, MI

Snow
The snow is falling outside
And it isn't stopping
So I keep on playing
In the white deep snow.

I make snow forts,
Snowmen, and a hill
To go sledding down
In the white deep snow.

When the snow is falling
I get my snowmobile going
To ride on the like
On the drifts the snow makes.
Brandon Misiak, Grade 7
Posen Consolidated High School, MI

Winter and Spring
When we see snow and rain come down
We know winter is here;
Oh how adorable to know
That springtime is so near!

In winter everything is so white
Even the top of the woods;
There are so many things to do
Some things might not be good.

Springtime brings all kinds of song birds
Most of them are pretty;
Springtime is my favorite time
For it I am ready.
Matthew Knepp, Grade 7
South Bogard School, IN

A Spring Day
The wind makes all the trees sway
Leaves blow away
The grass is warm
The flowers form

Butterflies dance all around me
They all soon flee
Little bugs run
Chasing the sun

The day is coming to an end
Night's 'round the bend
The moon does keep
Those that do sleep
Jessica Newkirk, Grade 7
Ruth Murdoch Elementary School, MI

Spring
After winter, when the snow melts,
When the air becomes wet and glum
At first it is chilly when felt
But it will be warmer to come

It rains and it pours, it never seems to stop
But the sun gets warmer every day
Then the leaves begin to pop
And before you know it, it's May

Everything begins to grow
For one single reason
Everything begins to show
To prepare for a new season
Michael Kalinowski, Grade 7
Assumption School, MI

Summer
Summer is the very best time
Fishing, hunting, trees to climb,
Swimming, camping boating too
There is also work to do.

Planting gardens and mowing yard
There is also work that is hard,
Cutting fields and raking hay
Putting in bales makes my day.

Feeding horses, milking the cow
Feeding the dogs that go bow-wow,
When we eat it is bed time
Summer is a happy time.
Jonathan Dale Wagler, Grade 7
South Bogard School, IN

Owl
The old dark owl,
A noble bird
Whose silent flight
Is never heard.
The cold, hard screech
Whose words are wise
With facts to teach
In minor sighs,
Its darkened drones
Of ancient folly,
Ring overtones
Of Melancholy.
Over a sleepy world he flies.
Singing chilling lullabies.
Elizabeth Bays, Grade 8
Stanley Clark School, IN

High Merit Poems – Grades 7, 8, and 9

The Beach
The waves crashing
The seagulls chirping
The sun beats down
The sand sparkles like the stars
The shells are picked up as quick as a jet
The castles made of sand
The screams and laughter from the water
The boat's horns drown out all sounds
The beach is the place of places
The love, the sun
The beach
Serena Clock, Grade 7
Oak Hill Jr High School, IN

Abby
I can still hear her loud ruff
Trying to forget her is tough
I cry every time I hear about her
I miss her every day and that's for sure
Her pretty little eyes are still in my heart
No one can ever rip us apart
I know she is in a better place
But my beating heart still aches
Every time it storms or rains
I know I will see her one day
Maybe someday in May
Alisa Zoller, Grade 8
West Side Middle School, IN

Love
Love is good
Love is great
Love will always steer you straight
Love is fine
Love is mine

Love will always blow your mind
Love is the thing that will keep us together
Love is mine and yours forever and ever
Love may not always be easy to find
Love is truly divine
Lauren Romel, Grade 7
Posen Consolidated High School, MI

Life
Life
No future path flows
Everything worries
Destroy yourself…gone

Life
Smiling friends rejoice
Crazy scenario written
Consider yourself…rescued
Constancia Pena, Grade 8
Culver Community Middle School, IN

Life
I sit in the room staring at the four walls that lie in front of me.
Writing a paper that I don't know what I'm writing for.
I hear a familiar sound, laughter.
There are many sounds of it being made, as I sit and wait.
I hear the swishing of swings from the wind blowing.
I hear voices now that are making a yelling sound.
Out of this room I hear the stomps made on the ground.
I turn around and look out the window.
Children, kindergartners specifically, playing hide and go seek.
A game I played 8 years ago when I was less than five feet.
Now I look at who I am now and what I was back then.
Wondering why I stopped doing it.
Oh I remember it was something adults called childish.
Now I have already hit puberty a woman I shall become as soon as high school's done.
There's no turning back 'cause *life has passed*.
I should have paid attention in class when they said you only live once so give it your all.
'Cause you don't wanna look back and miss out on what should have been.
Of course, only if you let it happen.
Ky'la Sims, Grade 8
Salina Intermediate School, MI

Ashley Renee Barnes
Through all our pains, you are always at my side,
No matter the problem, big or small
You've always stood so tall,
When you're around,
All the scary monsters and nightmares go away.
I'm so happy we get closer day by day.
Ashley, you are the sister I've held onto in all my "once upon a times…"
Thank you Ashley Renee;
For every tear you wiped from my face,
And every scar you quickly erased.
And every single heartbreak you've easily replaced.
Through life's ups and downs, you've never let us drown.
You lead us with every step you take,
You guide us by each mistake we make.
And I'm so glad you're the sister I have when I'm awake.
I love you, Ashley.
Thank you.
Clarissa Ramsey, Grade 8
Lincoln Middle School, IN

Who Are True Friends?
True friends are…
Your Puffs tissues when you're sad,
your steaming Campbell's Chicken Noodle Soup when you're sick,
your soft, cozy Snuggie when you're cold,
your GPS guide when you're lost,
your therapist when you're troubled,
your Chinese fortune cookie when you're confused,
your closet when you can't find a shirt to match your favorite shorts,
your ponytail on a bad hair day.
Your true friends always have your back.
Samantha Fogg, Grade 8
St Barnabas School, IN

Peer Pressure
I am falling
down, down, down
deeper into the dark abyss of friends?
dark, darker, darkest, light
It is there
I run down halls and 'round corners
I put up my hands to tell it to stay away
I back up but it still comes
Clang! A fence? A fence!
I can climb out
No pulled back to the abyss
I refuse to take them
the can with blue writing
and the box with white
No escape, no help
It is a terrible thing a very terrible thing
Peer Pressure
Casey Gross, Grade 8
Sherman Middle School, MI

Love
Love is peace,
Love is kind,
Love is the sun,
That brightly shines.
Love is real and always right,
From day-to-day,
And darkness to light.
Some love is just like the other,
But there is one special love,
That is only for the mother.
Most love is right,
To show how people feel,
The feeling of happiness,
That sits on the hill.
This is love,
This is me,
The love that I can only see.
Glynnat Moore-Horton, Grade 7
Hally Magnet Middle School, MI

Peace
What really is peace?
Peace is pleasure
Priceless
Amicable for all
Keeps our people together
Blooming with inspiration
Agreeable
Reconciliation between all
Perpetual
An equable goal
Worldwide
Peace is *powerful*
Miranda Dudek, Grade 7
St John Lutheran School, MI

Teddy Bear
I sit and wait
Until the night
When you hold me
So very tight.
I like to sit
Upon your bed
So I can cuddle
Up by your head.
There's very little
That I do
But it keeps those monsters
Away from you.
I'm very happy
That it seems
I scare away
All those bad dreams.
So now you know
That when you sleep
I'll be here
For you to keep.
Haley Ann Edwards, Grade 8
Verona Mills School, MI

Thanks Be to God
My family, my family,
They love me so dear.
My dad making dinner,
My mother so near.
With Princess on her left,
And me on her right,
I thank God for my family,
Together every night.
As I lay down,
Jake jumps in my bed.
I thank God for him
As he lies on my head.
As I awaken,
I see the morning light,
And thank God for the day
And the coming night.
My family, my friends,
I thank God for them,
And for my life.
I praise him. Amen.
Brandon Muir, Grade 7
St Clare of Montefalco Catholic School, MI

Trophy Buck, Trophy Buck*
Trophy buck, trophy buck
Oh what luck
I have finally found you, your time is up
You have many points on your rack
Pay attention and watch your back
Johny Koch, Grade 7
Whitehall Middle School, MI
*Inspired by William Blake

The Puzzle
When I start
a jigsaw puzzle,

I am anxious to
get done with it

to look back
and be happy with

what I've produced.
I realize this is just

how I want my life.
First, I piece together

the edges, my attitude, early
so that it'll be easier

to form who I really am later.
I try my hardest

but eventually I get frustrated
and want to quit, but if

I keep going and
persevere, I will be

able to finish and be pleased
with what I've achieved.
Ethan De Ruby, Grade 8
Kingsway Christian School, IN

Rainbow
Arched like a bridge,
a rainbow
sweeps the sky.

The vibrant colors glisten,
And I wonder if I tried
to reach the end of the rainbow
would I see
an overflowing pot
of gold
and
little, dancing
leprechauns.

Arched like a bridge,
a rainbow
sweeps the sky.

The vibrant colors glisten.
But where does the rainbow end?
If it even ends at all.
Madeleine Nichols, Grade 7
Detroit Country Day Middle School, MI

Stage Fright
She walks up onto the stage,
there's a hint of worry in her eye.

She gazes over the audience,
frozen and frightened.

Clutching the paper like it's her precious life.
Her nerves are overpowering her.

Her arms are tucked closely to her body
and legs glued together.

She tries to speak, but her voice is wobbling.
Swallowing hard, pursuing on,
staring blankly at her sheet and the floor.

The glares of others feel like lasers,
and the one spotlight, as if the sun is attracted only to her.

People smile for comfort,
but it only reminds her of where she is.

After she's done she swiftly moves her
weak and shaky self off the platform.
The pops of applause begin to rain out.

She sits down, relieved and slightly embarrassed.
Again.
Millie Trent, Grade 8
Kingsway Christian School, IN

Where I'm From...
I'm from divorced parents,
from living with aunts, uncles, and grandparents.
I'm from eight different schools
from eleven houses.

I'm from the city to the woods,
from the heat beating on my back
to freezing snow
up to my knees.

I'm from dogs, cats, ferrets, and squirrels
bouncing around in my yard,
from fish swimming
in fish tanks.

I'm from my sisters and brothers
picking on me,
from getting shot at
with an air-soft gun.
I'm from running into the woods
to hide from
my family tree.
Dakota Bartholomew, Grade 8
Kalkaska Middle School, MI

Breathless Night
I'm wide awake in the shadows of the night,
Fearing the moment my eyes would close.
I know the breathless night is coming.

I give up and my eyelids fall.
I'm sucked into this world of panic and helplessness.
This is what I dreaded — the breathless night has come.

These unending thoughts forbid to escape me.
I'm drowning and suffocating in fear.

Terror engulfs me.
I am so lost I can't find my way out,
I'm failing to navigate through this maze in such fright.

It's getting harder for me to breathe.
Time is running out.
Please get me out of this breathless night.

I have somehow escaped from this terror,
But it's a black hole I cannot run from.
I am dragged in further and I wish it would stop.

It wouldn't go down without a fight,
But I fought hard and succeeded
My eyes flew open; I'm gasping for air.
It's another breathless night I couldn't bear.
Camille Natividad, Grade 8
St Barnabas School, IN

The Fairy Necklace
The fairy necklace so beautiful
And delicate
Silver with pink jewels
Hanging from my neck

I tried not to
It was too tempting
I hung on to the delicate little legs
I swung them back and forth
Against the chain

After I did this a few times
It snapped
The place where it broke
Was rough and cold

I felt so bad
I couldn't tell you
So here it is

I'm sorry
For breaking the delicate fairy necklace
I know how much you loved it I'm sorry Mom
Kaytlin Boller, Grade 8
Kingsway Christian School, IN

This Calm, Peaceful Forest
The quiet, slow footsteps
Made by thick, heavy shoes
Is one sound to hear
In this calm, peaceful forest.

The sound of the branches
Cracked by coyotes and wolves,
Are sounds you may hear
In this calm, peaceful forest.

The cry of a robin,
The roar of a bear,
Are more sounds to hear
In this calm, peaceful forest.

So open your ears,
And quiet your voice.
Listen and learn
In this calm peaceful forest.
Lucas Liepert, Grade 7
Stanley Clark School, IN

Hurricane
The disaster is coming
  Hour by hour
    Minute by minute
      Second by second
It is here!
Boom
  Clatter
    Shatter
The eye has come,
We are scared
But just the next part.
The next part has come
Boom
  Clatter
    Shatter
Now just thunderstorms
My house is ripped apart but no worry.
I am alive.
Catherine Edmonds, Grade 7
Christ the King School, IN

I See Birds
A bird chirps as sun appears,
B lue as a sea.
C hirping as loud as can be.
D ucks are all around.
E verywhere I look I see birds,
F lying in the sky,
G oing up and up.
H igh up in the sky.
I see birds
Camille Ritchings, Grade 8
West Side Middle School, IN

Hit It Hard
Neon yellow with white lines
It's coming as fast,
As a cheetah catching its prey.
What could this possibly be?
A tennis ball, of course,
With top spin.
I quickly run and try to hit,
The tennis ball,
UGH!
It went into the net,
And I just missed it
By a tad,
I'm sure
If I made it over
It would have been
An amazing shot.
All I had to do
Is just hit it with an open face,
A little harder.
So now I know
For the next time.
Neela Podolsky, Grade 8
West Hills Middle School, MI

Don't Change Me
I'm a,
Ball spiking,
Bat swinging,
Boy smacking,
Pink hating,
Jean wearing,
Cello playing,
Converse loving,
Clumsy,
Girl!
Not a,
Pink loving,
Skirt wearing,
Nail painting,
Cheerleading,
Phone obsessed,
Drama attracting,
Frilly,
Self-Conscious,
Priss!
So stop trying to change me!!
Hannah Ashworth, Grade 8
West Side Middle School, IN

Happiness
Happiness rains down;
  as illuminating gold;
    flowing through my veins.
Alexandra Pace, Grade 8
West Side Middle School, IN

Thinking of You
Walking in the moon light
I am thinking of you.
Listening to the rain drops
I am thinking of you.
Smelling the flowers
I am thinking of you.
Eating pizza
I am thinking of you.
Sucking on a lollipop
I am thinking of you.
While writing this poem
I am thinking of you.
You do not understand
That I am the one for you.
But I hope someday
My dream will come true
To be with you,
But 'til that day
I will always be thinking of you.
Prince Prabhu, Grade 8
Ruth Murdoch Elementary School, MI

In the Greenhouse
Out in the greenhouse, there's lots of work
We all must help and will not shirk
Planting vegetables and flowers too
Plenty of work for all to do.

Geraniums, ferns, and sprengeri
Pumpkins, gourds, and squash for some pie
Better boy, Roma, Celebrity
Stone head, also Blue dynasty.

Daisies and mums will make a bouquet
Hot peppers and Rainbow Gourmet
Creeping Jenny and Lambsey will do
Incredible is some corn for you.

All these things and many, many more
Is what we eat and will work for
So let's be happy and not complain
And be glad for the gardens grains.
Carol Wagler, Grade 7
Green Acres School, IN

The Road
Many people journey the road
Paving their own trail.
Many people carry a load
Through sun, fog and hail.
When they finally come to the crossroads
And select a new route to take,
Many people travel the road
Full of choices to make.
Grayson Harding, Grade 7
North Rockford Middle School, MI

Game On…

B anging in the post
A ll we've done is win
S hots from all over
K lick-klick time's running out
E ven the coach is sweating
T ime is against us
B ench players changing the game
A ren't any excuses
L eave it all on the floor
L osing is unacceptable

Tyler Schoettle, Grade 8
St Barnabas School, IN

Sports

Sports keep me moving
Sports keep me learning
Sports keep me competing
Sports keep me motivated
Sports keep me occupied
Sports keep me satisfied
Sports keep me in line
Sports keep me living
Sports keep me having fun
Sports keep me on the run

Anthony Rogers, Grade 8
Perry Middle School, MI

Life

Memories fade
Feelings flow
Live today
And let yesterday go
Live your life
Enjoy the view
Smell the morning dew
Listen to the wind
Enjoy the sound
Soon you'll be flying off the ground

Katie Anderson, Grade 9
Gull Lake High School, MI

The Dream

Time goes by fast,
So fast that I get lost in the past.
I forgot what hope means.
I gave up on all of my dreams.
Caught in a fantasy,
With nothing to do
But scream.
I will hold on to forever
Until this dream
Meets reality.

Aliya Berro, Grade 7
Star International Academy, MI

Meet My Dreams

You started out a "Savior," the person this town needs;
But stardom can be hurtful, as crazy as it seems;
And after one accomplishment you really felt the heat.

You made a bad decision, one that's still with you today;
And your ranking slipped to "quarterback" as your fans slowly faded away;
But don't worry, for my fan hood will always stay.

After 3 seasons of redemption, remorse and regret;
You were hoping most people would be able to forget;
And after your clutch performance in Super Bowl 43 it would be hard to be upset.

Your rank flew back to "Savior," and your head was in the clouds;
But what you didn't focus on was how to deal with crowds;
And Mr. Goodell punished you for your performance out of bounds.

Your rank was down towards "failure" with trade thoughts and suspension;
And can he really change was everybody's question;
But my thoughts were what took so long for you to change direction.

You led us to the Super Bowl this year, even though it wasn't how we wanted it to be;
I know you've changed a great amount by watching you lead your team;
And my pride in you will be here no matter how much people tease.

I'm just a girl from Indiana, one of whom you've never seen;
But you'd think that we had met by how much to me you mean;
Ben Roethlisberger, as strange as it may be, meeting you is still my dream.

Maddie Mulinaro, Grade 8
St. Barnabas School, IN

Yellow, Camo, Blue, Green, Beige, Gray…Black

The yellow from the new playground equipment blinds you
The child's smile seems to spread from person to person, almost infectiously
as it sits above his blue shirt
his feet dangle.
The man is uncomfortable, but smiling as he holds the teeter totter down.
up and down
up and down
Strangers enjoying a new playground with a small clump of grass.
Then you see it, a long black smudge that seems out of place
No one seems to notice
It's a M16A4 standard issue military firearm
It came with her uniform.
Now you see
There's gray all around.
Where are these people?
Heavily accented laughing
How did this happen?
Why are those soldiers there?
Protecting our freedom!
Giving those Iraqi kids their freedom
and a new playground!

Nathan Hilbert, Grade 8
Kingsway Christian School, IN

A Celebration of Poets – Great Lakes Grades 4-12 Spring 2011

Suspicions
Suspicions
They make you anxious
Wary
You can't stop moving
Because you're right there
Next to them
You can't ask to confirm or deny
Your suspicions
That would be absurd
Stupid
What if you're wrong?
You'd look like an idiot
You'd feel like one too
The risk is too great
So you just remain unhappy
And keep your suspicions
To yourself
And see what happens
Because you hope somebody
Else will take away
Your suspicions
Tyler Lange, Grade 7
Fowlerville Junior High School, MI

Don't Be a Bigot, Just Get with It!
Racism is such an ugly word
The fact that people still practice
Is simply, just absurd.
Whether black or white,
Asian or Jew,
Always be polite,
It's the right thing to do.

All people are equal,
No one greater than his brother
Because in the next sequel,
We must all love each other
Diversity is what we need.
Don't judge an accent, look, or tradition,
Unity is the way to succeed
It's for our future…Have ambition!

All this hate, all this war,
What's the reason?
I don't know what it's for!
Let's all get along, and not commit treason.
Tessa Naman, Grade 8
St Hugo of the Hills School, MI

It's All a Dream
I'm going to smile like nothing is wrong
talk like everything is perfect
act like it's all a dream and pretend it's
not hurting me
Deisy Lucas, Grade 8
West Side Middle School, IN

So Much Depends Upon*
so much depends
upon

the president making
choices

and listening to
voices

of the people
who

make things better for
you
Lauren Lopez, Grade 7
Whitehall Middle School, MI
*Inspired By William Carlos Williams

The Protector
As the brown beast looks,
He stalks his prey with great stealth.
When daylight warns him,

He runs off to hide
Till his master wakes him up,
He sleeps in his bed.

Then when the day ends,
Till his master goes to bed,
He wanders around,

Guarding his household
From anything bad that comes.
He's the protector.
Aaron Harabedian, Grade 9
Lenawee Christian School, MI

My Uncle's Truck
Covered in dirt,
Red peeks out.
The exact color
Of an Easter egg.

When the engine backfires,
It makes a loud pop.
Making the passengers'
Hearts skip a beat.

Pulling into my drive,
I smile to the driver.
Heading for the door of my house,
I remember that
Dirt covered truck.
Tamar Jinkins, Grade 8
Covington Middle School, IN

Snuggie
If you are feeling cold,
Regular blankets get really old.
The snuggie will save you,
From a freezing Ahh-Choo.

It's a blanket with arms,
That never harms.
It looks great on you,
It looks fine on me, too.

They are easy to order,
You don't even need to cross a border.
You can text easily in them,
They're good to polish a shiny gem.

They sure do beat Sham-Wow
It can do more than just clean right now.
It keeps you super warm,
While in a drafty college dorm.

It's easy to eat in it,
I've even enjoyed a banana split.
It's the best invention,
With-in this dimension.
Patrick DePorre, Grade 8
St. Hugo of the Hills School, MI

The Yellow Swing in Spring
The sweet scent of flowers,
Freshly in bloom,
Bending and weaving in the
Lively cool breezes.

Everything freshly
Green with life,
Grass, leaves, stems, and
Four leaf clovers bringing luck.

Skipping through the yard,
Grass tickling her bare feet,
A carefree young preschooler
Dancing with pure joy and delight.

Prancing towards the play set,
Sitting on the banana yellow swing,
Marked with big, black sharpie letters,
Spelling out her name.

Swinging higher and higher,
Imagining her toes kicking,
The fluffy cotton clouds
In the bright blue sky above
Anna Cockrell, Grade 7
Detroit Country Day Middle School, MI

High Merit Poems – Grades 7, 8, and 9

The Power of a Song
Have you ever heard a song
A song that meant something to you
A song that made you laugh
A song that made you cry
A song that made you feel

That's the power of a song
A way to show real feeling
To tell the things that can't be said
To understand what can't be understood
To answer questions that can't be answered

A song is more than words being spoken in a microphone
A song is more than a beat
A song is more than something you listen to when you get bored
A song is more than a verse, A song is power

A song is an expression of ones deepest feelings
It tells the story of ones life in great detail
That is why a song can make you feel
That is why people have a favorite song
Not because you like the beat
But because it has its own meaning, that is the power of a song
Trea Harris, Grade 8
West Hills Middle School, MI

Different Keys
Keys
Silver, bronze, or even gold,
they are all different colors,
yet they're all just a key.

Keys
Short, average, or tall,
they are all different sizes,
yet they're all just a key.

Keys
Flat, dimple, or even corrugated,
they are all different shapes,
yet they're all just a key.

Keys
Loving, helpful, or caring,
we are all different,
yet we are all just humans.

Humans
No matter what the color, size, shape, or purpose,
we are all just human.
Nicole Wink, Grade 7
South Spencer Middle School, IN

Lead Them to Light
Sitting in this quiet room, I blindly feel for light
I've been here so long it seems, I can't tell if it's day or night.
To be where I am, isn't what you'd pick first
But to be where they are, I'd say it must be worse.
There was a time, we were one, we were just alike,
but now I'm different, smarter, wiser, right.
So I sit in this quiet room, watching you get worse.
I pray every day and every night, that you be rid of this curse.
I try to help, but you are too far…
I miss you here, It's getting dark…
People say I didn't help, only shoved love in your face…
But, I would never rush you, find light in your own pace…
If God is light, and also love, how could you walk away??
I'm not going to stop hoping. If you need me, here is where I'll stay.
Ali LeMond, Grade 9
Highland Jr High School, IN

When Teachers Call Me by a Different Name
I just hate it
When teachers accidentally say it
Even though they know who I am
They call me by a different name
They say the person who they name me
Exactly looks just like me
It makes me feel bad
It makes me feel mad
It makes me feel unrecognized
Even though I am organized
I always start thinking when this happens to me
What is so hard about my name to thee?
Our names are so different, I don't get it
I just don't praise it
Ankur Jain, Grade 8
Forest Hills Eastern Middle School, MI

The Spirit
My dear it's been years since I saw you.
I miss your laughter when I make jokes.
I miss your smile when you are around the grandchildren.
I definitely miss your cooking.
I'm sorry how I nagged at you.
I'm still living in our house that we built together.
The flower garden is blooming every spring.
I kept the painting that you made of me.
Honey I miss you so much.
I'm here on this earth without my dearest love.
One day I will see you again.
Vickie Kennedy, Grade 8
St John the Evangelist School, IN

Turtles
Gorgeous creatures swim.
From green to brown to turquoise.
Turtles swim slowly.
Cheyanne Finger, Grade 7
Perry Middle School, MI

The Day the General Fell
The day the general fell
from atop his great white horse,
the privates were all amourn,
every soldier felt a special remorse.
When news spread the commander was dead,
there was no colonel or captain to be head.

The rough fighters began a charge
of their own accord,
toward the menacing enemy horde.
As they looked across the battlefield,
they began to barrage their foe
with the terrible weapons they did wield.

When the smoke had cleared
and all was done,
the regiment was feared!
They had won,
for they fought their adversary well,
The day the general fell.
John Hopple, Grade 8
Culver Community Middle School, IN

Fifteen
Here I sit, at age fifteen
In an awkward stage somewhere between
Being a child with a wide open mind
And being an adult with ideas confined
Uncertainty surrounds me and questions abound
Regarding my past, my future, and now
Where will I be 10 years from today?
Do you remember those games that we used to play?
What if I hadn't done things like that?
Does this dress make me look fat?
How would things be if I didn't exist?
Excuse me teacher, what have I missed?
Will I ever be a happy, married wife?
Will this math ever be useful in life?
I'm only getting older, and can't go back
It's about time I get my life on track!
I need to live for today, and without a fret
So that later in life, I'll have no regrets
Yet here I still sit, at age fifteen
In that awkward stage somewhere between
Miranda Steward, Grade 9
Charlotte Sr High School, MI

My Grandpa
I may have not known you too well,
but I have always known you're swell.
Even though I didn't give much
it really hits me in the stomach with a punch.
In this situation you're gone and I'm in a tight place,
but now that you're in my heart you can't be replaced.
Nicole Woolwine, Grade 8
West Side Middle School, IN

Tranquil Trail*
Tranquil and calm
Is how the day starts
Kids awake,
Thud thud the basketball hits the ground as
It's accompanied by a LOUD
Scream of the children playing a simple game of tag.
BE-EP BE-EP the kids honk their horns on their very small bikes.
The moon f
a
l
l
s

Into the sky
And the day ends peaceful and tranquil
After all it is called
Tranquil Trail.
Maegen Myers, Grade 7
Whitehall Middle School, MI
*Inspired by Arnold Adoff

The Quarrel of Men
The lights of twilight
Glisten in the past
The peril of the Knight
To fight at last
With might at night
Is the destiny cast?
Drawing their swords
From left to right
For the honor of their lord
They will to fight,
Ho! what a gruesome chord
To be played at such a sight
They slayed the innocent with a mighty blow
Unaware of what they have done
They cast a shadow
Upon the setting sun
It will not shine again tomorrow
For the quarrel of men has begun
Ethan Miller, Grade 9
Columbus North High School, IN

Spring
It smells of summer in the air, yet too cold, too early.
The wind blows a breeze on the trees,
making them waver like arms swinging in the air.
The sun's rays warms the Earth up after a long, cold sleep.
She awakes, and stirs wildlife in the forests.
Then comes the squirrels, the rabbits, the birds.
Water awakes too, but drowsy,
making brooks and rivers flow like honey.
The grass grows green again, amidst from the melting snow.
It is Spring, they say, it has come after all.
Christopher Yun, Grade 7
Stanley Clark School, IN

High Merit Poems – Grades 7, 8, and 9

I Hate to See You Gone
All the times we had together
I hate too see you gone
Although I know you're doing better
I still haven't seen you for so long

If only I could see you again
It would be the best day ever
Just to see how you been
Would make my day forever
A.J. Gushwa-Williams, Grade 8
West Side Middle School, IN

Nature's Beauty
Take a look and smell within,
The beauty of flowers here and then,
Hurry now before they close,
For a good night's sleep you shall repose,
Then awaken to the morn,
To see your heart be torn,
As the bright red petals turn to weeds,
Now get some seeds,
To start the process over again.
Symantha Taylor, Grade 7
Perry Middle School, MI

So Much Depends Upon*
So much depends
Upon
Those last suspenseful
Seconds
Of a championship
Game
To make that winning
Shot
Drew Bolles, Grade 7
Whitehall Middle School, MI
*Inspired by William Carlos Williams

A Horse's Dream
You hear me in my stall
My hooves go clip-clop,
Because I am ready.
My dream is to race,
Because I move at a fast pace.
Sarah Rivard, Grade 8
Verona Mills School, MI

Spray
S pecial to my parents
P roud to be a wrestler
R eady as the whistle blows
A wesome at Black Ops
Y oung and wise
Luke Spray, Grade 8
West Side Middle School, IN

To Be King
All his fury, potential, and energy is released as he
Jumps from the helicopter. His heart beats
Quickly; at any moment it could simply stop

Expertly he carves down the mountain, dodging
Rocks and huge gaps in the snow.
It's him and the mountain, no one else matters...

There's no one to catch him if he falls, or guides him to safety, however,
He soars down the mountain; the man's eyes taking in
The gorgeous scenery behind their tainted goggles.

Beads of sweat form on his brow as he pushes on,
The mountain wants him dead and he knows it,
Yet fighting the overwhelming panic he remains focused.

And gains control. He then looks beyond to the snow covered
Mountains stretching upward to the bright blue sky.
Though everything hurts he smiles,

Restless with adrenaline pumping through his veins the athlete
Pounds his fists into the snow and throws his feet up into the air, completing a handstand.

Bits of ice are thrown into the air, they rain down like glistening pieces of confetti.
This is what it is to be king of the mountain.
To defy death and choose to live on the edge...to be king.
Jeremy Hendon, Grade 8
Kingsway Christian School, IN

Volleyball Nation
Dedication, reputation, preparation
We are dedicated, committed to this sport. We have a reputation for our ambition.
We have been preparing for this moment from the first second of practice number one.
We like to think of every little stroke on the game ball this way.

Situation, perspiration
It's fourteen-fifteen in the final game: we're down by one.
Our enemies have serve. Here's our sticky situation, like glue on your fingers after a project.
I have the aroma of perspiration that is dripping down my forehead, cheeks, and hands.
I roll my sleeves up for the pass as I pull back next to the libero from outside.

Indication, concentration, hesitation
The outside takes an approach, squats, and jumps.
She comes from an angle outside of the court and her shoulders align with my hips.
Before she jumps, it's already been indicated that the ball will be mine.
Bam, bang, boom! I concentrate as the ball shoots at me with downward power and speed.
I hesitate. Hands or platform? Platform. My pass goes right on target: our setter.

Sensation, celebration, coronation
I have this sensation, one to jump. I sprint from a little back corner to my open space.
I take my approach and leap into the air. I strike the ball down the line.
With no coverage, the whistle blows. The ball is dead. We won.
The crowd roars as we celebrate and cheer on the court.
We receive medals, small, but in our minds we are crowned the queens of the court, huge.
Carly Pugliese, Grade 8
St Barnabas School, IN

Purple
Plum, Lilac, Lavender, Violet,
All reminders of purple at hand,
Also found in the depths of the ocean,
As well as in the sky,
And on the land,
What comes to mind,
When I think of purple,
Is the beautiful night sky,
Shining with stars,
August flowers,
Grapes on a vine,
And autumn leaves line up in rows,
Storm clouds seen on the horizon,
Dark, windy, raining nights,
Evil things that lurk in the shadows,
Dark blues, blacks, and even grays,
So if you say purple isn't important,
This is what I will say.
Skyler Braun, Grade 7
Perry Middle School, MI

Street Music*
This street
My street
When the cars come rolling in
All you will hear is the sound
Crunch, crunch, crunch
The tires hitting all the
Holes and bumps
Making you jump,
Jump out of your seat
And one time a day
You can hear the train go by
Honking its horn
Like no one sleeping
Down by the lake
You can hear the frogs croak
Until that first day,
Of that cold bitter frost
Alaina Anderson, Grade 7
Whitehall Middle School, MI
*Inspired by Arnold Adoff

Dolphin
Dolphin, dolphin, swimming fast
like a bullet shooting past
blue tail moving up and down
with other fish swimming around.

Swiftly and precisely you move
through every crevice and every groove
of the sand on the ocean floor
through the depths of the ocean's core
like a jet away you soar.
Brianna Martinez, Grade 8
Bloomingdale Middle School, MI

The Stuffed Bunny
I used to go everywhere,
She'd never leave without me
Sure I'm just a stuffed bunny,
But to her I was the world.
She dragged me around,
Dropped me,
Lost me,
Cried on me.
I was many things,
A super powered bunny,
A jeep driver,
But most of all I was a friend.
I listened quietly and offered comfort.
I let her dress me up in fancy clothes.
I saw many hotels
And traveled from North to South,
I always was there for her,
I always will be.
Sure I'm just a stuffed bunny,
But to her I am the world.
Megan Drenth, Grade 8
Ebenezer Christian School, MI

Sunday Afternoons
In the afternoon sun,
near the red brick house,
along the sidewalk trots my dog, Tillie,
by my side.
Up the tree rests a squirrel.
Underneath, a cat hisses.
Without hesitation,
we cross the street
to walk our cul de sac
beside our neighbor's Rottweiler.
Later among the pansies, I lie peacefully.
watching the dogs run
over the hill,
between the maple trees.
In the fading sun,
off we go.
Back though the pansies
back though the maples
down the sidewalk,
to home.
Susan Ellert, Grade 7
Westside Catholic Jr High School, IN

Everything
Everything is anything
Everything is the world that surrounds us
Everything is the thing we do each day
Everything is the things we speak
Everything is the way we…
    Are
Liz Moore, Grade 8
Perry Middle School, MI

Summer
While walking along a road,
I saw a snail and a toad
I also heard the calling crow,
There was not a sign of snow.

Beside the big, wide river,
A long snake makes me quiver
Out jumps a fuzzy squirrel,
But it's gone with a whirl.

As I trudge slowly homeward,
Wondering how things are made
On my lips a praising song,
As I slowly wander along.
Marilyn Rose Knepp, Grade 7
Green Acres School, IN

Seasons
Summer, Fall, Winter, Spring
Seasons are a wonderful thing.
Rain, sun, snow and wind
The seasons go and come again.

Sledding, skating, skiing too
Lots of Winter fun to do
Fishing, swimming and softball fun
Things to do when Summer has begun.

Some places are always cold
Some are warm we are told
Some places are real windy
Some places have storm at sea.
Natheniel Wagler, Grade 7
Green Acres School, IN

Detroit
Detroit is a jungle with raging faces.
Detroit is crazy with many races.
Detroit is disruptive and unbalanced.
Detroit is wild then patient at stoplights.
Detroit is thriving and alive.
Detroit is full of fumes of exhaust.
Detroit is full of sirens.
Detroit is full of violence and gangsters.
Detroit becomes dark with moonlight.
Detroit becomes calm and quiet.
Detroit becomes peaceful and smoothing.
Detroit becomes full filled with streetlights.
Light that is only sound
The day is no more.
Hunter Creed, Grade 8
Perry Middle School, MI

High Merit Poems – Grades 7, 8, and 9

I'll Always Remember That Day
Kindergarten, 5 years old,
Sitting on a bench all alone.
About to cry,
So very shy.
At recess.

You walked up to me and asked
"Do you wanna play?"

I smiled and said yes.
We walked to the small bridge on part of the playground
On that sunny day.

We've been best friends since then,
Almost eight years.

And I'll always remember that day,
No matter how long it's been since then.

Lyric Silk, Grade 7
West Side Middle School, IN

Celestial Being of Night
The moon forms no light of its own.
It is cold, dark, and unnoticed
Like an anonymous stalker in the night.
But, from the scintillate sun
The moon catches light
And becomes a white disk in the evening sky,
The celestial being of night.
Imprecated in footprints,
Never stirred
Placed by astronauts prospecting the surface
Hoping to find something new
About the vast universe and its contents.
Moon, will you ever go away,
And abandon us with nothing to gaze at in the night?
Or to explore and learn new things?
Will you drift into the ever-growing Universe?
And leave us behind as we will leave you to expand to
New worlds, galaxies, and possibly universes.

Zack Bales, Grade 8
St Barnabas School, IN

Hidden Shadow
A dark vague forest
So silent and waiting
Something scurries and stirs the leaves
As the darkness reaches its peak
You can't even see a tree in front of your face
You feel a chill run up your spine
Then your only safety is to close your eyes
But even then only one fact remains
You can't escape
The darkness

Garrett Osborn, Grade 7
Perry Middle School, MI

Mom*
A malicious end to a
person uniquely aesthetic
Fading tragedy into
broken sympathy.
Flawless flying birds
mark the moment.
Perfect vision questioned?
The sear curves of my body tremble
As I realize the wait has ended
It has happened.

Lauren Large, Grade 8
Culver Community Middle School, IN
*Dedicated to my mom who passed away three years ago

Starting Over
M e and you we are two,
N ow do you even have a clue,
O pen your eyes and look at me,
P lease tell me can't you see,
Q uiet silence then you knee,
R eading my eyes then you say,
S orry please forgive me I didn't know a way,
T o say that I love you,
U pon what happened in the past,
V ery much that's the last,
W e can forgive and start over and this time not go too fast.

Ashley Bolen, Grade 8
West Side Middle School, IN

Miss Thelma Spencer
60 years, you spent your life on this earth
gone October 08, starting at birth
Crying for destiny, all night and day
sad that your illness took you away
I miss your laughter and your cooking
I know that down on me you will be looking
And right here, now I want you to know
from my heart and mind you'll never go
I thought of you just like a mother
I'll see you again, one day or another

Rhenna Alugaili, Grade 8
West Side Middle School, IN

Love
Love is your most passionate feeling
Love is what gives our hearts the power to beat
Love is the rhythm to your favorite song
Love is something only you can feel
Love is the rose petals leading to a chocolate montage
Love is why we are here today
Love is a trance only love itself can break
Love is what makes us who we are
Love is the warm fuzzy blanket around our heart
Love is more powerful than just I alone

Holly Lankford, Grade 7
Christ the King School, IN

Not Perfect

I know that I'm not perfect.
I have knots in my hair,
Holes in my jeans,
And barely anything cute to wear.
I see the sun,
Yet feel no warmth,
Without your guidance,
To lead me forth.
I didn't think I'd miss you,
As much as I do.
I want you back,
'Cause you're my boo.
I'm barely good at keeping secrets,
I'm bad at telling a lie,
I'm not the most coordinated,
But can be very sly.
I know that I'm not perfect,
And I hope that you don't mind.
I'm always on my best,
And yet one of a kind.
Caitlin Sall, Grade 7
Hudsonville Christian Middle School, MI

My Street Music*

As the wind   Bl o w s   through the trees,
the occasional car *rushes* by.

The leaves crunching beneath my feet,
the dew d
         r
          i
           p
            s
off the leaves of an oak.

As my dog trots along his fenced in yard,
a LOUD dirt bike motors on by.

A turkey gobbles very quietly,
As a squirrel scampers around a tree.
Snowmobiles drive by NOISILY,
While a deer chomps softly on a leaf.
Leah Thompson, Grade 7
Whitehall Middle School, MI
*Inspired by Arnold Adoff

To My Dog

Oh how much I miss you
I love you lots too
All the memories are oh so dear
How I would love to have you near
All your toys that laid around
Now can no longer be found
Megan Gould, Grade 8
West Side Middle School, IN

Simple Person

I'm just a simple person.
Nothing more,
Nothing less.

I'm not here
To start a revolution.
I'm just here to change
What people think
About life.

I don't want
To be known worldwide,
A change in history,
Or a miracle worker.
I just want
To make a difference.
Selena Nguyen, Grade 7
Christ the King School, IN

The Scariest Movie of All

Life is a scary movie,
You never know what to expect.
You sit up straight,
Heart pounding,
Waiting until the end.
Life is a scary movie,
You may love every second of it,
Or patiently wait until the credits.
Life is a scary movie,
You don't know what to trust.
But don't just sit there,
And watch it all pass by,
You can make a happy ending,
To this horror story.
Life is a scary movie,
So enjoy the show!
Charlotte Messner, Grade 7
Royal Oak Middle School, MI

Memories

All the memories on earth
Could not compare to mine
From tragic to aesthetic
Memories from heaven
Wrapped in chocolate papers
And fierce whispers of
Never being there.

In nostalgic moments
I often remember
Late night calls to memories
Lost in pain and weakness
Persistent and wretched to me
But mine forever they will be
Shoshona McNeece, Grade 8
Culver Community Middle School, IN

That One Fateful Night

He wasn't afraid of anything
Nothing could give him a fright
Until that one fateful night

Nothing was scary
Everything was nice
Until that one fateful night

Everything was funny to him
Nothing was creepy
Until that one fateful night

And on that fateful night
He was scared by his brother
And quickly wet his bed
But nothing used to be scary
Until that one fateful night
Nikolas Minanov, Grade 8
Grosse Pointe Academy, MI

Blind Friendship

It's strange to have a friend,
That you've never hugged,
Lightly touched their arm,
Or looked into their eyes.

But you,
Have touched their soul,
Felt their heart,
And by the warmth of your being.

A friend unseen,
Is not a friend untouched,
The eyes of the soul will gaze,
The heart will embrace,
The image will stand tall,
For you and I to see.
Emily Fisher, Grade 7
Perry Middle School, MI

Green

Green is the treetops
Towering in the sky
Grass dancing in the wind

Popsicles melting
In the sun
Fish filling lakes
And streams

Green is the color of happiness
Filling our hearts
Dragonflies flying in air
Out of reach
Brooke Steel, Grade 8
Perry Middle School, MI

High Merit Poems – Grades 7, 8, and 9

Emotions

Emotions are persistent
Deficient in exhilaration
They can be dangerous
Like a thunderstorm, always threatening the world

My emotions are exceptionally hazardous,
Truth is, they're forever serious, but
Like tonight's ecstatic clouds
Sometimes their display is entertaining

Often my emotions are counterfeit,
Like feet walking away
Enough malicious feelings
Never have the initiative of truth

I see my fat emotions
As one fat, horrendous bear.

Shianne Wagner, Grade 8
Culver Community Middle School, IN

Love

As I inch closer to love,
My life gets better as I go,
Things get better,
People get better too!
Life is getting worse,
But yet the inching love is getting better by the second.
Life will soon be filled with fears,
Only you can fulfill those fears.
My love has once again brought tears to my eyes,
Maybe I should rethink about him.
Am I really stressing this bad?
The world is now like a black hole,
I am still rethinking about him,
I don't know what to do.
The world is now full of fears,
No one knows what to do or what to think.
What will the world end up to be like?

Kristin Crawley, Grade 7
St Charles School, MI

All Knowing

It covers everything.
It is our friend and enemy.
It shields our faces and devastation's.
It knows our fears.
It creates our fears.
We tell it everything, and yet we tell it nothing.
It sees everything and we think it sees nothing.
It sees us cry, celebrate, wonder, think, and die.
It sees our emotions when others don't.
We think nothing of it and yet every day, it surrounds us.
It is our friend, our enemy and at times our ally.
It is darkness.

Courtney Morrison, Grade 9
Edsel Ford High School, MI

The Door

…and there I lay
on the edge of death and reality
the state in which only God can decide your fate.
I look now to the door
just a little bit closer
this is how it was supposed to be
in the end.
this is how I imagined it
all the pain,
the death,
the sorrow,
I know if I can get out of here
it will be all right
there's only one thing left to do…
I lay back, take a deep breath
and with that I silently close my eyes
and open the door, to the world unknown

Kathryn Martin, Grade 7
Forest Hills Central Middle School, MI

Next Year

We always whine and moan about school
It is hard, and seems like a waste of time
With all the homework, it isn't cool
Math, language and poems that have to rhyme

Though in hindsight, we see a lot of fun
Our inside jokes are too many to count
Cards, kickball, foursquare — all the games we won
We played teachers to watch their anger mount

Everything changes — we have no control
Just like next year when we go separate ways
We will no longer be seen as a whole
But we will hold on to all these days

Our decisions will start to have more weight
But give it a chance — next year could be great

Marissa Lane, Grade 8
St John Lutheran School, MI

Warmth in the Arctic

The cold air stings my body.
A howling wind swirls around me, making me shiver,
Then it stops.
As if the storm has been called off,
Like the sun is shining on my fur
Warmth spreads through my body.
Mama Bear's large paws wrap around me,
Shielding me from the icy wrath.
The way she protects me from this storm…
I know that I am safe.
Surrounded by her affectionate embrace,
I will always stay warm.

Taylor Orr, Grade 9
Allegan High School, MI

Sickly River
This river was once placid
And the heart of the forest.
    Now it is violent…
Animals would collect by its pleasant shore
And they would drink the cool water.
    Now they are gone…
Its vibrant blue waters shined
And glistened in the summer sun.
    Now it's dark and brown…
Once it flowed with a gentle hum.
And it sang in tune with the birds.
    Now it roars as it runs by…
Its water would bring life
And prosperity to the forest.
    But now it brings death…
    It is no longer the same…
It is corrupted and sick
And it pours itself into the lake.

And the lake, too, has become corrupted.
The river has contaminated it…
Joey Franc, Grade 9
Allegan High School, MI

Life
Long lasting,
living memories made.
A lot of choices chosen,
with consequences that follow.
As your own dreams come crashing
like waves on a beach,
you were born with a message
for people you can't reach.
Yes you may cry,
you may hurt
or be afraid to die,
but with strength, also courage
there are no worries,
so make sure that you always try.
So you push on the bridge
through the fog and the wind,
life seems so hard
when you're pushing to the end.
Yet it gets kind of easier,
as long as you have,
a very close friend.
John Nieto, Grade 9
Lenawee Christian School, MI

Picture on the Piano
So much depends upon
a picture
of a loved one, gone long ago
smiling approvingly as you play the piano.
Kaytlen Greene, Grade 8
Bloomingdale Middle School, MI

Friend
What is a friend?
Is it someone who is there by your side through everything,
Someone who won't turn away even on the worst day?
Is it someone who you can laugh with for hours,
Someone you share everything with?
Is it someone who knows your worst and is still there,
Someone who you can act dumb with?
Is it someone who makes you mad,
Someone who knows what to say at the perfect time to say it?
Is it someone who isn't scared of what others think just to stand up for you,
Someone who can stick with you through the trials of life,
Someone there when you just need a shoulder to cry on?
What is a friend?
Shelby Cleeter, Grade 8
St Barnabas School, IN

Ignored
Lights flashing with tight circles of people dancing.
Everyone else having so much fun.
My head turns as everyone dances away, into a tight circle, leaving me behind.
Like a wall with no way to enter.
I tag along, trying to get their attention, trying to be just like them.
I am ignored every time.
Why won't people notice me?
Why am I so alone?
These are the questions I've been asking myself for a long, long time.
The long time that I've been alone.
My heart aches as I realize that this is not the crowd for me.
I slowly walk away, and nobody even bothers to notice.
Once again, I'm ignored.
Margo Killey, Grade 7
Clague Middle School, MI

That Lake Over There
This town…is a NOT so NOISY town at all.
Well…except for that LAKE over there.

Always seem to hear the WHOOSH and CRASH of the white caps breaking.
Always seem to hear the RASPEY SCREAMS of the white gulls overhead.
Always seem to hear the BUZZ of those motor boats out there.

Always seems to be peaceful, in this…NOT so NOISY town…
Well…except for that LAKE over there.
Victoria Learman, Grade 7
Whitehall Middle School, MI

My Grandmother
My grandmother is an old-fashioned kitchen that never stops cooking.
She is the sun in the sky that warms the earth.
Eggs, toast, and sausage filling my stomach to the sky.
It is served on wax paper, while I watch the news.
But her smile is more filling than all the food.
Ramey Hamilton, Grade 7
Hally Magnet Middle School, MI

High Merit Poems – Grades 7, 8, and 9

Swallow the Medicine
The TRUTH
is just like the
most
disgusting, terrible, horribly-flavored
medicine.
The problem
is the cold.
Don't sugarcoat it,
you might get sicker.
Don't only tell part.
You won't get worse,
but you won't
get better.
It might be bitter at first,
but it's better in the long run.
Grab your mouthwash
and swallow that medicine.
Alexandria Printz, Grade 8
L'anse Creuse Middle School East, MI

In Finality
In finality,
the leaf will wither;
the beast will die;
the rock will crumble;
but I will remain.
Delicacies will pass;
luxuries will fade;
the easy life will be no more;
but still, I will remain.
In finality,
I will remain because they are frivolous;
I contain meaning, and they do not.
In finality,
I will remain because I have purpose;
I have a destiny,
and, in finality,
they do not.
Isaac Stansbury, Grade 8
West Side Middle School, IN

The Freedom of the Sea
The cool light blue waters of Hawaii,
Habitat to many wonderful creatures,
Including the humpback whale.
The freedom of such a beautiful creature,
Emerging from the cold blue water,
Like a new grown flower form the mulch.
Swimming wherever it wants to,
Not stuck in a cage forced to learn tricks,
For the entertainment of humans.
Just a harmless creature,
Roaming its habitat,
Free of harm and worry free.
Daniel Banooni, Grade 7
Detroit Country Day Middle School, MI

The Music
They lyrics fill my ears
The sounds pump me up
Help me focus
Block out
The unwanted
Unneeded sounds
Finish
What needs to be
Complete focus
Beautiful things created
The writing flows
Like the melody
It really speaks
It's a thank you speech
Gets your attention
Won't let go
Keeps you hooked
As if on repeat
Soon it ends
As must all things beautiful
As it ends
Another begins
Seth Kloss, Grade 8
Fowlerville Jr High School, MI

Pain
When the pain comes what will you do?
Will you sit there and act a fool?
Will you push it to the back of your mind?
Will you stand there and cry?
No, you will be strong
Will it take long, you ask?
Yes, to build your confidence
Do not be ashamed
To take pain
Yes there will be pain
Always pain
But the question is
Will you stand the pain?
Victoria Carmona, Grade 7
Ruth Murdoch Elementary School, MI

Snowflakes
Snowflakes of memory
Twinkle in the stars
Like a full moon
In its brightest shade.
They watch me
As I walk through this path
Remembering my every move.
For whom God gave us
This winter wonderland.
So enjoy them,
The snowflakes of memory.
Brandon Harthorn, Grade 7
Cedar Springs Middle School, MI

Dream Storm
The weather person said
there would be thunderstorms tonight
as I went to bed.
I curled up tight
and said goodnight
to the pillow beside my head.
Boom, went the music.
Crack, went the lights.
Then the raindrops started dancing
all in the light,
swaying to the music,
all through the night.
Then the sun peeked out
through the windows.
The grass glistened with dewdrops
and I guess the
rain did dance through the night.
Isabel Humphrey-Phillips, Grade 7
Verona Mills School, MI

Gone
I barely knew you when mom
spoke the words.
Ashley, I'm sorry, but Daddy's
gone.
Tears ran down my face like a
thunderstorm.
So much pain still today.
I miss you and all our silly
little memories together.
I wish you were still here
today.
You're gone, but I know one
day we'll see each other again.
Oh, I wish I could just
have one more day with
you.
I love you.
Ashley Bennett, Grade 8
West Side Middle School, IN

Death
What is death?
   An endless sleep
   Unknown and feared
   Experienced alone but by all
   A great change
   Obscured from knowledge
   A cold embrace
   A trip to a place beyond time
   Not the closing but the opening
   Something new and different
   Not an enemy but a friend
This is death.
Courtney Saunders, Grade 7
St John Lutheran School, MI

Family Devotion

Not all things are forever.
Hope can be crushed, trust be broken,
The firmest friendships can sever,
But family devotion remains.
At home, I can express
Who I truly am.
So what if I'm not flawless?
Why should they care?
They love me because they are mine
And I am theirs.
They see my troubles
And take them as their own.
No matter how small,
They support me and understand
I can't do it all.
I've heard them say
"You don't choose your family."
I know I would never.
I love mine so much, you see,
And I could thank God forever
For giving my family to me.
Lucie Ly, Grade 8
St Charles Borromeo School, IN

Me and Fate

I was a star
Special in everyone's eyes
But I have fallen from my place
Now I'm just on the outside
No matter what I do
It's never right
No matter what I accomplish
It's never enough
I used to know where I belonged
I used to be strong and brave
But now I'm scared and sad
I wish I could go back
And stop you but I can't
No one was ever there to comfort me
Everyone was there to tell me what to do
No one cared, I was alone in this world
I used to know who I was
But not anymore
I was a star
Special in everyone's eye
But I have fallen from my place
Sasha Chen, Grade 8
Fowlerville Junior High School, MI

Flaming Blaze

The intense crisp smell
The scalding hot fire glowed
The breathtaking smoke
Cameron Ritter, Grade 7
Perry Middle School, MI

Opaque Description

opinionated yet exaggerated
over the top hallucinated
my life

generosity overflowing
but not by my hands
by yours

you escaped
or more like was taken
by…it

I never knew the outcome
it was always hidden from me
but on the horizon it peaks

tear drops
beckoning for a solution
and then woefully disturbed

I now understand the power of love
what a broken heart can commence
because you taught me so much

goodbye dear one
proud to call you my friend
I love you
Kyle Diller, Grade 9
Beaverton High School, MI

Atop the Hill

Voices in the distance,
Headlights shining bright,
The leaves of an evergreen
Singing goodnight

But beyond all this
Stands a much greater sight,
For beyond the moon and atop the hill
Stands the lonely old oak

The oak whose limbs weave in and out
In a design that draws my attention,
As if stories are hidden inside,

Stories that are sent floating in the wind,
Stories of young love
And bitter loss,
Stories that even the fireflies
Can't tempt me from

And so I sit in wonder,
Atop the hill
And beneath the indigo sky
Mersadies Pierce, Grade 8
Lincoln Middle School, IN

In Which We Say

The red stripes wave
alongside the white,
adjacent to the fifty stars
surrounded by blue.
I stare at this political flag
as I read the Pledge of Allegiance
in which we say every day
we promise
to remain one nation
with justice for all.
I wonder
what it is like
in other countries,
people starved,
cities overcrowded.
I think about these ideas
and realize
how lucky I am
to be
in the land of the free
and the home of the brave.
Alexus Rhodes, Grade 7
Westside Catholic Jr High School, IN

Family

Family is important to me
They are the people you will always need
Through the good times and the bad
Or through the happy times and the sad
You always have someone there for play
Or to talk with all day
Sometimes you may fight
But everything is all right by night
Its fun to watch one another grow
And have someone you truly know
From working together or playing ball
There's plenty of fun for all
For me my family is large
With dad and mom in charge
There are five girls
Some with hair of curls
There are five boys
Who really make a lot of noise
My life is full of love
With blessings from above
Thank God for my family
Lucy Hemmelgarn, Grade 8
East Jay Middle School, IN

What Am I

I am orange and black
I hit the backboard for one
This shot wins the game.
Tyler Heim, Grade 8
West Side Middle School, IN

Suckers

Suckers come in every flavor you can think of,
Butterscotch is the one I love.
They can be made of chocolate, cookie, or even be sour,
I think I can eat one every hour.

Plain, is what suckers are not,
Filled with tootsie roll, bubble gum, or cinnamon to make them hot.
Blow Pops, Dum Dums, Tootsie Pops are just a few brands,
The great thing is they don't melt in your hands.

Suckers aren't always round,
But more shapes have been found.
Twisted, rectangle, and cone shape too,
Whatever the shape I'd like a few.

Suckers come in ever color of the rainbow,
Green apple, *Blue* raspberry, and coconut *White* as snow.
Multicolored suckers are a ton of fun,
Whatever the taste, shape, or color I love everyone!

Katelyn Nye, Grade 8
Perry Middle School, MI

Moon Light

In the moonlit night
A lone wolf howls
It howls for his pack
His pack has not returned.

He stares in the direction they went in.
The kind of stare that makes us ask questions.
Peaceful, powerful, pleading eyes shimmer in the moonlight.
As a tear falls down his beautiful, black face.

The wolf wines and cries.
He paces back and forth.
Then he lies down in the grass,
And gracefully falls asleep.

Jessica Holmes, Grade 8
West Side Middle School, IN

Rain

The rain pelted to the ground
Simultaneously with the tears streaked across her face.
One after the other, they fall.
She found it odd,
Every time she cried, it seemed to rain.
As if when she was sad God felt her every pain.
But when all her tears had been cried,
And her once wet cheeks
Had been dried,
She was left with one thing,
Complete and utter
Happiness.

Alexis Wilks, Grade 7
Cedar Springs Middle School, MI

Don't Blink

Don't Blink
    you might miss it
The colors streaming on the page
    like butterflies so beautiful
The creativity you use to express yourself
    is a bird taking flight; the freedom of the sky
It's private and special
    like a secret with your best friend
Or it's an amusement park
    loud and fun
Your pencil leads the way
    like the moon leads the stars
Your markers are the life of the sketch
Art is life
    From a blank canvas; empty and lifeless
To a masterpiece that's the sunset —
    vibrant and beautiful
Your paintbrush is the magic wand you use
    to color the world
So don't blink
    you might miss it

Yesenia Galvez, Grade 7
South Spencer Middle School, IN

Stop Me if You Can

Dribble, dribble, shoot, shoot
I take it to the hoop.
The orange ball of fury in my possession
Guides me to the hoop
So many ways to make points:
    Dunking — the ultimate show stopper;
Strength and integrity.
    Three-pointers — the magic touch;
Floating to the hoop like an angel with wings.
    Lay-ups — quick feet equals easy points;
Thank you for letting me by!
    Free-throws — Concentration and following through
Key skills obtained to take advantage of your opponent.
All the experience gathered continues to grow.
Stop me if you can…
For only the best will NEVER rest!

Beverly Bednarski, Grade 9
Posen Consolidated High School, MI

Dark Beauty

As I walk into an empty pit of darkness
I start to flame I am beautiful red and orange
I see I'm not alone
The empty pit of darkness
Turns to light
As I turn to ash
The pit goes dark
I burn out

Madison Smith, Grade 7
Perry Middle School, MI

What Color Are You?
Red,
black
or blue,
What color are you?
For red is angry,
Black is sick
and blue is just so lonely.

Would you feel
green or red if the world were to
end, because green is a big bowl of pity.

What color describes you?
Do you just feel the same?

What color describes you?
What color says your name?

For you are only human, your
color will always change, no matter
what the ring says, you will never feel the same.

Lexie Carie, Grade 8
L'anse Creuse Middle School East, MI

Short and Sweet
Life is a piece of candy
It comes in many different varieties
Some kinds cost more
Yet they might not last as long
Some will last very long
And some will claim to last long
But in the end
You never know till you try
Some of us get lucky
While some are given the bland candy
Most of them are very similar
But when an exceptional one comes
It changes the way the normal ones are made
In an infinite struggle for dominance
Even though one will believe he can rise above the rest
Until they all come to unity

Morgan Grougan, Grade 7
Royal Oak Middle School, MI

Sitting on the Sidewalk
I was sitting on the sidewalk one day,
When a young boy did come down my way.
It seemed he had fun as he ran in the sun,
For as he ran he looked quite gay.
Now, when he reached me, he sighed and sat down,
With a smile all over his face,
And he briefly explained, how joy he'd attained,
Before taking me out of that place.

Trevor Furst, Grade 7
Ruth Murdoch Elementary School, MI

Only One There
Embracing arms,
Loving hearts,
Never straying,
Only one there.

Strength as a tree,
Protector of his girl's heart.
Like a princess's knight, in shining armor.
Only one there.

The sky is the limit for him.
Loves you more that there are stars in the galaxy,
More that there are fish in the sea.
He protects you like a cheetah, protecting her cubs.
Only one there.

Teacher in being a monkey, in throwing a curve ball.
My teacher in splashing, sloshing, slashing, diving, and being.
A wonderful beautiful magnificent Mermaid
Only one there.

The wonderful man, that walks you down the aisle.
When you are dressed, in the white dress of your dreams.
Only one there.
Daddy.

Kaleigh Woolsey, Grade 8
St Barnabas School, IN

My Swimming Race
From a middle school race to a state swim meet,
I always have the same strategy.
A positive attitude and a focused mind
Are the key to getting a better time.

Once I step upon the block,
The rest of the world scatters away.
"Take your mark," says the official. *BEEP* goes the starter.
The clock starts ticking, and my body takes over.

My arms reach and pull.
My legs keep the beat.
Screams of motivation come from my coaches,
And shrieks of excitement escape my friends.

I power through the pain,
With my heart set on the goal.
I touch the wall with one final stroke.
I know I gave it my all.

Satisfaction fills my head.
This is what I train to do.
Every time I climb out of the pool, I think to myself
I love to swim!

Katy Smeltzer, Grade 8
East Jay Middle School, IN

High Merit Poems – Grades 7, 8, and 9

The Sensation of Summer
Summer,
Blue skies, annoying flies
Ice cold soda pops, any kinds of flip flops,
By a fan, skin so tan
Jean shorts, playing sports,
Mosquito bites, campfire ignites
Summer.
Lightning bugs, water jugs,
Fresh peach, at the beach,
Rays of sun, hamburger bun
No school, swimming pool,
Sun bleached hair, in a lawn chair,
Summer.
No worries or snow flurries,
Scattered stars, convertible cars
Full of fun, water gun,
Parties to attend and nights that never end.
Madeline Schabel, Grade 8
St. Barnabas School, IN

Change in Life
Grapes to raisins,
Apples to cider
Life is always a maze,
Even a path, yes, a dirt path
Maybe, leading you towards success,
Or somewhere to destruction.
Peculiar sights along the way
A chain of roses or twinkling stars
One day rain, snow,
One night stress, depressed.

But if you stay positive
Creatively laughing
Life may be exquisite
Grateful exhilaration to
Malicious melancholy
With a blink of an eye it can change
Kailey Heise, Grade 8
Culver Community Middle School, IN

Soccer
Black and white is on the ball,
I'm prepared to take on all!
The whistle blows, we're on our way.
We're all in sync to win today.

Passing, kicking towards the net,
Working side by side, a goal to get.
One final pass — a monster kick —
In the net the ball does stick.

Goal! Goal! That's the way
We won the soccer game today!
Kassie Butterworth, Grade 7
Hudsonville Christian Middle School, MI

Life
Life happens every day,
No matter what we try to do.
Various stages of it;
How do we do it?
Life happens every day,
From birth to toddler,
Life's decided for us,
No choices we can make.
Life happens every day,
From young child to teenager,
Choices start to come up,
It's up to us to make them.
Life happens every day,
From teen to young adult,
Obstacles, choices, and romances come,
It's up to us what we do.
Life happens every day,
From adult to death,
Challenges arise,
But life happens every day.
Rachel Buckley, Grade 8
West Side Middle School, IN

Running Blind
Calling your name, I hear only echoes
Searching for you I see only shadows.
Feeling the pain, feeling only shallow
Reaching for you,
Searching the rain,
Breaching my promise.
Keeps me going on
Keeps me running on
Keeps me running blind
Voices I hear them calling behind me.
Sights of you are burning inside me.
Feeling for you, vacuous beside me.
You're only in my mind.
You keep me running blind
Am I only wasting time?
Phantoms of you whisper my name
Shadows surround me, I shroud my shame
My face in the mirror, cast my vain
Why don't you give me a sign?
Why do you keep me running blind?
Nicholas Haynes, Grade 8
Westville Middle School, IN

Shamel
S aves chocolate
H ates salad
A mazing at the saxophone
M ellow
E asy to get along with
L oves to eat candy
Shamel Jordan, Grade 8
West Side Middle School, IN

The Life Below
As I dive under
A whole new world opens up
A place to be free

As the sun reflects
Off of all those crashing waves
I swim deeper down

As the fish swim by
I admire their colors
Their beauty and style

A shark swims by
In the reef, he haunts his prey
Waiting and watching

It's fascinating
It's the life below us
Magical and free
Mallory Reetz, Grade 9
Lenawee Christian School, MI

You and Me
The orange haze, off in the distance,
The green grass, tall from resistance,
the wind makes a beautiful sound,
As hot air balloons glide down.

The sun beams, fall on my face,
We keep walkin' at a comfortable pace,
The moment the waves hit the sand,
Together will be our hands.

You make me laugh every day,
My lips curve to the things that you say,
We gaze at the stars up above,
And think that this might be love.

Well we've only got one chance,
To make a thing outta this romance,
So take it slow and we will see,
How it turns out for you and me.
Zella Mae Patrick, Grade 8
Fowlerville Junior High School, MI

Baseball Is My Life
B ases that you can get safe
A ball that you can hit
S afe on bases that you go to
E veryone can learn
B leachers where fans sit and cheer
A home run people can hit
L aying out for a ball
L eaning to steal
Derrick Oley, Grade 8
West Side Middle School, IN

I Want My Life Back

I want my life back,
Where my parents didn't fight,
My brother got along with me,
I didn't have to wipe my tears to see,
I want my life back,
When I could text my brother,
I didn't get blamed
I want my life back,
My parents didn't call me a drama queen,
I didn't worry about grades,
I didn't get put in my room,
I didn't get yelled at for something my brother did,
I want my life back,
Where I got to see my grandpa,
My parents ask me how my day was,
I want my life back,
I got to see my brother every day,
My dad wasn't cranky,
I was like daddy's little girl,
Give me back my fairytale!

Emily Musson, Grade 7
Fowlerville Jr High School, MI

Every Time

Every time you smile
you make my heart race a thousand miles
every time I see you my stomach starts to sink
it's crazy to think
every time you say my name
it's hard to keep my heartbeat tame
every time you look at me
I know it's you the bender of my hearts key.
Every time you speak.
I look over to catch a peak
every time I get a whiff of your cologne.
It makes me dream of us alone.
Every time you sit by me
I picture us together holding hands by the sea.
Every time I hear you laugh.
My heart is overpowered by your loving warmth.
Every time we flirt
my mind just wants to blurt
it's really true.
I think I'm madly in love with you.

Shareece Yost, Grade 8
West Side Middle School, IN

This Girl

This girl she's beautiful, she's funny, she's amazing, she's cool.
When I see her my heart speeds up.
It's crazy I never felt like this about a girl…
Hmmm, but there's problem. She's taken…
What to do it's a dead end…
Man will she ever be mine.

Stephen Jackson Jr., Grade 9
Troy High School, MI

A Girl's Best Friend

His soft,
Brown fur
Brushed against my arm
As we lay
Staring out the window
He looked at me,
With those shining brown eyes
Even though he couldn't speak
In my heart I knew
He loved me.
Since I was a newborn
Up until I turned 13
He sat by me,
During thunderstorms,
Even homework.
Dogs are not only a man's best friend,
A girl's too.
Nike was not only my dog,
He was my brother,
And best friend.
I love you Nike and hope you are in a happy place.

Leigh Surugeon, Grade 8
West Hills Middle School, MI

Fly Away

Sir can you help me?
The young girl asked the man.
The man slowly shook his head and said,
I don't believe I can
Sir please let me explain,
You see I can't find my mom.
There was a big explosion,
I think it was a bomb.
The girl looked up at the man,
A sad twinkle in her eye.
Something stirred in the man's heart,
As the girl began to cry.
Now listen close please.
Remember what I said?
I know I can't help you,
Because your mother was found dead.
The young girls tears fell harder,
As the clock began to sing.
The man walked away, heavy with guilt,
And the mother flew to heaven with angel wings.

Olivia Pleiman, Grade 9
Gladwin High School, MI

Winter

Winter
A layer of snow sits perfectly sifted over every needle of the tree,
The wind whips across my cheeks,
And the sun ever so slightly peeks out from under the clouds.
Winter

Sam Fontana, Grade 7
West Middle School, MI

High Merit Poems – Grades 7, 8, and 9

Sweets and Treats
Sweets and treats
Good things to eat
Anywhere and everywhere you look
Even in a cooking book

Sweets and treats are not always bad to eat
Fruits and vegetables are also sweet

So next time you want something sweet
But not bad to eat
Pick up a fruit or vegetable
Because they are also very sweet
Kayla Flewelling, Grade 7
Posen Consolidated High School, MI

Say
If today was your last day
Would you fix your mistakes?
Or make your enemies pay
If you lived again tomorrow
Would you live it differently?
Or would you live it in sorrow
If you lived in the past
Would you appreciate it?
Would you want it to last?
But you live today
So will you live it to your fullest?
Only you get to say
Olivia Vargas, Grade 9
Plymouth High School, MI

100% Me
3% green eyes
15% angel
5% brown hair
10% devil
20% crazy
15% homework
25% horse back riding
5% lies
2% giggles

Add it all up
That's 100% me.
Torrie Mast, Grade 8
West Side Middle School, IN

Cruise/Voyage
Cruise
Dark, hollow
Waiting, eating, sleeping
Hoping land will come
Voyage
Lauren Dolmage, Grade 7
Trinity Lutheran School, MI

Creatures
As the sky turns dark blue,
As dark as the darkest sea,
The moon comes out
As shiny as can be
We all hear the whistling of the whimpering wind.
As the noise of many creatures arise.
One creature far from the rest,
Howls at the moon with content bulging eyes.
Fur as gray as rain clouds filled with rain.
This creature is slim, slim and sleek,
Out to scare children that aren't in their sleep.
These creatures come out to devout the week.
As the sky starts to lighten they all run away afraid of the light
That someone might see their bulging eyes and sleek gray coat.
Their night is over our day has come.
But beware of the creature that stirs in the night waiting for their time to come.
Little children
As the sky turns dark blue
As dark as the darkest sea.
Be sure to be snuggled tight inn your bed.
For fear of the creature that stirs in the night.
Korynn Hincka, Grade 9
Posen Consolidated High School, MI

Veterans
They fought in the war through thick and thin,
They were determined to win.
They stood tall through it all,
And trusted that they weren't gonna fall.
They are our veterans, who we are thankful for and pray for before we go to bed,
Because we still don't know what is to happen in the journey ahead.
The veterans that died and left their families behind,
We will always remember them in our mind.
We will always remember the veterans no matter where they are, nor how far,
If they are alive, or if they've past,
Because in our hearts they will always last.
I am so thankful for the veterans and all they've done,
Because they stayed and didn't run.
They sacrificed their lives for us, that takes a lot of trust,
So taking some time to thank them is definitely a must.
We honor our veterans loud and proud will every free breath we take,
Just think about all the sacrifices that they have had to make.
The veterans that are a live,
It took a lot of talent to make themselves survive.
They are people who took a chance to fight,
And that is why they stand on Earth as my heroes tonight.
Kayla Iser, Grade 8
Hopkins Middle School, MI

The Beggar
Sitting on all fours looking up at you from the floor, staring at you with those puppy-eyes.
Wanting you to pet his short soft hair, rolling around to get you to play on the ground.
Wishing you would give him a treat, while he sits at your feet.
Marty Curley, Grade 8
Bloomingdale Middle School, MI

A Final Melody
Tis true
We fought valiantly
But alas
Victory was not to be
And yet
I'm still filled with glee

Unavoidable
Death was upon us
Creating
A Cacophonous Ruckus!
Singing
A song titled

"The End"
Brandon Counter, Grade 8
West Side Middle School, IN

The Blond Girl's Smile
Into the blond girl's smile
I saw the light
When she smiled
It's like everything went
Black
I was standing there
Just waiting,
Waiting
On some one to get me out
Of the darkness
Then I cried
Someone please help
But no one came
And it was all because
I got lost in the blonde girl's smile.
Macie Trosper, Grade 7
Oak Hill Jr High School, IN

Sister to Sister
We always stick by each other
I never let you fall
You always have my back
You never let me fall
When I'm down you help me back up
When you're upset I comfort you
If you laugh, I laugh
If you cry, I cry
If you smile, I smile
If you fail I will help you through it
If you're in a bad mood I will cheer you up
My life with you is something special
We always stick by each other
There is never a dull moment with you
Sister's love each other forever!
Caroline McGraw, Grade 8
St Charles Borromeo School, IN

Daffodil Daydreams
I'm the one with the petals
Of every color that you know
Yellow, pink, red, and orange
The shades of the rainbow.

I'm the one with a strong stem
That jostles in the wind
Though hurricanes and storms may come
I do no more than bend.

I'm the one that still has hope
When winter snows do cling.
Expectant seeds are impatient to sprout
When they hear chatter of spring.

The soil in which I've come to lay
Boasts a comforting brown, no less.
And I have come to love the day
When my gardener's gloves are a mess.

The sun in all its amiable warmth
Sends down its rays to me
"And so begins another day,"
I think to myself happily.
Kelly McAvoy, Grade 9
Norwell High School, IN

I Hate Homework!
I hate homework!
I hate it, hate it, hate it!
We have so much,
I just can't take it!
I hate homework.

Homework in every class
Is just too much!
Homework in every class,
I've had enough!
Homework in every class,
"Ridiculous!" I say!
I hate homework!

My backpack weighs one hundred pounds.
My hands, they ache with pain!
I hate homework!

I hate homework!
Oh, do I!
(But maybe I could give it a try…
Maybe not!)
Gabriela Justice, Grade 7
Our Lady of Perpetual Help School, IN

The Sun's Smile
The sun glows,
The sky shines,
I wonder why
This doesn't happen
All the time.

I look around
For an answer
But I only see
My friend
And family.

I think, wait,
and wonder
But can't find,
Why this happens
Only some of the time.

Once it's dark
I realize
Why the sun is gone
And doesn't shine;
The moon has arrived.

My friend,
That's why
The sun doesn't shine;
She sleeps and doesn't smile
All the time.
Katherine Lorenzen, Grade 8
St. Hugo of the Hills School, MI

Silence
I was in my room
Sealed in tight
I tried to call
But there was only silence
Only silence
I called even louder
But still nothing
There was only silence
Only silence
I called again
No one called back
There was only silence
Only silence
I was in panic no one could hear me
There was only silence
Only silence
The silence drowned all my cries
There was only silence
Only silence
That's when I realized
It was all a dream.
Justin Fraser, Grade 7
Ruth Murdoch Elementary School, MI

The Golden Gates

I'm sick, I'm dying
There is no cure
My life will be over soon
I put people in tears
I hate people feeling sorry for me
I brought this upon myself
My heart is on a time line
Like a watch is on a wrist
I could cry myself to sleep
And make myself look weak
My life is over but another one has begun
I can't wait to meet the ones I never have
I can't wait to see the ones I've missed
Life never really ends
Just stops for a while
Then you climb the amazing enchanted stairs to the
golden gates where they will be waiting on the other side
Grandfathers, Grandmothers, Great ones at least.
Uncles, Aunts, even a cousin
The ones I have not met.

Shane Monahan-McLearon, Grade 7
Fowlerville Junior High School, MI

The Pursuit of Happiness

The pursuit of happiness,
to be successful,
to work hard,
to go for your dreams,
to be what you want to be,

Do you want to be successful,
to have a good family,
well you have to work at it,

Irritation, overcomes me,
when people don't care,
don't care about their grades if they're bad,
don't care about a college degree,
or the future of themselves,
their family,
You, nobody else, has to decide,
if you want to make money,
or just sit on the couch worrying about your future,
You decide.

Daniel Broerman, Grade 7
South Spencer Middle School, IN

The Light

We used to play and run all night long
Until something happened that was oh so wrong
Yes we ran and played until the darkness of night
When that voice, oh that voice pulled her into the light
Now I know that she will live no wrong
Because now she can play and run all night long

Jordan De La Rosa, Grade 7
Whitehall Middle School, MI

Army

I've seen you twice,
I think it's stupid,
We're brother and sister!
We're supposed to be close,
Army,
You're in the army now,
I don't know how,
I'm supposed to go 3 years without knowing,
Much about you,
Army,
Your daughter was just born,
Little Kennedy,
That's my niece,
I don't even see her!
Our brother and sister relationship is breaking,
Army,
I wish you could be home,
So we can act like brother and sister,
But it won't happen,
Please be Army Strong!

Darth Musson, Grade 7
Fowlerville Jr High School, MI

Letting Go

I can't say it was easy letting go of you,
But tell me, what else could I do?
I'll admit I spilled a whole lot of tears,
Losing you was one of my worst fears,
I see that you're happier where you were sent,
You left too early, you shouldn't have went,
It's hard not hearing you around anymore,
Now that you're gone, my heart is so sore,
I'd do anything to see you just one last time,
But it's impossible, so why do I bother writing these rhymes?
It's the closest I'll get to bringing you back,
You were a huge part of my life that I'll forever lack,
There's a place for you in my heart, now and forever,
I'll never forget you, not tomorrow, not ever,
You were always that one,
That made me happy to wake up to see that bright shining sun,
Letting go of you may have caused pain,
And those tears I shed were just like rain,
But the only choice I had was to let go of you,
Tell me now, what else could I do?

Alyssa Lysher, Grade 8
Fowlerville Junior High School, MI

Flowers

She softly touched the moist flower petals and buds colorful
All full of excitement
Roses filled the air with beautiful colored scents
The morning's full of color
The ground covered with beautiful flowers
All the flowers stood strong

Taylor Ramey, Grade 8
Lincoln Middle School, IN

The Pessimist
nothing goes my way.
nothing good will come out of this.
my life is just a waste.
no one can help.
no one cares about me.
everyone hates me.
there is nothing I can do.
this happens every day.
I sit in sorrow, until tomorrow,
when things start going my way.

no one hates me
my life is not a waste
anyone can help
anything is possible
many things go my way
everyone cares about me
there is a lot I can do
I'm always happy
good things will come out of this
I am no longer a pessimist
oh how I wish this were true.
Dylan Cuc, Grade 7
Fowlerville Jr. High School, MI

Hard Lessons
I messed up a lot in my life,
I acted like I hated my dad,
I'm, now glad,
That I can have him next to me,
Well guys I'm coming home.
I'll never forget my mistakes,
What is a house without loved ones,
It isn't is it,
Well guys I'm coming home.
It's time to make this bad house,
Just a memory,
I'm sorry guys,
I'm coming home.
I messed up a lot at school,
I wanted people to think I'm cool,
I've learned hard lessons,
Forgiven my mistakes,
I've straightened up a lot,
I'll still mess up now and then,
But no one's perfect,
I'm finally back home.
Travis Skaggs, Grade 7
Fort Branch Community School, IN

Spring
Bright sunlight shining
The cold raindrops dripped off,
Bright purple tulips.
Emily Sarkisian, Grade 7
Royal Oak Middle School, MI

Can There Be Two of You?
Is it possible to have two of yourself?
Or is it just more than one personality?
Is it two-faced to have more than one personality?
What if you feel you can't act like you when you're around certain friends?
Are you hurting yourself more than anyone else?
Do you have a friend, or friends that change the real you?
Is it bad to change?
Can you still be the "*old you*" after you change?
Do you lose people that mean a lot to you because you
Changed?
Is it worth losing them?
People say change is a *good* thing
But is it really?
Changing is a risk.
The true question is, is it a risk you are willing to take?
Livvy Schipp, Grade 7
South Spencer Middle School, IN

Lightning
I look out over the lake
Dark clouds are forming
A storm is coming
Lightning flashes before my eyes while I stand on the front porch
The screen in front of my face is the only thing separating me
from the deadly bolts
It dances across the lake and the sky fascinating everyone on the front porch with me
All of the sudden, lightning splits the sky and lake in half
Then the thunder rolls across the sky shaking the wooden frame of the cottage
It starts to pour down rain showering the sand, making the road flood
A strong wind starts to whip through the air
We then shut the curtains on the front porch with a long battle with the wind
We look out and the lightning is even more fierce than before
And before we know it, the storm is gone
But the lightning is still dancing around in our heads
Andy Scheel, Grade 7
Stanley Clark School, IN

This Man
This man's favorite quote is, "Everyday's a holiday, every meal's a feast."
Which makes sense, because he's always happy and never mad, most of the time, at least.

This man has given me a wonderful and privileged life,
But it wasn't handed to him; he had to earn it with a lot of hard work and strife.

This man taught me right from wrong and to just always do my best.
He would always practice my sports with me, until I felt I was better than all the rest.

This man always makes me laugh and is like a little kid, in a funny way.
Even when you're upset, he always knows just the perfect thing to say.

These reasons and many more I'd like to add,
Are why this man is my hero, if you're wondering who he is, this man is my dad!
Cassidy Komorowski, Grade 8
St. John the Evangelist School, IN

High Merit Poems – Grades 7, 8, and 9

Blizzard

The little boy wandering outside became lost,
with only the clothes on him and a tiny
knapsack.
He couldn't help but keep thinking about that
day. It was like a blizzard in his head.
They were playing up in the tree, just a gentle game
of monkeys and tigers.
They were fighting of course,
He wanted to be a horse
But his older brother didn't like it.
His older brother threw a punch,
And sent him off to pack a lunch.
Mom got mad like the March hare.
When the little boy freed himself of the
dreadful memory he found himself back home.
Now he knew it was a mistake to leave.
He realizes that as they welcome him with open
arms and tear-filled eyes.
No matter what, his family will always love him.

Kirsten Salois, Grade 7
Fowlerville Junior High School, MI

Music Note

Music is a way to express yourself.
The notes running together to crea
te wonderful, beautiful song. It's
al   m
o   st
impossible not to enjoy it. There is
N   o
th   in
g   As
Rew   ar   ding   as
Doing w ha   t you lov e
To do and then   have people cl
ap and cl   ap and cl
ap fo   r you.

Andrea Foerster, Grade 7
Royal Oak Middle School, MI

Friday

a dash of homework
a hint of trouble
a cup of laughing
5 new friends
1/2 cup of shopping
2 T of texting
3/4 t of ice cream
3 cups of good times

add the homework to the texting, then
the friends to the laughing, and the trouble with
the ice cream, mix it all together and add
the good times and you get my crazy week.

Shelby Rachwal, Grade 7
West Middle School, MI

Now Is the Time

Twelve years of love, happiness,
And preparation
For this day to dawn.

While the sun shimmered through my curtains,
I received the wake up call of a lifetime

As I processed what my mom said,
A chill raced through my body.
Tears poured
Down my face
My heartbeat was loud, hard, and fast as I realized,

The time has come —

When we arrived, they came out to meet us.
I walked away — crushed.
Cautiously came back and then they left.

We gazed at one another
And I said my last words:
"Shadow, I will always love you."

My dad and I watched as her eyes
Slowly
Close
Knowing that we will never see them open again.

Zoe Lang, Grade 9
Allegan High School, MI

Native American

I am Native American.
　My skin is dark brown,
　As brown as the soil I live on.

I am native.
　I was here centuries before the white man.
　My family and I lived on this land long before the white man.

I am resourceful.
　I only take what I need and use every piece.
　The white man takes a lot but uses very little.

I am a slave.
　I am bound by chains,
　To mine the white man's mines and die by their whip.

I am dying.
　I am dying from the white man's diseases.
　I am dying from hunger because of the white man.

I am Native American.
　My skin is dark brown,
　As brown as the soil I lived on.

Sarah La Foe, Grade 8
Covington Middle School, IN

The Seasons of Time

When spring comes in fresh
The blossoms do bloom
The summer brings heat
And mosquitoes that bite
Bright colorful leaves
Each autumn does bring
And winter brings beauty
When birds do not sing
The newness of spring
Acrid summer heat
Bright autumn colors
The stark wintry cold
No season can boast
That he is the best
Each season is special
Each is unique
They all form together
To create the years
The years of our life
Each a precious gift

Jonathan Logan, Grade 7
Ruth Murdoch Elementary School, MI

My Future Is What I Make It

Every morning
I wake up,
With a new gift from God,
A new day.
A day full of wonderful new opportunities,
Time to focus on what the future will bring,
Not what the past has already given me.
My future is an open door,
It is what I make it,
I am behind the wheel,
Heading into my future.
My future is in front of me,
Like three different paths,
I get to choose where I go.
It may be the right decision,
It may be the wrong one,
This is my life,
It is what I make it.
This is a new day,
It is what I make it.

Haylee Weiss, Grade 8
St. Barnabas School, IN

Family

F un and cheerful,
A lways there,
M ine to love,
I s always in my mind,
L oving and caring,
Y ou will always be there for me.

Alex Garberick, Grade 8
West Side Middle School, IN

Night and Day

You see
Night
You see
Day
You see
Life pass
Day by day
Week by week
Month by month
It goes by
Fast
Doesn't it
So hold on to it
Hold on to those
Days
Hold on to those
Weeks
And
Hold on to those
Months,
Live day by day

Emily Colston, Grade 7
Fowlerville Jr High School, MI

Rain

There is rain outside my window,
There is rain outside my door.
There is rain, although
I can see it no more.
The rain has ceased outside,
Gone for today,
But has instead migrated inside;
It came with no delay.
In fact, it is no longer raining at all —
There is a storm, a hurricane,
Perhaps even ice fall.
Though you cannot see the rain,
I can feel it in my being.
Perhaps one day you come across me,
You will see that it is raining.
It first began as a light rain, barely
Anything more than a drizzle.
But then, one day, it all became
Far too much to handle.
So here is my tale; a sad one, I know.
But hopefully the rain will one day go.

Daniella Umana, Grade 8
Ruth Murdoch Elementary School, MI

Who Am I

I am black and white
I live in tall bamboo trees
I make cute babies
who am I

Mikala Mack, Grade 8
West Side Middle School, IN

Moto Mania

Get on your gear
ride to the line,
engines are revving,
life's on the line.

Waiting for the gate to drop.
Hoping and hoping to get the hole shot!

To the first turn I race.
In the lead as I squeeze the corner
holding the competition behind.

Jumps up ahead, air to be had.
Yes! I'm alive!
But the whoops yet to concur.
I hold down the throttle and bounce as I go.

Finally I see it.
The finish line at last.
Just as the competition blew right past!

Connor Schwartz, Grade 7
Hudsonville Christian Middle School, MI

Reflections

I look in the mirror, and see a girl
A girl who has feeling
A girl who has pain
A girl who is shy
I see a girl who is lost
She needs patience
She needs love
She needs care
All of my own reflections
I look in the mirror again
There's a girl who needs help
A girl who's confused
A girl who's scared
I see a girl who's strong
She needs happiness
She needs freedom
She needs attention
She's crying out for someone
Someone to save her
All of my own reflections

Taylor Caldwell, Grade 7
Canton Charter Academy, MI

Dalton

D oesn't like school
A lways tries to be on time
L ikes to play the PS2
T alks here and there
O n time to classes
N ice and neat.

Dalton Briggs, Grade 8
West Side Middle School, IN

High Merit Poems – Grades 7, 8, and 9

School Friends
I have so many friends at school.
Some are weird and some are cool.
Many are unique and have their own styles,
But my uniqueness beats them by miles.
I don't mean to brag or get them mad,
But my friends understand and never think I'm bad.
My friends tell me jokes,
That make me want to choke.
They're so lame and funny,
Just like my pet bunny.
We like to hang and go to the mall,
and talk about our weekends as we walk down the school hall.
We like to mess with our teachers,
By hiding in the bleachers.
We hate homework and despise it all,
But who cares we know it all.
My friends and I like to laugh and play,
And put up quite a display.
My poem is just about to end,
And I can't wait to hang with friends.

Brittney Byrd, Grade 8
Ruth Murdoch Elementary School, MI

Where I Am From…
I am from a big gray house with two doors,
   from a terrible city where crime revolts.
I am from a big school that never ends,
   from the back alleys of Detroit where
   everyone hates everyone.
I'm from gangland and bullet holes
   where I walked to school,
   to find there's no other place to be.
I'm from streets broken by speeding cars
   to big explosions.
I'm from a bad accident that changed my life
   from glass and ice
   to hospitals and stitches
under my bed are the fears of getting hurt,
   of being in misery all my life,
wondering what could have been instead
   of what could be,
I'm from place to place abiding by no will
   but with only a family.

Austin Santos, Grade 8
Kalkaska Middle School, MI

My Sister
At three I was blessed with a little sister.
At fourteen she's still my best friend.
She's my therapist, advice column, and teacher.
Through the years we've had loads of ups and loads of downs.
As we age I shall look to her
For my every problem and issue.
Forever I'll be thankful for my little blessing.

Libby Buhl, Grade 8
Lincoln Middle School, IN

Love, What Shall I Compare to Thee?
To Love, what shall I compare?
Shall I compare thee to a new morning rain,
   Or a bright double rainbow?
Shall I compare thee to end of the universe,
   Of which none may know?
To Love, what shall I compare?
Shall I compare thee to the lilacs blooming?
Or shall I compare thee to a glittering moon?
Shall I compare thee to a glorious lake,
Filled with a vast array of mallards and loons?
To Love, what shall I compare?
Shall I compare thee to a warm summer day,
   Or a rose plated in gold?
Shall I compare thee to an ancient ruin,
   Dusty and riddled with things of old?
To Love, what shall I compare?
Shall I compare thee to an unborn child,
   Still resting in its mother's womb?
No, I shall compare thee to three things,
   Three nails, a cross, and a tomb.

Ethan Lambert, Grade 7
Portage Christian School, IN

The Best Journey
Life is a climb
It's a long journey
There are some tough spots along the way
But, it can be exciting and adventurous
You want to reach your goal in the end
Life is a climb
Along the way you have wonderful moments
Each and every day is filled with something new
There are lots of troubles you have to overcome
Plans are always changing having to come up with new ones
Life is a climb
There are valleys you have to overcome
You may get tangled along the way but friends and family
Are there to help along the way
But, when you reach the peaks they can be the best times
Life is a climb
Once you reach the top your journey is done
You can't go back now and try to change the mistakes
You have made it through life
Be glad you made the best of your journey

Kaitlyn Davidson, Grade 7
Royal Oak Middle School, MI

Charlie
My best friend is gone from my view
Without you here, I'm not sure what to do
Playing Frisbee with you was second to none
Even though you would only use the same one
Seeing you made the sun shine
I hope you know you will always be mine

Taylor Hupp, Grade 8
West Side Middle School, IN

Thoughts of a Hunter
I sit waiting,
Watching,
Consuming,
Not food,
But time.
Is it time that controls me?
Or me that controls time?
Preoccupied,
I turn my head away from an engaging book,
Looking,
Searching,
Hoping,
For something to come out of the mantle of darkness
We call a forest.
I am prepared to take advantage
Of anything that fits my sights.
Anxious, my patience begins to wane
The most difficult with hunting
Sets upon me:
When you are ready but weary of a long wait.

Conor Reilly, Grade 8
West Hills Middle School, MI

Black
Black was considered dirt.
All that pain and slavery, it hurt.
We tried to live like a human, but you shoved us aside.
We tried to do things in a civil way,
But you started a fight.
It's not a cry that you hear at night,
It's not someone who has seen the light.
These are the words that you hear,
From the knight.
The one who gets me from day to night.
Black is everywhere,
But you might not see it.
It's in your house, and you even talk about it.
Black cars, black pictures, black houses, black chairs,
Man there's even black pencils.
So then why did you ignore the black people?
The *human* beings, the ones who worked in your house,
Who cleaned your dishes, who washed your floors.
But now I see that all of that's changed.
It's like it was never even there.

Chrystal Porter, Grade 8
Ruth Murdoch Elementary School, MI

In Wings
My dad was a friend, a man, a teacher.
He was also a disciplinary, strong, a preacher.
He is missed, more every day
My heart has been broken, since he went away
but thinking of him, and in wings, is his best feature.

Mesay Taylor, Grade 8
Lincoln Middle School, IN

How to Set the Example
Being the oldest can be hard, as well as tiresome,
but I like anyway.

I have to set the example and show my sister that
she should not do this and how she should not say that.
Sounds easy right? Well…it isn't!

I keep her out of trouble, and I look out for her
when my parents aren't there.

Sometimes we fight, but later I feel awful about it.
Being the oldest, I apologize first.
I do this because I have to set the example.

It is impossible to stay mad at her.
She is my sister after all and the only one I've got.

God gave her to me, this precious gift from above.
No matter what happens between us I still have to love her
and set the example,
like a big sister should.

Kayla Stradford, Grade 8
Kingsway Christian School, IN

Fifteen Years Later
Fifteen years later I hope to still have some fun,
Whether in cold Michigan or the California sun.
Maybe I will have a hover car,
Or a house made of sticky tar.
I hope I'll be a video game tester,
And be in college for at least a semester.
I know my sister will be a teacher.
So for a few years I will miss her.
I hope to have a big red house,
With a big cat and a little mouse.
In fifteen years I'll be twenty seven,
And by that time I'll wish I was still eleven.
But by the time I'm twenty four
I'll make my dad remodel the floor.
That's what my life will be like
Fifteen years later.

Charlie Bonkowski, Grade 7
Royal Oak Middle School, MI

Within You, Without George
You have brought music, you have brought inspiration,
you have brought Happiness among the nation.
Cancer is deadly,
and while you play us a medley,
we remember your name sadly.
We will remember you forever,
George Harrison.

Cris Cerda, Grade 8
West Side Middle School, IN

Desert

The endlessly long ocean of sands
I can feel my life slipping through my hands
So hot I'm almost walking on glass
I wish I could leave, get out fast
Like a tall tower with no top
It seems the desert has not stop
I am lost forever, forever lost

I walk, I search, I run
Look for an exit but I find none
I'm left here to die under the sun
I'm starving, I'm thirsty, I'm done
Being lost in the desert is never fun
It's overtime and nobody's won
I am lost forever, forever lost

Sadly is how my story ends
Exhaustion or starvation it all depends
If only I could make amends
With those I've wronged I'm very sorry
Life in a desert is no safari
I'm on my way to heaven, be there on the 'morrow
I am lost forever, forever lost

Isaac Bancroft, Grade 8
Perry Middle School, MI

Can You Hear It?

The whistling of the trees,
The colored leaves,
The crisp weather,
It's fall.
Can you hear it?

The white stuff falling from the sky,
The hats, mittens, scarfs, and gloves,
The sound of snowball fights and snow forts,
It's winter.
Can you hear it?

The endless showers,
The blossoming,
The buzzing bees,
It's spring.
Can you hear it?

The tank tops and new apparel,
The pool and bathing suits,
The kids screaming as they eat their ice cream,
It's summer.
Can you hear it?

Sara Abate, Grade 7
West Middle School, MI

A Feeling from Inside

A message, a thought
deep inside your mind
unique and special towards the ones you love

A message, a thought
written millions of times
for hope or desire, screaming to get out

A message, a thought
for sympathy from within
nowhere to be found through evil times

A message, a thought
disciplined by sanity,
so, therefore, not proclaimed sincerely

A message, a thought
fierce and massive
bashing, anxious to be announced

A message, a thought
deep inside, not denied
waiting to escape

Mickella Hardy, Grade 8
Culver Community Middle School, IN

Friends and Goodbyes

As I stare around the classroom,
Looking at my friends.
And I'm anxious because the year is
Almost to its end.

It's definitely not going to be easy,
Saying all my farewells.
I'll miss them,
Even though I know that it might not be the complete end.

I remember we all hung out,
Laughing and yelling,
Without a care in the world.

We will always have our memories;
Some not as good as others.
I will always remember the good,
and erase the bad.

I don't feel like saying goodbye,
To all my friends.
I don't ever want this year
To come to an end.

Kaitlyn Kay Eckstein, Grade 8
St. Barnabas School, IN

Hurt

I loved you to death.
But you didn't care, and left me.
I wanted to be with you till your last breath.
What made you change what you used to see?

How could you do something so cruel?
I did everything for you.
And you just used me like a tool.
What else could I really do?

I was sick and barely able to move.
You showed kindness and compassion.
Now I will, to you, prove,
That I can handle this in a mature fashion.

After all this I am back on my feet,
To get what is rightfully mine.
Eventually, a strong future I'll meet.
Until then, I'm doing just fine.

Jessica Munroe, Grade 8
Anchor Bay Middle School North, MI

Without You

Mom, without you there would be no me
Your love, your compassion, your guidance
Have made me who I am today
Without you I don't know what I would be like
Tying to make it on my own, with no goals
Without a purpose, or direction
You showed me the way to go
To preserve, to accomplish, to preserve
Without you there would be an empty space
I could never fill, no matter how hard I tried.
Without you I would be incomplete
I guess what I'm trying to say is that
Without you I'm nothing,
I love you Mom.

Jonika Scott, Grade 8
Ruth Murdoch Elementary School, MI

Mind's Eye

Hoping, wishing, wanting, dreaming.
Private to me my thoughts and desires.
Always with me to carry me higher.
My thoughts, hopes, dreams may seem foolish to some.
My dark and light side, although, has yet to come.
In my mind's eye, every thing's strange.
More intense and focused, maybe a little more…sane.
No one can reach me here, in my small special space.
It's all my own, a place no one can taint.
Searching in awe, for my meaning of life.
Even though it does hurt me and causes me strife.
Here in reality, I'm comfortable and "on track."
But in my mind's eye, I am anything but intact.

Hayley West, Grade 8
Perry Middle School, MI

First Tee

Standing on the first tee,
The air sparkles with an early morning mist
And golden rays of light spill through the trees.
Mowers roar in the distance — I ignore the sound,
And focus my gaze on the far away flag
Waving gently in the morning breeze.
Choosing my target, I rehearse my swing —
Loose grip,
Arms relaxed,
Knees flexed,
Back straight.
The club glides back then swoops downward
And sweeps the ball from the tee.
I stand frozen,
Watching the ball soar into the sky,
Then return to earth
Landing on the rolling fairway.
Returning the club to my bag, I set off…
My day on the course begins.

Calvin George, Grade 9
DeKalb High School, IN

Love and/or Falling in Love

A musing
B reathtaking
C razy at times
D aring
E asy to do
F rightening
G ood feeling
H as its ups and downs
I n everybody's hearts, no matter who you are.
J oking or not it's serious to one another
K eeps coming and coming
L ovely
M ake people go crazy!
N ever stops.

Keyla Jenkins, Grade 8
West Side Middle School, IN

The Game of Indiana

Swoosh!
Screams and cheers,
as the crowd goes wild,
and the buzzer sounds,
and the fans storm the court.
The court quickly turns to a sea of crimson,
as the golden boy is lifted on the throne of shoulders.
The game has ended,
but the story has just begun.
It's a game of pride,
and a game of passion.
But most of all,
it is the game of Indiana.

Jimmy King, Grade 8
St Barnabas School, IN

High Merit Poems – Grades 7, 8, and 9

My Life
I have come so far,
in thirteen years.

I have witnessed life.
I have witnessed death.

I have been through rough times.
I have been through the best times.

I have witnessed health.
I have witnessed cancer.

I have seen love.
I have seen care.

I have come so far,
in thirteen years.

Kristina Steward, Grade 8
Covington Middle School, IN

Emptiness
What is it?
What can it be?
Loneliness
From emptiness
Inside me
Depression, aggression
Anxiety, pain
A deep hole within me
That seems to remain
I cry out for help
I want him to hear
To take away
And end the tears
Can't figure out how
Can't seem to get through
He doesn't know my heart
What should I do?

Haley DeFord, Grade 8
West Side Middle School, IN

Your Daughter
She continued to cry,
Because I had actually tried.
I worked so hard to achieve,
To make her actually believe
That I can be,
That I will be,
The daughter she'll be proud of
And the daughter she'll always love.
I'll try to never let her down,
So I won't have to see her frown.
That's what daughters do,
When they love you.

Madi Hanson, Grade 8
Covington Middle School, IN

Sleeping
I am a cat
Elegant and soft

I am a cat
Smart and small

I am a cat
Loving and loyal

Careful and kind
Well trained and
Deserving

I am a cat
Living and liked

I am a cat
Calm and kind

I am a cat
Fluffy like down

Quiet and peaceful
Long and slim

I am a cat
Simple and sly

I am a cat
Sleeping

E.C. Going, Grade 7
Fowlerville Jr High School, MI

Never Ending Fire
As high school awaits me
Just out of reach
I dream if my grandparents
will see me
graduate
From heaven or earth
I do not know
But they will always be looking over me
In eternal grace they will wait
For me
Walking beside me
No matter what
good times
we have always had
But what would happen
If they were suddenly gone
like a door
slamming in my face
a never ending fire
forever in my heart

Zach Marsh, Grade 7
South Spencer Middle School, IN

Play-Doh
A soft squishy
factor in every ones' life.
The many shapes and sizes
the many objects you can make,
the smooth feeling
as it forms in my hands.
The colorful objects
crazy and slick,
the intense feeling
of such a genuine blob.
O, the joy it gives me
when it's in my hand,
the prints it leaves
can always please.
But when it's gone
I get so sad,
'cause all I can say
is come back and play.

Jake Luck, Grade 9
Lenawee Christian School, MI

Grandmother
She was nice and caring
Smart and daring
Courageous and religious
Spontaneous and ambitious

Fearful and respectful
Thoughtful and never doubtful
Funny and happy
Always laughing

She was a loving wife
She had a caring husband
She had a dozen smart children

She is in Heaven now
Looking down at me
Wishing me
To be the best I can be

Megan Schilling, Grade 7
St John the Evangelist School, IN

Worry
Worry,
Every morning you worry
Cold, hot, or raining
Every day you worry
Did I get all my school work done?
Every night you worry
Am I in trouble? Do I get to play?
Worry is everything in life
You just keep on repeating it until you
Die

Cody Bickel, Grade 7
South Spencer Middle School, IN

I'm From…

I'm from forgotten memories, fading away
to joyous moments staining my heart,

I'm from harsh thoughts changing my ways
to screaming parents I'll always love,

I'm from warm tears flooding my vision
to mistakes I always make,

I'm from riding bareback through the woods
to high price horse shows in Lansing,

I'm from troubled friends
to helping hands,

I'm from scraped knees and broken bones,
to dark nightmares and sweet dreams,

I'm from good grades
to hopeful Harvard,

I'm from playing sports
to painting nails,

I'm from silly gossip with friends
to stupid rumors that stalk the halls,

I'm from mixed emotions about life
to wondering what would happen if I lost mine.

Ariel Sabrina Newton, Grade 8
Kalkaska Middle School, MI

Little Red Pieces

He tore out my heart
Left it abandoned in the dirt
But you found it
You took the red organ in your hands
Promising it would never be left that way again
I believed you
But I didn't know
Didn't know you were going to destroy it
My heart
It was already broken
And you just cut it into pieces
Smaller and smaller
Shrinking that red organ
If you can call it a heart anymore
Because little jagged pieces
Don't amount to anything
It cannot be weighed to a whole
All that's left are these little red jagged pieces
Scattered across the floor
In remembrance of what used to be
Of what is no longer

Mariah Grove, Grade 9
South Knox High School, IN

The Fight to Keep Going

I undergo this
agony of disbelief and
pain swirling in my chest.
The memory of our paths becoming one,
with each step
sketched perfectly with love comes rushing back.
The feeling of
caring and assurance was
substituted for pain and anger,
leaving me stranded in sorrow.
But,
the time to
regain strength and hope has arrived.
The light above is
shining radiance upon me,
brightening my new path, and helping me prepare for
the vigorous climb.
With each step, the message of who I am supposed to
be comes closer to sight.
Though, narrow treacherous turns lie ahead,
nothing will stop me again from my destiny.

Alessandra Fistrovich, Grade 8
St Barnabas School, IN

Spring

It rains all day long.
When the rains stops, the birds sing their songs.
A rainbow appears in the sky.
Its arc of colors greets every eye.
Spring flowers bloom.
The growth of daffodils, tulips, and daisies zoom.
The sweet smell of fresh green grass
greets every inchworm as they pass.
My-oh-my the large blue sky
is filled with cotton candy fluffed clouds near and high.
Bunnies hop and frogs chirp.
The bugs flying above make the fish slurp.
As the days get longer, the sun's bright rays stay
and the children play outside all day.
As the wind blows about
I am so happy I could shout!

Jessica Kerrigan, Grade 8
East Jay Middle School, IN

Soccer

I see the green field.
The players are ready for action.
The whistle blows and the game has begun.
I watch the players running.
Each player is trying to be the first to reach the ball.
Legs are kicking and elbows flying.
Every person is desperate to make a goal.
The season has begun.
Just kick it!

Lyndsey Gourley, Grade 7
Selma Middle School, IN

Amoretti

He laughs at me,
"You arrogant fool,
You seem to have forgotten that one simple rule.
The one you spoke of long ago,
Never to drown of that undertow.
But you see,
Our love was that sea,
And you let yourself drown,
Let us fall deep down."
It's almost impossible,
I barely reply,
"I hope you can see,
What you've done to me.
Left me here to bleed,
Still aching with need."
I was sure he'd whine,
But he had nothing to say this time.
Far away,
He is from me.
I'm glad he's not stuck here,
Because I'm still stuck in that sea.

Amanda Minkkinen, Grade 8
Mill Creek Middle School, MI

Him

You stole my heart, you kept the key.
Nothing's better than when you're with me.
Your eyes are gentle. They shine like the sea.
That's how I know you're smiling for me.
I can't breathe when I think of you.
I can't speak when I talk about you.
There's not much more I can say;
You've taken my breathe away.
You appear just like a dream to me. When the waves are
Flooding the shore and I can't find my way home anymore;
That's when I look at you.
When I look you,
I see forgiveness.
I see the truth.
You love me for who I am.
When no one else does.
You're my light, my everything.
My love for you will never fade away.
I love you with all my heart.
You hold the key for now,
You hold it till the end of forever.

Kelsey Hart, Grade 8
Covington Middle School, IN

Great Grandmother

Today I see you again,
Even though I don't want to see you like this,
Seeing my family members and my friends,
Knowing I'll never ever again get that kiss on my forehead.

Kaleb Summers, Grade 8
West Side Middle School, IN

Ode to Friendship

The day I met you I found a friend,
and a friendship that I pray will never end.
Your smile — so sweet and so bright,
kept me going when day was as dark as night.
You never ever judged me, you understood my sorrow,
then told me it didn't have to be that way
and gave me the hope of a better tomorrow.
You were always there for me,
I knew I could count on you
you gave me encouragement when I didn't know what to do.
You helped me learn to love myself,
you made life seem so good.
You said I could do anything I put my mind to
and suddenly I knew I could.
There were times when we didn't see eye to eye,
and there were times when we both cried,
but even so, we made it through
our friendship hasn't yet died.
You are so extra-special to me
and so to you I really must say,
you are my one true friend.

Hannah Mount, Grade 8
West Side Middle School, IN

Purple

Purple is a color that can be also violet
Purple is one color that doesn't rhyme with anything
Purple is a color of a flower
Purple is the color of the noon sky
Purple is dark or light
Purple is my mom's favorite color
Purple is grape
Purple is a plum
Purple is lilacs
Purple is a balloon high in the sky
Purple is nail polish on your toes or fingernails
Purple is a crayon
Purple is royalty
Purple is jelly beans
Purple is eye shadow
Purple is purple

Bailey Scott, Grade 8
Perry Middle School, MI

Softball Mornings

The smell of hot chocolate
Flows through the air.
You can see the sun,
Peeking up over the treetops like a baby peeking from a crib.
The roar of cars zooming by,
And fields being plowed.
Gloves snap as wild throws
Are caught.
Players are getting on fields and ready to play.

Meghan Hall, Grade 8
Covington Middle School, IN

A Celebration of Poets – Great Lakes Grades 4-12 Spring 2011

For Now
I trust you,
and you trust me,
but so far you haven't told me anything
about your life
or how you are.

When I ask, you say
it's just too big of a scar.

I want to know
just tell me please.
It will help incredibly.

How you don't listen,
you disagree.
I tell you that it is not fair to me.

I wish one day
you could tell me everything,
about your life
and how you are.

For now
you decide to live with that scar.
Sara Porter, Grade 8
L'anse Creuse Middle School East, MI

Spring
Sounds come alive and fill the warming air
joyful birds can be heard everywhere
listen now and hear the sweet call
playful cubs shall give it their all

flowers start a blooming
hummingbirds are truly zooming
the frosted air releases its chill
light snow covers the ground…still

buds shall open into the world
for their whole life they have been curled
babies of all breeds are ready to explore
to entertain, there are adventures galore

after a long winter's cold
many are feeling quite bold
though child's fun you can't spoil
their clothes begin to soil

sun seeps through the cracks in the blinds
of the welcomes of summer this reminds
bask in the warmth, the glory of spring
for melting hot days it will later bring
Abby Austin, Grade 7
Walker Charter Academy, MI

Sunny Days
Sunny days
Girls and boys like to go out and play
Kickball, basketball, baseball.
Why they might even play volleyball!
Rainy days
Kids just sit and stay.
My! What a waste of a day!
They wish to go out in the sun,
So they can have fun!
But when the rain stops,
They'll think, "let's hop!"
So they go out and splash
They get dirty in a flash.
Some people may ask,
"Why do that? It's such a dirty task!"
Emily Westgerdes, Grade 8
East Jay Middle School, IN

Rollercoaster of Life
Life is full of changes,
So buckle up for the ride
You have to make hard choices
And let your spirit never die
Stay true to your heart
And close to your friends
You have to go through the changes
With your head held high
You may not like the new changes
But you may like what they become
And when the ride is over
You'll exit your seat
You'll look back with a smile on your face
And you'll say
Look at all the changes I beat
Brittany DeLong, Grade 8
St Barnabas School, IN

Winter Days
In these cold Winter days
We are always glad to see sunny rays
But we still enjoy a Winter day
We'll just go out with a sleigh.

My hobby is to skate
At a very fast rate
we all like to play fox and geese
And look who can get caught the least.

I like my brand new sled
Which is all nice and red
We all like to sled out on the road
"But children be careful," we are told.
Viola Graber, Grade 7
Green Acres School, IN

Where I'm From
I'm from memories of good and bad.

I'm from long days on the beach,
getting sunburns on my shoulders
and sand in my swimsuit.

I'm from the frightful trips to the hospital,
sitting in the waiting room for my sister.

I'm from playing outside in the spring
and watching movies in the fall.

I'm from sad rooms
filled with relatives that I don't know.

I'm from cold days in the winter,
sitting by the fire
and drinking hot chocolate.

I'm from little memorials in the backyard
to animal graves covered in wildflowers.

I'm from colorful chilled days,
raking till my hands hurt
and swimming in a big pile of leaves
that fell from my family tree.
Sara Kate Shipp, Grade 8
Kalkaska Middle School, MI

The Strength of Me
I am strong,
Like a rock
I am weathered away by pain,
But my soul remains deep inside
Where nothing can disturb it.

I am strong,
Like a tree
The whispering winds rattle my branches,
But my roots remain planted
Where no tempting voice can disturb them.

I am strong,
Like a soldier
Standing guard with an emotionless face,
Like him my secrets will be forever hidden.

The wind will blow,
And I won't follow,
The shadow is cast,
And I won't hide,
The door is closed,
And I won't stop,
Because of the strength I have inside.
Sarah Elam, Grade 8
St. Barnabas School, IN

Spring Rain
As I look and wonder why
The flowers bloom and start to cry
Give me more nourishment, give me more rain.

The smell of spring wonders the air
And I start to bear a sudden scare
That winter will be upon us once again.

As I watch the rain pour down
I have to frown but I know spring is coming,
That I know is true

The side walks glistens
The birds chirp and the puddles dry,
As I ride by.

Children come out to play
Running through the day,
Happy and gay.

As the flower buds grow,
The earth beneath me starts to glow
And the people walk to and fro.

When the sun sets,
And the day is done
I hope tomorrow will be as fun.
Nina Bournias, Grade 8
St Hugo of the Hills School, MI

Tell Me Why
look, look around you
do you see all the homeless on the streets
or do you stand there and watch someone die
please tell me
tell me why

why are there people dying
why are there teenagers on drugs
why are there people drinking and driving
please tell me
tell me why

tell me, do you care for the soldiers
fighting for you and me
for the young children with nothing to eat
please tell me
tell me why

look, look around you
do you see someone changing the world
do you see someone taking one step to success
please tell me
tell me do you
Megan Stafford, Grade 8
Centreville Jr High School, MI

Love That…
Love that you care
Only about who I really am

Love that you're there
Whenever I need you there

Love that you hope
To see me standing there

Love that your love
For me is as big as the universe

Love that feeling,
Knowing that you'll be there forever and always

Love that every time you're near you whisper in my ear
"I love that, too."
Maria Dorado, Grade 8
Bloomingdale Middle School, MI

My Golden Watch
Tick tock tick tock time passes on.
My watch, my watch
O how I'll miss it if it gets stolen.
This watch means a lot to me.
My father left it to me when he died.
It reminds me every day about him.
It doesn't have hands
It's a digital watch.
My dad's watch now mine.
Goes off at eight o'clock
To let me know when the good TV shows are on.
My watch, my beautiful watch
I will never let it out of my sight.
I will not let anyone wear it.
It means too much to me.
My watch, my watch
Is with me wherever I go.
David Steffen, Grade 9
Lenawee Christian School, MI

Mississinewa 1812 Battle Re-Enactment
I always like 1812 best.
You can hear the chirping of the clay bird fest.
Smell the smoke lingering in the dusty fall air,
(you can't find this elsewhere).
You see trappers and Indians and food galore,
Shops full of toys and tools and more.
Camp fires blazing and crackling and burning,
Battles cracking and burning and booming.
Canvas tents stained with age,
It's like were on stage!
For this travel back in time we are blessed,
I always like 1812 best.
Bradley Belcher, Grade 7
Oak Hill Jr High School, IN

My Headphones!!!

When I was little my house was a war zone
Every day, parents screaming, baby crying
Hungry in every way

No lights on
So in my bed, I would lay
Staying up all night and some nights there I'd stay

The walls too thin
I would cover my ears and sit in the dark alone
A small sense of comfort I would grab my headphones

Engulfed by the small beauty of hidden sound
Taken away from these chains no longer bound

Like a bird I was able to escape the ground, pleased with myself for this new device that I found

Like a portal to a different place
The music made my mind escape and my heart race

The freedom of music even though I felt alone
When I needed to leave
I would simply grab my headphones

Khalil Upshaw, Grade 9
Detroit Academy of Arts & Sciences - Medbury Campus, MI

Boundless Love

Oh, Daughter of the Sun, how long will you continue to abandon your love, the moon?
The moon, in its subtle beauty, sprinkling light down upon the darkened world;
And you, the Sun, in your Olympian beauty, bearing down upon the world in all your glory.
Your light shines in all the corners of the universe, creating a resplendent sight to behold.
The moon, casting velvety strands of pearly light down among the very darkness that embraces every rock among the gardens.
Oh, Daughter of the Sun, how long will you abandon your love, the moon?
How the Moon longs to share the light with you, the Sun,
And fill every space that is hidden in darkness.
You, the Sun, as omnipotent as you are, needs someone to fill the prodigious void that looms in your very soul.
A void of darkness that not even you, the Sun, in all your majesty can replete.
Your loneliness consumes the bottoms of the seas, and stretches beyond the mountains topped with snow.
Oh Daughter of the Sun, how long will you continue to abandon your love, the moon?
The moon greets companionship with a joy that is enough to stretch beyond your perch of triumph.
The Sun, the Moon, in all their splendor, fill the heavens with the very light that spreads across the galaxies.
Oh, Daughter of the Sun, ignite the cosmos with the power of Venus, that you and the Moon both share.

Brittany Ronto, Grade 8
Ruth Murdoch Elementary School, MI

Life as a Weeping Willow

My life as a tree with a bad name The world thinks my name brings shame I know I'm not bad Maybe a little sad But I am nothing depressing But full of happiness as I say sway in the breeze My leaves at ease Nothing to say with kids around me at play I do not mind that the other trees boast about being strong and powerful For I am not the boasting type But rather quiet in the place with the trees I see the world change around me all the time From green to hot then I lose my leaves and become quiet cold My old trunk says it cannot last any longer I tell it every day to hold on to what means most to you I know what means most to me is seeing life every day Knowing how some people love looking at my swaying branches And others hate how I am weak and bad for wood This makes me slightly happy though My life has been full of adventures even though I'm a tree

Brianna Moore, Grade 7
Ruth Murdoch Elementary School, MI

The Big Old Oak Tree

The leaves sway
On the old oak tree
That has grown
In my front yard for many years

It's impossible to climb
The branches are too high

When I was young
The tree symbolized
fun
enjoyment
As I grew older
The tree became one
To hold me up
There are rocks beneath
The old oak tree
Planted firm and sturdy
moss has begun to grow
and now I don't try to climb
I sit at the bottom
and enjoy

Kaitlyn Powers, Grade 7
Fowlerville Junior High School, MI

Winter

The snow falls
like little dancing angels
wintering the world
in a wonderland of sparkling diamonds
the wolves run wild
the bare trees are beautiful
a red bird stands out in the white
perched on a willow
the wind blows wishes
of wonder and wisdom
to all who hear
winter's whispers
and wonders

Alicia Porile, Grade 7
Stanley Clark School, IN

Friendship

Friendship is like a
Roller coaster. It's always
A thrill with the ahhhs
and the ooohs. Friendship
Is when you call your best
Friend at 2:30 am because
You just remembered something silly.
Friendship is like pb and jelly, it's a
good combination!
You and me we're stuck like glue!
Friends through thick and thin!!

Rachel Mark, Grade 7
Fowlerville Junior High School, MI

A True Champion

Pride in his heart
Intimidation on his face
What is a champion?

Aggression in his soul
Winning in his mind
What is a champion?

Overflowing with talent
Bravery pulsing in his veins
What is a champion?

Practicing 'til perfection
Attempting the impossible
What is a champion?

Taking chances
Exceeding expectations
What is a champion?

A warrior, fighting to the end
Competing with his rivals
What is a champion?

Defending his dignity
Protecting his goals
A true champion.

Dominic St. Peters, Grade 8
St Barnabas School, IN

Wake

I wake,
to my dear surprise,
to find myself
above the skies.

Soaring, gliding,
feeling firm and tall
above the clouds;
above it all.

I see a river,
I see a creek,
I see a desert,
so bare and bleak.

I see a meadow
with grass and trees.
I sense a tempest,
but feel a breeze.

I glide down to meet it,
but what does it seem?
All of this was only a dream.

Joshua Leady, Grade 7
Christ the King School, IN

The Person I Call My Hero

He's a big teddy bear
He has brown hair
And loves to cuddle
He loves afternoon naps
He works hard
He saves people
And heals the sick
But he never complains
He reads scripture at Mass
And prays with me at home
He's known as a saint
And always sings the loudest to God
He's a true American
He loves his country
And he loves his family
He loves humanity
He helps with school projects
He makes dinner
And cleans the house
He is…My Daddy!

Meg Lanham, Grade 8
St John the Evangelist School, IN

Three Ways to Look at a Bunny

1
A really big and fuzzy furball.
It doesn't have a mouth to talk.
The only way a bunny can get around
is to run, hop, or walk.

2
Bunnies of all kinds are quiet, and
that's how it's usually meant to be.
Even when they make quiet and funny
noises, they are still a super cute
pet for me.

3
If they could talk, I wonder what
they would say.
I think they would make dad get out
his wallet and pay.
If I picked a regular body color,
it would probably be brown.

Danielle Booms, Grade 7
Verona Mills School, MI

Monster

Look in the mirror, and what do you see?
Standing right in front of me?
The monster was there a second ago
But now, there are wings and a halo.
How can you be so easily deceived?
There's still a monster in front; it's me!

Molly Sage, Grade 8
Culver Community Middle School, IN

Water: A Blessing and a Curse
Water,
Clean, pure, fresh and cold;
A blessing for life.
Mist and rain,
Falls, oceans, and springs;
Breathtaking.
Water,
From where life sprung,
The source of life

Water,
Polluted and stinking,
Dirty Lakes and streams;
Storms and death,
Rancid.
Water,
The destroyer of civilization;
A curse of earth

Marley Higbee, Grade 7
Ann Arbor Learning Community School, MI

The Color of Time
A day in the life of my Crayola 8-pack,
   As the colors spring to life, relax and sit back
Beginning with the hue of the vast dancing sky,
   A most perfect and majestic blue passes on high
Morning arrives gradually through the rays of sun,
   Yellow brings new life 'til sunset is done
Under foot is the brown of the soil that feeds
   The healthy plants that blossom and do good deeds
Blades of thick grass rest in the afternoon heat,
   Green life all around, colorful beauty, a treat!
Orange fills the landscape with the crispness of fall,
   Brilliant leaves and bright pumpkins honor nature's call
The garden stands regal with fragrant purple flowers
   Waiting anxiously for a drink in the cool evening hours
Red is the beacon of the 4-way light,
   It flashes its message, first silent, then bright
When the sun slips away and black fills the air,
   Such a wonderful day, colored with hope and care

Catherine Dunn, Grade 8
East Jay Middle School, IN

Limo Fun
What I remember about that day
is my hair flowing down my back in cascades of curls
and my shimmery blue dress glinting in the sunlight
and descending the front stairs towards my friends
and myself, beaming from a fun party
anticipating excitement with my friends
glad to spend the evening celebrating my friend's 6th birthday

nothing about being overwhelmed by a colossal limo
nothing about feeling small in a giant party

Melissa Connop, Grade 7
Detroit Country Day Middle School, MI

Friendship
A friend I once held close, has disappeared into space
Where possibly can she be, she has left us no trace.

I see this girl often, but only in my dreams
This girl is gone forever, or only as it seems.

Our friendship was torn apart, we were such great friends
But only until, she started following strange trends.

She never showed up to play, she stopped caring about school
Her phone became her life, she became a fool.

Has this girl really left, or has she been here all this time?
All I know is, she committed a crime!

Now that I look back, she was here all along
She ditched me for her new friends, don't you think it was wrong?

Enough of the trashing, we still hang out some
It doesn't matter to me, what she has become.

I can't change her, she will be herself
She'll just sit there, and put me back on that shelf.

When she looks at me once in a while, she will surely know
That I am sitting here, I will never go.

I will still be there for her, until the very end
Don't I have to, she is still my friend!

Hailey Browne, Grade 7
Canton Charter Academy, MI

What Makes You Smile?
What makes you smile?
Is it the birds in the trees
Singing their tiny hearts out?
The bees pollinating the ever so beautiful flowers
That will one day be in our windows for the world to see?
Or is it your family?
Or your friends?
Could it be the love of your life?
How about the satisfaction of helping someone in need?
What makes me smile you ask?
I smile when I laugh.
I smile every time I see a friend,
A familiar face.
I smile at a happy thought
Of family and friends.
I smile to cheer up a friend who is sad.
I smile at a song or a movie
That digs deep and touches my heart.
That's why I smile.
So just think.
What makes you smile?

Jaron Kirshenbaum, Grade 8
West Hills Middle School, MI

High Merit Poems – Grades 7, 8, and 9

My Mother

My mother is the grand merry-go-round
sitting in a park of modern-day roller coasters, containing majestic,
polished gold and silver horses, proudly hosting green, striped saddles.
Children squealing in delight giving their parents the I-never-want-to-leave expression, hoping the moment will never end.
Shrieking "Can you see me mommy?" and "Over here daddy!"
The proud parents wave, some with tears of joy slowly welling from their eyes, watching their children grow up before them.

My mother is the cool, crystal-clear water slowly trickling onto a shriveling brown plant,
in a barren desert sand and bead-size pebbles everywhere.
Vultures circling overhead in the ocean-blue sky, no clouds visible.
The plant, sits there, uncared for, abandoned.
The loneliness, the feeling of being lost, the forlorn sinking in.
It tries in vain to edge away from the sun. Harsh, searing, scorching,
burning everything in its proximity, laughing deeply the plant's existence.

My mother is the last, warm but gentle summer breeze,
on a cool fall day, causing the leaves to dance in the wind.
It is a beautiful sight to witness.
Coffee bean russet, Cardinal feather scarlet, lemon peel yellow.
Scattered in all places where the eye can see, aerial acrobatics in the sky. Swirls, nose-dives, and sharp turns everywhere
towards the ends of the earth the end of time
the ends of one's imagination and beyond.

Janith Jayatilake, Grade 8
Detroit Country Day Middle School, MI

Forever and Always

We hear you giggle, the whole family loves to hear, and you turn our frowns upside down into greatly needed smiles.
When you say "Hi" it's as if an angel just flew over our shoulders, your tone is high; we al love to hear it every day.
You talk more and more each day, learning as you go.

Your high fives to Papa, we all love to see. You blow kisses to me, they feel as if a butterfly just landed on my face.
The sunshine hits your head, the little streaks of red show that you're almost two.

No doubt about your mommy loves you dearly,
When you say "Mommy" or "Momma" our hearts melt when she smiles back at you
To sit and hold you is a treat, as I read you a story you snuggle close, this I love the most.

Rain or shine you love to see the new arrivals of spring, summer, and winter.
The puddles you jump in, you get soaked but you love it with that great big smile.
"Mine," "Ditto," "Dog, dog," the words you learn from the one you hold close to your heart.

Elizabeth Oswalt, Grade 8
St Barnabas School, IN

All About Taya

Taya —
Nice, Funny, Sweet,
Sister of Blake and Braylon,
Lover of shopping, movies, and flowers,
Who feels happy around brothers, scared at the doctors, and love around my mom and dad,
Who needs more friends, water parks, and family,
Who gives laughs, love, and care,
Who fears spiders, mice, and sadness,
Who would like to see a famous person shake my hand, people being nice to each other, and my granddad get better,
Who lives in a white house on Ravena.

Taya Smith, Grade 7
Royal Oak Middle School, MI

Dreams

I open the door to a place I knew long ago
Same dusted blue walls and matching pale furniture
All so old, and yet they make me feel so young.
Picture frames line the small table, each holding within it a memory
Of a stranger whom I used to know so well.
Books scattered on shelves the years sat heavily on
Within the stories are bookmarks, peeking out the tops
And next to them sits a tiny piggy bank and I can remember the days when it meant the world.
Desk still stands tall with papers shoved tight in its wooden drawers
Notes to friends, letters to Grandma, certificates
All the little things that used to matter to me.
Closet filled with clothes much too small
Graduation outfit, first job interview skirt, prom dress
Each absorbed a time I cherished and always will.
Bed of many emotions where I laid just thinking of who I wanted to be when I grew up.
Rock star, scientist, veterinarian. Never accomplished one.
But looking back now, my life still feels like a success to me.
I take one last look, give a broken goodbye and I close the door in silence.
Then, when the tears all pass,
I take a deep breath and I know that I grew up to be just who I always dreamed of.
And I let that be enough to live the rest of my life.

Ella Rohlfs, Grade 7
St Bartholomew School, IN

Life Choices

In life you have choices and you make them.
Cold or warm? Sweet or sour? Right or wrong?
Some people don't know how to make right choices.
They start listening to the wrong voices.
They start to fall.
Hoping someone is there to answer their call.
Hoping someone is there to catch them.
Hoping someone is there with fast legs to fetch them.
The sad news is there's not a single soul of forgiveness with their arms wide open, willing to make the catch.
And run fast to make the fetch.
When you make bad choices you regret them. Why?
Because it hurts to fall a hard fall.
And not have anyone answer to your S.O.S. call.
Walking alone because of the bad choice.
Having to listen to your own hurtful voice.
It's either a yes or no, not a maybe so.
If you're faced with a hard decision make the right one.
The one that will make a benefit in your life.
It's your life; listen to the helpful voices that say "make right choices."
This is the final call for you to start making life choices.

Haley Forbes, Grade 9
Beaverton High School, MI

Old Age

Old age, everyone grows old, it has its advantages and disadvantages. But being old means that you have experienced life. When you're old you are wise, stubborn, and brittle. The bad part is sometimes you can no longer keep up with others. And a lot of times have a lot of problems. But it doesn't matter you should enjoy the time you have to yourself now that you are old. Because everyone grows old.

Tyler Weisweaver, Grade 8
West Side Middle School, IN

High Merit Poems – Grades 7, 8, and 9

I Am Who I Am
I am who I am, I can't understand
Do you like what you see?
Do you hate who I am?
To look in the mirror, and cry at the sight
I know you too, look in despite

Surgery, cosmetics, sickness, and more
Without it all, I'd be called a bore
You say I don't need, that's just a lie
Leave the house without makeup on?
I think I'd rather die

Something needs to change,
Not myself, I feel fake
Am I ugly? Am I pretty? Did I make a mistake?
No need, no care, I mustn't satisfy
I am who I am
My heart will never lie.
Mattee Martin, Grade 8
Perry Middle School, MI

War Is Peace
War is not without peace,
Peace is not without war.
How could you say something is peaceful without war?
How could you say it's wartime if there's no peace?

How is War…Peace?
How is Peace…War?
War is Peace,
And Peace is War.

War is greater than Peace,
Peace is greater than War.
If there's no War,
There is no Peace.

War is not without peace
Peace is not without war,
And neither is Freedom.
Joshua Curtis, Grade 8
Perry Middle School, MI

Batch of Love
To make a batch of love
you need an open heart.
You mix happiness with a splash of being yourself.
Mix well and put in a pinch of tenderness.
Then pour in a cup of kindness,
then a half a cup of selflessness.
Mix with a blender
then make little balls of joy.
Put them on a pan of caring.
Bake at the temperature of 143 degrees.
Haley Haines, Grade 8
St Charles Borromeo School, IN

Tough
Choices are like lemons…
  Some sour, some sweet,
  Some rotten, some spoiled.

Choices are like a dark hole…
  It's like someone putting a blind fold
  On you and telling you to run.
  It's dark, it's scary, and sometimes you lose your way.

Choices are like weather…
  Weather can be stormy, it can be sunny,
  It can be cloudy, it can be devastating.
  So, how do you find your way?

Choices can be tough
  But if God leads you to it,
  Then He will get you through it.
Alexis Annee, Grade 8
St Barnabas School, IN

First Winter and Then to Spring
A soft blanket covers the city street
Gorgeous flakes touching the tip of your nose
Cold as can be — certainly not a treat
Everything dead even a red rose

Snowball fights and sled races here we come!
All the children want to come out and play
Every child's hands, feet, and head all numb
They all hope to come out another day

Tomorrow is here and full of wonder
The snow has melted and disappeared
All the people question Mother Nature
Even though they all might think it is weird

Spring is on its way — you all will soon see
You should all be joyful and even happy
Garrett Monroe, Grade 8
St John Lutheran School, MI

Roses Budding in the Quiet of the Night
Roses budding in the quiet of the night
Afraid to show their true selves to the light
Birds singing the hollow of a tree
Afraid that to their sound someone might perceive
A butterfly in the night gracefully floating
Afraid that a person may take noting
These are all things of beauty
And so are we as humans with the duty
But for some reason we are the things that stay in the shadows
Yet sometimes we cannot even say a simple hello
I am like this you see
And I will try to show the true me
Elizabeth Bierlein, Grade 8
St Lorenz Lutheran School, MI

An Ode to Hockey and Golf
Hockey and golf are passions to me
On the ice or on the green
I can't think of a better place to be
Either place provides the best scene

I play hockey on the '97 Flames
We won Districts and States
A fight to win every game
One can say it must have been fate

Golf 2010, marked my first competitive year
In my division overall ranked first
Not bad perhaps for a starting career
I did not have any beginner curse

Whether fun is on the ice or on the tee
I've met friends for a lifetime
I purely love it, for what it can be
I wouldn't change it for a dime

I love what these sports have given me
A push to be the best I can
Sports are the golden key
Just look at me and you'll see!
Dylan Deogun, Grade 8
St Hugo of the Hills School, MI

Week
Mondays are madness
Mondays are sadness
Because school has arrived
and you feel like you want to die

Tuesdays are modern
also mild
but not wild

you can't wait until
Wednesday is over
so the week will
be almost over

Thursdays are terrifying
you can see it in your eyes
waiting for Friday to arrive

Friday it's Friday
everybody cheers
hurting my ears

the weekend has finally begun
it's time to have some fun!
Makenzie Wyzlic, Grade 7
Fowlerville Jr. High School, MI

Resurrection
There's something burning deep within,
It's time to forget my regrets and sins,
A life of lies and crime,
The true me is always hard to find,
It's time for me to have a resurrection,
Its time for me to make the connection,
To who I am and I want to be,
Because now they seem pretty far to me,
To revive from inactivity and disuse,
I'm giving it all my attention,
With a broken heart and jaded mind,
My real identity, I know I will find,
In a world to me which was not kind,
It might be my worse fear,
It's too late to cry, I don't have one tear,
I'll forget my mistakes in past years,
This might be a dream,
It might be my nightmare,
All I know is that it's my new obsession,
I was given the name Asia,
It means resurrection.
Asia Butler, Grade 9
Trillium Academy, MI

Dream
Recently, I had a dream.
In this dream was my grandfather.
This is dedicated to him in loving memory.
So close your eyes,
And just dream:
I see you standing in the church,
In your white button-down shirt
Your hair remains white,
Your smile remains grand.
I ask you questions
About my future
Wondering just what life
Has in store for me.
When I ask about you,
You tell me you are staying with friends,
And you tell me about your journey.
I listen.
You tell me you finally made it.
To where, I wonder.
You tell me.
Heaven.
Claire Migliore, Grade 8
Stanley Clark School, IN

Ice Cream
Milky, creamy, and cold
Chocolate, vanilla, and berry bold
A creamy mountain in a bowl
Will always make you full
Rebekah Townsend, Grade 7
Whitehall Middle School, MI

No More
There it was
On the floor
Broken into pieces
It was no more
While I watched
My essence soar
It was then I realized
It was no more
As it lay there
With a shattered core
I couldn't fully grasp
It was no more
I sat and marveled
How it was torn
From my life
It was no more
With sorrow and doubt
I stood and mourned
My broken soul
It was no more
Emmanuel Saint-Phard, Grade 7
Ruth Murdoch Elementary School, MI

Here They Come
Klick-klack,
Tap-tap-tap,
The soldiers of God march toward me,
Klick-klick
It's my time to go,
Tap-tap-tap
Here comes the soldiers you cannot see,
Knock-knock,
They knock on my door, the sound is low,
Creek-creek-creek
The door opens in a moan,
Knick-knack,
A voice, speaks in a low tone,
He says, "It's time to come home."
Tap-tap-tap
His face finally shows,
Klick-klick
The bare skull comes close,
Klick-klick, tap-tap-tap
Today I march home.
Seth Persinger, Grade 8
Covington Middle School, IN

The Fall
Leaves are turning colors
They are blowing in the wind
Whirling around, and around
Rusting on the ground
As they're falling without sound
In the mildly cold air
Kenzie Oakley, Grade 8
Lincoln Middle School, IN

High Merit Poems – Grades 7, 8, and 9

Over the Green Gem

When I was young I used to wonder where you were
You were never at my piano recitals
Nor my soccer practices
I scanned the faces of happy families for you
But you were never there
My parents told me that you were across the ocean
More than 60,000 miles away
When I was young I used to dream of soaring across the sky
In order to catch up with you
Or swimming across the ocean in order to see you
Sometimes I dreamed of gliding across the sea to meet you
Now that I am older I understand
Those things are not possible
Now that I am older I understand what love means
So really, how big is the ocean?
How wide is the sea?
How far can my love reach to you?

Ellen Zhang, Grade 8
Boulan Park Middle School, MI

Eyes

Looking in her eyes I could tell she was sad,
But she tires to cover it by smiling and looking glad.

You could see the emotions in her eyes,
If she were to break down and cry it'd be no surprise.

She looks like she's been hurt before,
Looking like her heart is sore,
But when she smiles you can't see it anymore.

She needs to let her feelings out,
Maybe to scream,
Maybe to shout.

Is she sad? Is she mad?
She is scared to let her feelings show,
But maybe it's best to let somebody know.

Maegan Brown, Grade 8
Perry Middle School, MI

Bad Day

Struggling moments I've faced since dawn,
Revolting regrets I will loathe from here on.
Conflicts and trials blockade my way,
While comforting words has no one to say.
It's a wonder how quickly the world falls to shreds,
Hopes for tomorrow lie burdened and dead.
Thin ruts converge into one massive hole,
For forgivable slips I pay a large toll.
I believe I've been cursed, not a thing's going right,
Like I'm trapped in a war and losing the fight.
Though my day has been horrid, it isn't all bad.
Now I deeply appreciate good times I've had.

Katie Grieze, Grade 8
Heritage Jr/Sr High School, IN

Autumn

The green leaves browning in the autumn sun,
Not as hot as summer but in the same;
Red or purple in the dark sky is done,
The favorite in me all like its name:

Oh so gracefully the leaves dance in sync,
Doing the tango in fresh autumn sky:
All nature comes together like a link,
All beauty is seen by the little eye:

My heart swoons for this time of the ole year;
The sun sleeps soundly: cannot bare a lie:
It all works in unison like a gear,
To myself this moment will never die:

My partner in life comes one out of four,
I will mourn until it comes here once more.

Matthew Fodera, Grade 8
St John Lutheran School, MI

Reflections

Dark brown eyes, sleepy but curious
Almond shaped, beneath prominent eyebrows mysterious
Often behind clear glasses
Perched on a narrow bridge, looking serious
Nostrils slightly flared, like a racehorse victorious

Disheveled straight black hair, I never comb it
Pale smooth skin, marred with an occasional zit
Hopefully not in great masses
Facial hair — actually peach fuzz — I admit
No danger of cutting myself with a shaving kit

Pondering, I look into the mirror
And wonder about my future, near
Will I be in classes
Or have a successful career
Because I have no idea what I want to be, I fear

Marcus Lee, Grade 8
Bloomfield Hills Middle School, MI

Room with No View

The only thing I'm sure of is
20 years and 18 if I'm good.

Day and night.
I stare at the cement wall as if its going to change.
Reaching out of the hole just big enough
My two hands can fan fit through, I grab my breakfast.
It's been years since I have seen my wife or daughter
I think.
Why am I here?
I'm not sure.
I woke up today, in a room with no view.

Savannah Julien, Grade 9
Allegan High School, MI

I Am Who I Am
I am who I am
No one can change it
I am who I am
No one can break it
I love myself for who I am
Not what others want me to be
So…
I am who I am
No matter what people say
I am who I am
Every single day
Jasmine Petry, Grade 7
Oak Hill Jr High School, IN

Miles to Go
Many miles to go
down this long, empty street
Trying to find myself
in one of those ugly taxis

It is driving me far, far away
from my home, family, life
My identity is gone
I lost everything

In those still many miles to go.
Cheyenne Earl, Grade 8
Bloomingdale Middle School, MI

The Lock
Inner feelings locked away
People try to beat the lock with a hammer
They get nowhere, the lock won't bend
The key was lost long ago
Tears streak my burning red face
Behind a pillow of shame
Running makeup gets repaired
They hide behind my cold outer shell
Pain will always be there
Secrets seep through the cracks of the door
Nothing can penetrate my lock of sorrow
Clarissa Heilman, Grade 7
South Spencer Middle School, IN

It Is Fall!
Fall is the best time of the year.
Honking of geese we always hear.
The leaves are turning from their green
Snowflakes falling will soon be seen.

The smell of corn is in the air
Being harvested everywhere.
Thanksgiving is in that season
Being thankful is the reason.
Travis Devon Wagler, Grade 8
South Bogard School, IN

Dad?
I know he misses me, my dad.
I do believe that he still loves me, I know.
I moved away from him, from Kentucky to Indiana.
I feel so stupid for doing that, now.
But instead I put myself first, blindly, stupid!
I don't even know what was going through my mind when I left him.
It felt like someone squeezed my heart until it turned to ash, and fell into my stomach.
I didn't even think at the time, but when it was all real, when I got there, it hit me, stupid!
I try to keep my chin up, but I miss him too much.
Why did I leave him?
Can I get through this? No!
Should I tell mom? NO! She is just so happy here!
When can I see him?
Can I ever?!
Please, please can I see him?
But there is a four foot glass between us, then I watch as he evaporates
"Come back!!"
Hanna Shadowen, Grade 7
South Spencer Middle School, IN

Picture Perfect
It's funny, isn't it?
How someone on the outside looking in knows nothing, but they act like they know it all.
Like they know for a fact nothing could make us fall.
Boy, are they wrong.
They think we are so strong, and I guess in one way we are, but in the other, not so much.
Together forever?
Maybe, but probably not. I guess that's just life you know?
If you have to go, go.
If you want to sing, sing.
How about laughing?
You know what is right.
Don't put up a fight.
Don't question if you don't want the answer, but the truth is you know it.
We all do.
So picture perfect?
Maybe, but probably not. I guess that's just life.
Kate Owens, Grade 8
St. Regis School, MI

One Way to True Beauty
What is true beauty?
It is not the physical appearance of a face,
But of what is on the inside, the heart.

The truth of the thriving heart,
The want of spiritual beauty,
These are far more important than the beauty of a face.

For it doesn't matter the beauty of a face,
Because to be truly beautiful, you need to have a pure heart.
God is the key to true beauty.

Beauty is not of a face, but it comes from the One who purifies the heart.
Danniele Rydzinski, Grade 9
Lenawee Christian School, MI

Friendship

It's more than just having things in common,
It's understanding each other.
It's having a bond that no one can break
Friendship.
Is knowing someone better than they know themselves
It's not one big thing, it's a million little things
It's always being there
Friendship.
Is having thousands of memories, even if they
aren't all happy
Sometimes it's like being in World War II
Friendship.
Is actually keeping your promises
It's fighting, but finding a way through it
Friendship.
It's that one person who will help you
through anything

Grace Kirkpatrick, Grade 7
South Spencer Middle School, IN

Heartbroken

I still remember the day when you left
You took my dream, that for you they just were a bet.
You simply took my illusions and painted them black
Without hesitation, without turning back.

I stood out in the rain the whole day.
But then you were there and you swept me away.
I guess that's what I waited for
But I never believed that things happened for a reason before.

I wish I could press reset to remember all the good times
That of course is impossible now that you said goodbye.
I'm trying to fake through
But there really is nothing that I can do.

You left me heartbroken.
You proved me right to say that in the end there's no perfect man.

Adriana Celis, Grade 8
West Side Middle School, IN

The Prey

The cheetahs lay in the tall green grass,
Waiting patiently,
Stalking the animal.
The mother gives a quick glance of readiness;
This was the signal.
A nearby antelope runs by
And is hastily hurled to the ground.
With a quick
Rip
And
Tear,
It sprawls in the dead grass.

Brad Gillette, Grade 9
Allegan High School, MI

Danger

Surrounded by trees and rushing water
with the cracking of sticks being trampled on
from down under
suddenly with silence filling the air
with a gunshot that rang from somewhere in there
terrified animals scramble through the woods
trying to find an unharmed home
to escape the fright
in the dreadful dark night
just as the sun set over the hills
it leaves the sky with a
signal light
saying everything will be fine
until tomorrow
turns into
night

Sara Hendzel, Grade 7
Perry Middle School, MI

You're My Mom

You're like a flashlight
Guiding me through life
You're a book
Taking me through new adventures each day
You're a sweater
Keeping me warm
You're a first aid kit
Keeping me safe
You're Taylor Swift
Entertaining me each day
You're a heart
Loving me
You're my hero
Teaching me to the best I can be
And you're my mom

Madelyn Mans, Grade 7
West Middle School, MI

Life

Life is rather humdrum sometimes.

But for some, life is like a precious diamond
They have a vision that the sun will shine brighter
They'll have a home to go to

No more chaos just trying to survive
No more coercing them to live in the dark alleys
No more crying, wondering if they'll see tomorrow
To come out of a mysterious, blurred space
Into one that is smooth as frosting on a cake
To make a difference in the world
These are stalwart, wild warriors
Fighting for brighter days
Fighting for a better life

Katie Blocker, Grade 8
Culver Community Middle School, IN

Seasons

The first season of a year is winter — from that point, the trees and wild animals are left for dead. There a person's life has turmoil, sadness and agony — all the pain in the world. From those

horrible times comes spring, the lively season with joy that has been sealed inside from the cold and bitterness. Your heart begins to repair, your mind has come to a cooperate rate, and bliss has

taken over. And then summer arrives — audaciousness awakens with everlasting happiness. The solstice brings a soothing feeling within your soul. A smile was born from the dark, low scowl. But

we all know that trials must intervene through your gracious success. Fall has come with struggles, with winter returning with its curse all over again. That is life — it has many challenges and trials

that come for us to face, and we stumble because we cannot be in control. Our confidence is lacked, for "the spirit is willing, but the body is weak." Life is a difficult piece to comprehend. The

provocations and demurs are predators and we are their prey. But we learn from them, for when they come again, we are prepared.

Faith Montgomery, Grade 8
Kingsway Christian School, IN

There They Go

There they go to where no one shall know,
As they drift down the hall the tears slowly begin to fall.
Memories made, memories lived and memories yet to be made.
This may or may not be the last time that they are together.
But for most, it isn't and all the while there is still one more event.
One more thing left to do, one more memory to be made.
It's almost over but one thing is left.
The time has come and there they go.
Up on the stage they hold back tears while looking confident.
This last event that will break some apart, for finally it is over.
The time has come and there they go.
As they leave one by one they each say goodbyes and give farewells.
They stare out the window at passing objects thinking about the great times through the years.
To where they will go only one shall know.
Others together forever, while others not.

Christian Widduck, Grade 8
St Barnabas School, IN

Tears in the Wind

Sometimes it seems like the wind sweeps over my tired soul,
as if searching for something it cannot find.
All is void and empty. I'm hit with emotions as they roll over me like silent cries
over the ocean mist, as they take me captive.
The gentle hush of the wind's gentle touch, carries me away.
The rustle of leaves dance and float in the air, and I'm calm as my thoughts drift away with them.
Memories haunt me, as the wind sweeps over me.
The smell of earth and dirt fills me somehow, reminding me that I'm not alone.
Wisps of thick hair circle my face, slapping my eyes, as the peel away and entangle in the air around me.
Slow tears roll down my cheeks, cold against the howling wind.
I stare ahead of me, as the wind continues to search me, as I wonder what it is it cannot find.
But in this moment, I'm — free? Suddenly, I want this to last forever, whatever this is, *this* unnamed peace.
But in this wind, I feel free…

Sydney Wilding, Grade 8
Corunna Middle School, MI

How to Live with This Burden

I set my alarm for 2 a.m.
   just to see if I'm doing all right,
     because anything can happen at anytime.
I try to remember to test before I eat,
   but I have done this so long,
     I can tell when something's wrong.
I have memories of when I was a little kid,
   when everything was normal,
     I hold them back, knowing that's not the case anymore.
I don't think of the day at the doctor,
   because every time I do,
     I see the tears in my parent's eyes.
I do all of the things I used to,
   because I tell myself I can,
     even though sometimes I can't.
I smile when I think about it,
   because there's no way out,
     not for anyone like me.
I hate living with this burden,
   but I'll get through it,
     because I can handle living with this responsibility.

Kyle Castner, Grade 8
Kingsway Christian School, IN

A Friendship to Last a Lifetime

We've known each other for quite some time.
We've been there for each other through thick and thin.
We are closer than close could ever be.
There are no words lost every time we are together,
even if time has passed since we've last seen each other.
We've laughed, and we've cried, and you are like my sister.
My life would never be the same without you.
Now as we grow, we are going in different directions.
I know I can still count on you,
that phone call to make me laugh,
to talk about our day,
to cheer up, to listen to, to lean on.
Our different directions will not keep us apart,
it will only strengthen our bond.
My friend, my sister, we've worked all of our lives,
on our friendship to last a lifetime.

Brady Stephens, Grade 8
St Barnabas School, IN

Theater

It's inspiring and beautiful in many ways. The song and dance brighten sad, sad days. It's the drama, the props, and the costumes and colors. It's heart and soul like living the life of another. It's patience and nerve, and as sweet as sugar. It's blood, sweat, tears. It's not just one thing or another. Though some call if fright, I call it lime light. It's cheer and sadness, and something I believe. It's staged and comfortable. It's theater, it's me.

Samantha Parker, Grade 7
South Spencer Middle School, IN

Running

I ran from my past
I ran from my failure
I ran from my town, from you from me
I ran fast
I ran slowly
I ran away
I run to my future
I run away from my pain and grief
I run from yesterday, I run for today
I run into you
I run into a shelter, a safe haven, a place made for me
I run into love
I stay in my shelter, my peaceful sanctuary
I love my peaceful sanctuary that doesn't need to be quiet
I love the one that I ran into
I love the one that found, and gave me the world
And it is because I love you that I run from you
I run from you because you don't deserve my past
Then you run to me because you say you love my future
I ran to you, I run from you, I ran for you,
Just like you will always run for me.

Sharon Quartey, Grade 7
Ruth Murdoch Elementary School, MI

Just Imagine

Just imagine —
what the world would be like
if there was no hunger, no poverty,
no war, and no incurable diseases.
Would we all be grateful for what we have?
Would we help others in need?
Would we all be friends?
A lot of us would probably be stuck up,
living the perfect life.
Having these things make us who we are.
Not having hunger, poverty,
war and incurable diseases,
would be a miracle —
but that's life and for now
we can just imagine what life would be without them.
Just imagine!

Autumn Horn, Grade 9
Beaverton High School, MI

Friends

They're by your side
even for the emotional roller coaster ride
They're on your speed dial
and they shed tears with you once in a while
They're there for you through thick and thin
no matter what they're genuine
We'll be old in our Depends
but we'll still remain friends

Taylor Kline, Grade 8
West Side Middle School, IN

Ode to Music

O music!
Your presence in this world
that of no other;
in most homes,
you are to be found,
one form or another.

Any genre of you:
classical, rock, jazz, pop,
or any other, is always desired
somewhere.

With your soothing melodies,
dissonant chords, pounding bass,
squealing trumpets, thirty-second note runs;
everyone loves something about you.

O music, you are pie;
everyone loves you.
No matter what happens,
everyone will always love music.

Will Pierce, Grade 9
DeKalb High School, IN

Balancing Act

Standing looking down, at the wire
The wire I stand on, my life trusting in it
Taking it step by step, concerned in every footfall
My hands extended keeping my balance
Looking at the wire, as it cuts the world in half
Leaving me watching as the two sides fall
Nothing but white below me, leaving me alone
My balance slipping, tipping from side to side
The wind comes rushing around me
Tearing me off my tightrope
Falling gazing into nothing but white
Fearing there is no bottom
Finally seeing a color, a sliver of blue
Coming rushing toward me, hitting the surface
Diving into the warm running water
Taking me down river, speeding along passing scenes of my past
To end at a fall, water stays around me
Hitting the bottom, finding it dark
Wrapped in cloth, standing up to have them fall off
Looking at the bed I rest in, where my dreams always form
Where my dreams always haunt me

Wyatt Lawson, Grade 9
Riverton Parke Jr/Sr High School, IN

Life Is Music

Life is music coming from an electric guitar.
Life is distorted,
It will make you confused,
It will make you understand.
Life is sweet,
It will make you charming,
It will make you excited.
Life is smooth,
It will make you calm,
It will make you relax.
Life is over driven,
It will make you fast,
It will make you crazy.
Life is controlled,
Life is the guitar,
You are the guitarist.

Joshua Marchand, Grade 7
Royal Oak Middle School, MI

The Cross

What a
beautiful,
terrible
sight.
The cross that held my Savior joined by a sunset
amazingly crafted by the One that hung on that cross.
Yet
once again
God's power
exposes the
tricks of
Satan
as just
a shadow
compared to
God's radiance.

Jonathan Bayless, Grade 8
Kingsway Christian School, IN

Someone

Someone out there is waiting
Someone is looking at the sky
Someone is having a baby
Someone is having they're first kiss
Someone is trying to be the best they can
Someone wants to be adopted
Someone wants to feel and be loved
Someone is thinking that they should help their community

Sarah Ash, Grade 8
Perry Middle School, MI

The Path

A path is chosen every day
We walk along, and make our way.

Though times get tough, and you're struggling to see
The good things in you and me.

Take a breath, sigh and relax
For you will never get tomorrow back.

Brandon Dietz, Grade 9
Posen Consolidated High School, MI

M.V.P.
Basketball is my favorite sport
I like the way they dribble up and down the court
I keep it so fresh with my Nikes on
I'm like Moses Malone when the game is going
I like the way they take it to the hoop
My favorite pass is the alley oop
Then there's the pick and roll the give and go
That's basketball finger roll let's go
When I take it to the rim I'm not a punk
So look out below here comes the slam dunk
I shake it left and I shake it right
Check me out now guys I'm out of sight
I pump fake the shot and you fly by
Then I shoot the shot and the ball flies high
As the ball soars the air off goes the buzzer
Then heart skipped a beat like no other
The shot goes in and I just smiled
Then I looked over to the right and the crowd went wild
I looked at the coach and asked who was MVP
And the coach lifted me up and said it was me
Angelo Suggs, Grade 8
Ruth Murdoch Elementary School, MI

Volleyball!
Volleyball
Shoes, socks, jersey and spandex
you got that
and you're ready to go
Volleyball
Looks of floor burns from diggin the ball
Sound of the girls cheering for their warm-ups
The crowd roars when you spike the ball
Volleyball
Taste of you Gatorade in a time out
never tasted so delicious
The butterflies in your stomach
When the score is 24 to 23
in the final game of a tournament
Volleyball
The last serve could cause the whole game
They think it's not coming over the net
then the ball plops on their side of the court
and they don't budge to go for it
You feel like you have just won the Olympics
Claire Roberts, Grade 7
South Spencer Middle School, IN

You and Me
The best times were under that big old oak
Just you and me
Sitting on the porch all night long, waist deep in thoughts
Of you and me
Laughing on the beach, chasing the seagulls
It was just you and me
Or taking a long walk through the cornfield just to talk
About you and me
Having a family dinner because you were almost family
Oh you and me
Lying on the ground watching the stars
Just you and me
Sinking deeper and deeper into my ocean of thoughts
Of you and me
Sitting on the beach waiting for the sunset
It was just you and me
Or splashing in the pool talking
About you and me
Laughing at our parents who think we're in love
Oh you and me
Hannah Fenwick, Grade 7
Ruth Murdoch Elementary School, MI

I Love the Beach
I love the warm waters washing onto shore.
I love seeing the seagulls take flight and soar.
The dolphins are my friends,
I hope this day doesn't end,
Because I love the beach.
The waves gently clean off my feet.
The birds in the sky sound so sweet.
I make footprints in the sand,
And I hold a starfish in my hand,
Because I love the beach.
I dive into the ocean
And feel the wave's motion.
I climb onto the reef,
But my stay is very brief,
Because I love the beach.
I'm at home in bed,
And I feel sorrow in my head.
I stroke my dog,
Because my head is in a fog,
Because I love the beach.
Erin Collins, Grade 7
Christ the King Catholic School, IN

Stolen Youth
They don't speak of the things they spoke of,
long ago, before the flames,
chaos, burning left them blind
to the things they saw.
Long ago, long ago
Megan Yeager, Grade 8
Culver Community Middle School, IN

Michigan
The B ^{U} M ^{P} Y roads are now being raced upon

the rustling of the trees when the cool wind blows
The waves gently splashing as the sunset overlooks Lake Michigan
Autumn Crummett, Grade 7
Whitehall Middle School, MI

Dream World
Gliding on a butterfly's wings
into a world of slumber and dreams
Reality begins to fade
thoughts and ideas flood in.
Fluctuating upon the calm air.

Choose one!
Grab it!

The breathtaking adventure
that seems like forever,
comes to an end.

Reality gives gesture,
and brings you back,
to existence.
Riley Dare, Grade 8
Culver Community Middle School, IN

Just a Dream
The dream,
I wish to be true,
Was the dream I had,
About me and you,
We were in love at last,
But it's all a dream,
Of the past,
My nightmares of the day,
Have come to haunt me,
Because of the feelings I have,
That taunt me,
I keep it all hidden inside,
Because I know it shall never be,
But when the night comes back,
To spare me,
My dreams come and reunite me.
Rachelle Roese, Grade 7
Mount Clemens Middle School, MI

Nature
From the bluest skies
To the greenest trees
I see the eyes
Of you and me
With all these colors
With all these shades
I get these wonders
About my charade
If I see the iris
I see the truth
If I see an ibis
I see not uncouth
Oh through eyes one uncovers
Things not said but are discovered
Jordan McDaniel, Grade 9
DeKalb High School, IN

Dogs, They're Dogs
Dogs, with their waggly tails,
Dogs, with their sharp, pointy nails,
Dogs, eating all they can reach,
Dogs, not always allowed at a beach,
Dogs, with their strong sense of smell,
Dogs, not always obeying very well,
Dogs, some with big ears and long snouts,
Dogs, some with large, droopy mouths,
Dogs, helping in search and rescue,
Dogs, who will always stand by you,
Dogs, whether their wild or tamed,
Dogs, some unknown or named,
Dogs, some odd shapes and kinds,
Dogs, mine has a very small mind,
Dogs, mostly a cats worst foe,
Dogs, don't see what the cats know,
Dogs, mankind's partners through time,
Dogs, protecting us without even a dime,
Dogs, they will always be cool,
Even if they always drool!
Stephen Andrews, Grade 7
Fowlerville Junior High School, MI

In the Beginning
In the beginning,
all was blissful.
The days were
bright and quiet.

All I ever loved
was how you
made me feel
around you.

In the beginning,
you were mine
and I was yours.
Perfect days went cold,
the day you left.

Why did you have to leave me?
In the beginning we were together,
but now all the love and fire,
that we had is gone.
Taylor Tosh, Grade 9
South Spencer High School, IN

Baseball
being all around
never touching the ground
hitting you in the air
but I won't be there
running to first base
but you will never see a smile on my face
Trey Lax, Grade 8
West Side Middle School, IN

The Greenest Grass of All
Life is a meadow
Full of flowers and grass
They wilt and grow back
As time comes to pass

Life is a meadow
To be frolicked with glee
Surrounded by trees you are trapped
And yet you are free

Life is a meadow
Seemingly clear and true
Up until a tree
Appears in front of you

Life is a meadow
And your spirit lives on
Frolicking there
Until the meadow is gone
Chance Maddox, Grade 7
Royal Oak Middle School, MI

Pride
With eyes as fierce as a warrior
He spots his prey,
Digs his sharp claws into the earth
As he moves in beat with nature

Locked on like a missile
His strong stride increases,
Golden ocean crashes
Leaving little error for the unfortunate

Moving rapidly upon arrival
One last courageous leap
And the blue victory will be earned
Proving dominance and seniority

Suddenly, a boisterous roar rings out
The two animals become one,
As crimson spills
The end of one life, the joy of another.
Emily Ghena, Grade 9
Lenawee Christian School, MI

The Dive
Screeching loudly,
The eagle dives,
Darting down,
Straight towards the ground,
The bird as fast as lightning,
It snaps out is wings,
And glides a heartbeat,
Above the ground.
Matthew Burns, Grade 7
Assumption School, MI

High Merit Poems – Grades 7, 8, and 9

Give a Little More!
Today I'm going to give a little more
Forgive and forget the bad things
Smile just a little bit brighter
Each day is a gift and not a given
Live life a little bit fuller
Dream a little bit bigger
And give it your all
Because
You just might not be here tomorrow
Tori Lauer, Grade 7
Perry Middle School, MI

The Media
It waits,
Like a hunter
Waiting to make its kill.

It prowls,
In the shadows of my soul,
Waiting to destroy my very being.

I am at war.
Kaitlynn Kimmel, Grade 8
Rockford Christian School, MI

Regret
Every day, unique thoughts are
lost in embarrassment.
People twisting them
so I regret telling them.

It was ridiculous to think
they would understand
Everywhere I go they whisper them
Now all that's left are the scars
Samantha Reed, Grade 8
Culver Community Middle School, IN

Anticipation
Anticipation
Impatient, hopeful
Waiting, wishing, sobbing
Cut off from civilization
Awaiting
Laurel McGerty, Grade 8
Trinity Lutheran School, MI

The Clumsy Dinosaur
There once was a dinosaur
Who thought that he could soar
He tried it one day
Crashed into an x-ray
And was later thrown out the door
Amanda Veenstra, Grade 8
Ebenezer Christian School, MI

Branches, Blowing in the Wind
In the glorious night, branches blow in the breeze.
They blow so heavenly it as if angels have come down from earth
and are dancing with joy in their hearts.
The branches feel rough and hard,
they feel like sand paper rubbing your arm.
I hear the branches crumbling, crackling, swaying all evening long.
When I hear their beautiful song, I feel joy and life near the soul.
They smell like the trees on which they rest on.
When I see the branches swaying with rhythm, I know that I am alive.
The branches are like doves flying through the night,
delivering messages of our God to all.
The branches songs are immaculate
for they are the true spirits of the night.
Every night I hear the branches
rumbling, crackling, swaying all evening long.
When I see those beautiful, pretty branches,
I know that I am alive.
Savannah Shaver, Grade 7
St John the Evangelist School, IN

Life Isn't Fair
Down the street is a orphan child
lonely, depressed, wanting friends
then comes another child, foolish
Humiliates the orphan child
the child weeps, and memories of the past condemn him
carelessly, the foolish child walks away
While the lonely child weeps in despair
Where was his family? Where were his friends?
All abandoning him for the riches of life
living selfishly in a titanic mansion, with good fortune
Life is unfair for the innocent child, who all his life has
been abandoned and done nothing wrong to deserve this
Night falls, and comes him his shining star for a chance to a better life
On comes a couple, desiring a child,
yet can't naturally because of a rare disease the woman has.
The boy's heart swelled with joy, and chose to go with them.
No words can describe how he felt to be once again in a loving family!
Nesreen Ezzeddine, Grade 7
Star International Academy, MI

Months, Months, Months
January is very cold, but it never gets old
In February I like to rest in bed, but Valentine's Day is coming ahead
March is beautiful and very green, it makes me feel like a jumping bean
April has a lot of rain, it is a very big pain
We are going to have fun today, it is the very merry month of May
July is coming very soon, but for now it is only June
July is the best, I get no rest
August is the start of a new school year, I cannot wait for it to be done, dear
In September the leaves turn yellow, it makes the tree look like a jolly fellow
October is the month of Halloween, I am going to be Lightning McQueen
November is the month of Thanksgiving, you can surely make a good living
I get gifts in December, I will always remember
Rachel Schurman, Grade 8
DeMotte Christian School, IN

Swing, Swing*
Swing, swing, swinging fast
Hopefully this next pitch will last
Strike one strike two crack
Around the bases and back
Brittney Loudermilk, Grade 7
Whitehall Middle School, MI
**Inspired by William Blake*

The Fall
Leaves
Yellow, Green, Red,
Blowing soft in the wind,
Their colors bring me happiness,
Fall Plants
Kandace Kettler, Grade 8
Lincoln Middle School, IN

Push-Ups and Pull-Ups
push-ups and pull-ups are very hard
but not if you work on them every day
you build up muscle to the sky
but you can't be lazy
then they won't be so hard
Garrett Paulson, Grade 8
West Side Middle School, IN

The Season of Spring
The bird chirped loudly,
letting the animals know,
spring will soon be here,
with its new beginnings,
saying the past is the past.
Jade Brown, Grade 8
Lincoln Middle School, IN

War
War
It's all around us
Soldier's fate on the line
Why are humans so cruel?
Sadness
Tristen Howitt, Grade 7
St John Lutheran School, MI

Army Boots
There was a pair of army boots
That made the sound of toots
Whenever he walked
Whenever he talked
They copied the sound of his glutes
Grant Greyson, Grade 7
St John Lutheran School, MI

The Darkest Day
On the run though you may be, you cannot escape, you cannot flee.
Today the sun won't shine on me. Darkest night we'll ever see.

The clock strikes 1, 11, and 17. Our plight, it will not be seen.
Alone in the loneliest way; we find no comfort on the darkest day.

Processions the streets align; processions inhabit only my ind.
People gather. Come to pray. The thoughts blotted in the darkest way.

Time warps, speeds up, then stops; we feel only the coldest rain drops.
Chills our bones that do decay; as our minds slowly fray.
Slowly the heat will pass away; we'll forget the things we did not say.

All comes to no avail. More quickly now, we will become frail.
Our skin will inevitably pale. The highest mountain we did not scale.

The lowest valley we did not cross, as our body's encroached by moss.
The greatest hill we did not climb, as our bell it finally chimes.

The cure avoided by our demise. Our mother sits and cries.
As we leave they will stay. No comfort for them on the darkest day.
No, they're the ones that will pay.

But through the darkness shines a light; intensity so ever bright.
In the cold of the darkest night; on the step arrives the collected might.

The will to live not move on. Our lives dwindle but will never be gone.
In the frost of the darkest day, shines a blue jay in the brightest way.
Kyle Beyer, Grade 9
Lakeview High School, MI

Brothers
Brothers are crazy, fun, and wild.
Brothers can be annoying.
Brothers are cute, no matter how they look.
Brothers are amazing.
Brothers are made and put here by God.
Brothers are put on this Earth to annoy, but also to be loved and cared for.
Brothers come in all shapes and sizes, but they should all be loved the same amount.

Brothers are all different.
Some are messy, some are clean,
Some eat like a pig, some barely eat at all,
Some are loud, some are quiet,
Some shouldn't eat sugar,
Some are really laid-back, some are crazy as can be,
Some are ornery, some are sweet,
Some love to laugh, some are serious,
Some love to read, some just want to play,
Some are athletic, some are academic,
Some are both athletic and academic.
All are beautiful human beings, no matter how young or old.
Brothers are all different, but we should love them all the same:
Totally, irrevocably, and with our whole heart.
Sierra Tippmann, Grade 7
St Charles Borromeo School, IN

To Be Somebody
I work so hard to be somebody
but what if I'm a nobody
life now is a daily struggle
It's so hard to enjoy
I want a job
but where do you work
to try to be somebody
A doctor
Lawyer
Counselor
will all work for me
But what if I mess it up
what if I turn out to be a nobody
Emily Martin, Grade 8
Ovid-Elsie Middle School, MI

Nature
Up! Up! in the sky
Where clouds are high
And birds fly

It is in the fall
The leaves are falling
The cats are crawling
And the people call

I live in a trailer
It is so boring
It is brown
And people are snoring
Ashley Shadley, Grade 8
Thomas A Edison Jr/Sr High School, IN

My Favorite Season Is Fall
When colors are very bright
Leaves drop like a ball
And pumpkins are in sight
Ghosts and goblins running wild
Always causing such a fright
And costumes cover every child
That walks throughout the night
Warm apple cider warms the heart
And donuts fill the tummy
Leaving a taste of tart
That is really yummy
The time flies by fast
The seasons never last
Jonathan Brunet, Grade 9
Posen Consolidated High School, MI

The Sea
I swam in the sea
Among all the sharks and whales
In the cold water
Michelle LaFave, Grade 8
Holy Name School, MI

High School
High School
What will it be like?
Exciting?
Nerve-wrecking?

I know it will have more freedom
but what if…
What if it's not what it's cracked up to be?
They say it's better
than elementary and middle school combined,
they could be wrong.
High School
It could be a dream
or a nightmare.
Then you're stuck in the middle trying to wake up from a nightmare.
High School
Is it scary? Hard?
If so, then why do people go there just to drop out?
Hope High School is what its cracked up to be.
Bailey Forston, Grade 7
South Spencer Middle School, IN

Soccer
Soccer is fun
Soccer players are always in motion
They train for days for a game
Strikers practice their aim
Defenders practice how to claim the ball
And proclaim their territory
Midfielders practice sending the ball to the striker with one powerful kick
Trying to make it hard for the other team to defend the goal
Even though all these players have fame, they are hard to be tamed
And they feel a lot of pain to get where they are
It is a war on that field
That's why it appeals to so many fans
These players and their coaches always have a plan in mind
And at the end of the day, if they are successful, they will be on the newspaper headlines
And at the end of the season, we will see who is better
Every region in the world has a champion
The grass can get so wet the cleats get mold on them
And then the players get sold to other teams
But it is every kid's dream to play on a soccer team
Matheus Silva, Grade 8
Ruth Murdoch Elementary School, MI

Music
Music
the beat,
the sound that jazzes up any person for any moment any time,
that you are unaware and need to be soothed into the heart of music,
shocked with senses that flow through your body, brought to you by music,
the sound that flows, through your blood, stream,
to stimulate your senses, with rhythm and beat the way of
music.
Augustino Hartnagel, Grade 7
Stanley Clark School, IN

Ocean
The warm ocean breeze
Blows the salty smell
From the ocean waves
Towards me which makes
My body fade to total calmness

I relax and fall
With the rhythm of
The boat as it rocks
Upon the waves
As if my body was only on the water

The birds sing above
The waves beat the side
As the winds whip
Through the trees
I sit and dream

The warm sun smiles
On my cheeks
The hot sand tickles
Beneath my feet
Warmth fills my body

As I relax upon the beach
Emily Booth, Grade 8
Perry Middle School, MI

Captivated the Nation
Butler, small university in Indianapolis,
They were unexpected and unknown.
They were underdogs and underestimated,
and captivated the nation.

Butler, home of 4,000 students,
They were David versus Goliath.
They were fan favorites,
and captivated the nation.

Butler, played as a team,
Through every situation.
They believed, and triumphed,
and captivated the nation.

Butler, had an amazing run,
They were confident and never gave up.
They achieved the impossible,
and captivated the nation.

They were one game short,
A couple of shots and fouls away, but
The country will never forget
The run the bulldogs had as they
captivated the nation.
Bryan Doerr, Grade 8
St Barnabas School, IN

Relax
Relax, in my mind, out there,
all around me, everywhere,
all I see, all I hear,
my paradise gone is my fear,
is all I need to think about,
no one yelling, or in need to shout.

A great way to end a bad day,
let my mind go blank as I drift away,
no one near or far,
as I drift away really far,
all I think about is no one helping.

I need peace and quiet,
not thinking about another riot,
everyone everywhere,
peaceful and quiet air,
is all I need,
is all I think.
Relax.
Jade Killingsworth, Grade 8
Perry Middle School, MI

Drifting Like Paper Planes
Like a paper plane
a seagull
drifts aimlessly.

Over the water,
across the world,
drifting to its destiny.
Free from trouble,
released from worry,
concentrated on the horizon.

Like a paper plane
a seagull
drifts aimlessly.

Time goes slowly,
like a turtle walking.
Drifting for months and years.
But where will it go?
To wherever the breeze takes it, it's destiny.
Shiva Sachdeva, Grade 7
Detroit Country Day Middle School, MI

Andrew
A nxious and likes to try different things
N inja taskful as can be
D isagreeable with others
R eally hyper at home
E njoys playing music
W reckless at times
Andrew Manthey, Grade 8
West Side Middle School, IN

The Story of Us
What you chose to decide
Made me die inside
You'll never see what you did
You ran away like a lil kid

I thought what we had was real
But it wasn't the real deal
What you said hurt.
You were such a jerk.

You'll never see my tears
Not in a million years
Maybe one day you'll come near.
But until then there will be more tears.

Maybe it's a test
To see if it's for the best
I guess what you said is true
It's just not working for us two.

You left a scar
Then ran away so far
If you come back to me
Is what I'm waiting to see.
Katelynn Chandler, Grade 8
Covington Middle School, IN

The Sea
The breeze of the sea
Is so comforting to me.
I'm the great blue sea,
The world revolves around me

If it weren't for I,
There would be no sky.
If it weren't for me,
There would be no sea.

I am the bravest of brave,
Heard through my wave.
I am home to fish, whale, and shark
And have a bite as big as my bark.

No greater is my mite,
Than a storm at night.
My fury is vast,
Whipping through you so fast.

So loud is my roar,
Heard from shore to shore.
You can run but you can't hide,
Never doubt the fury of my tide.
Drew Gallagher, Grade 8
St Hugo of the Hills School, MI

Night

Oh how I love the night,
It is such a stunning sight.
How the stars shine so bright.

Fireflies light up around me,
As I am filled with glee,
Though, I must whisper softly.

Everyone is asleep.
While they are counting sheep,
I mustn't make a peep.

I tip-toe around,
Trying not to make a sound,
Making sure I won't be found.

In need of midnight snack,
I'll hurry to get back,
In order to hit the sack.

I zip down my zipper,
Take off my second slipper,
With a chance to gaze at the Big Dipper.

I turn off my light,
Looking at the sight,
Oh how I love the night.
Maria Becharas, Grade 8
St Hugo of the Hills School, MI

My Phoenix

I know someone who is beautiful
Hair is lake brown
curled with streaks of vanilla
Eyes are summer leaves
Book of poetry in left hand
Love and honesty in right
Inside, she is the phoenix
Image of strength and power
Heart beating, beating, just like a drum
A drum with which we both dance to
A dance that is simple yet complicated
A dance that claims one to the other
Nothing can freeze the phoenix's dance
No one can claim this phoenix

For she has already been claimed
For her claimer is the mallet
She is the drum
Always together
Working side by side
Together as one and one together

Forever
William Redd, Grade 8
Lincoln Middle School, IN

The Chase

My beagle tracks
the scent of a rabbit
through the bushes,
across the barren field,
and under the thick brush.

Buried in the weeds
the rabbit
conceals itself,
attempting to puzzle
my companion.
Suddenly, the hare bounds
across the field
then dashes out of sight.

Without a trace,
that cottontail is gone.
Tristen Watts, Grade 7
Westside Catholic Jr High School, IN

Ode to Grandpa

you entered this world
knowing your love
and left it knowing the same
Grandpa
it was fun to know you
and hard to let you go
Grandpa
I had no choice
God is greater than the power I have
Grandpa I wanted you for myself but
God wins between me and Him
Grandpa I can't wait to see you in heaven
but until I get there guide me
Grandpa
without you I am nothing
I love you and miss you lots
I hope to see you soon
Bethany Neel, Grade 8
West Side Middle School, IN

The Simple Task

Your life may seem dark
Like the devil's left his mark
You're depressed
Like you're not blessed
You've lost all hope
You're at the end of your rope
But God can make way
In your disarray
All you have to do is ask
It's just a simple task
Get on your knees and pray
And God will take your cares away
Ivette Ruban, Grade 8
Ruth Murdoch Elementary School, MI

Black

Black is a dark secret,
Kept deep in your mind,
The color of space,
Black is blind.

A horrific nightmare,
Sadness and shame,
Oozing dark tar,
Suffering without pain.

Thundering storms,
Are the color of black,
A shriek in the night,
A slinking black cat.

Depression is Black,
Screaming your name,
From deep in your mind,
Black plays its game.
Alexa Ross, Grade 7
Perry Middle School, MI

Schoolwork

My math is not yet finished
My history not quite done
The others are out playing
This isn't very fun.

In spelling I have a question
My writing is too hard
This English is so tricky
I have to stay on guard.

Vocabulary is boring
It takes so very long
Reading isn't very hard
It's just to get it done.

But summer is now coming
And I can hardly wait
Hearing the last school bell ring
And I'll be through the gate.
Ruby Miller, Grade 7
West Hastings School, IN

No Longer

You are no longer with me
I am no longer filled with glee.
I cried the day you went away,
I hate that you no longer live today.
I loved the way we used to play,
I no longer live this way.
I can no longer see you tomorrow,
my life is only filled with sorrow.
Johnathon Attkisson, Grade 8
West Side Middle School, IN

The Big Catch

The sun rises and the whispering winds howl,
And birds begin to chirp as I knew it was the start of a beautiful day.
As I begin to suit up for the day outside,
I ask my mom can I, can I, can I go fishing
The words hang on shout from my mother's facial expressions.
I wait and wait for the phone beep the end, as soon as I hear the beep
I'm nipping at her shoulders with the question of can I go, can I go fishing,
I wait and finally I hear the words I want to hear and
Of course as all moms say, "Be safe and don't get into any trouble."

With rugged shoes I stretch out for the metal rod that will soon be my only friend on the clear lake.
The first cast is out and I swiftly reel it back in to see if the fish I dreamed of was at the end.
Many hours go by and the motion of casting reeling is stuck in my head,
But the only other thing I need is that fish.
Casting and reeling, casting and reeling, casting and reeling from dusk to dawn.
My final couple of casts are coming and I throw out one cast and nothing.
Here comes my last cast let's make it a good one, I say to myself, "This will be the fish."
I cast it out and I feel something the fish I wanted,
I reel it in and it's the shoe I lost a week ago,
But I have to remember there's always tomorrow.

AJ Neu, Grade 8
St Barnabas School, IN

Mondays

Waking up and going to school, Mondays are definitely not cool.
If I had my own way, I would ban Monday as a day.
I'd probably leave the spot empty, because we already have plenty.
If you go to school will always depend, whether or not you want to see a friend.
Weekends are always so deceiving, because Monday is soon to come and you're left grieving.
English, History, Math, and Science, I'd much rather show noncompliance.
Lunch is the only thing I look forward to on a Monday, but it's always much better on a Sunday.
All day long, so much homework, but at the end of the day there is always a perk.
Going to class, and hearing a long speech, I'd much rather be in California relaxing on the beach.
Looking at the bell, waiting for it to ring, wondering about the great things that it will bring.
In math class working with all those numbers, I would love to go home and have a nice slumber.
Junior High is so dreadful and boring, I'd much rather take some friends and go exploring.
Sometimes on Sunday I almost cry, seeing the weekend drift right by.
I hate being cramped up in a classroom, I might just explode and go BOOM.
Spelling tests aren't that hard, but history tests make me feel barred.
All day writing notes, anything that floats the teacher's boat.
When we have those crazy ITBS test, it makes me feel like a mess.
When you think about it, Mondays shouldn't make you feel blue, because you lived one more day anew.
We should be happy we lived another day, even though it had to be Monday.

Nina Woodard, Grade 8
Ruth Murdoch Elementary School, MI

Star Gazer

Serious, Star Gazer stares at the stars, sitting silently staring in silence. The sincere scenery makes him sigh. The sparkling stars sit in Star Gazer's glance. Splitting the sky according to the star constellations, Star Gazer studies the stars in the sky, from star to star never stopping till the stars stop shining.

Star Gazer
Star Gazer
Gazer of the stars
Star Gazer

Ashley Faulkner, Grade 7
West Middle School, MI

High Merit Poems – Grades 7, 8, and 9

The King

Showtime, in L.A. Staples Center,
The king is in the house

The adrenaline gets to him,
And before he knows it,
He's airborne, level with the rim

It's a good feeling,
Looking at the bright reddish-orange rim,
Cameras flashing and everything in slow motion

The crowd witnessing every move,
And the spotlight is on him

Wearing a dark blue "Cleveland 23" jersey,
Pride is not in doubt

But the players wearing white jerseys
Have a weird feeling in their stomachs
Knowing what lies before them

The crowd stands up when
He jumps like that,
And before they know it,
He's at the rim, throwing
It down with authority.

Elijah Huff, Grade 8
Kingsway Christian School, IN

Soldier Support

An injured soldier lay on the ground,
Crying in agony as bullets flew through the air.
Others fell around him but there was not a sound,
No one stopped to help the soldier and no one gave a care.

I woke up with a jolt and sweat on my face,
The image stayed in my mind with a battered heart.
At least at school I would be in a happy place,
I was ready for the day to start.

The image came back as we were making crafts,
They were for the soldiers across the sea.
I sat silently for a while, I heard nothing, no laughs,
How could I help them more, they're fighting for me?

I put my heart into this card as well as my soul,
It was the least I could do to put a smile over there.
I put hearts, smiles, a thank you, this card was my goal,
I went home quickly and got on my knees in prayer.

There was the soldier again, but different this time,
He was with someone holding him up with a card in his hand.
It was then that I realized what had helped him to climb,
Just my little card gave him the support to smile and stand.

Danata Paulino, Grade 8
St Charles School, MI

Best Friends

We laugh so hard we cry
And we mutter hurtful things

We fight so much, it's hard to believe
That we have stayed friends all this time

If I were you I wouldn't have forgiven me
For all the horrible things I have done to you

And yet, somehow the more we fight
The stronger our friendship

We can tell each other everything
Then turn around and talk about each other

Typical teenage girls
But while most don't stay friends, we still deal with each other

People start to wonder how we are friends
But we know that it won't change anytime soon

We are best friends
We know everything about each other

We will always fight
But we will always know from the inside that we are best friends.

Olivia Roedel, Grade 8
Fowlerville Junior High School, MI

Missing Moments

Cancer:
Noun.
A malignant and invasive growth or tumor.
Because of cancer I lost my grandmother and my best friend.

It will take you at any age.
In her case, 64.
It's way too young to die.

She lost so many moments with me.
Getting glasses,
Braces,
Winning contests,
Days laying in the sun soaking up vitamin D,
And the most important celebration: my Bat mitzvah.

She will never see me get married
Or have my first child.
These are moments everyone should live to see.

I see her in the casket:
Face blank,
Eyes closed,
Never to open them again.

Rebecca Bloom, Grade 8
West Hills Middle School, MI

A Celebration of Poets – Great Lakes Grades 4-12 Spring 2011

Me, Myself, I

I look
Look around
Wonder why
Why they yell
Yell at me, my brother, my sister
Do they know?
The pain they cause?
Is it, anger, regret?
That's why
I must
Must go
Break away and fly
To somewhere I can't hear them
Somewhere they can't cause pain
Somewhere, where I can't hear the regret and anger, in their voices
Just somewhere
Somewhere
I can be
Me
Myself
I

Caitlin Matney, Grade 9
Trillium Academy, MI

Ode to the Sun

Oh, what would the world be without you?
Probably dark, dull, sad…
Everything wouldn't be here without you.

You bring us life, the feeling of heaven,
Where everyone is smiling, because of your gift.
The gift of warmth, underneath my skin

There wouldn't be any summer fun without you,
Cool, pool water and hot, mushy sand.
All of that would be gone.

Oh, what would the world be without you?
Probably dark, dull, sad…
Everything wouldn't be here without you.

Kristyn Cook, Grade 8
West Side Middle School, IN

You Come Too

You come too
Come with me to my hiding place
You come too
Come with me to the crisp air of early morning
You come too
Come with me to the land I call home
You come too
Come with me to the cool fog of freedom
You come too
Come with me to the country

Noel Milliman, Grade 8
Bloomingdale Middle School, MI

The Best Work of Art

Life is a blank page,
Waiting to become a work of art.
We are the artists,
Starting off with nothing,
But through time,
Creating something magical.
Our lives are filled with wonders and excitement,
Just like a work of art.
Some people take hold of the brush with confidence and pride.
Others take advantage and never get to see the final product.
Sometimes the angles will be off,
Or the wrong color in the wrong spot,
There is no such thing as a perfect picture,
There is always going to be mistakes,
You just have to make them into something beautiful.
So when you run out of room on the page,
And the art is finished,
You will be proud of the picture you left behind.

Samantha Sanders, Grade 7
Royal Oak Middle School, MI

Where Will I Be?

Fifteen years from now I hope to complete law school
I wish to be smart and not a fool
I wish to go to Duke and play football
Maybe on a scholarship, so I don't have to pay it all
I don't need to be famous, just maybe well known
I'd like to have a wife, kids, and a beautiful home
I will be an attorney, and a good one I swear
Be cool, calm, collective, and let nothing get in my hair.
I'll be able to look everyone in the eye
Always tell the truth and never a lie
If I play football I'll give it my heart to be the best
Work my hardest so I can beat the rest
Be a good safety, maybe win a Super Bowl
And to the game I will give my heart and soul
Either way success is my only goal
Won't make bad decisions, won't pay the toll
I'll shout it out loud so everyone hears
This is where I'll be in fifteen years

Joey Jenkins, Grade 7
Royal Oak Middle School, MI

In the Dark

In the dark
Yet it is light
But all I feel is cold
In the dark I feel alone and hope someone will find me
I sit here wanting to just be saved
I miss the way things used to be
And now they have had to change
So I sit here
In the dark
Waiting to be saved

Jazlyn Fox, Grade 8
West Side Middle School, IN

High Merit Poems – Grades 7, 8, and 9

Heart to Heart

The first beat of
Life. So tiny and fragile. Innocent and
unknowing of the troubles

of the world. It grows rapidly with its owner,
pulsing with excitement.
That unforgettable rhythm

pounds in every chest.
The issues it's born with are at times unbearable.
However, it always finds a way

to keep itself going.
But with issues or not, it was made
and formed perfectly,

It beats from the beginning and will beat
to the very last
moment

Of a long and
fulfilled life.

Aislyn Galford, Grade 8
Kingsway Christian School, IN

The Melting of Life

Life is ice cream
So many colors and flavors
Many good
But many many more bad
Life is ice cream
It melts and it is gone forever
Some melt faster than others
But eventually all of our ice cream melts
Life is ice cream
In our life, we find a perfect ice cream to be with
We play
We talk
We are there for each other when we are sad
Then when we age
Both of our ice cream will melt together in peace
Life is ice cream

Cody Moyer, Grade 7
Royal Oak Middle School, MI

Basketball

B asketball is an amazing sport
C ounting down the steps until you get to the hoop
D efending and marking up players so they won't score
E ven getting the rebounds, and taking it up the court
F ouling out when you have to
G etting the ball and passing it to someone else
H aving to stop playing when the buzzer from the clock goes off
I am then going and shaking hands with the other team

Juan Cardoza, Grade 8
West Side Middle School, IN

Where I Am From

I am from a little green house
   with daffodils and tulips.
I am from love and laughter;
   fun and happy times.
I am from good ol' folks
   and the land of leprechauns.

I am from blue eyes and green;
   redheads and freckles.
I am from Laura and Mark
   and from what's yours is mine.
I am from a blessed union
   shared by two hearts.

I am from "My Old Kentucky Home"
   and songs of the south.
I am from the Irish of my Mummum
   and the southern grace
of the green grass and rolling hills of Kentucky.

Allison Brothers, Grade 8
St Barnabas School, IN

Basketball

Basketball
Fast running
Out of breath
Running down the court
I dribble past the defenders
Leaping in the sky
I hope to make it especially from the free throw line
I close my eyes and start to fly
Palmed the ball in my hand stretching for the rim
The ball goes through the hoop and we win the game
Everyone is very happy including me
They put me up on their shoulders as we celebrate
This night will never end
We just won the championship game.

Alex Algee, Grade 7
St Bartholomew School, IN

Thank You Mom

Mom, you are very special to me
I love you as can be
You are caring, loving (no matter what), funny and sweet
You are also very tidy and neat
Thank you for all you've done
I am glad that we have a strong bond
For I can tell you anything
Our bond is also stronger than ever
I know it'll last forever
Mom, I admire you and I think you are great
There's nothing about you that I could ever hate
I also have one more thing to say…
I hope that you have a wonderful Mother's Day!

Kayla Hodges, Grade 7
Wagar Jr High School, MI

Ode to the Super Bowl

It's that time again when friends meet and greet
And can be very bittersweet as they bet against one another
As they don their old jerseys and put on their colors
As they root all around the nation from sideline to side chair
And some people even pull out their hair from excitement and cheer
Which could be from drinking a little too much beer
But when the Super Bowl starts, everyone cheers
But not for the teams, as it may seem
They cheer for the commercials, both funny and cool
And once it's all over…
They wait 'till next year!

Matthew Homsy, Grade 8
Grosse Pointe Academy, MI

To John Lennon

John Lennon you were good
With the Beatles you made history
Alone you said always dream
You sing to the ones you see in the light and dark
You're with singing legends, singing with them
Alone or not you made music what it is today
You died unexpectedly, no one would have thought
Now you sing for you and for all of history
Since you have been gone you've inspired me
Now I will take the next step and take your advice and dream
John Lennon made history you will always have me dreaming

Eric Holt, Grade 8
West Side Middle School, IN

Blank Soccer

Soccer is life.
Soccer is sweaty.
Soccer is slippery.
Soccer is itchy.
Soccer is winning.
Soccer is like a party when you get a goal.
Soccer is like a headache when some guy trips you.
Soccer is like noisy birds as the crowds go wild.
Soccer can be like wild animals when the team tries to get the ball in the goal.
Soccer is as fun as swimming in the river.

Kalyn Frizzell, Grade 7
South Spencer Middle School, IN

Grandpa

Oh how the good times come and go.
Standing at the foot of your bed,
Watched you take your last breath.
Now it's time for you to go.
You spread happiness and joy,
The cancer played you just like a toy.
It came, it went, it came, you went.
Your passing left a dent.
Oh how the good times come and go.

Gabby Warner, Grade 8
West Side Middle School, IN

Sand Swept

Misty air fills my lungs,
Icy water laps at my skin,
Seagulls hover above my head,
Ice cream melts in tiny rivers onto the sand,
Beach-goers display their paint-box towels,
And sunbathe until the shower-filled clouds gather,
Palm trees tower over the glossy sand,
And the breeze whispers against my toes,
I am at the beach,
With the sand on my feet and the palm trees tower over my head.
A mere speck, on the sand-swept shore.

Serena Alway, Grade 7
Stanley Clark School, IN

The Beach

The sun is shining on my face
The water is glimmering on my skin
The breeze is cool against my neck
The smell of ocean tickles my nose
The feeling of seaweed as it touches my hand
The feeling of a beach is unforgettable
The way the water makes you calm
The way the sand keeps you warm
The way the sun shines off the water
The way the water is clear and blue
The feeling of a beach is unforgettable

Olivia DeMarco, Grade 8
Sacred Heart Elementary School, MI

Fight

FIGHT

Whenever someone says cancer
Everyone shivers in fright

Could you imagine a world where all are content
And no one has to die from that terrible sickness
Never cower away from a word

WIN

Dustie Pier, Grade 8
Culver Community Middle School, IN

Buddy

Buddy is my favorite dog
I never ever would like any other
My dog is special
Funny
And most of all, overactive
He is my friend and I'm his
But he still puzzles me
At why I can't figure out
That he has his own personality
But he's still my favorite dog

Colin Sollars, Grade 7
Oak Hill Jr High School, IN

Paintballing Battle

Empty the contents of your bag,
And get ready for capture the flag.
Put on your goggles and your mask,
Slip on your vest for the coming task.
Get your ammo and load your gun,
And now for the count, 3, 2, 1, RUN!
Race to your base over the hill,
And post some guards with superior skill.
Now run with your squad into no man's land,
Make them move stealthily by your command.
Finally the call goes up from teammate Jeremy,
He looks and exclaims, "It's the enemy!"
Duck behind some trees and brush,
To catch the enemy off guard with a rush.
As they quietly walk around,
Aim your guns without a sound.
Pull the trigger and watch paint fly,
And knock them all down, every last guy.
Now you find the flag, so go back were you came,
And dance with victory, you have won the game!

Christian Long, Grade 8
Ruth Murdoch Elementary School, MI

Time

Time is something we can't control.
Every second goes by quicker than a blink of an eye.
Every minute is consistent like a metronome.
Sixty beats make up an hour,
Twenty-four of those make up a day.
Before you know it,
It'll be tomorrow.
Today will be yesterday
And yesterday will be forgotten.
All the laughing and crying,
All the memories and treasures
Will be lost in time.
We all reminisce about our past
Because we can't bring it back.
But in the time to come,
We are left with endless possibilities
To dream, adventure, and live.
For better or for worse,
We'll have to wait and see.
Time is something we can't control.

Xinlei Zhu, Grade 8
West Hills Middle School, MI

Without You

Days without you are like days without the sun
The darkness is a pain that makes me want to run
But when I see your face
Everything falls back into place
Then I'm back in your arms
Forever and always safe from harms

Sierra Purcell, Grade 9
Lakeview Jr/Sr High School, IN

Seasonal Changes

Summer
Hot, humid
Buzzing, humming, singing
Blooming into warmth
Hearing the buzzing of the bees in summer.

Fall
Chilly, pretty
Changing, blowing, swirling
Colorful leaves
Sweet smells of hot apple pies and warm, cinnamon donuts
Seeing the maple trees in our wonderful neighborhood change
To fall, right before our eyes.

Winter
Cold, icy
Freezing, chilling, piercing
Icicles hanging everywhere, in the below-zero air
Breathing in the smoke of the fire, in winter.

Spring
Flowers, gardens
Warming, raining, springing into action
Turning white coldness into green beauty
Smelling all of the freshly-sprouted tulips

Jessica Lynn Wells, Grade 7
Cedar Springs Middle School, MI

One Last Chance*

In an instant,
Everything can change.
A baby is born
A soldier dies
Trees become bare,
And flowers begin to bloom.

It seems as if
The second
We close our eyes,
We miss something.
We missed the butterfly, fluttering
Above our heads.
The robin hatchling, crack it's flamboyant
Blue shell, with its minuscule beak.

In a flash,
We wish we had more time.
More time to be with the one
We love.
More time to cherish the memories.

And in a blink of an eye,
We miss our chance.

Emma Fellows, Grade 8
West Hills Middle School, MI
*Dedicated to my Grandma Marilyn who passed away 4/7/11

Colors

Shades of blues,
Hues of greens,
Painting out a colorful scene.

Yellows, purples, oranges, reds,
But no black or white,
They're waiting for night,

When the moon is out,
Then they come out to play.
And the colors slowly, fade away.

Until the sun comes out again,
That's when the colors come back.
And in their presence you will find, beauty does not lack.

For shades of blues and hues of greens,
Yellows, purples, oranges, reds,
Dance, spin, and twirl about, painting a picture in my head.

Sydney Abbott, Grade 7
Oak Hill Jr High School, IN

S.S. Dreamscape

In the dark of the night a storm brews in the sky
I hear it in my dreams; in my bed, snug and dry
Just as gentleman sleep descends slow over me
A ship's bowsprit bows low to clasp hands with the sea

The stars hold the gentle clouds in the dark and night
Just as they hold the masts in my ship's northward flight
The wind tears at the roof top with howls and screams
But even the wind cannot rouse me from my dreams

For raindrops tell great stories of sailors and ships
Where they once fell down as mere droplets and drips
When the dark spewing clouds fill the drain pipes with hail
In my dream air is filling up billowing sails

Maria Styma, Grade 9
Posen Consolidated High School, MI

My Dream

A snow white unicorn of my own, I dream of it nightly.
With its unicorn horn towering high,
shining like a star so brightly.
Thinking as I lie.

I would never deny.
I would ride it into the night so lightly.
Every night it would sing me a lullaby.

I wish this adventure would come to me daily.
I would hope it would never die,
and when it disappears I would think of it silently,
goodbye, goodbye.

Marie Drogt, Grade 7
Ebenezer Christian School, MI

The Cherokees' Tears

When the act was being signed that night they did not even know
They would be leaving their homes they loved, not wanting to go
The Cherokees were the last to leave
They had no more tricks up their sleeves
They started to walk on a cold winter's night
Some left behind to die no longer to see light
Walking barefooted crying and cold
They were guarded by soldiers like sheep that had been sold
Many thought they would thrive
But over 4,000 did not survive
They had no water shelter or food
The soldiers were not in a very good mood
The people tried to stay strong
Asking the question "What did we do wrong?"
They were punished by one signature, that's it
No more Cherokees with their strong wit
Their ancestors try to go on some more
This signature they continue to feel to the core

Madyson Davenport, Grade 9
Wainwright Middle School, IN

I Wish for Summer

I wish for summer now and then,
I wish for summer again and again
For warmth and rain and sticky flip-flops
For ice cream and shorts and colorful tank tops
I miss chlorine-filled pools and mosquito bites,
I'd much rather have them than blizzards all night
I miss the playing in the park,
And I miss catching lightning bugs after dark
The parades, the beach,
The sand in my feet
No school, tan skin,
And hot, humid wind
Pink sunsets, green leaves
And climbing tall trees
I wish for summer's hot, midday sun
I wish for summer, but it is far from begun
I guess I'll just have to wait 'till then,
Until summer comes again

Mary Blewitt, Grade 8
St John the Evangelist School, IN

A Completely New Look

Wash, trim, cut
Hair falling on the floor
Wash, trim, cut
Getting shorter with every snip
Wash, trim, cut
Millimeters then inches
Wash, trim, cut
My hair is piled on the floor
Wash, trim, cut
A completely new look when I see myself in the mirror

Natalie Fowler, Grade 7
West Middle School, MI

Different

Everyone is unique,
In every way.

Everyone is unique,
That's okay.

Everyone is unique,
That's what we know.

Everyone is unique,
I know so.

I am matchless from you,
You are exclusive from me.

Every person is different,
I certainly agree.

We are all uncommon, one of a kind,
There is no match, not one that you'll find.

We are all different,
That's okay.

Everyone is unique,
In every way.
Katie Leigh Dotson, Grade 7
Fowlerville Junior High School, MI

My Mirror

To organize, to classify thoughts
As mirrored eyes stare at me
Poking, probing at everything I do,
Our hidden mistakes fly out at you
But you try to take me away
From the direction I see ahead

A highlighted trajectory waits for you
My useless thoughts; my twisted soul
Marks what you will never come to know
Your echoed scream taunts violently
My negligence corrodes your mind,
Guide me back to life that never heals

Girl looking back at me
Do not fade or look away
Our eyes will burn through the mirror,
Holding us safe inside, Together
You know the way; and I have the time
To run in patterns we've already gone

I believe in you blue eyed girl
And I know we'll make it out
Of the maze in the mirror
Whitney Hopkins, Grade 8
Culver Community Middle School, IN

Secret Depths of the Heart

My heart is like the ocean
Growing deeper as you go
Discovering many secrets
Finding feelings that will grow
My pride is like a bird
Soaring through the sky
Taking sudden turns
But still remaining high
My Smile is like a tree
Growing bigger every day
And when I get chopped down
I know I'll be okay
Because you're by my side
Every moment, everywhere
I can always count on you
To guide me anywhere
Laura E. Wesley, Grade 9
Wapahani High School, IN

Father to Son

Son…
Listen to your elders son…
For they know more.
They know what's right.
You son do not…
They know what's wrong.
You son do not…

You should respect your elders son.
For you are young…
And they are not.
You don't ask yourself for help, my son.
That is what your elders are for…
Help.
Always ask for help…
My son.
Greg Tippmann, Grade 8
St Charles School, IN

Tree Frog

I hop around from tree to tree,
croaking through the summer's breeze.
Swamps are places that I live,
fills the woods with joy and thrill.
With my feet they help me cling,
then again I sing and sing.
Hopping around is what I do,
it's lots of fun for me and you.
As my days pass by and by,
I leap up into the majestic sky.
Being a frog is lots of fun,
laying under the mighty sun.
My voice is shrilling, happy and bright,
hopping through the summer night.
Bailey Kolenda, Grade 8
Rockford Christian School, MI

My Life

I am white.
I have gold hair.

I am fourteen.
I have pets.

I am a person.
I have brothers.

I am a sister.
I have friends.

I am a girl.
I have loved.

I am proud.
Rebekah Walters, Grade 8
Covington Middle School, IN

Mr. Unknown

He jokes
Unknowing
The death
Of his words
And the loss
Of spirit that
The prey
Receives.
The prey
Of the punished,
Are punished by
The reminiscing
Words in their heads,
The words
Of
Mr. Unknown
Josie Wanner, Grade 8
St Barnabas School, IN

Thoughts

Wise words of wisdom,
and pointless paraphernalia,
run circles around my head,
like kids in a track meet.

Ignoring them is not an option
a lucky but rare understanding
like a college textbook,
so complex and technical.

I don't even comprehend these
whispering voices,
omniscient words of wisdom,
that make up my thoughts.
Madelyn Strycker, Grade 8
Culver Community Middle School, IN

No Man Lives

No man lives
to truly know oneself, but
they have to look at another.   By

seeing others ordinarily,
sparks something unique.

To truly know oneself,
they have to look at the past.   The

one who knows nothing of the past
times will have no future.

To truly know oneself,
they have to feel darkness.   Fear of

the darkness of the body,
the darkness of the mind,
the darkness of the soul.

To truly know oneself,
they have to know   the pain of

either side of the
thin veil that is   death.

Tristan Fuller, Grade 8
Rockford Christian School, MI

How to Be a Bibliophile

Do you sing?

No I don't sing
I don't dance
I don't act
I don't play sports
I don't do anything
Or do I...

The pages of the book turn
And I absorb the word on the pages
I'm in a foreign world

Turn the page...

In the middle of the desert
Underwater by a shark
Running through the woods from murderers

Turn the page...

Books can take me
Anywhere
And in a book I can do
Anything

Blaire Coleman, Grade 8
Kingsway Christian School, IN

Snow

The snow is light and glimmering
The sparkle draws my eye
It hides the barren ground
As it falls from the sky

It alights upon my nose
And I laugh with delight
It is as light as feathers
On this cold, winter night

It falls now so softly
That I can hardly hear
That fine, white powder
As it drifts past my ear

I stick out my tongue
And there the snowflakes land
Melt to water, freeze to ice
Now gritty as the sand

This cold, frozen wasteland
Can hardly have a scent
But the air smells crisp and chill
I hope it won't relent

So now what is glimmering and soft and light and cold? Snow.

Colleen Dosch, Grade 7
Christ the King School, IN

Seasons

Spring the time when all the trees bud
And when the ground is mushy with mud
When the farmers go out to plow
It's very important to know how.

Next is Summer working hard
Like mowing lots and lots of yard
Also helping with the hay
Nice to rest in the shade.

And when the corn grows nice and tall
Almost ready to harvest, then comes Fall
Bringing in corn and tomatoes
And lots of squash, pumpkins, and potatoes.

Apples, peaches, and green beans
And cherries, plums, and gourds can be seen
Next is Winter, so very cold
Sometimes the ice and snow get so old.

But there is also fun things to do
Like ice skating and sleighing too
That sure is amazing how God plans
And all the rain and snow he sends.

Mary Viola Knepp, Grade 7
Green Acres School, IN

My Pencil

Today was the worst day yet, I thought my day was set.
The thing I used to appall became the most valuable thing of all.
Today when I was leaving the bus, I must have left my pencil through all the fuss.
I didn't even realize my loss, or even the fact that my shirt was stained with sauce.
But when it was time for the test, I wasn't at my best.
It felt that I searched for it everywhere known to man; but I realized that I had looked only in my tin can.
Before I even realized it the bell began to ring, the chain reaction made my heart sting.
As the teacher was picking up tests, she looked at me confused as she stopped by my desk.
To make the long story short, I got detention and that sort.
I ended up missing soccer practice that day, as I sat in detention wiping my tears away.
I walked home with my head down, as I carried on my face the biggest frown.
All because of that silly pencil, that striped blue and orange utensil.
All of a sudden I heard my mother's voice, for some odd reason my heart did not rejoice.
I looked around but the setting was totally different, the place looked just like my comfy basement.
I wiped my eyes once more, this time I clearly saw my room door.
But I came to realize that it was all just a dream, a dream about my pencil and me.
Never again never will I, forget the pencil that made me once cry.
My pencil and I my pencil and me, together forever through all quizzes in school we will be.

Joy Ngugi, Grade 8
Ruth Murdoch Elementary School, MI

Thanks

I believe thanks is in order for all the wonderful things I have:
The fresh air full of bright blue skies, and warm windy weather.
For my bed, inviting and comfortable for me to sleep on every night.
The dinner I have on the table every night made with Mom's great home cooking touch.
My furball dog, Frodo, who's always ready to play and run.
The home I have to stay in where I am always safe and content.
The PS3, pool table, piano, and guitar, because without these I would be bored to death.
All my friends and memories I'll cherish forever (some more than others.)
My school (unluckily, yes boring as it is) where I can get an education to prepare me for the future.
All the sports I can play to my heart's desire. Football, basketball, soccer (woohoo!), and everything else.
Let's not forget music with every beat that rocks the nation (or rap or country or blues).
All the miraculous medical technology we have available to help everyone.
Natural gifts giving us the power to do whatever we want to do.
I take all this for granted every day, where others across the world have almost nothing of anything.
Where you can't say, do, or be what you want because of fear, poverty, oppression, and disease.
Think about it today before you start to say something is unfair,
Remember what you do have and be thankful that you have it.

Mikey Reeves, Grade 8
St Barnabas School, IN

Sports

Football is a wonderful sport to throw, kick, and score. The first touchdown 7 points. It's fun, even though the game is hardcore.

Now soccer just the same but no throwing with your hands (even though that may be lame) just your feet to pass kick and score, this sport may be not hard core. But fun as can be even with just two people maybe even you and me.

Baseball as I hit a home run, the bat slams the ball but as the ball falls I'm already back to home plate. With the winning score, my team jumps up, and says I'm the best, I say, no, there's no I in team, then I go home to rest.

Now basketball, what can I say, everyone knows it's the best sport in this generation today, as I hit a three, score a free-throw or drive it in for a easy lay up, my heart starts pounding, I take a deep breath to find myself passed out asleep, now it's time to get up, I run out side and guess what I did, what's that you say, yes, grabbed a basketball to play with today for the rest of the day.

Jessica Peterson, Grade 7
West Side Middle School, IN

Death

You can cry that she is dead or be happy that she is alive.
You can close your eyes and hope she's there when you open them,
or you can open your eyes and see all she has left.
Your heart can be empty because she is not there for you or be
filled with love you had for her.
You can forget about today and live yesterday, or be happy for
tomorrow because of yesterday.
You can only remember that she is gone, or cherish memories
and let it live on.
You can cry, close your mind, be empty and turn your back,
or you can do what she'd want you to do: Smile, open your eyes,
Love and go on.
Death is not the biggest loss in our lives; it's what dies inside of
us while we live.
So as sorrow passes over the families fate has hit, we soon
grow over the death, Love again, but we will never forget those
who have passed.
As I type this poem, tears stream down my face as I think of
how she suffered.

Gino Costantini, Grade 7
Fowlerville Junior High School, MI

Time to Say Goodbye

You share many years
You shed many tears
You share many laughs; you two are halves
You understand each other like no other
Then time goes by
Then they leave
Oh how I grieve
I'll miss you so much
Let's stay in touch
Let's not forget or regret all of this
It's hard to move on now that you're gone
I have no choice I hear another voice
But just remember you won't be replaced like a tube of paste
I'll leave you in my heart even though we're apart
But for now I must say goodbye

Grace Yoon, Grade 8
Ruth Murdoch Elementary School, MI

Who I Am

I am
Cheerful, gleeful, delightful.
Showing the world my smile as I laugh.
Showing respect is important to me.
Kindness is important to me.
Being truthful is important to me.
Happiness is no crime.
Dishonesty is wrong, but useful for cheaters.
People are getting crueler.
The truth is buried too deep.
All we need is joy.
I am

Paige Robinson, Grade 7
St John Lutheran School, MI

Swinging for the Stars

Under our endless summer skies we swing life away,
Every night we would kick our legs and shoot for Mars.
We lay in the grass and watch the cloudless day,
Every second of sunlight seemed to fade away the scars.

Countless hours filled with our favorite bands,
Every song we played was never left unsung.
Every day we left summer's foundation as it stands,
That night recapping the time that we had swung.

Summer was constantly held up by chains and plastic,
As we pushed ourselves to race the inevitable sunset.
Waking up each day just a little more enthusiastic,
Making countless mistakes we were unable to stet.

Back and forth we sway, the wind runs through our hair,
During that summer not one of us could be held by bars.
And we keep on singing as if we never had a care,
Come next summer we will be swinging for the stars.

Stephen Lyon, Grade 9
Dewitt High School, MI

The Brother I Never Knew*

The brother I never knew
I wish I could bring you back just to meet you
Could the stars bring you back
Could my heart bring you back
My love is too strong to even think about that
You died on my birthday
When I found out it really hurt me
I had just turned three
Too bad I never got to meet you
We would have been close too
I wish life would flow into you
So I can give you a kiss
I'ma really miss you!

Lyric Bell, Grade 7
Hally Magnet Middle School, MI
*R.I.P. Quinton June 14, 1983 - June 15, 2001

Time Twister

As time runs out…
The clock ticks mocking our people in shame.
Laughing till the last tick…
Waiting till we're all happy…ruining time.
Precious time lost.
Happy memories lost in the ticking of the clock…
Hopes dissolve.
Friends disappear.
What is this?
The dark timing of despair and fear.
Is time falling into a twisting nether?
We're seeping deeper into a black hole…
Tick, Tick, Tick, Tick, Tick…

Tanner Wathen, Grade 7
South Spencer Middle School, IN

High Merit Poems – Grades 7, 8, and 9

He's Always There for Me

He's always there for me,
With a smile on his face,
Or just sitting there laughing at his own jokes.
But sometimes I forget, ignore, or cherish
Those special times I share with my brother.
His scruffy brown hair and bright blue eyes,
And a smile that just makes your day.
But our relationship is like the weather,
You never know when the lighting is going to strike.
You never know,
when the sun's going to come out.
When we fight I feel like hiding,
Like a turtle sliding into its shell.
But eventually the turtle comes back out,
And eventually we make up.
My brother is like a tree.
It never stops growing,
But in his case he will
Never,
Stop,
Loving me.

Danielle Sherman, Grade 8
West Hills Middle School, MI

I Am Who I Am

I am not the prettiest
I am not the most popular
I am not a "chip of the old block"
But I am who I am and I am proud to be
The band geek who is in love with Pep Band
I am proud to be the girl who wants to learn
I am proud to be the girl who believes Marching Band is a sport
I am proud to be athletically inept in anything
I am proud to be a multiple instrument musician
I am proud to be the girl who compliments everyone
I am proud to be the girl who finds joy in reading
I am proud to be the girl who spazzes during movie credits
The girl who loves riding on airplanes
The girl who lives on note cards
The girl who will wait for her prince
Because I am who I am and this is me

Alexa Gail Colinco, Grade 7
Center Grove Middle School Central, IN

Springtime

In springtime when the days are clear
The birdies chirpings we do hear
When warm showers and sun are seen
The pastures and the grass turn green
the butterflies flutter in the air
The children love the weather so fair
When plowing the garden and planting seeds
Then it's not long till we fight the weeds.

Hannah Wittmer, Grade 7
Green Acres School, IN

Tears of the Rainbow

If you're not the same color as me and my friends,
then you don't know the feeling of harsh reprimands,
and you don't know the crackle of a leather-made whip,
or the marks left behind when you catch the tip.

You don't know the feeling,
or the heavy heart beating sound,
when the horses come reeling,
large white bed sheets all around.

You don't know the struggle,
or the horrible fight,
to rush from safe house to safe house
through the cover of night.

You don't know the feeling,
but you know that it's true,
to be stared at and looked at
as if you were in a zoo.

Roy Benjamin Jenkins, Grade 8
Castle South Middle School, IN

Eternal

Since when was it said, that from all great things,
Some part of it had to be lost…
Terrified of our hearts becoming one,
I tried to let our bodies fill the void,
I tried to mask my fears,
But still,
Every single one of those days,
You were still there,
You were still there, in my heart…
If we could have shared a deep love,
I thought,
Even if someday,
Our time here were to end,
I could imagine I'd be loving you for all eternity…

Nicole Brockway, Grade 7
Westville Middle School, IN

Basketball

What is basketball?
A contact sport.
A strategic series of 5-on-5 match ups.
Something that requires dedication and motivation.
A working process.
A game that can lead to success.
Something people can base their lives on.
Something that can cause heartbreaks and champions.
Something that is only mastered after years of practice.
A hobby and a job.
A life-changing experience.
That is basketball.

Tyler Kivela, Grade 7
St John Lutheran School, MI

Broken Puzzle
Pieces are put together but also fall apart.
Once a person you love is sick the puzzle slowly falls apart.
While sitting by their bed holding onto their hand, it cracks and you cry knowing you're losing them.

Side by side, hand to hand, knowing it's their last, your puzzle is now in half
180 out of 360 and you know it won't go back. I guess it was suppose to represent
My heart because I knew he wouldn't be back.

I know he loved us all a lot and we all loved him too.
He was like superman and surprised us when we were blue.
But now our puzzle is broken, the puzzle that represented our hearts.
He meant the world to us and he will never be forgot.

Taylor Price, Grade 7
South Spencer Middle School, IN

Nature's Beauty
High above me, I feel the trees tower, like a Goliath, they stand there for years, with tales of long ago.
The sun shines above me, I feel it warm my skin, it's a light for the entire world,
it sits silently, not a sound it makes.
The waves of the ocean, magnificent and graceful, they rise and fall again,
as they journey to far off lands for the rest of the world to discover.
The majestic mountains, with beauty unlike any other, rule over the grounds below it,
a queen unlike any other.
I see the clouds high above me, they go unnoticed in our everyday world, as they appear,
and flutter away, and disappear, and anxiously await to be born again.
The beauty of nature is all around, it is out there to enjoy, to discover, a true treasure for the entire world to see.

Daniel McCauley, Grade 8
St. Barnabas School, IN

Just the Beginning
Grab all the stuff,
and head to the car.
You first arrive,
and open the large metal door.
Hear the clank,
and think there's no going back now.

Walking down the long narrow hall,
thinking to yourself, which room's mine.
Finally you're there,
all the faces innocent as yours.
All the groups,
already beginning.

As time progresses,
difficulty increases.
The big projects,
multiple tests in a day.
More responsibility,
more opportunities to make wrong decisions.

It's been so long already,
but I'm only halfway through.
This is just the beginning.

Grant Rafferty, Grade 8
St Barnabas School, IN

To See in Black and White
What if everything were black and white?
If humans were like dogs,
oblivious to the wondrous colors around them.

Sometimes people only see in black and white too,
only noticing the big picture,
not looking into the shaded grey area in the middle
which reveals so much more to a story
than what is just on the cover page.

Some people can see those wondrous colors,
which further inspire them to make the world theirs,
helping to create a path for those who haven't
traveled across the line between the darkness and the light,
to experience those wondrous colors for themselves.

Alas humans are not dogs,
seeing in black and white or color,
is an option.
Seeing those wondrous colors or just darkness
is a choice.
Will you be oblivious or experience the wondrous colors
of life?
Or will you stay hidden in the dark?

Brooke Reiter, Grade 7
Detroit Country Day Middle School, MI

High Merit Poems – Grades 7, 8, and 9

A Battlefield of Love
Hold me tight and close
the warmth I get from you
brush my hair back smooth
hum a beat of tune
take me to a far away place
where nothing comes with pain
a magical mystic place
to sleep upon my protected face
I dream of love and happy endings
thank you god for tending my sendings
Michaela Galaske, Grade 8
West Side Middle School, IN

The Meadow
In the meadow
in the meadow I enjoy so
the tall grass and in the winter the snow
in the meadow the wind blows
and the sun glows
in the meadow birds fly
trees bend and twist in the breeze
rabbits hop hole to hole
as I sit here
and write
Dustin Kerckhove, Grade 7
Stanley Clark School, IN

19 Lines in One Day
19 lines in one day?
What am I supposed to say?
Wheat turns into hay?
Children don't like to play?
My birthday is not in May?
I'd like to stay
Come what may
I still don't know what to say
Because 19 lines in one day
Is too much!
Daniel Ghisolf-Astacio, Grade 8
Ruth Murdoch Elementary School, MI

Jaylin Ivory
You were so young
smart, sweet, and fun.
I'll remember the jokes you told
trying to find life's hold.
The dreadful cancer
took you away from all matters.
You never got to fulfill your dream,
playing basketball so fierce and mean.
Now you're gone but that doesn't matter.
All you need know is I'll love you forever.
Dana Franklin, Grade 8
West Side Middle School, IN

Autumn
The whistling wind blows
And makes the leaves drift,
They float to the ground,
The temperature drops
And flowers wilt
The lack of sunlight and warmth
Killing them slowly,

The trees are bare
And the fallen leave's colors have changed
Red, Orange, Yellow, Green

I embrace the chilly wind as it lashes against my face
Say goodbye to the heat of summer until next year falls upon us
Say hello to the chilly days and the cold nights that lays within the season
Kids run around in sweaters, playing in the leaves

I walk alone
With the leaves crunching beneath my feet

The sky is sunny with no clouds
How could it be so cold with so much sunlight?

The animals gather their necessities, preparing for winter
They run around and play before their annual slumber

This, my friends, is Autumn
Cierra Collins, Grade 8
Alma Middle School, MI

Blue, White
The enormous sky
The gigantic boats on sea
The bunched up clouds
Jacob Hannah, Grade 7
Perry Middle School, MI

Mother
You gave me life.
You gave me courage and hope
to help me accomplish my dreams
which makes me thankful for you.

You gave me trust
and also love
for this makes me a happier person
which makes me thankful for you.

You helped me succeed
and because of this
I'm living my dream
which makes me love you.
Kaila Brusdahl, Grade 8
West Side Middle School, IN

Hot 2 Miles
Faster Anna. Harder.
give it all you have. I need
to run my hardest and dream
my biggest.

It may be hot but it will be over
soon. pass more people one after
other.

Come on there are people cheering for
me. close to the finish line, cheering.
is getting louder. just crossed the
finish line. I did it.

My coaches come up to me. why?
what's wrong? wait…I won?

I proudly walk up on stage, smile, and
receive the medal I have always wanted.
on it, it says:
FIRST.
Anna Horak, Grade 7
St Bartholomew School, IN

Summer
I am summer.
You like me because
I'm warm.
I give you dark, dark tans.
You go to
My beaches on my
"Happy Days."
Tiffany Jaworski, Grade 7
Verona Mills School, MI

Nobody
A nobody can do things,
That are unimaginable…
Different, unique.
And yet…you never notice them.
Just cause you don't get that a nobody…
Can be…
Special.
Michaela O'Hanlon, Grade 8
Christa McAuliffe Middle School, MI

Weather
Cold
Goose bumps, jacket
Snow, ice, shiver
Weather, temperature, wonderness
Sun, run, play
Sweat, shorts
Hot
Katelyn Flinn, Grade 8
Covington Middle School, IN

The Memories I Hold
You made me cry,
When you left without saying good bye.
Those cold and deserted nights
With you not by my side.
I saw you once,
But then you were gone.
It was just a picture
I dreamt of again.
Now you're gone
Too far away.
Can't even say hello
To that lonely old grave.
I will love you now,
And forever I hold
The great old times,
I've never told.
Kayla Allen, Grade 9
Posen Consolidated High School, MI

Withered Flower
Weak and withered flower
Is dying on its death bed
Screaming for someone
Trying to keep its last breath
Picked, dumped, deserted little flower
Erica Nixon, Grade 8
St John Lutheran School, MI

Fire
Burning, angry light
Destroys all things in its path
A silent enemy
A tsunami on land
Crackling, hot, vicious flame
Brett Wagner, Grade 8
St John Lutheran School, MI

Summer's Dream
Summer sun shining
laughter filling the warm air
green grass all around
Kristin Mallard, Grade 8
Holy Name Catholic School, MI

Parguera
Oh the parguera
A bay glowing in the night
Brighter than the sun
Xan Pérez, Grade 8
Holy Name School, MI

The Fall of Summer
Autumn is now here
Leaves are falling everywhere
It is cooling down
Christian Jamesen, Grade 8
West Side Middle School, IN

Food
The scent fills your house
The satisfaction to say it's yours
Nobody else's
You have the right to say that
You made it
Tasting a new creation
Awesome
Makayla Johansen, Grade 7
South Spencer Middle School, IN

Winter Hunt
It's calm and cold
Dark but still bright
A lone wolf howls in the night

Walking through the field
Snow crunching under your boots
You find a good spot then you just sit tight

You sit in the shadows
Quiet and still
Just waiting, waiting for a kill

Then you hear a twig snap
Your heart beats fast
You raise your rifle
Then the mighty predator in now your prey
John Zaborney, Grade 9
Posen Consolidated High School, MI

Rice
A tiny granule of grain
Brown or white like man
Coexist in peace and harmony
Without hate or war or crime
Are wiser than man will ever be.
Tyler DeRosia, Grade 9
Posen Consolidated High School, MI

Grades 4-5-6 Top Ten Winners

List of Top Ten Winners for Grades 4-6; listed alphabetically

Kate Bowling, Grade 5
Stilwell Elementary School, KS

Rachel Edwards, Grade 6
Heritage Preparatory School, GA

Jessica Hodge, Grade 6
Highland Elementary School, NY

Darby Holroyd, Grade 5
Indian Hills Elementary School, KS

Shaylee Jerabek, Grade 5
Traeger Elementary School, WI

Anne Elise Kopta, Grade 6
Hamilton International Middle School, WA

Victoria Martin, Grade 5
Mornington Central School, ON

Hannah Pincus, Grade 6
Kittredge Magnet School, GA

Rachel Roberts, Grade 6
Ode Maddox Elementary School, AR

Sophie Williams, Grade 4
W R Croman Elementary School, PA

All Top Ten Poems can be read at www.poeticpower.com

Note: The Top Ten poems were finalized through an online voting system. Creative Communication's judges first picked out the top poems. These poems were then posted online. The final step involved thousands of students and teachers who registered as the online judges and voted for the Top Ten poems. We hope you enjoy these selections.

Spring Time
Spring time is almost here
The birds singing out there cheer
The grass is all turning green
Our mower blade is keen

There are buds on the trees
Surrounded by buzzing bees
Soon we'll have fresh fruit to eat
That will be a good treat

We go and plow the field
Where soon the crops will grow yield
When we come in with it done
Then it's time to have fun
Dwayne Amos Stoll, Grade 5
Green Acres School, IN

On the Farm...
On the farm there's lots to do
Forking straw and milking too
In the loft we have some hay
For our horses that say neigh.

We have pigs and some sheep too
And many cows that say moo
We have crops of wheat and rice
And we have some pesky mice.

We have a pond with some ducks
And some chickens that say cluck
We have some cats that say meow
And we have a big brown owl.
Rachel Diane Wagler, Grade 4
South Bogard School, IN

When I Started School
When I started school in 2007
I was happy as could be
I just thought it was so cool
Lots of friends I'd make you see

With my buddies Jared and Steve
We had a lot of fun
From school it was hard to leave
By playing out in the sun

In lots of trouble we would get
And the teacher would punish us
In our seats we'd have to sit
To remind us not to fuss
Stanley Eugene Wagler, Grade 4
South Bogard School, IN

Metaphors
A garden is a forest
Of sweet and sour mist.

A rainbow is a butterfly
Leading itself to adventure.

A hand is a promise
Of trustworthiness.

A smile is a caterpillar
Waiting to be changed.
Tabby Traver, Grade 5
Staunton Elementary School, IN

Red
Red is like the sound of a big red
fire truck zooming down the road.

Red is like the smell of a big sweet
rose in the bright green grass.

Red is the taste of a red hot candy
fresh from the candy store.

Red is the feel of my soft red
blanket keeping me warm.
Bailey Wenning, Grade 4
Morgan Elementary School, IN

My Hero
My special angel
My shoulder to cry on
My sweet friend
My guide for life

Always there for me
Always keeping me on track
Always giving me advice
Always loving me to pieces
Always caring for me so dearly
My Hero
Julia Schwark, Grade 6
St John Lutheran School, MI

Snow Is the Best
I love snow because it is like
A wonderland of white stuff.
Snow is like cold white powder
That falls like rain. Also in my
Opinion I think that snow is as
Fun as your birthday. Also snow
Is like ice but not that, it is as soft as
A pillow that you gently lay your head
On. Winter is my favorite season of all.
Beau Andrews, Grade 6
St Simon the Apostle School, IN

My Little Puppy
I found a little puppy
Along the roadside ditch,
I picked him up and saw
That he had a little itch.

I then took him home
And gave him some food.
After several hours
He was in a better mood.

We were playing by the tree
When he rolled in the mud.
So I gave him a bath
In the big, gray tub.
Myron Lee Knepp, Grade 4
Green Acres School, IN

The Toad
One day, when hoeing weeds,
I looked down toward the road
As I was looking down there,
I stepped on a great big toad.

I felt something squishy,
And look down by my toes
I thought I saw something big
Oh, my! There he goes!

I was laughing so very hard,
And surely thought I'd die
When I saw he was squished flat,
I almost had to cry.
Anthony Steven Knepp, Grade 4
Green Acres School, IN

Butterflies
Soaring, soaring all around,
Making, making not a sound.
They are very powerful,
They are very colorful.
Fluttering to every flower,
They have so much power.
There's a lot of types around,
A net full probably weighs a pound.
They are very helpful,
When it comes to flowers so colorful.
I named one Bower,
And I named one Flower.
Soaring, soaring all around,
Making, making not a sound.
Shelby Wargel, Grade 4
Chrisney Elementary School, IN

High Merit Poems – Grades 4, 5, and 6

Tumbling
From the car
Into the door
Warm up
The routine
Near the judges
Right over the floor
After the tumble
Past the crowd
1st place!!!!
Kassie Tanana, Grade 5
Dodson Elementary School, MI

Spring
Spring is the best
It is not a pest
You can play outside
Not inside
Drip, drop comes the rain
Finally no cold pain
Come let's climb
It's Spring time.
Christina Varghese, Grade 4
Floyd Ebeling Elementary School, MI

My Fluffy Friend
A mazing, **b** rave,
C ute, **d** ifferent, **e** xciting,
F unny, **g** angly, **h** appy,
I gnores me, **j** olly, **k** ind,
L iving, **m** oody, **n** ice,
O ld **p** uppy, **q** uick, **r** uns, **s** nuggles
T ug-of-war, **u** nusually, **v** ery stinky,
W hite spots, **X** tra special, **y** oung, **Z** zz.
Elizabeth Clemons, Grade 4
Morgan Elementary School, IN

Laughter Makes Me Smile
Laughter is extraordinary
It always makes me smile
It's so much prettier than frowning
Even if it's just for a short while
A smile is an upside-down frown
That always helps you through
When your troubles seem overwhelming
A smile can cheer you!
Zoe Korelitz, Grade 4
Akiva Hebrew Day School, MI

My Favorite Sport
Basketball
exciting, diversion
lay up, run, shoot
I'm joyful when playing
B-ball
Abigail Hottell, Grade 5
Hendry Park Elementary School, IN

What My Soup Said
What my soup said,
Was words I didn't know.
As I laid in bed,
About a week ago.

As I ate my tasty soup,
The letters turned and sped.
The O's would make a little group,
The words that I misread.

I didn't eat a spoonful,
I didn't eat a bite.
The letters would always roll,
The words would just fight.

This is what my soup said,
I saw some words I knew!
Eating the soup filled up my head,
and finally I was through.
Abigail Roberts, Grade 4
Liberty Elementary School, IN

Clear the Way
Rain dance wash away.
Blues return to blue skies soon.
Clear the way before the moon,
Comes and makes its mark.

Swarming words,
Settle down,
And carefully leave just one:
Let only 'Peace' remain.

Firing bullets,
All around
Why can't it all leave,
And just leave us with happiness?

So much happening everywhere
Let us clear our minds
And step towards perfect time –
Of world peace for all.
Kavya Chaturvedi, Grade 6
Detroit Country Day Middle School, MI

Winston
His little tail sways
Fast running partner
Sharp claws
Couch ripper
Begging cute eyes
Chewing bones
Meat lover
Bark, bark
Andrew Beyer, Grade 5
Dodson Elementary School, MI

Ocean
What is an ocean?
A swimming place,
A boater's home,
A surfer's dream,
A fish's palace,
A shark's restaurant,
And a wonderful place to be.
That's an ocean!
Carley Allison, Grade 5
Wayne Gray Elementary School, MI

Ode to Rocky
Ode to Rocky
when you try to sleep you purr in my ear.
Ode to Rocky
you love peaches.
Ode to Rocky
you are a big fat furry orange cat.
Ode to Rocky
I love you.
Jaden Pohle, Grade 4
Morgan Elementary School, IN

Blue
Blue is like the sound
of rain on the roof.
Blue is like the smell
of blue flowers growing in the soil.
Blue is like the taste
of blue Kool-Aid on a hot day.
Blue is like the feel
of the ice on a pond on a winter day.
Dexter L. Feeler, Grade 4
Morgan Elementary School, IN

A Friend
What is a friend?
someone who hangs out with you
does not yell
shares
plays with you
tells funny jokes
tells the truth
That is a friend!
Alina Wainscott, Grade 4
Bailey School, MI

Sunset
S himmering on the ocean surface
U nder the great blue sky
N ever ending water
S parkling in the evening sky
E verlasting rays peek out
T onight on the beach
Nathan Lee, Grade 6
St Simon the Apostle School, IN

The Wild Ride
Bright colored steel
12 dark cars
Over heating engines

Big blue sky
Simmering sun
Darkness far away

The heavy wind rushing
Structures rumbling loudly
Birds humming away

How many have enjoyed?
Can it last forever?
Why can't we ride again?

Risky amazement
Feared fun
I'd hate to see it go

A fun experience for all
A fun experience for all
A fun experience for all
Ali Sobh, Grade 6
Star International Academy, MI

An Ode to Bella
Bella you are my cousin's new dog.
Bella you are so cute and so small.
Bella you like to bite.
Bella you like to bark.
Bella I love you so much.
Bella I love playing with you.
Bella you like to play with Joe.
Bella I wish I had you.
Bella I blow you wishes every day and
I really really love you.
Lucy E. Watts, Grade 4
Morgan Elementary School, IN

I Am From
I am from a bunny,
and three cats,
from two dogs,
Kasper and Lilly,
I am from a flute,
and going to Disney World,
from listening to Corbin scream all night,
I am from nights filling up scrapbooks,
from long summer days and nights
at Grandma's pool with sister,
I am from a family tree,
from memories,
pictures.
Olivia Parker, Grade 6
Knox Community Middle School, IN

Shades of Gray
I don't know which most consumes me:
the screaming rush of life
or the silent dark of night.

I don't know which is more out of reach:
understanding the things I've seen
or leaving those things forgotten.

I don't know which speaks louder to me:
the visions shouting in my head
or the sleeping voice of my soul.
Ivy Harford, Grade 6
Pinewood Middle School, MI

Silver Stream
The silver stream glistened,
and the trees around me shook.
I stopped to listen.
I heard the birds sing,
and the chimes around me ring.
All was quiet,
there was no riot.
I felt the rain kiss my hand,
as I watched it fall onto the sand.
The silver stream glistened.
I stopped to listen.
Sarah Jacobson, Grade 6
St Simon the Apostle School, IN

Snow
Snow is falling
Softly falling
Twirling
Swirling
Spinning
Floating gently in the air
Everyone stops to stare
Gives everyone a chill and thrill
Quietly falling
Helping for some
Beautiful to all
Kristen Bensen, Grade 6
West Middle School, MI

Chocolate
Ooey gooey chocolate.
It tastes like heaven above.
When I unwrapped my first Hershey bar,
It was just like true love.

Just to be honest, it's an addiction.
I need to go to the store.
Hey look! There's a chocolate truck.
I need to buy a lot more.
Brenden Seewald, Grade 4
St. Raphael School, MI

Brown Furry Companions
Looks like a wooden plank
With big webbed feet.
It's a semi-aquatic animal
With a sensitive bill.
Can lay an egg
Only one that can.
And a big broad body
With fuzzy
Fur.
With a dark, dark
Figure staring
At my feet.
Caleb Christensen, Grade 5
Addison Panther Elementary School, MI

3 on 3 Champs
Shouting like a howler monkey
2 to win, 2 to win!
We're up to 2-10.
We need a shot
Screen, screen
Boom,
Chad is open.
Catch, shoot
Going,
Going,
Going.
Swish, it's in!
Chris Markules, Grade 6
Assumption School, MI

The Hit
Helmet on,
Ready,
Waiting
Staring,
I'm ready to swing.
The ball,
Coming,
Coming,
Coming,
CRACK! Like a rocket,
Up it flies,
I run to first base.
Julia Adams, Grade 6
Assumption School, MI

Truth/Lie
Truth
Thankful, nice
Truthful, right, cool
Warm, awesome, mean, hasty
Hating, lying, wicked
Lie
Paige L. Julian, Grade 5
Hendry Park Elementary School, IN

High Merit Poems – Grades 4, 5, and 6

My Room
Entering my room,
Admiring my room,
My eyes feel comfortable.
Bed, desk, closet,
Dolls…etc.
Lots of things
Fit and live in my room.
Not really messy,
My desk and bed
Need a lot of place to live.
My roommates,
We are a little family.
Always welcome
New family members.
Feels like…Heaven
There is no place
That makes me comfortable
Like this —
It's my favorite place
In the whole world!
Da-in Kang, Grade 6
St Bartholomew School, IN

I Thank the Lord for Spring
In the spring the flowers bloom,
In the spring it is very cool.
There are a lot of flowers I assume,
But it is not warm enough to play in a pool.

I thank the Lord for spring!

If I were a bee,
I would buzz over the sea,
I would go up high, way up into the sky,
And look at God's creation in the spring!

I thank the Lord for spring!

In the spring the sun goes down later.
Then we get to see more of God's creation.
Like butterflies and alligators.
On spring break, I take a vacation.

I thank the Lord for spring!
Paige Williams, Grade 4
Hillcrest Baptist Academy, IN

Kitty
Tiny golden paws
The golden black fur
Waiting for joy
Attacking the toy mouse
Back and forth
Back and forth
Scratching the cat nip
Getting treats
The green eyes staring
Waiting to be loved
Playing with the toy ball
Back and forth
Back and forth
Eating every hour
Playing with the toy ball
Back and forth
Back and forth
Getting a drink after playing
Fighting with his older brother Lucas
Sleeping in my loft
Wilson Berryhill, Grade 5
Dodson Elementary School, MI

Ages of the 3ds
In March,
you were new and
shiny, you were clean
and interesting you were
reliable and new

In April,
you gave me
entertainment and
still you give me
reliability

Now,
you are a
relic that
represents
Nintendo
and fun
combined
into one
Austin Shammas, Grade 6
Knox Community Middle School, IN

The Horse of the Night
I am the Pegasus of the sky
Look up at me
with your magnified eye

Gently galloping throughout the night
Look up at me
I'm a beautiful sight

I look up at you
with my magnified eye

Near the Big Dipper is where I'll see
the white winged horse
of Greek mythology

From summer to fall
On a very clear night

I try to find him
He's not up right
Haley Koss, Grade 6
Sashabaw Middle School, MI

Fall
Fall is great.
It's time to create,
Brand new memories.
While you watch the trees,
Let go of their leaves.
Let's listen to the bees,
While they hide in ease.

Fall is fun,
It has just begun.
Time to play,
And have a great day.
Leaves are crunchy,
The sound they make is funny.

Time to pick up pumpkins,
And collect them in bins.
Halloween is right there,
It's time for a scare.
Fall is a time to care.
Zeinab Beydoun, Grade 6
Star International Academy, MI

Christmas
Christmas! Christmas! Christmas
is here! Let's all give it a holiday
cheer! I see presents all around,
Up on top and on the ground.
Hooray! Hooray! Let's all hear it!
Who has got the Christmas spirit?
Hannah Roberts, Grade 5
Hendry Park Elementary School, IN

Christmas
Fun
Friends
Family
Presents
It is a fun holiday.
Christmas
Brooke Berger, Grade 4
Mentone Elementary School, IN

School
S ome times fun,
C onsecutive learning,
H aving to multiply and divide,
O utstanding place,
O utside recess,
L earning new stuff.
Praveen Prakash, Grade 4
Dibble Elementary School, MI

A Celebration of Poets – Great Lakes Grades 4-12 Spring 2011

Grandma and Grandpa
My grandma

She loves to watch birds
She loves me
I am free
To see birds

Grandpa

He likes to ride horses
I am proud of him
He goes down to the lake
To swim like the wind
Kyle Sutherby, Grade 5
Gobles Elementary School, MI

My Room
My room is
Where I express
Myself
Do what I
want to do
To
Have fun
Imagine
I am in the
NBA finals
Hitting the
Game winning
Shot
Sam LaVelle, Grade 6
St Bartholomew School, IN

Sisters
She is older than me
I am younger than her
She goes to middle school
I go to elementary school
She likes white milk
I like chocolate milk
She likes fish
I like turtles
She likes pink
I like purple
She has curly hair
I have straight hair
She is my sister
Jennifer Bressler, Grade 5
Dodson Elementary School, MI

Cat
My sweet cat Miley
Thinks she is a tiger when
She pounces on leaves.
Lenah Beck, Grade 5
Northern Heights Elementary School, IN

Cheetah
The snow is a bounding cheetah,
Fast and ferocious,
With sharp teeth and tearing claws.

But also with soft eyes
And slick fur,
As she dances through the forest,
Like a leaf in the wind.

And at the end of the day,
As the sun drifts below the trees,
The beautiful animal tucks away
In her dark, dark cavern.
Taylor McClain, Grade 6
Mendon High School, MI

Close Game
Two seconds
Free throws
All eyes on me
Down by 2
Dead quiet
I shoot
Missed
Second shot
Nervous
Made it
Down by one
2,1, Hooooooonk
Game over
Cam Patin, Grade 6
Assumption School, MI

Bullies
Bullies…they are everywhere,
on the sidewalk and in your school.
Bullies…push and shove
They don't know,
what you are feeling inside,
pain…
They bully to feel good
about themselves
bullies…do not care about you.
They hit and call you names,
that miserable feeling never goes away,
it stays inside you,
forever…
Kelsea Sherrill, Grade 6
Linton-Stockton Elementary School, IN

Weather
Leaves fall in the frost,
There's a lot of rainy days,
And short days coming.
Hannah Mervine, Grade 5
Ballard Elementary School, MI

Missing Milo
Labor Day weekend,
I remember
The lingering smell,
Of puppy breath
The way I threw you away,
Like an old candy wrapper
Your footsteps haunt me
It all left me for life
Your blissful eyes,
When I played with you
I love and miss you Milo
I wasn't ready to say good-bye,
Nor let go.
Victoria O'Bryant, Grade 6
Knox Community Middle School, IN

Baseball
Baseball is a wonderful game,
It's going to be a hall of fame.
It is a wonderful thing to do,
If you mess up everybody gives you a boo.
There is no crying in baseball,
If you cry you are a goofball.
A home run is hard to hit,
You catch a baseball with a mitt.
We pray before each game,
Then we have a good ballgame.
Our pitchers throw really hard,
They strike everybody out,
Then they will go on the bench and pout.
Nathan Lamar, Grade 4
Chrisney Elementary School, IN

The Goal
3 to 3
Opponent closing in
The juke, the fake
One on one
Nervous,
Waiting,
Ready!
The perfect steal
Going down the ice like a jet
The perfect move
The back hander
Top shelf!
Unstoppable.
Gabe Rabbers, Grade 6
Assumption School, MI

Rainbow Flowers
Many different kinds
They are a living rainbow
Tall, small, short and fat
Rieley Jonca, Grade 4
Dodson Elementary School, MI

High Merit Poems – Grades 4, 5, and 6

This Is How I Do It
Basketball is my favorite sport
The sound of the dribble as
I move up and down the court.

I cross everybody
Break through high and low
Shoot my 3 pointers
I'm a one man show!

I'm like a kid Michael Jordan
Dunking my ball like Derrick Rose
Spinning with style and grace
Camera's flashing, they got my trademark pose.

I am the show stopper
Free throw's going in
Swoosh!!! through the net
one, two, it's game. I win!
Jalen Dunscomb, Grade 4
Thea Bowman Leadership Academy, IN

Fishing
Lakes, river, streams, and bays
Have fish in big and small sizes
The species numbers can amaze
And have so many surprises

Your line in the water feels so light
You know that something is there
That monstrous fish gives such a fight
It almost feels like a grizzly bear.

Its bite is as hard as a rock
Its body, so shiny and colorful
When you land it, it's as big as an ox
This makes it way more wonderful.

With that beautiful mount hung on the wall
You may not stop staring at it al all.
Brenden Gorney, Grade 6
St Mary Cathedral School, MI

Winter
As the first snowflake falls, little kids cheer.
It's a sign that winter's here.
My mom moans,
while my dad groans.
We pull out our snow clothes and zip them up tight,
we make a snowman who looks just right,
but then in February, the snow starts to melt.
I loved the way the snow felt.
The little kids cry,
and the adults sigh.
Now it's time to say goodbye.
Andrea Chipman, Grade 6
Jean K Harker Middle School, MI

A Softball's Seasons
In summer
your leather shell starts to get scratched up,
while you soar off the bat through the sky,
you amaze thousands of kid's eyes.

In fall
your yellowness starts to fade,
and sometimes we lose you in the leaves,
but don't worry, we only lost you once.

In winter
you wait for us to come outside,
but we can't, it is too cold,
someday you will be too old.

In spring,
you love the feeling of gliding through
the moist air,
and someday you will tear up to shreds.

I keep the shell of you,
because you remind me of precious memories.
Tonya Conley, Grade 6
Knox Community Middle School, IN

Thinking of You
Thinking of you late at night,
Thinking of a reason to call,
Wishing I could hear your voice,
Hoping I'm on your mind,
Thinking of you in the morning,
Not a day goes by,
Dreaming of you in the hallway,
Hoping you never say good-bye,
Wishing you could feel the way that I feel,
Please pick up the phone,
Hope you'll listen to my message,
It's only for you, I'm writing a poem for you, to say I love you,
Wish I could stay but I can't stand the limelight,
Hope you can understand,
I love you more than spring and even fall,
I love you more than words can describe,
Now it's hard to say goodbye,
You're fresh in my mind,
Your velvet voice whispering my name,
Your beautiful face to answer my call,
Oh I wish you could see what your presence does to me.
Alexis Winquest-La Ponsie, Grade 6
East Elementary School, MI

Chuawa
The circumstantial charming cherry chocolate
Chomping chuawa charmingly chased a
Chickadee that chose Charoflucarbon Street.
William Yahl, Grade 5
Sunman Dearborn Intermediate School, IN

Cats
I love cats,
Cats are a lot better than rats.
Rats are nasty and small,
Cats are the best of all.
Some are fuzzy as a bear,
Some don't have any hair.
They can play with balls,
They land on paws,
Even when it falls.
They scratch with claws.
They bite with jaws.
I love cats.
Dakota Brinksneader, Grade 4
Chrisney Elementary School, IN

A Drummer's Drum
I see the golden trumpets
In front of me
They are saying "good job."
I feel the stick springing off me
My head hurts every day
The vibrations tickle my side
Hitting like a punching bag
My silver rim holds me together
When the golden guys leave
I do not have anyone
To talk to
I am lonely…
Michael Thompson, Grade 6
Linton-Stockton Elementary School, IN

Why?
Why? A very common question.
Why do I have to?
Why am I happy?
Why am I sad?
Why is he mad?
Why is my life hard?
Why am I here?
Why aren't I there?
Why, oh why, oh why?
But at the end of the day,
Rather in hatred or in glory,
"Why" is just a word.
Taylor Kempf, Grade 5
Holy Redeemer School, IN

Stars
Stars, oh stars,
why lost in the
mist of the
darkened night, oh
stars how I wish
I could reach you someday.
Joe Pena, Grade 5
Ballard Elementary School, MI

My Teacher
She is Mrs. Dean
I am Avery
She talks
I listen
She cracks a joke
I laugh
She demands
I respect
She goes
We follow
She shhh's us
I shut it
Avery Olson, Grade 5
Dodson Elementary School, MI

Grandparents
G reat at everything
R eally cool
A nything's possible around them
N ever lazy
D andy people
P arents, they are!
A lways having fun
R eally smart
E nchanting
N ever late on my birthday
T ogether with me
S tupid, of course not!
Bryce Logsdon, Grade 4
Morgan Elementary School, IN

My Special Shell
If I give my special shell to you,
I hope you would take care of it,
Keep it near to you…
Take it with you
Wherever you go,

Without my special shell
I would feel empty
Like something was missing,
I would hope,
You are keeping it safe
And near to your heart.
Jennifer Weaver, Grade 6
Linton-Stockton Elementary School, IN

Cars
Engine powered
Four wheeled
Machines
That produce
Harmful fossil
Fuel
Drake Bernauer, Grade 6
St Simon the Apostle School, IN

I Wonder
I wonder why the sun comes up
I wonder why it shines

I wonder what makes the sky blue
and if it ever cries

I wonder who invented ties
and if that person's died

Everything comes from something,
so now it's time to say goodbye
Anna Staltari, Grade 5
Heritage Intermediate School, IN

Family and Love
Family and love.
This is all you need in life.
They keep you happy.
God gave this to us.
He gave it to us with love.
Give love back to him.
Your family keeps you safe.
They will always protect you,
keep you by their side.
They will never let you go.
Family and love.
Elena Silva, Grade 5
Northern Heights Elementary School, IN

High Dive
"Don't be a chicken,"
It is clear and scorching
Like boiling water,
Butterflies are tumbling
In my twisted stomach,
The crashing water
Is a million feet down,
I close my eyes…jump fearfully,
I drop down…down…down,
Then…splash!
"No, I am not a chicken"
Allie Walton, Grade 6
Linton-Stockton Elementary School, IN

Spooky Graveyard
I was in a frightening graveyard
On a frigid terrifying night
Alone and dismayed
Like a mouse running away from a cat
By myself
Just roaming around
Glancing in the distance
All I observed was nothing
But fog…and darkness.
Mikyla Rhodes, Grade 6
Linton-Stockton Elementary School, IN

Flowers

F lowers swaying.
L ady bugs buzzing.
O rangutans swinging.
W ind blowing.
E ating hot dogs.
R eady for spring.

Josh Pequignot, Grade 5
Northern Heights Elementary School, IN

Clouds

Clouds
Puffy, white
Floating, moving, raining
They are shapes in the sky.
Feathery

Matthew Witzerman, Grade 6
St Simon the Apostle School, IN

Dogs!

Dogs
Loud, fast
Licking, barking, running
My best friend
Super smelly

Emily Abriani, Grade 6
St Simon the Apostle School, IN

Jobs

Jobs
So hard
So very boring
Get lots of money
Jobs

Alec Najem, Grade 6
St Simon the Apostle School, IN

Tiger

Tiger
Graceful, orange
Running, jumping, eating
They love to play with their tiny cubs
Big cat

Glendin Hayes, Grade 5
Perry Central Elementary School, IN

Candy

Candy
Yummy, chewy
Dissolving, chomping, sucking
Cherry flavored Jolly Ranchers
Sugar

Alexis Donahue, Grade 4
Bailey School, MI

I Love My Family

There is a loving grandmother who's waiting at the door for you, or in the family room waiting to telling you and your sister a story.

There is a caring dad that helps you with your homework, or is in the kitchen making all the yummy meals!

There is a working or busy mom who is willing to spend time cuddling with me and the whole family!

In homes there is a sweet sister who's usually doing her homework or just hanging around the family room.

But

When you don't have a family the world is a place without love, and without love you will feel sad.

Paige Posada, Grade 4
Dodson Elementary School, MI

What Makes Me Smile

A lot of different things make me smile.
I wonder what makes these things make me smile.
My heart begins to burst with joy.
I think these things bring about a happy smile to me.

What makes me smile is doing well on a test.
Because I was taught by the best.
I receive a reward for all my effort.

What makes me smile is going out to eat with my family and niece.
My niece makes me laugh when she pretends to be somebody's mom.

What makes me smile is helping others.
Caring for those who need a helping hand.
I feel warm inside by giving my best and nothing less.

Keondra Exford, Grade 4
Thea Bowman Leadership Academy, IN

Two Cousins

Two terrible singers
Two corn lovers
Same Grandma
Two reading lovers
Two kickers at night
Two brown eyes
One taller, one shorter
One does not have a phone, one has a phone
One has a brother, one has a sister and a brother
One was born in the city of Incheon, one was born in the city of Ansan
One is younger by four months, one is older by four months
Two cousins

Jin Yoo, Grade 4
Hampton Elementary School, MI

Autumn
Autumn leaves
Breeze through the trees.
Down to the yard
By the pumpkins and mummies.

Apple cider is insight
While kids in costumes
Glide through the night.

Scarecrows or donuts
The choice will be tight.
While cider mills open shop
With a profit that is right.

As lanterns light up the night
Autumn leaves
Breeze with flight.
Kyle Mendes, Grade 6
Eagle Creek Academy, MI

3-Point Shot
Basketball
Faked a pass
Dribbled between the legs
3
Jump stop
2
Pumpfake
Knees bent
Follow through
Down by 2
1
Bounces on the front of the rim
Anticipation
Goes in!
The ref shoots up 3 fingers
We win!
Buzzer beater!
Jake Westman, Grade 6
Assumption School, MI

Winter
I can't wait until it's here!
The season winter is really near!
The snow will come down from the sky,
And the birds will leave then fly.
The snow will land on the ground,
I will play in it with my hound.
I throw many snowballs with my arm,
They hit my hound with no harm.
I hear sleigh bells ring,
If it's Santa I wonder what he will bring.
I hope he will bring me a toy,
The season winter will bring me joy!
Will Strobel, Grade 4
Chrisney Elementary School, IN

Eagles
Eagles,
Fast,
Swift,
Huge,
Predator,
Fluttery,
Anxious,
Strong,
Rapid,
Towering,
Proud,
Grand,
Amazing,
Terrifying,
Exciting,
Ferocious,
Eagles.
Camden Kuntz, Grade 4
James R Watson Elementary School, IN

The Best Bear Ever!
My best friend, I still remember
the lime green of your fur
and your big happy brown
eyes glossy in the sun.
I remember everywhere
we went together showing you off,
losing you so many times but
always finding you again.
Playing on the back porch,
going to the grocery store,
dressing you up like a doll,
coloring with you purple, green, and blue.
I miss those days in preschool together,
But now you are muddy green
it seems you're not happy anymore
because we aren't together every day.
You are still on my bed lonely and crying.
Libby Atkins, Grade 6
Knox Community Middle School, IN

Grandparents
G reat at making pies
R ockin' people
A lways by my side
N ever letting me down.
D ressed up on Sundays for church
P resident at fishing
A nnoying, no way
R eally caring people
E ntertaining all the time
N ew things they teach
T errific people
S traight forward, "Always looking ahead"
Farrah Hiser-Smith, Grade 5
Morgan Elementary School, IN

Basketball
Dribble down the court
With the basketball in my hand
Crossing people out
Foul! I get two foul shots

The team cheers me on
Swish! One basket. Swish! Two
One minute in the game
If we lose the coach is to blame

Five seconds left
All tied up
Sweat on my face
Made a jump shot and won the game!
Richard A. Walker, III, Grade 5
Dodson Elementary School, MI

Camping
Camping is cool,
the lake is like a pool.

You can hike,
or you can bike.

You can tell a story,
that ends in glory.

You can look at the stars,
and hope you see Mars.

Camping is fun!
Sarah C. Hasik, Grade 6
St John the Baptist Elementary School, IN

Boys and Girls
Boys
Fun, trouble
Tackling, eating, sprinting
Pranks, strong, perfume, shopping
Clothing, designing, dressing
Cars, hair
Girls
Ian Aldridge, Grade 4
Concord Ox Bow Elementary School, IN

Sports
Baseball
awesome, extreme
catching, throwing, hitting
baseball, bat, glove
basketball, hoop
shooting, jumping, rebounding
fun, exciting
Basketball
Evan Powell, Grade 5
Hendry Park Elementary School, IN

The Color of Expression
Green…
Oozing of self-confidence
The fruity taste of a crisp, green apple
Green…
Like the waxy texture of a peaceful candle
The smell of a raw, earthy world
Green…
As the color explodes
The world goes dark…dark…dark
Bouncing off the walls
Sticking in my mind
Green…
The color of expression
Mikayla Lannan, Grade 6
Linton-Stockton Elementary School, IN

One Last Time
My great-grandparents
They enter my thoughts all day
My great-grandpa and grandma
Their lives…
Blown out like a flame
They were like second parents
All the cherished memories
That cannot be relived
Such generous people
They spoiled and loved my brother and me
Now they are gone
I wish I could hug them
One last time…
Justin Rippy, Grade 6
Linton-Stockton Elementary School, IN

Piano
I push down a key,
Sound rises.
Now higher,
Now lower,
Each sound delights me.
I am tempted to play some more,
But I can't teach myself.
I guess I'll just have to wait.
As I stare at the empty space,
Where a music sheet is supposed to be,
I start wishing that there was one there.
I guess if there was one,
It would be no use to me.
Alyssa Bergman, Grade 5
Hendry Park Elementary School, IN

Rivers
Rivers are wicked
The fish jumped from the river
Rivers are thrilling
David Gestwicki, Grade 6
Holy Name School, MI

Music
Nicki Manaj. Trey Songz have great songs
Hear their music all the time
I listen to it all day long
It's never out of my mind
Always hearing my favorite song
Nicki Manaj. Trey Songz have great songs
Hear their music all the time
I listen to it all day long
It's never out of my mind
Always hearing my favorite song
Joie Smiley, Grade 5
Dodson Elementary School, MI

Wolves
Leader of the pack
In the luminous Alaska wilderness
Beautiful howls fill the midnight air
Deep blue eyes look towards the sky
Sharp claws scrape the rough earth
Oil black fur that blows in the Alaska breeze
Travels swiftly in the night
Silhouette shadows
In front of the bright moon
Across the December frost.
Rachel Elliott, Grade 5
Dodson Elementary School, MI

Valentine's Day Is Lovely
V enice is the city of love
A ll people think of hearts with love
L earning about love
E verything reminds you of love
N ice getting married today is lovely
T ime to share with those you love
I sn't this the best loving holiday
N ice day for lovers
E ating truffles everyone loves
S ome people fall in love
Wendy Unland, Grade 6
St Simon the Apostle School, IN

personal
cassandra
wild
lover of gymnastics
who feels friends are important
who needs family and friends
who gives hugs when they are sad
who fears the unknown
who would like to see new york
resident of u.s.a.
lester
Cassandra Lester, Grade 6
Martin Middle/High School, MI

Wakeboarding
I put on my life vest
Jump in the water
A chill runs up my back
Of fear and excitement.

Pull on my boots
One at a time
I reach for the rope
Position my body
I concentrate, take a deep breath
And relax

I hear the roar of the engine
And the boat tugs me forward
My muscles tense
I pull myself up
I feel like I am a fish on water
I hear my family cheering me on
Like the first time I got up
And it's a very happy feeling!
Wakeboarding can take you away.
That's why…I AM A WAKEBOARDER!
Marina Hughes, Grade 6
St Bartholomew School, IN

Basketball
B est sport ever
A ndrew plays it
S wish
K nock the ball away
E veryone likes it
T echnical foul
B asket
A lways play fair
L ost the ball
L OSER
Andrew Corravo, Grade 4
Dibble Elementary School, MI

Will the Fall Ever Leave?
Red, orange, yellow leaves
Will the fall ever leave?
Leaves are falling, now it's hard
For people to clean up their yard
Red, orange, yellow leaves
Will the fall ever leave?
The children can't go outside
It's hard for them to stay inside
The squirrels get food ready for the snow
Will the fall ever go?
The animals are starting to hide
Because it's time for fall time to stay inside
Red, orange, yellow leaves
Will the fall ever leave?
Sara Aldelahmawi, Grade 6
Star International Academy, MI

I Am From
I am from the swish
of the basketball
and the sound of a gun
firing at a deer
I am from my dogs guarding
the family and
playing at all times
I am from the wind
blowing in my ear
and making a whistling noise
I am from bruises,
scrapes and scratches.
I am from the fresh cut grass
the smell so sweet.
I am from fresh cooked
deer on the table
the dirt flying from ATV's
I am from Friday —
the best day of the week.
Gavin Majchrzak, Grade 6
Knox Community Middle School, IN

Springtime
Springtime is the best time of all
When barefoot we all may go
Friends gather round, you can play ball
The sun has melted the snow.

Birds are starting to build their nests
In branches high up in the trees.
With work all done. Let's take a rest
And feel the nice and cool breeze.

Helping others to mow the lawn
Picking the strawberries too.
Planting the garden is so fun.
Milking time, cows start to moo.

Let's thank God for all He gave us
For our food, our clothes, and shoes,
Let's thank him for our large garden
For watching us all year through.
Teresa Joanne Knepp, Grade 6
Green Acres School, IN

Fall
Adirondack Park
Beyond the grassy treetops
Among the leafy orange trees
Across the white and blue sky
Within the orange and green trees
Upon the leafy ground
Is the most wonderful place
Of New York
Sydney Reinhardt, Grade 6
Knox Community Middle School, IN

Around the House
Around the house there's lots to do,
Cooking, cleaning, baking too.

Out in the garden pulling weeds,
Get a hoe to plant some seeds.

Go inside and mop the floor clean
Wash windows and make them gleam.

Run upstairs to straighten the room,
Get the dustpan and the broom.
Leah Renae Knepp, Grade 4
South Bogard School, IN

Running in the Fields
A strong smooth animal
As shiny as the sun
With a brown furry mane
Running wild in the fields
Dashing over anything in the way
As fast as she could possibly go
The athletic beast running wild
She was fierce with bony legs
Leaping in the breath of air
The beautiful energetic horse
Catherine Mayfield, Grade 5
Wayne Gray Elementary School, MI

The Powerful Wind
Gliding to the wake
Pop high through the air
Do an outstanding one-eighty
Feel the rush of crazy wind
Push against you
Land gently down
On the glassy water
See the little ripple beside you splash
The sensation of a great trick
Now a smile
Drew Rokita, Grade 6
Wayne Gray Elementary School, MI

Rushing Creeks
Cold water rushing over pebbles
Little boys and girls playing
Scaly minnows swimming
Peaceful place to get away
Leggy water-spiders dancing across water
Green ferns swaying in the wind
Refreshing to cool off
Playful children skipping rocks
Warm sunshine reflecting off creeks
Mud sliding off the bank
Meghan Gordon, Grade 6
Wayne Gray Elementary School, MI

First Shot
Rebound
Get the ball
Dribble, dribble
Running down the court
Heart pounding like a race horse
Speeding,
Racing,
Blaring,
Stop and shoot!
Ball goes up!
Wobbles,
Twists,
Wiggles,
Ball goes in!
As confident as ever
The very first shot I have ever made!
Emily Adams, Grade 6
Assumption School, MI

Ice Cream
Ice cream's so delicious
It always makes me wish
That I had more ice cream
It feels like a dream
Maybe I'll chime
In for some lime
Or take a dip
For some chocolate chip
It seems like a fright
Without caramel delight
And to give you a hint
I just adore mint
If I cannot decide
I'll just sit here and cry
So I'll take them all
And hope they don't fall
Aditi Hukerikar, Grade 4
Dodson Elementary School, MI

Katherine
Your perfect little cheeks
are pink enough to make
me want to call you Rosy

Your pretty little smile is
a pocket full of sunshine

Your shiny brown eyes
are just like your curly
hot cocoa hair

You're my short shadow
with pink and purple
colors in between
Corinne Nedeau, Grade 5
North Muskegon Elementary School, MI

High Merit Poems – Grades 4, 5, and 6

Pigs
P oopy and stinky!
I cky and slippery!
G ooey and ooey!
S oap would do the trick!
Connor Davis, Grade 5
Northern Heights Elementary School, IN

Daddy
Daddy, Daddy, please don't go
We will miss you
Please don't go.
I love you, Daddy,
Jasmine Jacobs, Grade 5
Northern Heights Elementary School, IN

Cedar Point
Windy, exciting, wild, awesome
Scary, fast going to the top
The place fills up quickly
Extremely exciting going in hoops.
Neel Patel, Grade 5
Dodson Elementary School, MI

Waterfalls
Splashing water fall,
Flowing down the river, stream
Gently falling.
Kelley Devernay, Grade 4
Hampton Elementary School, MI

Ice
I ce is on my pond
C racking when you step on it
E veryone falls in
Brennon Pelland, Grade 6
West Middle School, MI

Halloween
A witch at my door,
Bright houses with lights so cool.
Trick or treat! Yum, yum!
Megan Coultas, Grade 5
Ballard Elementary School, MI

Grass
I love the green grass
you can run around in it!
Go out and have fun
Lydia Kay Tuckerman, Grade 5
Hendry Park Elementary School, IN

Sun
The sun knows power.
The sun knows how to make its minions worship it.
It knows its teacher pet planet is Earthy, keeping it too torrid but not too frosty.
It knows how to chastise the planets for getting off track by sending sweltering weather.
It does not have a dwelling, for it just uses its heat to keep itself sultry.
The sun knows how to melt the ice away like vacuum sucking up dirt.
It takes a break every six months so it can recharge like a tired battery.
Cameron Kight, Grade 5
Dodson Elementary School, MI

My Hamster
Oh hamster, oh hamster, why do you bite a lot.
Oh hamster, oh hamster, why are you so little.
Oh hamster, oh hamster, are so funny and weird also.
2 Hamsters takes the places of my first hamster that died.
I think my Hamster is 2 months old.
Oh hamster, oh hamster, you have the best coat of gray and black streak on his back.
Oh hamster, oh hamster, you are the best hamster for me.
Corey Funk, Grade 4
Morgan Elementary School, IN

Where I Am From
I am from a big, known, place that got bigger by years.
I am from a sweet, easy life that got one step harder every day.
I am from eating saucy pasta for dinner and breaking down a sticky stack of pancakes.
I am from a place with a long chain of historical events.
I am from a place that is partly hot and partly cold.
I am from an enormous country called America.
Shreeya Ramesh, Grade 4
Hampton Elementary School, MI

America
America looks like birds singing in the trees, a rainbow with beautiful flowers.
It feels like beautiful grass, sand from the beach and water from the ocean floor.
America tastes like baked cookies that just came from the oven, tacos and enchiladas.
It smells like beautiful roses that came from beautiful gardens, plants just born and nature.
America sounds like beautiful songs from birds flying.
America is my home.
Ana Sanchez Montalvo, Grade 4
Hampton Elementary School, MI

Seasons
The sunny season of summer, smeary sundaes on sizzling sidewalks
Fades into fall with floating fragrant leaves flung in filthy heaps
Winter waltzes in with wandering winds and whimsical snowflakes
Sprinkles and showers, skipping rope and flowers, song birds sing in spring
How can I find a favorite when each has features so fabulous?
Sara Spicer, Grade 6
Martin Middle/High School, MI

Where I Am From
I am from family pictures, chicken and rice, and Barney Blues Clues blankets.
I am from hamburgers, "Do your best and never give up!" and, "We're going to Cedar Point!"
I am from Patrick and Joey and potato chops filled with meat and rice.
Jonathan Jajjo, Grade 4
Hampton Elementary School, MI

Kittens
I like kittens,
Any kind of kittens.
Fluffy kittens,
Gray kittens,
Long haired kittens.
Kittens in a tree.
Kittens on the table.
Any kind of kittens.
I like kittens.
Sydney Young, Grade 5
Jackson Christian School, MI

Turtles
Turtles, I love you so
With your shades of green
Light, dark, or very colorful
Shapes, lines across their shells
I love them all
I will travel to ponds, rivers
And oceans — I don't care
As long as I get to see
You…TURTLES
Madi Kilmer, Grade 5
Heritage Intermediate School, IN

Me
I am a fifth grade girl,
My hair and eyes are black,
I like to play with dolls,
And bounce them on my back.

The day my nieces come
I'd love to just skip school,
But I cannot do that,
I'd disobey the rule.
Rosetta Jean Knepp, Grade 5
South Bogard School, IN

Basketball
Basketball
Orange, round
Painful, jumping, falling
Screaming, exciting, nervous, cheering
Game
Ben Joseff, Grade 4
Crestwood Elementary School, MI

Sunny Days
Remember those sunny days
When we used to laugh and play
The sun in our faces
And how we would run to places
Oh, yes
I remember those sunny days
Abby Faurote, Grade 6
St Simon the Apostle School, IN

The New Year Treat
Firecrackers all over the place
All the red colors are next to my face
All the dragons on the street
Sure is a nice New Year treat
Cooking food on the grill
Really is such a thrill
Working together on the meal
Words can't express how I feel
Being here at the celebration
With me my family and the entire nation
Sure gives me a feeling of admiration
Marwa Moubadder, Grade 6
Star International Academy, MI

The Sounds of Nature
The sound of blue jays chirping delightfully
In the beautiful, morning sunrise
The pleasant sound of woodpeckers
Gently pecking on a maple tree

The sound of dairy cows
Mooing constantly in the pasture
The sound of the cool wind
Easily blowing the silver chimes

The sounds…of a perfect day.
Madison Millick, Grade 6
Linton-Stockton Elementary School, IN

Ghost Soldier
I walk as the raindrops cover my tears
The trees stare and taunt me
Delicate flowers spread across the yard
Weeping silently
I hear an echoing gunshot
I see a sobbing woman being handed a flag
It hits me like a rock
My funeral…my funeral
As they mourn…I sink into the icy ground
No one hears my silent scream
I am gone.
Mary Moore, Grade 6
Linton-Stockton Jr. High School, IN

The Beast
BOOM! is all you hear
Lava and magma staining the sky
The beast has risen
Ash and its raining fire
The souls of hell unleashed
Screaming all around you
The beast breathes his last breath
The souls recede and everything is silent
The beast has died
Jake Sturtevant, Grade 6
Wayne Gray Elementary School, MI

Red
Red, the color of spicy salsa
On a crunchy tortilla chip
Red, the color of juicy strawberries
Popping into my mouth
Red, the color of hot peppers
Burning my tongue worse than a sunburn
Red, the color of dark blood
Pumping through my body
Red, the color of my heart
Kody Nelson, Grade 6
Linton-Stockton Elementary School, IN

Shooting Star
A star soared across the wonderful sky
It blasted by like a bird
Caught in the stormy wind
I love spying the constellations
They shine like no other
I better make a wish
I hope it comes true
Looking at shiny stars in the gloomy night
Just hoping one will come true
Katie Sawdey, Grade 5
Wayne Gray Elementary School, MI

Hockey
On the ice
Upon the puck drop
On top of the guy I just checked
Across the offense men
Pas the defense men
In front of the net
Between the goalie's legs
Past the goal line the puck goes
OVERTIME WINNER
Nick O'Donohue, Grade 5
Dodson Elementary School, MI

Ice Cream
Ice cream
creamy, cold
eating, licking, laughing
you won't be able to stop
Yum
Kristen Caldwell, Grade 6
St Simon the Apostle School, IN

A Colorful Day
All the colors of the leaves
yellow orange red please
walking by the colorful monkey bars
gazing up at shooting stars
when the sun and moon come to meet
It is time to go to sleep
Ayelet Pollock, Grade 5
Akiva Hebrew Day School, MI

High Merit Poems – Grades 4, 5, and 6

Flower
With petals like silk,
And leaves as green as emeralds.
Reach out into the sun,
And bring life inside of me.

Waiting for the morning mist,
To get a refreshing drink.
As cool as ice,
To keep me healthy.
Sarah Lloyd, Grade 6
Fort Branch Community School, IN

I Like Bikes
I like bikes
Any kind of bikes
New bikes, fast bikes
Slow bikes, old bikes
Bikes in stores
Bikes on trails
Bikes with reflectors
Any kind of bikes
I like bikes
Julia Maguire, Grade 5
North Muskegon Elementary School, MI

The Movies
Through the parking lot
Between two cars we stop
Toward the big building
Under the roof
Down the line
At the ticket booth
Toward the theater
Into our seat
Action!
Catherine Christenson, Grade 5
Dodson Elementary School, MI

Italy
Italy's
Famous church
The Vatican has
A great man called
Pope
Parker Hopkins, Grade 6
St Simon the Apostle School, IN

Brandy
B randy
R agtail mom
A wesome mom
N ice looking
D ances good
Y oung lady
Gavin Klemczak, Grade 5
Northern Heights Elementary School, IN

The Atrocious Monster
thunder screaming in the clouds
lightning flaring toward the ground
wind whipping at your windows
trees cracking like shot
rain pelting the ground
hail crying to come in
the giant ocean like puddles
as the water washes back and forth
Bethany Valdez, Grade 6
Wayne Gray Elementary School, MI

Amazing Animal
Wolves are gray, brown and white.
They have large powerful ears,
sharp eyes for great seeing.
These animals are strongly built,
long sharp teeth for tearing up their meat.
The thief in the night was so deep,
running, smelling here and there.
Wow, wonderful wolf.
Maggie Holbrook, Grade 5
Addison Elementary School, MI

Autumn Leaves
Autumn leaves,
Red, yellow, brown,
All crumpled up,
Falling to the ground,
They cannot stay,
It's time for them to go,
For they cannot survive
The harsh winter's cold.
Jaiden Shipley-Snider, Grade 6
Martin Middle/High School, MI

Green
Green is like the sound
of wind whistling in the grass.
Green is like the smell
of a bass I just caught.
Green is like the taste
of a sour Granny Smith apple.
Green is like the feel
of my football jersey hitting my arm.
Cameron Hodge, Grade 4
Morgan Elementary School, IN

Chess
Why can't I win at chess?
Is it because of the stress?
My strategies include the Queen,
But my opponent is keen.
Although when I do achieve,
The opponent's strong pieces I do receive.
Lucas Daunhauer, Grade 5
Holy Redeemer School, IN

Springtime
Springtime is almost here
And it's warming up outside.
Hear the birds sing so clear
When we all go for a ride.

It's time to mow the lawn
Cause the grass is turning green.
The flowers are blooming
The prettiest you have seen.

Soon we'll plant the garden
Then the weeds will also grow.
It seems there are a bunch
It is time to get the hoe.
Christina Leann Wittmer, Grade 5
Green Acres School, IN

Candy
Candy is dandy!
When you share with others!
My friend likes candy, her name is Mandy!
But it is not loved by many mothers!

When I eat candy I get a tummy ache!
But it is yummy!
It is way better than cake!
I love it even though it ruins my tummy

But when I eat candy I feel very dandy
Everybody should like it, yes yippee!
Candy is good and very handy!
It makes me feel kind of flippy!
Madison Packer, Grade 5
Dodson Elementary School, MI

Crazy Killers
Evil giants
Deadly
Tallest thing ever
Don't try
Climbing these
Awful skyscrapers
Mount Everest is the worst
Many have died
Trying to claim
This huge beast
But some have tamed him
Some have finished their journey
Slinking there way up
These ancient wonders
Brendan Nicholl, Grade 6
Wayne Gray Elementary School, MI

Change

Every day I watch you grow
From small to tall
Short to long
Your fur a bright red
To a dusty color.
You once smelled like pumpkins
And shampoo. You were a playful puppy.
You were fat but not chubby.
Now you are a grownup dog.

The new puppies we got,
Think of you as a mother.
You watch them grow like I did you.
You keep them in line But at one time
You, yourself, thought our other dog
Clairie Bear was a mother to you.
I saw all of the changes and knew you were
Not a little puppy anymore.
Brian Tobin, Grade 6
Knox Community Middle School, IN

The Capture

The water is warm, I have no doubt
Today, tonight, the frogs are out
Trees, bushes, more vegetation
The pond in the woods is my destination
When I get there I cannot shout
Today, tonight, the frogs are out
The moment is tense
My presence they sense
Their hopping is stopping
Their swimming beginning
Jumping, squirming and swimming about
Today, tonight, the frogs are out
Reaching, catching, victory
They try to hide where I can't see
I let him back. It was a pleasure.
I cannot disrespect Mother Nature.
Green or brown; Slim or stout
Today, tonight, frogs are out
Jillian Campbell, Grade 5
Detroit Country Day Junior School, MI

Miami Heat

M asters on the court
I nternational all-stars
A wesome at the sport
M y favorite team
I mproving all of the time

H awk eyes to scan the court
E xcellence is the name
A lley-oops
T eam work is the best
Trenton McElfresh, Grade 5
Perry Central Elementary School, IN

The Many Colored Bird

You with your many colors
Curved beak, strong legs, upright stance
You eat the food
That nature provides

You go back
Back 5 million years ago
To when only time could tell

With your sharp claws
You climb and swing
Through the jungle treetops
Where you fly

Strong, direct
Charismatic, colorful
Intelligent, musical
You are the many colored bird
Lily Frost, Grade 6
Wayne Gray Elementary School, MI

Animal

Lining up, the gun goes off.
Like a lion, I catapult forward.
Red, blue, gold; all disappear.
I am faster than a galloping horse,
A speeding jaguar,
A diving falcon.
The finish line is near.
Red is in my sight lines.
The finish line is nearer.
　Nearer
　　Nearer!
Red is closer still.
Like a wolf, I shoot forward.
Red fades; dust in the wind.
Savor the victory.
I am the alpha!
I am supreme!
I am the victor!
Katie Cruickshank, Grade 6
Assumption School, MI

Guess Who?

He has circles for ears,
His head is almost half black
And half tan
No shirt,
Black body
Red pants with two buttons
White gloves on his hands
And yellow shoes!

Guess who! Mickey Mouse!
Jose-Luis Angeles, Grade 4
Hampton Elementary School, MI

When I Was a Kid

When I was a kid,
I loved the color pink,
no…blue,
no…green,
How 'bout purple ink?
When I was a kid,
I wanted to be an artist,
no…a teacher,
no…an actress,
How 'bout an author?
When I was a kid,
I liked volleyball,
no…soccer,
no…basketball,
How 'bout softball?
When I was a kid,
I liked everything,
So making up my mind,
Was a fantasy.
Ivana Khreizat, Grade 6
West Middle School, MI

My Gentle Breeze

My room
My gentle breeze
My block of quietness in a tough situation.
My room
My personal hiding spot
of stuffed animals
of a heaven for children.
My room
My solitary space
is what I dread every single day of my life.
My room
My nightmare arena
where I'm expelled to when I'm angry
home of my terror.
My room
My gentle breeze
My personal hiding spot
My solitary space
My nightmare arena in a tough situation.
Clayton Stine, Grade 6
St Bartholomew School, IN

War

The war is no bore.
It is hard core.

We want freedom,
So we have got to beat them.

War can mean a lot of lives lost.
We have to pay a high cost.
Kevin Beddow, Grade 5
Staunton Elementary School, IN

Fall

Before winter, and after summer.
Life is such a bummer.
Raking leaves, all day long
In the fall birds sing songs
I like to jump in the leaves
In the fall people like to believe.

Sitting watching the clouds very still,
I make a vase so I can be filled.
Children jump around and play tag
Bringing home leaves in a bag
Away everyone loves to go
And go to places that no one knows

To bad summer went
No one to give a mint
Luckily winter is coming to town
No one to see with a frown
Lots and lots of rain
So goodbye and see you again.

Yasmine Hamka, Grade 6
Star International Academy, MI

Desert Demon

A hot dry night
A rattlesnake slithers
Fast as a cheetah
Across the open desert
It crawls to a bush
To take a nap
Along come 2 people
Who awaken the snake
As they get closer
They hear a ringing rattle
But keep on going
Then out of nowhere
He hears his friend scream
That's when he saw
The Rattlesnake
On that hot, hot night
The rattlesnake rests
Alone in the bushes
Never disturbed again

Nathan McLouth, Grade 6
Wayne Gray Elementary School, MI

Summer and Winter

Winter
Cold, white
Freezing, snowing, sleeting
Sleds, snowboards, beaches, boats
Shining, swimming, raining,
Beautiful, bright
Summer

Elizabeth Griffith, Grade 6
Knox Community Middle School, IN

Stay Strong

When they try to knock you down,
just get back up again.
Remember to stay strong, don't frown,
and you will always win.

Don't ever let them put you down,
not one little bit.
No matter what they say or do,
just smile and ignore it.

Life is a roller coaster,
up and down and everywhere.
When they make it a disaster,
just remind them you don't care.

Don't ever let them put you down,
not one little bit.
No matter what they say or do,
just smile and ignore it.

Erin Miller, Grade 6
Mary Evelyn Castle Elementary School, IN

Where I'm From

I'm from music,
From guitars and drums.
I'm from technology,
From computers and cellphones,
iPods and video games.
I'm from Hershey,
The city as well as the candy.

I'm from faith,
From Catholic schools and churches.
I'm from the pool at my old house,
From swimming all the time,
With family and friends.

On the walls of my house,
Are pictures of my family.
I'm from the memories,
Each one of them holds.
I'm from the comfort of my home.

Evan Raymer, Grade 6
St Bartholomew School, IN

Believe

People who believe in themselves
Can achieve anywhere else
Just put your mind in START
And study for the ARTS
Just believe in yourself
Your dreams will come true
I'll promise you will make it
All the way through

Lonell Dixon, Grade 6
DSA - West Langston Hughes Campus, MI

World Peace

In a world filled with peace,
All fighting and sadness would cease.
Everyone would get along
Even birds would sing their song
There wouldn't be sick or poor
There wouldn't be any war
No one would have to spill any blood
There wouldn't be disasters like floods
No one's going to sing the blues

We'd only win; never lose
When push comes to shove,
We'd still be filled with peace and love!

Nicole Drylie, Grade 6
St John Lutheran School, MI

In the Hole

Wipe the sweat from your face.
Deep breath
Crowd going silent.
This is it.
Putter goes back and hits the ball.
Rolling
Yelling
Twisting
Turning
Waiting
Hoping
AND THEN...
It sinks into the hole!

Alan Adams, Grade 6
Assumption School, MI

Hannah and Mother

H ave I ever broke my arm? No!
A m I good? Yes!
N ever gave up.
N ever stole anything.
A lways awesome.
H ave I gotten hurt? Bunch of times.

M ight get a car soon.
O ught to have a son.
T ogether with me and my sister.
H as she broken her hand? No.
E very time she is awesome.
R ight-handed.

Hannah Norskov, Grade 4
Morgan Elementary School, IN

Swaying Trees

Trees sway with the wind
The owls hoot from the treetops
Wind blows through the trees

Brett Stalboerger, Grade 6
Holy Name School, MI

Ode to Grandpa Grant

Grandpa Grant you always made me happy. I was sad when you died. I got to see you on Thanksgiving and sometimes between Thanksgiving. I still cry sometimes, but I'm getting through it. I really wish I could see you one more time. I used to do puzzles with you or draw. it was hard for you because you're old. You died at 87 or 89. You died in the hospital because you broke your leg. Your wife let me get something out of the glass cabinet. I got two bells to remind me of you. I miss you very much.

Ashley Prince, Grade 4
Morgan Elementary School, IN

Ode to My Cat Spot

Spot you are the best cat ever. When I wake up in the morning you are sleeping on my pillow. Sometimes you climb up the tree. You always try to scare your mother. Sometimes you make my mom say oh brother! Spot, you meow all day till I come home. You hate it when I brush you with a comb. Sometimes when I read a book you sit in my lap and purr. You get scared when you get a giant burr. Spot you see, you mean so much to me.

Carly Alderman, Grade 4
Morgan Elementary School, IN

Perfection

As I open the wrapper I see a great mass of deliciousness and smell the sweet cocoa and sugar fused together to create this masterpiece. As I dive into the first bite of perfection, I feel the warm creamy concoction dance around in my mouth. The urge to taste it again is irresistible, so I take another bite. It feels like a dream as the fantastic crunch combines with the explosive flavor that seems too huge to be real. My senses almost burst as I finish the spectacular bar of chocolaty goodness.

Matthew Gordon, Grade 6
Home School, MI

I Love You

I know you love me, I know you care, that's why I gave you this little teddy bear.
Our love is expressed in a way that's not known, that's why I'd let you rule while sitting on a thrown.
You could rule my world, I'd bring you everything on a silver platter, I'd make you heart shaped pancakes out of buttermilk batter.
So if you understand, let me take your hand, and there I would put a little teddy bear.

Maddisson Soper, Grade 5
Liberty Elementary School, IN

I Am

I am flexible and sporty
I wonder if someday I will be a star
I hear the world saying, "Elli, Elli"
I see me playing with friends every day
I want every Nintendo game
I am flexible and sporty

I pretend I'm a teacher
I feel lonely in my room
I touch red berries outside
I worry when I lose a friend
I cry when my mom cries
I am flexible and sporty

I understand I am not perfect
I say treat others the way you want to be treated
I dream I will be a teacher
I try to do my best in softball
I hope people say I am nice
I am nice

I am Ellianna Monroe Downs

Ellianna Monroe Downs, Grade 4
Floyd Ebeling Elementary School, MI

Me as Myself

I'm from tasty Chicken Alfredo,
from the soccer ball in my room,
and from the Jackson himself Michael Jackson,
I'm the monkey in the tree,
with branches I climb,
as if they were my own.

I am from dodge ball dodges and Jolly Ranchers,
from Reshon Fegan to Jackie Chan,
"From hold your horses" to the Chicago White Sox

I'm from Family Guy,
to the stitches in my head,
I'm from the basketball court,
from Denise and Dennis.

In the closet the Thompson machine guns,
memories from family guns.
I'm from those family memories,
Before my birth before this day,
They waited for our family,
to grow on me.

Desmund Thompson, Grade 6
Knox Community Middle School, IN

Where I'm From

I am from Dragon Tales and Little House on the Prairie,
To dark chocolate Hershey's bars and Hamburger Helper.
From the dark black cowboy boots sitting in the corner.
To country music and Alan Jackson.

I'm from building model cars and making posters,
and from climbing the small tree in the back yard.
From Play Station 2 and Xbox 360 games,
to Call of Duty and Sly Cooper.

I'm from "Just try it, you'll like it" and "Do your best,
just keep practicing, you'll get it."
From "Git R Done" and "Would you please stop it!"
From the freckles on my face that each tell a story,

to the glasses I wear to help me see the world.
I'm from fishing and camping.
From finding and catching frogs and bugs.
And from crashing my bike, four-wheeler, and go-cart.

I'm from a lifetime in Knox.
From a picture in the year book,
From a long line of family,
All the way down to me!

Jaimie Lemke, Grade 6
Knox Community Middle School, IN

Zoey

In the winter,
You watched me,
As I cradled you,
The warm touch of your fingers,
You're my favorite of them all,

In the spring,
You came to hunt eggs,
I was holding you close,
Searching for your eggs,

In the summer,
Your sister and I helped you swim,
You trying to paddle,
Your short black hair, now blonde, floated.

In the fall,
The big pile of leaves called you,
We pounced in the swimming pool of leaves.

Now you're five reading big kid books.
The bigger you get, the more worried I get.
What if you get too old and do not want me?
But I know in my heart that you will always love me

Allison Marshall, Grade 6
Knox Community Middle School, IN

Kirby

Oh Kirby, oh Kirby you are so fluffy.
You bark at your shadow.
You bark at yourself in the mirror.
We sometimes call you a dorkdog.
When I let you out you turn around and scratch at the door.
You're a dog that eats a lot.
Your record is five seconds for eating a weenie.

Alex Shaw, Grade 4
Morgan Elementary School, IN

Mrs. P,

Mrs. P, is peaceful and playful!
She loves to paint pretty portraits and go to parades!
Mrs. P, likes to eat popcorn and peaches!
She loves to wear pants that have patch's and punk rock clothes!
Mrs. P, hates porcupines!
She loves O but hates Q!
Mrs. P,'s favorite words are pop, popping, and popcorn!

Madison Cashero, Grade 4
Dodson Elementary School, MI

Forgotten Love

My mind is open to reality now. I might as well not frown.
The kissed was missed and the heart is broken.
But all is okay my love is a token, maybe hurt but never broken.
Life is filled with obstacles, some are left unsolved.
But if you look at them with a open mind they soon will be resolved.
I am a new person now I am going to try over.
I am no longer worried about you or any other.

Cydney Gardner-Brown, Grade 6
University Preparatory Science & Math Middle School, MI

Heart Knows

A heart knows when to slow down from its beating race
When to thump slowly when you sleep
When to stop when your life is done
How to beat rapidly to show that it's time to slow down,
Like a warning police office or a speedometer
When to tell you what to do,
A heart knows.

Emma Patrick, Grade 4
Dodson Elementary School, MI

Beatles

B ring the beat in my head
E xcited for the concert
A stonished by their look
T hink they rock or think not
L et's hear their awesome music
E ven the best song is HELP!
S ing and dance enjoy playing with the Beatles

Savannah Pratte, Grade 6
St John Lutheran School, MI

Spring

It's spring,
So let's sing.
I like to swing.
While I swing, I sing.
It's fishing season,
The fish won't bite because they have a reason.
The water is warm,
There is a worm.
I love to be outside,
I play on the slide.
I love spring,
So, let's sing.

George Green, Grade 4
Chrisney Elementary School, IN

Green

Green, the color of juicy green apples
Towering from an apple tree
Green, the color of my finger nails
Sparkling in the bright sun
Green, like the hot-earthy August
Exploding in the warm air
Green, like the gooey play doe
Splashing and snapping with joy
Green, the color of zinging green cars
Screeching in the parking lot
Green, the color of a bright flickering TV
Humming in my ENORMOUS multicolored room

Katelynn Lawrence, Grade 6
Linton-Stockton Elementary School, IN

Me

My life can sometimes be boring
And other times it's soaring
I hang with my best friend all the time
We laugh so much that people think it's a crime
It takes me forever to do my hair
But I always finish with no time to spare
I listen to music all day long
I know every word to my favorite song
I think summer is really cool
Because we get time off of school
And when I'm down
My friends always know how to take away that frown

Hannah Muehlbrandt, Grade 6
St John Lutheran School, MI

The Bond Between a Mother and a Daughter

The bond between a mother and a daughter,
Is completely unbreakable.
When the daughter is crazy,
The mother makes her feel lazy.
When she is hurt,
The mother reminds her of her beautiful birth.

Victoria Shahnazary, Grade 5
Academy of the Sacred Heart, MI

Ohio State!

My favorite football team is Ohio State
We win the coin toss and kick off first
Our defense is hot right out of the gate
Our offense is on the bench, waiting with thirst

Running as fast as a cheetah, half back Dan Heron breaks free
The defense chases but cannot catch him
They soon give up and just let him be
24 yards he ran, we're on our way to a win

The defense takes the field, it's thrown…interception!
The offense is back to secure the game with a score
First play, Pryor and Posey hook up on a touchdown reception
The clock hits 0 and the stadium gets louder than a lion…ROAR!

The game is over and we have won
The Big Ten is ours, we're number one!

Christopher Gregory, Grade 6
St Mary Cathedral School, MI

Rod Hockey

I own a game called rod hockey
The players are very slick
My dad is really good so occasionally he'll block me
My offense is really quick

Every game we play to ten
I have only beat my dad once
He beats me over and over again
Even though I've owned it for months

I am awesome at passing the puck
My dad is good at scoring
Sometimes I score with a bunch of luck
We score so much it gets boring

Rod hockey is so much fun
We play until the day is done

Nathan Wahr, Grade 6
St Mary Cathedral School, MI

Ode to Charley

Ode to Charley
how you're a black cat.
Ode to Charley
how I got you when you were a kitten on my birthday.
Ode to Charley
you had a lot of nicknames.
Ode to Charley
you loved our baths especially mine.
Ode to Charley
I loved you then and I still love you no matter what.
Ode to Charley
why did you have to go.

Samantha Masterson, Grade 4
Morgan Elementary School, IN

High Merit Poems – Grades 4, 5, and 6

No Way!
Whoosh!!!
32-32
Dribble, Dribble
Stomp, Stomp
8-7
Dribble, Dribble
Stomp, Stomp
6-5
Dribble, Dribble
Stomp, Stomp
4-3
Shoot, Shoot
Whoosh!!
2-1-0
Buzzzzz, The buzzer is like a bee.
The fans jump up.
Like a cheetah on its prey
Roar!! Roar!! The fans are like a bunch of lions.
32-34!! US!!
"No Way!! We win!" The Coach yells.
Trophy Time!!
Thomas J. Buursma, Grade 6
Assumption School, MI

The Four Seasons
Wonderful, snowy winter is here,
When certain animals play, like deer.
When the snow is glistening white,
When children have a snowball fight.

The snow has melted, the cold is gone,
So, beautiful, enchanting spring is on.
When flowers are growing,
When birds are crowing.
That's when spring is here, my dear.

The weather is warmer,
And it's a scorcher,
So that means summer is nearly here.
The water's good for swimming,
So we can swim until the light is dimming.

The air is getting colder now,
So let's all take a bow,
For bone shivering fall.
When once again, you're walking through the school hall.
Emily Wood, Grade 5
Thomas M Cooley School, MI

Bobbi
I remember the sound of her beautiful voice
When she was telling hilarious jokes
I remember the look on her glowing face
When she was serious, and when she was joking
That day when I last saw her
When she was in pain, but not showing it
I remember trying to make her laugh
To make her feel better,
But sometimes I think it hurt to laugh
She had cancer
One day, it was gone…then it came back
Worse than ever
The doctors said they were sure
She was going to pass on
To the next level in life
But I had faith in her
I wasn't going to quit on her
A few days later, she passed on
I'll never forget her
Now she's in Heaven…not hurting, safe
I love you Aunt Bobbi, I'll see you someday
Emily Sullivan, Grade 6
Linton-Stockton Elementary School, IN

Ride in the Mist
At first, I cannot see anything,
the mist is as thick as fresh
peanut butter
Then, some mist dissolves away,
revealing the still, blue-green waters of the ocean
I peer out from my seat and
watch as the calm waters are
sliced
by the sleek craft
The once still waters are now waves,
crashing into the boat,
sending water and
frothy,
sea foam flying
Dark shapes loom up out of the mist
As we draw nearer, I realize that the silhouettes
are just buildings on the shore
As we step out of the boat,
the sun appears from behind a cloud,
soon to burn the mist away
until the air is crystal clear.
Sanjana Kulkarni, Grade 6
Stanley Clark School, IN

White
White is like the sound of snow packing down when you walk on it.
White is like the smell of a white daisy blowing in the wind.
White is like the taste of a scoop of whipped cream on a piece of pie.
White is the feel of my kitten as we settle in on a cold winter's day.
Mabel DeVore, Grade 4
Morgan Elementary School, IN

Green
Green is like the sound of tall grass blowing in the wind.
Green is like the smell of fresh cut grass.
Green is like the taste of a sour apple.
Green is like the feel of an apple in your mouth.
Evan Lasley, Grade 4
Morgan Elementary School, IN

Beaches
Beaches
Sandy, hot
Tanning, running, swimming
Relaxed, calm, joyous, stressless
Florida
Marley Muhlada, Grade 5
Sunman Dearborn Intermediate School, IN

Green
Green is like the sound of grass waving in the wind.
Green is like the smell of ripe bananas being picked.
Green is like the taste of color-dyed green eggs and ham.
Green is like the feel of shag carpeting tickling my feet.
Jobe Whitman, Grade 4
Morgan Elementary School, IN

Pink
Pink is like the sound of a pink dress swishing back and forth.
Pink is like the smell of a candle burning.
Pink is like the taste of pink sour strawberry.
Pink is like the feel of a pink fluffy coat on a winter day.
Emma Wise, Grade 4
Morgan Elementary School, IN

Blue
Blue is like the sound of dolphins going through the water.
Blue is like the smell of the open salty ocean.
Blue is like the taste of blue lemonade.
Blue is like the feel of my Morgan Elementary shirt.
Amber Lenz, Grade 4
Morgan Elementary School, IN

Blue
Blue is the sound of a dolphin singing in the hot summer water.
Blue is the smell of a fresh painted wall.
Blue is like the taste of a fresh-picked blueberry in the cool breeze.
Blue is like the feel of a soft blanket keeping you warm.
Everly Yocum, Grade 4
Morgan Elementary School, IN

Trophy
I am yours when you win
If you try I will be on your shelf in no time
What are you competing for?
Work hard, I'm not plastic I'm a true trophy.
Chance Roddy, Grade 5
Hendry Park Elementary School, IN

Peppermint Grass
Peppermint grass,
Roseberry flowers,
Honey sunset in the warm summer evening,
But what I really love is the pomegranate sea.
Megan Trulock, Grade 4
Dodson Elementary School, MI

The Skies of the Day
Stare out your window
Into the morning sky
The treetops swaying in the wind
Blocking the morning sun in the clear sky
It rolls into the afternoon
The sun beams down
The clear sky holds very few clouds
While the sky creeps dark into the night
With the sun gone to rest
And the moon and the stars awake
All the stars hold a picture in the sky
Some of the stars form the dippers
With some sailors using them as maps in the night
The morning soon comes again
With a new story to tell every day
Kelly O'Brien, Grade 6
Christ the King Catholic School, IN

The Monster in the Closet
I am a big frightening monster
You know me for my giant shadow stalking on the wall
My mother is dreadful nightmares
My father is a misty white invisible ghost
I was born in a child's room
I live in a dark echoing closet
My best friend is the pitch-black darkness
Because it helps me hide
My enemy is the bright shiny light
Because then I can be seen and I will be the one that's frightened
I fear wonderful thoughts and dreams
Because they are not thinking of me
I love to frighten children at night
Because I love to see the scared look on their faces
I wish the world would be completely terrifying for children
Austin LeBert, Grade 5
Dodson Elementary School, MI

I Am
I am a giant blue wave
You know me for splashing the land when I hit the shore
My mother is the dark blue sea
My father is a raging hurricane waiting to smash into the land
I was born in the deep depths of the ocean
I live close to my mom and dad, always getting closer to the land
My best friend is a big plump rain cloud
Because he rains on me and makes me bigger
My enemy is the red sizzling sun
Because he burns me and I get evaporated
I fear big gray rocks
Because it hurts to land on them
I love the colorful fish of the ocean
Because it tickles when they touch me
I wish I will be a colossal wave when I crash into land
Michael Kaledas, Grade 5
Dodson Elementary School, MI

You

You took my hand, you showed me how to live.
Now you're gone.
I would give anything to hear your voice,
sadly death is not my choice.
You took one last breath
then you left.
I want you near.
I need you here.
Grandma, I miss you.

Samantha Love, Grade 6
Sherman Middle School, MI

Ice Cream

Ice cream, ice cream, kids scream for ice cream
Chocolate, strawberry all different kinds
When we eat, it's like a dream
It blows our minds!
Chocolate, strawberry all different kinds
When I hear that song
When we eat it it's like a dream
I'm sad when it's gone
Ice cream, ice cream kids scream for ice cream

Arianna Alva, Grade 5
Dodson Elementary School, MI

What's in the Polar Region?

The frigid weather haunts the freezing animals.
The polar bear finds it complicated to balance on the slender ice.
The seal below him feels alike to the frozen, petrified iceberg.
Frigid weather just laughs.
What clever tricks I have!
Although, the wind and snow are safe.
They are weather themselves.
Coldness everlasting inhabits this region.
Guests are not welcome in this kingdom of coldness.

Devin Kennedy, Grade 5
Dodson Elementary School, MI

Ode to Leah

Leah, Leah, you're so cute
Sometimes you cry it makes me feel bad
You always wear purple
You're only 8 months old
When you smile it makes the world go around
I love you, Leah!

Jalynn Lori, Grade 4
Morgan Elementary School, IN

Nothing Better

There's nothing better than getting a letter,
There's nothing better than a really soft sweater.
When I'm in a pool,
There's no getting wetter;
And I think there's nothing better.

Jack Kozyrski, Grade 6
St Simon the Apostle School, IN

Darkness

Darkness surrounds me,
Darkness takes over the sky,
As the light fades away,
The darkness cannot be broken.
As this dark gloomy evening,
Carries all hope away.
The darkness sucks all the happiness out of you,
As if a vacuum cleaner is sucking out your insides.
I sometimes think the darkness is everlasting,
And that I will never see light again,
The thought is terrifying,
The darkness has stayed for what feels like,
Twelve years long.
I am depressed upon this dark day,
I am empty

Bryce Douglas, Grade 5
Perry Central Elementary School, IN

Towering Walls

Towering walls,
In this ghetto so small,
Seem like giants to me.

Towering walls,
There's no chance they'll fall,
But no one can find the key.

Towering walls,
From which dead bodies they haul,
And throw them out to sea.

Towering walls,
Taking the life of almost all,
Leaving living people wishing their families would still be.

Sami Lofman, Grade 4
Akiva Hebrew Day School, MI

Life

Why is life such a pain?
It gains all the sorrow.
All of the lost hearts,
the darts in the hearts.
But when you have someone to cry to,
they will dry the tears.
So just look in the mirror…
and smile.
Think of the joy it is to have someone love you,
and only you.
Few people have that.
So just smile…
and dial the person who loves you.
And say hello,
and say I'm always here for you.

Vittoria Lange, Grade 6
East Elementary School, MI

It All Ended So Quickly

We went there at midnight, you and me. Just seeking a peaceful place away from our troubles. We don't talk; we just lay there, relishing our time together. You were my life and all I ever cared about. We fell asleep with comforting thoughts flooding through our heads.

I woke up and reached to my side, seeking the warm presence of you touch. Instead, I found the smalls grains of sand that covered our secret beach. I sat up, expecting to see you on the dock fishing or swimming in the ocean water, but saw that I was alone. Its less than a minute before I see it.

A note.

It was perched up on a rock, waiting to be read. I got up, took the note, and sat down. I had a bad feeling about what it could say, and those thoughts were correct. Each sentence makes my eyes swell up more and more, until that first tear comes dripping slowly down my cheek. I sit there for hours before I stop crying.

I crumpled up that note and threw it across the sand. It took me a few minutes to realize that I was alone. You were all I had, and you were what kept me living. I take one last look over my shoulder at all my troubles and wasted years before I dive into the ocean, into a place without pain or sorrow.

Every day I look down at you and her. You seem so happy, happier than you ever were with me. Years and years go by, and I see that you are my past life, and that my life up here is what makes me happy. Not you, or what we used to be, but living in peace. Finally.

Isa Hoban, Grade 6
St Stephen School, MI

The Absolutely, Positively, Not So Scary, OK Maybe a Little Bit, But Just a Little Bit, I Think Really Creepy Monster

The absolutely, positively, not so scary, (OK maybe a little bit, but just a little bit, I think,) really creepy monster
She has pointy, pink, polka dotted horns,
Filthy rattail hair,
One eye patch
One eye,
No ears, just empty vacant holes
An extra-long elephant nose
Teeth that say she doesn't brush them,
Trust me, it shows!
A super long giraffe neck
A watermelon chest
Five foot long scaly arms
Short slimy legs
Big hairy feet,
Toenails that are green…I hope she painted them!

Annie MacLean, Grade 4
Hampton Elementary School, MI

Where I'm From

I am from the big white house on the corner playing outside imagining my life when I was in kindergarten
I am from following my mom around watching her cook and clean in admiration
I am from waking up going to my first day in kindergarten wondering how my neighbor is doing with her first day of school
I am from the swing set, the books, and the movies
I am from the early mornings and the late nights with my friends
I am from going to Frosty Treats every night only to get the same thing
I am from bouncing between dance and play practice only wanting to curl up with my book
I am from divorced parents
I am from a little apartment for 2 years, still glued to my books
I am from a remarried mom, now in a big orange stucco house on Hewitt Street
I am from a supportive mom, and a great dad
They are why I believe in love and friendship
I am from ever changing life

Sandra French, Grade 5
Bothwell Middle School, MI

High Merit Poems – Grades 4, 5, and 6

The Endless Sound
I awake to hear the continuous sound of the waves,
As they pound on the shore, the everlasting white foam
Rolling to the sand.

I watch as the sun rises, hearing none of the repeated
Excitement of the figures below me,
Nor the shrieking and yelling of my older cousins who are
Asleep peacefully inside.

The only two sounds I hear are the most comforting:
The soft creaking of the white, straw chair, on which I rest,
And the waves that sing me their beautiful song of
Endless sound.

Briana Baker, Grade 6
St Simon the Apostle School, IN

The Hog and the Frog
There once was a hog
Who went outside with his brother frog
They decided to go to the local well
But the hog fell.
The frog panicked and got out a rope
Then he slipped off like a bar of soap
Now they sit screaming for help
No one could hear them
Even with a yelp
Their neighbor Mr. Spout checked to see what was going on
Anxiously waiting to finish mowing his lawn
He got them out as quick as a shout
Oh thank you for Mr. Spout!

Clare Nalezyty, Grade 6
St John Lutheran School, MI

Dad the Best
D ad
A wesome
D ad's always there

T ruffles is your nickname
H onest
E xcellent

B est dad in the world
E veryone loves him especially me
S moky Mountains is your favorite vacation place
T urbo was my dad's dog

Brooke Shively, Grade 4
Morgan Elementary School, IN

Dinner
The house fills with smells right before dinner,
The steak and potatoes have just simmered,
When I smell these smells, I am a winner,
Because of my mom's homemade dinner!

Caleb Shannon, Grade 5
Hendry Park Elementary School, IN

Wonderland
Alice knelt on her knee
And peered through the large hole.
But all she could see was black.
She crept closer…and fell down…down.
She landed upside down.
Alice saw a white rabbit in a waist coat.
"In this place flowers talk and sing.
Rabbits are dressed in petticoats and have hand watches…
A cheshire cat disappears and reappears."
Said Alice in complete bliss.
"This must be wonderland."

Solei Porter, Grade 6
Lake Linden-Hubbell Elementary School, MI

Hope
Hope is something that was given to all,
But has been thrown away, by so many.
It is believing that good things will come,
and the bad things in life, will cease to exist one day.
Don't give up hope because of fear,
and don't give in to the pessimistic thoughts.
For hope is offered to you after you've lost it,
Don't throw it aside, because you fear you will lose it again.
For one day, when you have accepted hope after you've lost it,
You will be given happiness in a place,
where all of your hoping, has paid off.

Maddie Elliott, Grade 6
Karl Richter Campus, MI

The Shy Beast
Big black silver back,
Creeping, crawling, through the Congo.
Sprinting through the rain forest,
He is quiet as he thumps through the jungle.
Protecting his family he thumps on his chest.
He climbs a tree every once in a while,
When hunters come to take his fur.
The females groom the silver back,
But he is too powerful to groom them.
He learns lessons in his long life,
The shy, social silver back.

Garrett Bernath, Grade 5
Wayne Gray Elementary School, MI

Grandma, Oh Grandma
Grandma, Oh Grandma, I miss you so much.
I don't want to sleep, I don't want to munch.
You died on Halloween,
I think that's really mean.
I wish you were here, right in front of me.
You loved me, you fed me, you rocked me to sleep,
and now you are gone and it's making me weep.
Grandma I miss you, I miss you really bad.
Grandma, Oh Grandma, please come back.

Keimon Gordon, Grade 6
Palmer Park Preparatory Academy, MI

Who I Am?
I am from cherry jolly ranchers
the fabulous taste in my mouth.
I am from the bright gleaming purple
when I see it just hits me.

I am from bubble gum
that juice comes out like I am going
to drink the best juice in the world.

I'm from the trophies from
past soccer games
the trophies shine like the sun shines
when I go past my room, it shines like the sun.
Zaida Chacon, Grade 6
Knox Community Middle School, IN

The Crazy Lopper Whopper Maniac Monster
The Crazy Lopper Whopper Maniac Monster
has
A large red mohawk hairdo,
13 large red eyeballs around his head,
A large triangle nose,
Big pointy shark teeth,
With a French mustache,
Big dark lips,
A hard boulder chest,
Soft yummy chocolate arms,
Rainbow colored hands,
Hard metal robot legs,
And big sharp alligator feet!
Sudarshana Lakshmi, Grade 4
Hampton Elementary School, MI

Basketball
He's in my hands.
Full of air, but so energetic!
Just wanting to bounce to the hoop,
Make the noise SWOOSH!

He likes to go somewhere, anywhere,
He's never gone before,
The place he gets the most excited
Is when he's at the court.

He likes to shout, scream,
Shoot, and jump from hand to hand.
Sometimes so unpredictable but will always be fun!
Josie Edick, Grade 5
North Muskegon Elementary School, MI

Black
Black is like the sound of a headache in the dark.
Black is like the smell of blackberry pie freshly baked.
Black is like the feel of my fat black cat that thinks he's a dog.
Jacob Slaughterback, Grade 4
Morgan Elementary School, IN

Flowers
Flowers have a very pleasing aroma,
They grab you by a hook and reel you in.
There are so many kinds they'll make your head spin.
Their fragrance fills the air and makes you grin.
By the end of the day you will be in a coma.

As you walk through the flower garden,
Roses standing tall, thinking they are so smart.
Cosmos whispering about their big heart.
Daisies acting foolish, playing the child's part.
You might turn and say, "I beg your pardon?"

So as the sun sets each day,
The Roses are still deep red.
The Cosmos all wanting to go to bed.
The Daisies asking to be fed.
So it must be time to walk away.
Morgan Yingling, Grade 6
Leo Elementary School, IN

The New Kid
Hi, my name is Sidney,
please call me Sid.
I'm going to share a story
about the new kid.
His name is Tyrone.
He likes to be called Ty.
Let me tell you one thing,
he is very shy.
It wasn't our idea.
He just showed up in our grade.
And at recess time, with Ty, nobody played.
All the kids played ball in the sun,
while Ty sat there and had no fun.
I walked over to Ty and asked him if he wanted to play.
He looked at me with a smile and said ok.
You should treat a friend like you would want him to treat you.
It shouldn't matter if he's an old friend or someone new.
Eden Gilan, Grade 5
Akiva Hebrew Day School, MI

Cheer
I love to cheer, I can't help myself
Cheer is so much fun
I just need to share my spirit with someone else
When it's done I'm glum
It is so much fun when flipping upside down
My teammates are so funny
You go round and round
But it costs a lot of money
You travel everywhere
My mom brings me there
Sometimes I get scared
My mom deeply cares
Payton Olson, Grade 5
Dodson Elementary School, MI

Basketball
His heart was racing
The game was tied
All he wanted was to get inside
Inside the game to hear the crowd cheer his name
Then he heard it, Damon get in the game
Now was his chance
To collect all the fame
His heart was racing faster than before
All he wanted was to make a score
20 to 20
The scoreboard read
10 seconds left the referee said
He grabbed the ball
His hands sweaty and slick
And ran down the court hoping he didn't trip
He shot the ball from half court line
Please please he said this is my time
He heard the ball go through the net
He turned to the crowd and said you haven't seen anything yet!
Damon Hooker, Grade 6
Fort Branch Community School, IN

A Blank Piece of Tree
There it was,
Sitting on the table,
Laying over top of my sketchbook,
Praying to impress someone.

He can't wait to be displayed,
Maybe on a wall,
Maybe he will be first place,
Or maybe even take home a trophy.

He used to be a tree,
But now it is something magical,
An impression made of lead,
On a white piece of tree.

Just a few curving lines,
And scratches from erasers,
But I have always known the piece of paper as…
My drawing.
Jimmy Cobb, Grade 5
North Muskegon Elementary School, MI

Signs of Fall
The sun is still shining, but there's a chill in the air
Leaves are still green, but trees seem more bare
Birds chirp and caw, flying from tree to tree
Woodpeckers are pecking, somewhere around me
Some trees start to color, yellow, orange and red
Squirrels and chipmunks scamper, looking to get fed
Branches sway and rustle, as squirrels jump and climb
Signs of fall are here, it's that time
Jenna Lee, Grade 5
Bloomfield Hills Middle School, MI

My Favorite Sport
Heading down the court
with the ball in my hand.
Looking at the goal
making a plan.

Blocking people out of my way
trying to make the perfect play.
Getting closer and closer to the goal
panicking, in shock and losing control.

Concentrating to make a shot
there is a person in front of me almost forgot!
The arching ball is now in the air,
all I can do is stare.

The ball swooshed through the net,
just like a jet!
Brooke Lasher, Grade 5
Perry Central Elementary School, IN

A Close Win
39-37
My team is down by two!
5 seconds on the clock
I dribbled down the court with my right hand.
Then to my left
Juked him out.
3 seconds
Dribbled between my legs
He fell to the ground.
1 second on the clock
I pulled up from half court
SWOOSH!
The basket doesn't count
I traveled
Boos rained like hail
I collapse to the court like a bowling ball because of the call.
Eli Katt, Grade 6
Assumption School, MI

Football
Football is so fun
It's better when you have won
Touchdowns are so great
Interceptions are kind of lame
YAY a touchdown
It's even better when you know you have won
Quarterback throws the ball
Interceptions are kind of lame
YAY a touchdown
Quarterback throws the ball
Touchdowns are so great
YAY a touchdown
Football is so fun.
Hasif Bhatti, Grade 5
Dodson Elementary School, MI

Spring Has Sprung
As the tulips come,
We know that spring has sprung!
As the birds chirp,
We know that spring has sprung!
As the little animals lose their winter coat,
We know that spring has sprung!
When the monarchs have come,
We know that spring has sprung!
When April showers bring May flowers,
We know that spring has sprung!
When allergies come,
We know that spring has sprung!
When the grass turns green,
We know that spring has sprung!
And on March 20th…
That is the day spring has officially sprung!
Kaitlyn Lohe, Grade 6
Fort Branch Community School, IN

Forever…Gone
That tragic night
My dad's face…bright red
She is gone
Into that starry night
I need to hear her laugh
Once more
Pain gushes…through my heart
Thoughts make me cringe
The night she went
Away
Sobs…I am so sorry
She will never…ever
Be forgotten
Her blood runs through my veins
I am hers
Forever…
Kassidee Kleist, Grade 6
Linton-Stockton Elementary School, IN

Volleyball
The ball is mine,
So is the court.
Waiting,
Waiting.
Tweet the whistle blows
It seems like the net is 1000 miles away!
I held the ball up…
BANG!!
I hit the ball
It's going
Going
YES! It made it!
The crowd goes wild
We won the game!!
Erin Leatherman, Grade 6
Assumption School, MI

Two Siblings
Two tennis players
Two sets of brown eyes
Two piano players
Two in Student Council
Two with brown hair
Two Michigan State lovers
Two funny people
One shorter, one taller
One glasses, one contacts
One high voice, one deep voice
One long hair, one shorter hair
One goes to Hampton, one goes to Reuther
One writer, one reader
One likes mild, one loves spicy
Two siblings
Sara Ang, Grade 4
Hampton Elementary School, MI

Libby
Her eyebrows over her eyes
The arched beard on her snout
Her stub tail wiggles a mile a minute
Chews on my shoes
Makes big paper messes
Barks at anything that moves
Loves to go for walks
Runs for her toys
Likes to eat
Pointy ears are curious
Eats her food quickly
Loves the outdoors
Has soft, salt and pepper fur
Likes to wrestle with the cat
Bark, bark, bark
Jacob Skwirsk, Grade 5
Dodson Elementary School, MI

Mashed Potatoes Imashination
M ounds of white cotton balls
A nd a couple water falls
S nowballs cover here and there.
H eaps of snowballs everywhere.
E very bite is so delicious.
D o you think they are nutritious?

P eople eat them 'round the world.
O n a plate they can be swirled.
T he gravy pools like little lakes
A nd goes so well with two grilled steaks.
T asty taters for everyone!
O h, I like taters a ton!
E xciting endings come right now.
S mashed potatoes are so good! How?
Maria Bustamante, Grade 4
Divine Child Elementary School, MI

Cemetery Tears
Crying…
Heart throbbing
In my chest.
Searching
For Grandma.
I see her hiding
Among the saddest of souls.
I follow.
My limbs trembling…
I collapse onto her tomb
Sobbing, "Grandma!
Please, Grandma!
I want to see you again!"
I walk away,
Hoping that she remembers
That I will not forget her,
Ever.
Christina Hayden, Grade 6
Linton-Stockton Elementary School, IN

Blue
Blue is the beautiful color of the sky.
The awesome vacation
By the blue ocean water.
As I sit down on the crumbly sand,
The strong beach breeze hits my face.
Blue makes me think of a blue jay
Passing by swiftly.
My last name starts with a "B"
Just like blue.
Yum! Out comes the blueberry pie.
I like blue Gatorade.
My chair at school
Is a cool bright blue.
I think of the Colts because
They are blue.
I like blue!
How about you?
Macy Brinkman, Grade 5
Staunton Elementary School, IN

Rain Forest
In the rain forest I hear sounds,
There are hardly any mounds.
There's a lot of rain,
Sometimes the sky will let it drain!
Sometimes there are flowers,
And maybe some showers.
Some flowers die,
But not the sky.
There's a lot of trees,
But not so many bees.
There are some logs,
And so many frogs!
Kendra Weyer, Grade 4
Chrisney Elementary School, IN

I Remember

The day I sat outside the door, waiting for an answer
Two days before my birthday

I remember the life changing day, when everything changed
I sat outside the door listening, I could make out very few words

Cancer, Port, Broviac, Stay…

I knew very little about any of these words
The doctor's booming voice echoed I sank my head into my knees
The door opened and my dad came out,
he said "Here," and took my hand

He led me into the room but my heart and soul still sat
I feared what was behind the door, but I followed my dad
I gripped his hand and closed my eyes,

I held my breath and opened…
Without thinking I fell, a hug to my sister

I saw

Pumps, buttons, tubes, and tears
My sister was crying, and so was I
I sat and hugged her

Love

She had Leukemia…
I remember

Grace Goszkowicz, Grade 5
North Muskegon Elementary School, MI

Stay

When He takes me,
the utmost high,
will He see me boast
or see my shy?
Will I be rewarded
the Kingdom of Heaven
or perish down under
in refusing His body unleavened?
When a blistering tornado hits the highest volcano,
will I sit in front of a TV and stare?
Or will I step up and help all the people of the city
who are gentle, lost, and in need of urgent care?
When I see you slip and when I hear you cry
will I offer a hand with all hope?
Are you going to grasp it, trusting me forever,
that I am willing to help you up the slope?
I don't know what I am doing, alone,
or why I am here this way,
but when I ask you to help me through it,
please tell me that you'll always stay.

Lauren Pham, Grade 6
Kraft Meadows Middle School, MI

Dogs

A loving animal
B oxers are awesome
C ats hate them
D aschunds are short
E veryone loves them
F at sometimes
G olden Retrievers are adorable
H ot when they run
I could never hate one
J apanese poodles are so small
K ool and cuddles a lot
L abradors are amazing
M utts are the best
N ever ever bites me
O ld Yeller is my favorite
P oops a lot
Q uiet, I wish
R oads with cars they like to chase
S hih Tzus are wonderful
T otally my favorite animals
U nique as can be
V iolent sometimes
W agging tail
X traordinary
Y ou love them
Z ooming so fast

Hallie Hinton, Grade 5
Morgan Elementary School, IN

Friendship

Friends are like dogs,
Loyal and true,
They always stick with you.

Playing, having fun,
All day in the sun.
Brightening up your day
In so many different ways

Always putting a smile on your face,
And taking you to a happier place.
We share good times and bad,
But quickly forget the things that made us mad.

Mary, Megann, Julia, Kaley, Blake,
Just to name a few.
They all have nicknames for each other too,
Mare-Bear, Meggy, Jules, K.K., and B.E.E.
I know that when I'm around them all I have to be is me.

Cassandra Plummer, Grade 6
Mendon Middle/High School, MI

Getting a New Pet

Getting a New Pet is like petting a Caged Tiger.
Getting a New Pet is like riding down Niagara falls.
Getting a New Pet is like feeding a Panda Bear.
Getting a New Pet is like climbing a 100 Foot Tall Tree.
Getting a New Pet is like eating 10 pounds of Ice Cream.
Getting a New Pet is like going Sky Diving.
Getting a New Pet is like Bungee Jumping off a Cliff.

Taylor Rardin, Grade 6
Martin Middle/High School, MI

America
America looks like the nice people of different cultures pledging to the great, big American flag.
America feels like the hot, brown, tickly sand that is inviting me to play and build in.
America tastes like all the different delicious cultural foods together waiting to fill my small, hungry tummy.
America smells like the new, fresh, clean, autumn air that I can play anything I want in.
America sounds like nature's great, big, roar with the happy celebrating people welcoming America — their home.
America is my home.

Alexander Popa, Grade 4
Hampton Elementary School, MI

America
America looks like flowers bursting with colors, people full of energy and buildings with proper structure.
America feels like the bumpy rocks, the wet water and the smooth leaves of a plant freshly grown.
America tastes like smooth, oily pizza, crispy, crunchy tacos and spicy, hot piping rice.
America smells like sweet mother nature, food burning in an oven and the shavings of sharpened pencils.
America sounds like the smooth waves of an ocean, a sweet fragile bird and the crashing cymbals of a band.
America is my true home!

Rhea Gupta, Grade 4
Hampton Elementary School, MI

Fall Festival
A tree with an apple and lots and lots of leaves
A scarecrow protecting corn with the cool wind and a breeze
A hay ride takes place outside by the games, without the caramel apples it wouldn't be the same
A pumpkin is being painted and everyone's having fun
It makes me really sad to know that the day's finally done

Carly Wenzell, Grade 5
Eagle Creek Academy, MI

The Hunger Games
The Hunger Games was the most amazing, awesome, violent, jarring, speed-rap of a novel that I ever read! It always had constant, nonstop suspense. The only reasons I stopped reading were to eat and sleep. It made me boom with excitement! It was brilliantly paced and perfectly plotted. I was so obsessed with this epic novel, for, in *The Hunger Games*, winning means fame and fortune, but losing means certain death. This book is perfect for boys and girls because it's violent, but also romantic. Suzanne Collins writes the amazingly epic novels, her fans read them.

Elizabeth Schaefer, Grade 5
Crissman Elementary School, MI

Mrs. Schmitt's Classroom
Smells like, fresh salty pretzels in the air.
Feels like, riding a bumpy, extremely fun roller coaster at Cedar Point.
Sounds like, beating music in your ear.
Looks like, a sparkling, bright, beautiful, colorful, happy, nice, packed classroom with lots of fun things in it.
Tastes like, fresh air, smooth and sticking to your tongue.

Samantha Paulson, Grade 5
Crissman Elementary School, MI

Ode to Dupont
Your fur gleams in the sun, and your eyes are so beautiful. Your toys don't stay long, neither did you. You were killed by accident, by your owner, and they are sorry for what they did. You died peacefully, and I wish you wouldn't go. We named you Dupont because of number 24, Jeff Gordon and his brand Dupont. You love your food and your toys. We still have your 3 favorite toys. You're a miniature pincher and you have a stubby tail. You will always be in my heart until forever ends.

Samantha Marples, Grade 4
Morgan Elementary School, IN

High Merit Poems – Grades 4, 5, and 6

Rain
Drip
  Drip
    Drip
      Drip, drip, drip
rain on the window

Drop, drop, drop
I hear the rain fall

Tap, tap, tap
the rain on my head

The rain is falling down
to the ground
Mayghan Tubicsak, Grade 5
Heritage Intermediate School, IN

My Daddy
He is old
I am young
He loves playing golf
I love dancing
He likes kittens
I like puppies
He goes to work
I go to school
He comes home around 8:00 p.m.
I come home around 4:00
He has his own laptop
I have my own trampoline
He is my dad
I am his daughter
Morgan Holmlund, Grade 5
Dodson Elementary School, MI

Fritzz
Waiting in her cage
Her head peeks out
Her tiny shell
Thinking in her brain
Feed me
Taking very tiny steps
As she peeks up her head to nibble
Teeny blue eyes staring me down
Waiting for a move
So adorable
Twinkling eyes
Wanting food
Crunching on lettuce
Yummy!
Amy Dunford, Grade 5
Dodson Elementary School, MI

Demons Unleashed
An amber monster screaming
with anger blood red lava everywhere
hiding till its perfect time
to pounce on its prey
a demon rising
to burn the forest down
black ash gently floating
dead silence when it tires
just when you think it's over
ROAR! SPLASH! BOOM!
the devil is summoned
he's coming after you
rushing down the side
of the volcano
humans retreating to safety
but its to late
the topaz eyed beast
is here to stay.
Cassandra McCombie, Grade 6
Addison Middle School, MI

Because of You
Before I was born,
You looked after me in your stomach.

Because of you,
I know how to do the right things.

When I do bad things,
You still love me.

Since you encourage me,
I am a good a person today.

When I am with you,
I feel secure.

Since you are good to me,
I will love you forever Mom.
Cameron Watson, Grade 6
Berrien Springs Middle School, MI

Two Sisters
Two glasses wearers
Two readers
Two girls with brown hair
Two girls that like to play around
One hornet, one falcon
One long hair, one short hair
One taller, one shorter
One dark brown eyes, one light brown eyes
One crazy, one not crazy
One loud, one not loud
One dancer, one clarinet player
Joelle Shavers, Grade 4
Hampton Elementary School, MI

Hearts
Hearts
Beautiful, love
Kissing, hugging, grateful
Mesmerizing everyone each day
Beating, pounding, pumping
Red, caring
Spirit
Tayler Huff, Grade 5
Perry Central Elementary School, IN

Blue
Blue is like the sound
of my blue brush going across the paper.
Blue is like the smell
of a blue berry pie fresh from the oven.
Blue is like the taste
of blue cotton candy.
Blue is like the feel of my blue blanket.
Autumn Williams, Grade 4
Morgan Elementary School, IN

Flowers
F lowers are pretty,
L ovely they are,
O pen in the sunshine,
W ith a lot of colors,
E very flower has a color,
R eally pretty bouquets,
S pring is when they come out!
Allison Matthes, Grade 4
Dibble Elementary School, MI

Mom/Jessica
Mom
small, nice
loving, caring, sharing
purses, kitchen; phone, computer
arguing, fighting, working
tall, mean
Jessica
Jakelyn Skorup, Grade 6
Knox Community Middle School, IN

Spring
I can tell spring is in the air
I can smell it anytime
Winter's gone by far
Summer's just around the corner
Colorful flowers blooming around me
It's just so beautiful
I love it because it's spring
Haley Miller, Grade 4
Concord Ox Bow Elementary School, IN

Lovable Grandparents
G reat at making supper
R eally huggable and lovable
A wesome
N ice
N ot mean like papaw
Y ou are the best

A lways watching Nancy Grace on TV
N ame Carla Nevil
D oing chores all around the house

P erfect
A lways being lazy
P icky about everything
A funny person
W ill always remember you
Chelsey Arnold, Grade 4
Morgan Elementary School, IN

Laughs Always Last
Laughs always last.
I can remember
my grandmas warm smile,
her soft hand's hugging me.
Laughs always last.

I can remember
her with her Bible in hand,
her in her rocker,
her lovely voice singing, "Holy Night"
Laughs always last.

How I miss her cooking
How I miss her,
but I can remember.
Laughs always last.
Taylor Kinney, Grade 6
Knox Community Middle School, IN

Fear
My heart pounding…
I leap off the platform,
All of a sudden…SNAP!
I glance up…everyone is rushing to me,
Frightened, I look at my arm
I was shocked,
Before I knew it
We were in the crowded car,
I look up…I see the massive hospital,
Strangers rush me
To a tiny room,
They attach some strange machines to me,
I knew I broke my arm,
My heart was pounding…
Adam Sanders, Grade 6
Linton-Stockton Elementary School, IN

Beauties in Springtime
Down through the meadows
Are beautiful petals;
On lots of flowers
You can look at for hours.

Down at the little brook
Is where you can go take a look;
For a big turtle shell
Or even a cute little snail.

Down to the woods you go
Looking for animals that you know;
Hoping to see a deer
Before it bounds away in fear.
Christopher Dean Yoder, Grade 6
Green Acres School, IN

School
There are seven boys in my grade
When we go out we got it made
We like to play outdoor games
But can't go out when it rains.

When the bell starts to ring
We all go in to sing
Then our lessons are assigned
"Stay busy" we want to keep in mind.

Then it's time for a break
And our dinner starts to bake
Springtime is finally here
We are all filled with cheer.
Daniel Hernan Graber, Grade 4
Green Acres School, IN

Baseball
Heavy hitter all game long
From the first pitch
To the fade of dawn

Corn dogs, corn dogs, nacho cheese
Give me some peanuts please

Swing, swing hit that ball
Surprise those outfielders
And make them fall

The final roar of the crowd
That final swing…
If you lose it will really sting
Keith Wertman, Grade 5
Heritage Intermediate School, IN

Snow
Falling, falling, prettily
Snow is looking right at me
White as white can be
Covering everything I see
Snow is crunching under my boots
In a long crunch, crunch trail
I feel like I am flying in the sky
Because the snow's so high
Snow brings many things, good and bad
But when it goes away it makes me sad
But then I think about next November
When I will look out the window and say,
Falling, falling, prettily
Snow is looking right at me
Riley Whitaker, Grade 6
West Middle School, MI

Spring
Springtime is a beautiful time
When we hear the pretty wind chime
We also do lots of fun things
Like going outside on the swings

There is lots of work to be done
And sometimes it's not very fun
Sometimes the sun is very hot
Then we don't want to do a lot

Then Easter is in this season
Do you know the very reason
Jesus died on the cross for me
So that everyone can be free
Bethany Sue Wagler, Grade 5
Green Acres School, IN

Springtime
Spring brings plenty of things to do
Planting flowers and mowing too,
Raking gardens and seeding things
Imagine all the work it brings!
Not to mention hoeing yet
Grab your hoes, hurry, and let's get,

In the garden to weed the plants
So tonight mom can still wash pants.

Hear the birds singing as we hoe,
Eggplants and corn, row after row
Rest will come after we are done,
Each evening when it's setting sun.
Glenda Jean Wagler, Grade 5
Green Acres School, IN

Brothers
Brothers
Brothers
Brothers

Older brothers
Younger brothers
Little playful silly brothers
Fat funny twin brothers
Those are just a few.
Sneaky brothers
Spying brothers
I've got four brothers
Loving smart friendly
Mean brothers too!
Creative brothers
Hungry brothers
Don't forget skinny brothers
Most of all, best of all I love my brothers!
Jada Pavelko, Grade 4
Bailey School, MI

Wooden Porch
I'm just a wooden porch
I sit here in the cold,
Getting splashed
With rain, swaying,
Back and forth.
A year later
I start getting broken down
Piece by piece
With the thrash of the wind,
Hitting me,
Just like a kid
Getting bullied.
I finally collapsed,
And broken
D
O
W
N
Justin Reinke, Grade 6
Sashabaw Middle School, MI

I Miss You
I miss you when I wake up
And I miss when I go to sleep
Just to remember you
Always makes me weep

I wish I could see you again
And I wish you were with me
You always made me happy
And that was the way
You were always going to be
Sian Rhodes, Grade 6
St Simon the Apostle School, IN

Summer and Winter
Summer
Blistering, sweltering
Fishing, baseball, hunting
Sports, blossoms, windy, frosty,
Snowflakes, snowing, icing
Nippy, frigid,
Winter.
Jaron Underhill, Grade 5
Perry Central Elementary School, IN

There Are Differences
Sister
Girly, stylish
Running, singing, acting
Girl, adorable, Boy, funny
Jumping, falling, running
Handsome, loud
Brother
Alexis Halls, Grade 5
Hendry Park Elementary School, IN

Blank
Absolutely barren
Nothing present
Nothingness controls, nothingness rules
Hollowness about
Total blankness rules
This blank piece of paper controls
Total blank
Clayton Estelle, Grade 5
East Elementary School, IN

Animals
Bear
Ponderous, king size
Charging, eating, killing
Carnivore, salmon, tree, nut
Squeaking, jumping, running
Diminutive, fun size
Squirrel
Jaxon Davis, Grade 5
Hendry Park Elementary School, IN

Tiger in the…Zoo?
In the forest waiting
For me to come out and play with
The tiger
It
Has
A ball of yarn to play with
A ball
Garrett Lilley, Grade 5
East Elementary School, IN

Tsunami
Running jumping leaping
Trying to get away
Oh please giant wave
Let me survive today
Drowning drooping dying
Many lives you took, none you gave
Scared afraid alone
Only thinking why Lord why
Silent as I open my eyes
Thank God I'm alive
Kiara Williams, Grade 6
Palmer Park Preparatory Academy, MI

The Sun
The sun is big
The sun is round
The sun is orange
The sun grows crops
The sun has an interior
The sun has an atmosphere
The sun gives off light
The sun gives off heat
The sun gives off energy
The sun is made by God.
Jacob Correa, Grade 6
St John the Baptist Elementary School, IN

Rainy Day
Rainy Day, Rainy Day,
You make me so sad,
I can't come out and play!
Rainy Day, Rainy Day,
You fill me up with sorrow.
I'm hoping for sunshine tomorrow.
Rainy Day, Rainy Day,
I know it's for the best,
Well,
At least I can stay in and rest!
Christine Campbell, Grade 6
West Middle School, MI

Dolphins
I watch as dolphins
Jump up in the air and
Land on their backs,
Cute as can be.
I lean over the boat
And pet the dolphins.
Just as I have to leave,
A dolphin jumps over
My dad's boat in surprise…
Splash! I'm covered in water.
Brittany Brown, Grade 5
Perry Central Elementary School, IN

My Uncle Phil
You had the best parties.
You watched me when I was young.
You took me on rides through the woods on the golf-cart.

You're my Uncle Phil.
I went everywhere with you. From just going to the fair, to going all the way to the Dominican Republic.
We went fishing together, too!

I loved every minute I was with you. But now you're gone.
All your love, fun, jokes, and laughs.

They're all gone. You brought everyone you knew to tears.
Every second at your funeral I couldn't breathe.
Because I knew I lost something huge in my life.

I never forget you, and I hope you won't forget me.
No one else will forget you either.
For we all know you're with the Lord.
He's keeping you safe and away from danger.

You had a great life,
And you're the one who made my life better.

Hunter Wolford, Grade 6
St Bartholomew School, IN

A Container All About Me!
In a world filled with craziness and wackiness lies a container.
A container all about me! In other words, my room.
The place where it's all me.
My pictures, my bed, my desk, my games, my own compartment where I do my own homework.
With beautiful decorations, my room is colorful, exciting, unique, crazy,
a whole different world in a wacky world.
My cage, my jail, the place I'm sent to after a fight with my brother.
The box I sit in for my "talking to" from my parents.
A place where I used to pretend, playing boats and
my stuffed animals and sail the seas.
The location for sleepovers and fun. Where friends can hang out and laugh.
But the peace won't last. My little house, in a bigger house,
is being robbed and attacked by a little child and his blocks;
my brother and his stuffed animals.
OK, so my room isn't perfect.
Blobs of clothes and homework lay all over the place.
I still like it though messy or not, because
it doesn't smell bad or anything.
There's a vanilla scented air freshener in there.
But this is still my container, all about me.
Everything here is MINE, MINE, MINE! And nothing but mine.

Alexandra Nusawardhana, Grade 6
St. Bartholomew School, IN

Rocky
My dog is like a gift from God. He sleeps with me at night, as if he were another pillow.
He protects me and watches over me like a guardian angel. He is a best friend who entertains me
and makes me happy. My dog Rocky is basically a "man's best friend."

Jake Burkhart, Grade 6
St Simon the Apostle School, IN

Poetry
Poetry is very wonderful,
It tells the poets emotions
While also telling about other poems
Poetry is very wonderful
It can tell about anything it wants
Even mythical creatures
Poetry is very wonderful and amazing
Daniel Kerber, Grade 6
St John the Baptist Elementary School, IN

Silence
I sit in my room all day
I look at the light until it's gone.
I ride in my car and listen to one song.
I go to sleep with a cross
Made out of stone
'Cause God is always with me
So I know I'm never alone.
Timya Mallett, Grade 4
Thea Bowman Leadership Academy, IN

Basketball
Basketball is one of my favorite sports
You get a lot of exercise on the court
When you dribble down the lane,
You pass to your teammate
He passes back
Help, help —
It's a defensive attack!!!
Jeremy Yoder, Grade 5
Heritage Intermediate School, IN

Beautiful Jamestown
Jamestown island
beneath the clear, sunny sky
On the short, stubby grass
Along the bumpy, poky trees
On the mossy, winding water,
Near the slow, murky, creek
Virginia
Lucas Jesuit, Grade 6
Knox Community Middle School, IN

Flames of Fury
Flames of fury roll in
Like a tide
On a windy day
Grabbing everything
And ripping it apart…
Flames of fury,
Also known as love.
Amelia Carey, Grade 4
Dodson Elementary School, MI

Car Crash
When I was 1 year old
We were in a car crash
Our car flipped over 7 times
It was like a Halloween bash.

So came the ambulance
And also the cops
So we went to the hospital
then I heard a pop.

We went to the hospital
To see my mom
We felt sorry for her
Then came Dr. Tom

My mom was half out of the car
It was really bad
She went into surgery.
It was really sad.

At the hospital
My dad and I were fine
Then I just remembered
It was my mom's 2nd time.
Sabrina Phillips, Grade 5
Crissman Elementary School, MI

Lightning Storm
In long strips of light
day is done and now for night

The clouds roar in
coming as fast as they please
lightning has struck
shooting down many, many trees

The night comes to day
to the destroyed little bay
people are shocked
their town has been rocked

Hopes and dreams are gone forever
wondering if they will ever return
losing all ways in which they are clever
even their chance to learn

No more chances, no more hope
no more wishing
that this will all go away
you have lost it all
nothing can ever bring back
a true perfect day.
Brian Blust, Grade 6
Sashabaw Middle School, MI

All About Sports
I like football,
　But not soccer
I like hockey,
　But not basketball
I like Falcons,
　But not Vikings
I like leaders
　But not followers
I like UFC,
　But not boxing
I like Notre Dame
　But not Purdue
Brandon Ryan, Grade 5
Holland Elementary School, IN

Two Best Friends
Vali and Stacy
Have
Two lip sticks
And two girls in the same class.
Two head bands
Two stickers of the same color
Two Selena Gomez fans
One Salsa dancer
One Soccer player
Lots of practicing
And one good friendship!
Vali Raheem, Grade 4
Hampton Elementary School, MI

My Peaceful Shell
Outside my shell are the beautiful waves
Of the blue ocean.
The stripes of a running zebra in the safari.
The rigid walls of a large brick.
The calming sound of crashing waves
Flooding the sandy shore.
The sweet taste of soft air
On a stormy spring morning
Outside my shell I see the sun setting
On the endless horizon
Over the sparkling blue ocean.
Audrey Reed, Grade 6
Linton-Stockton Elementary School, IN

The Shot
I was open
Between the 3-point line
And the free-throw line
Aaron drops the ball
Rolls to me like a lost puppy
Pick it up
Shoot
Goes in.
Quin Cowen, Grade 6
Assumption School, MI

Families That We Can Help Change
There are families like mine that are lucky
To have a roof over our head, food to eat,
Clothes on our backs, shoes on our feet.

There are many families that have lost their home
that have children wondering when
Will I eat again, wear new clothes and
Shoes.

There are families like mine that can afford
New toys, games to play, things to do, to bring
Me to soccer every week.

These are the most important things in your life
but just remember your
Families will always be there for you.
There are families not as lucky as mine
but we can help change that.

Brenna Heins, Grade 4
Dodson Elementary School, MI

For My Mom!
In my mother's hands,
I see years of hard work to support my family.

In my mother's smile
I hear years of singing and talking to me.

In my mother's legs
I see miles and miles of running and walking.

In my mother's heart
I feel warmth and a loving person
willing to do anything for me.

In my mother's touch
I smell the great food she makes my family.

Love
Brendan

Brendan Hampton, Grade 4
Dodson Elementary School, MI

I Am From
I am from iPods,
from the guitar in my closet.
And playing in the woods,
I am from the tree house
That has a hundred cracks.

I am from Star Bursts to chocolate bars,
from Clint Eastwood and Zac Brown.
from "Calm down" and the Chicago Black Hawks.

I am from Invader Zim
To the scar on my side
I am from pro hockey

In the attic are family mementos
of when I was young.
I am from those mementos.
That I always treasure.

Quintin Risner, Grade 6
Knox Community Middle School, IN

Where I'm From
I'm from the small suburbs of Chicago,
from height and brown eyes,
from black and white.
I'm from adoption.
I'm from Easy Bake Ovens, and from Paper Dolls.
I'm from Sneaky Snake and sticks.
I'm from kickball and Don't Steal the Bacon,
from backyard football and Tag.
I'm from riding bikes and hiking,
from Lynard Skynard and Neil Diamond.
I'm from Bobby Sherman and Audrey Hepburn,
from Heath bars and Milk Duds.
I'm from Here Come the Brides and Lost in Space.
I'm from Box Car Children and Mad Magazine.
I'm from words like "Groovy!" and "Totally Tripendicular!"
I'm from dreamers of teachers and astronauts.
This is where I'm from.
This is me.

Kendall Gerken, Grade 6
St Bartholomew School, IN

Volleyball
V alue It,
O ut we all scream,
L ots of work,
L oads of fun,
E ither spike it, either pass it, either bump it,
Y ou would not know it, it is a volleyball thing,
B ump it hard,
A ll the time to be the best,
L oading your brain with facts,
L earning the moves and the right way to do it

Terissa Roark, Grade 5
Perry Central Elementary School, IN

Rainy Days
Have you ever felt under the weather?
But, you knew you had to pull yourself together
On an important day
You knew you had to stay

All around you was rain
And you couldn't feel better about it
The clouds were gray
But on a rainy day
You knew you had to stay

Christina Gonzalez, Grade 6
West Middle School, MI

High Merit Poems – Grades 4, 5, and 6

Ode to Mom
Oh Mom, you think I'm funny.
You sometimes what me to be a bunny.

Oh Mom, you like my cat.
You think she's fat.

Oh Mom, you love your daughters.
You always make us feel good.

Oh Mom, you know what I like.
You always know what to get when we got to McDonald's.
Casey Arnold, Grade 5
Morgan Elementary School, IN

Horses Running Free
Horses, horses running in the wild,
Their manes swaying loosely.
Their hearts pounding full of freedom
As they run free with the eagle.
They gallop through the lake
    Splish, splash, splish
        Like it's just a small puddle.
Their nostrils flaring as they finally settle down
For a quick nap.
They are beautiful, amazing creatures
As they awake and fall asleep.
Mariah Brown, Grade 5
Staunton Elementary School, IN

Ray of Hope
A cloudy mist suffocates the air,
blinding the ones who cry out,
hoping someone reaches for them.
And when all hope seems lost,
a small beam of light creeps through the mist.
It touches the hearts of the despaired.
Soon, the beam expands
and smothers the dark mist out of existence.
The hopeless are soothed by the light.
And the ray of hope
becomes a sun.
John Collins, Grade 6
St Simon the Apostle School, IN

Smiling Rain
The rain smiles as it falls
With its big bold drops
Of water from the sky.
It laughs its way down,
While groups of rain become stronger and stronger.
As you may say
It's not a very bright day.
But, with one condition,
You can still have fun watching them smile.
Zaynah Taleb, Grade 6
Star International Academy, MI

Leopard
leopard, spots so dark,
he will make his mark,
he will leap through the day and into the dark
stalks around with glowering eyes
until it finds its prey tonight,
so watch out
its prey it will find,
and who knows what this prey may be
so remember, with its spots so dark
leaps through the day
and into the dark...
Owen Eveler, Grade 5
Heritage Intermediate School, IN

Diabetic Life
My life with diabetes is so crazy amazing.
A life full of health, meters, and shots.
With high blood sugars, low blood sugars.
So mixed up between high and low.

Can't do certain stuff but can eat certain things.
So caught up between life or death.
Between sweets and no sweets.
Happy with my life, able to still eat.
Ok with my diabetic life.
Ok with my friends, too.
Christian Dodson, Grade 4
Thea Bowman Leadership Academy, IN

White Rabbit
White as snow
Fast as lightning
A rabbit.
Leaping swiftly in the breeze
Then landing with a thump
Its soft fur brushes against the powdery snow as it leaps again.
Now on a solid ground it runs
A vehicle missing it by inches spews gray smoke
Dirtying the rabbit's coat
Leaving a revolting smell
It cringes but sprints off the road as another one arrives.
Maya Malouin, Grade 5
Miller Elementary School, MI

My Grandma
Grandma Ruth,
I love you as much as God loves you,
You mean the whole world to me,
When you were diagnosed with cancer,
I thought I was going to lose you,
You stayed strong while believing in yourself,
I am proud of you,
Now we can run, play, and feed the hogs in the summer,
I am happy you are still with us.
Samantha Shidler, Grade 6
Linton-Stockton Elementary School, IN

Scuba Diving

I dive down with a splash
Right into the deep blue sea
Nothing compares to this not even cash
I feel like life revolves around me

The water around me swiftly flows
The dolphin swims around me laughing as I pass
The water flows right through my little toes
There are many fish, but not any bass

I'm down so deep I can't see the sky
I've not even seen one fraction of the oceans
An ocean is like a party, in it time will fly
The ocean acts up most of my emotions

I see bubbles from my tank and I'm running out of air
I must go up, but I just want to stop and stare

Elizabeth Harbin, Grade 6
St Mary Cathedral School, MI

Duck Hunting

When we get up early
I know exactly where we're going
I know we'll get some action surely
Even though it's snowing

We drive to the swamp, of all places
Dad sets up the decoys in the shallows
There's so much camouflage we can barely see each other's faces
We're there so early, we watch the early morning yellows

When, finally a bird comes in
It's the time we're least prepared
Yet, BANG, one duck in the bin
Never shall one be spared

One duck trip is over
Now it's time to start another

Nick Torsky, Grade 6
St Mary Cathedral School, MI

White Wonderland Christmas

The white wonderland in front of my face
is so amazing, I stand in awe of
its astounding beauty. Snow looks like lace.
It's almost Christmas time, season of love.

The trees are bare, leaving a place for snow
to rest. Children are building snowmen and
women, they slide down the hills of snow, through
they must drag their sleds up hill and through land.

Snow is delightful, it is clean and white.
The many houses around me are filled
with Christmas spirit, goodwill, love, and light.
Even in the cold, our hearts can't be chilled.

The birth of Jesus Christ started it all,
a gift straight from Heaven, not found at a mall.

Alissa Jagger, Grade 5
Northern Heights Elementary School, IN

Madeline

Madeline, the love of my life
On a hot summer day
Our love will quickly take us to a beautiful place
Where there are birds happily splashing through a bird bath

The only one I love forever and always
No matter what…
You make me smile as the moments last
My girl who loves me and I her
She's my honey buttercup kitten

Madeline my spark
My honey buttercup kitten loves her sweet cupcake puppy
Honey buttercup kitten I love you
Until my heart almost blows up

I love Madeline

Reily Anderson, Grade 6
Linton-Stockton Elementary School, IN

Spring

Spring is a beautiful thing,
It makes you want to dance and sing!
Swirl around and touch the ground,
Land with a bound.
Animals give birth in the spring,
Embrace the magical thing.
Listen to the beautiful sound,
In the background.
It's nice to sit on the porch swing,
And listen to the bells ring-a-ding.
You won't have this much fun year-round,
So exclaim "Hooray" when spring comes to town!

Sara Hanebutt, Grade 4
Chrisney Elementary School, IN

The Hopeless Sight

As I step closer, I can hear the sobs from everyone…
It is painful to see his pale, stiff body
I feel warm tears stream down my face,
I know I cannot cry
I have to be strong…
For my little brother.
I am waiting in the soft velvet chairs
As they say, "We are gathered here today…
For Cory Barnes."
My father's death…
The worst thing an nine-year-old girl could experience…
The hopeless sight in front of my eyes…

Corianne Barnes, Grade 6
Linton-Stockton Elementary School, IN

High Merit Poems – Grades 4, 5, and 6

God's Creation
I walk along the sandy beaches,
And the beautiful sunshine's bright.
The ocean's water rushing in,
And oh what a beautiful sight.

But let's remember God created,
All the ocean and all the land.
Yes, he made the heavens and Earth,
And all by His almighty hand.
Karlin Miller, Grade 4
West Hastings School, IN

Losses of War
Among the war-torn battlefields,
Bullets soaring everywhere,
Bang! Crash!
Soldiers in agonizing pain,
Dread of death in each of us,
Smash! Boom!
The horrid terror…
Immense worry is unfolding,
Among the war-torn battlefields.
Christian Bedwell, Grade 6
Linton-Stockton Elementary School, IN

The Lightning
The lightning dances at midnight
It always does the cha-cha,
And the salsa.
One night I saw the lightning dancing,
It got mad at me.
At midnight the lightning came back to me,
I asked "why did you get so mad?"
The lightning replied "I dance alone."
I said "Let's dance together."
Jamila El-zein, Grade 6
Star International Academy, MI

Bearded Dragon
Run
Spring, lay
Run, sprint, walk
Nice, loving, awesome, cool
Lizard
Chloe Van Eck, Grade 4
Crestwood Elementary School, MI

Heaven
H eavenly Father
E verlasting life
A ngels
V ery special
E verlasting love
N ever dies
Kyle McCain, Grade 5
Northern Heights Elementary School, IN

My Beloved Cooper
You were my best friend
I always loved you as much as you
loved me
One rainy day I heard you died
I ran away and cried instantly
You were my favorite dog
You loved all of my best friends
They all loved you dearly
Every time I think of you, I begin to cry
That depressing Tuesday evening
I walked out to your wet grave
I sat down and sadly told you how I
loved you
If I ever get a new dog
It will never replace how I feel about you
Some people think it is good bye
forever
But I will remember that you are in
my loving heart
I will always love you, Cooper,
My best friend ever
Cortney Booker, Grade 6
Linton-Stockton Elementary School, IN

Family
There are children looking for homes
and seeking for food
and always worrying
if they will wake up the next morning.

There are moms with the soul
to make you feel better
and always be by your side.

There are dads that are always
filling your heart with joy and laughter
as his humor fills the house.

There are homes with sisters and brothers
that fight
but we always have a fan of love

But when you don't have a home
the grass is the ground
the stars are the night light
and the wind is your fan.
Connor Bates, Grade 4
Dodson Elementary School, MI

The Moon
The moon is like a balloon.
It floats in space like airspace.
We sometimes put people on it to study it.
Maybe we can live up there one day.
Andrew VanNoort, Grade 4
Liberty Elementary School, IN

Turkey
It was a sunny day
People working
Fountains spitting
Wind yelling through the air
Birds singing everywhere
The days were as bright as the sun
The nights were dark and clear
Twilight was never near
Birds Chirping around us
The wind blowing through my hair
The fountains splashing everywhere
People chatting through the air
How big is it?
Will I get lost?
Will I have fun?
I feel scared.
I feel ancient.
I feel amazed.
Wow!
Wow!
Wow!
Amal Kassem, Grade 6
Star International Academy, MI

Singing
Frightening to some
To others just a breeze.
Need to know if
you're truly good or
it's just your imagination.

Worries that someone
will say, "You sing bad."
Or "Ha, you call that singing?"

You have to get yourself up.
Give it the best you can.
Don't give up, follow your dreams.

One day you
could be famous.
You will never
find out your dreams
until you try.
But someday
you will…
Amber Amor, Grade 6
Knox Community Middle School, IN

Apples
I love apples and you do too
So let's have apples every day.
Apples are so great
Apples are good for your heart.
Ross Kirkpatrick, Grade 6
St Simon the Apostle School, IN

Ode to Seasons
Oh goodbye snowy winter.
No more sparkling spring.
Goodbye rosy summer.
Fall leaving me.
Now back to cold snowy winter.
Abigail Schaffer, Grade 5
Morgan Elementary School, IN

Space
S omething's out there, I know there is
P laces of untold treasure's
A liens taking over planets
C onsists of what they're doing
E ventually we will find out
Jacob Wenz, Grade 6
St John Lutheran School, MI

Woman from France
There was an old woman from France,
Who loved to sing and dance.
She really was nice,
Who made good Mexican Rice,
And wore the most beautiful pants!
Julianna Leo, Grade 4
Hampton Elementary School, MI

Summer Days
Bright sun
Shining so bright
Hanging high in the sky
Warming up the Earth and my eyes
So bright
Hannah Light, Grade 5
Staunton Elementary School, IN

Spring
Spring time is here and children play
They go out during the day
They play with the grass
With a ball they pass
They have fun in the month of May
Sanjna Pradhan, Grade 6
Detroit Country Day Middle School, MI

Winter
Smells like hot cocoa.
Feels like cold air.
Sounds like snow crunching.
Tastes like snow falling from the sky.
Looks like white ice cream on the ground.
Keigel Johnson Jr., Grade 4
Dibble Elementary School, MI

Where I Am From
I am from my grandma's fantastic cookies that I make with her
I am from my friend Noelle that moved to South Carolina
I am from my great 5th grade teachers for 2009
I am from eating the delicious ribs served at the Dead Wood, the place that my dad owns
I am from swimming through the huge waves at grand haven
I am from the skiing trips to Salt Lake City Utah
I am from my family's annual Christmas party with Santa
I am from the snowy Christmas mornings opening presents by the tree
I am from my sweet baby cousins Noah, Alexis, Natalie
I am from my gold fish Ginger that eats food like its candy
I am from my gold metal I won at my first ice skating competition
I am from my wonderful, loving family
Mikaela Hazergian, Grade 6
West Middle School, MI

Where I Am From
I am from refreshing air and the taste of sweet ice cream.
I am from people asking me if I think I look like my middle school sister.
I am from a picky cousin that likes to pull my hair.
I am from an awesome dad that used to throw me in the air.
I am from a lovely mom that takes me shopping everywhere.
I am from a very long winter that makes me want to put on three coats.
I am from a crazy sister that climbs tall trees in a flash.
I am from an adventurous mom that can speak three languages.
I am from a Roman Catholic family that goes to church every Sunday.
That's me! I am from Michigan!
Ornela Shtjefhilaj, Grade 4
Hampton Elementary School, MI

Blue the Color of Fun
Blue, the color of my party dress that I quickly slipped into
Blue, the color of the flowers on my pretty silky dress
Blue, the color of my jacket that warms me as I wear it
Blue, the color of my nail polish sparkling on my smooth nails

Blue, the color of my head band that softens my hair
Blue, the color of my sparkly hair clip shining in my dark hair
Blue, the color of my dangling earrings that sing from my ears
Blue, the color of my glamorous necklace that dangles from my neck
Blue, the color of my shoes that dance as I walk into the sunlight
Katie Cross, Grade 6
Linton-Stockton Elementary School, IN

An Ode to My Papaw
Oh Papaw, Oh Papaw, you are the best
Oh I know how you love me so but
I know with all your heart
Oh so you can rest
I bet you're the best
Oh Papaw I know my nickname is snake because I would climb in bed
I miss you so
It hurt to see you go but
I love you so.
Madison McCorkle, Grade 4
Morgan Elementary School, IN

I Will Always Have It
There are homes with mothers who check on the
children for anything they need,
And some homes without mothers.

There are homes with fathers who have a sense of
humor as jokes fill the evening air,
And some homes without humor.

There are homes with sisters who drive you nuts
but love gets caught on,
And some homes without love.

There are homes with grandpas, who build you
activities with their money so you're not bored,
And some homes can't afford that stuff.

I'm blessed with what I have and will always be.
I know there are children out in the cities, cold
and hungry. I wish everyone had a nice, kind, and
loving family in a warm house with food and
water, and know they will always have it.
Ethan Touma, Grade 4
Dodson Elementary School, MI

What I Found in My Bedroom*
What I found in my bedroom:
A big grandfather clock,
One of The Hulk's socks,
A big dog,
And a patch of fog!
A steamboat,
And a Vermeses fur coat,
A big juicy booger,
And a pig as big as my bed!
A magic hat,
And a big black bat.
A wishing stick,
And a half of a bit pick.
A very thick log,
A big fat hog,
A soccer ball
And a one eyed doll.
And one more thing, I must confess,
A note from the world,
CLEAN UP THIS MESS!
Kunal Bhatia, Grade 4
Hampton Elementary School, MI
*Patterned after "What I Found in My Desk" by Bruce Lansky

Green
Green is like the sound of a tractor moving,
Green is like the smell of a sour green apple,
Green is like the taste of a juicy cucumber,
Green is like the feel of grass tickling my neck.
Ella Hoehn, Grade 4
Morgan Elementary School, IN

Piles of Candy Corn
Candy corn is all around,
I can't even touch the ground!
I look for my house, but all is gone.
I'm thirty-six miles above the lawn!
I dig and jump and climb and pound,
But I am on the top of a huge candy corn mound!
All I see is white, orange and yellow,
So I turn around and start to bellow.
Can't you see, I am above the tree?
Hello? I'm here! It's me!
All the people heard me bellow,
But they couldn't see me among the yellow.
I threw a piece of candy corn down,
And it hit Mrs. McGumphrey, who started to frown!
I wave my arms for all the people to see,
And, uh-oh! Down comes the candy corn, the candy corn and me!
Madelyn Roe, Grade 5
Black River Public School, MI

Your Heart
In my mother's kitchen
I breathe not just delicious air…but a story!

In my mother's eyes
I see a spirit that opens up a new world for me
Like a book

In my mother's adventures
I feel her in my bones,
Going from place to place!

In my mother's hands
I touch not just wisdom, but faith

In my mother's voice
I hear a strong, smart and beautiful woman
Drew Harper, Grade 4
Dodson Elementary School, MI

Jack and Mack
Jack and Mack,
What are the odds?
Jack and Mack, here comes the smack,
Here come the wads!

Uh-oh! Now they're hitting!
Now they're using their feet!
Someone might be quitting!
I wonder who will find defeat!

Uh-oh! Now they're doing something really strange!
I think they're hugging!
That's so out of their range!
I just darn wonder what they're thinking!
Emily Cobb, Grade 4
Liberty Elementary School, IN

Hunting
Young men go hunting in fall.
Shots are heard everywhere.
The deer are fleeing for their lives.
The hares are fleeing everywhere.

The animals are in danger.
The animals are being shot.
They all have very good meat.
Some hunters shoot a lot.

We hear the shots ringing in the woods.
Some hunters shoot a lot of meat
Some shoot not one animal.
Some shoot a buck that is neat.

Didn't you have a gun to hunt?
Didn't you get to have a shot,
At meat-bearing animals?
Some end up in a hot pot.
Kevin Kauffman, Grade 4
West Hastings School, IN

Spring's Here
Spring's here,
Flowers blooming,
Trees budding,
Warmer weather,
Sunny days,
Riding bikes,
Sports are starting,
Long walks,
Summer's coming,
Flying kites,
Rainy times,
Warmer nights,
Longer days,
Playing outside,
Hiking trails,
Winter's done,
No more coats,
Because…
Spring's here!
Lauren Warner, Grade 5
Patterson Elementary School, MI

My Star
They glow,
They shine.
There is a special one,
That is mine.
My star,
My sun.
My own,
Very special one.
Katelyn Bender, Grade 4
James R Watson Elementary School, IN

My Front Porch
Summer
your brand new forest
green paint glimmers in the sun.
In fall
leaves rattle together as they
are blown across you.
In winter
freezing snow sits on you
while kids run around throwing
snowballs at each other.
In spring
the melted snow drips off
you like sweat, and your
once beautiful paint chips
and cracks.
Another summer
you rest sitting in the sun,
as a new beautiful
color fills your floors.
Blue.
Haley VanVolkenburg, Grade 6
Knox Community Middle School, IN

Sam's Ode to Legos
With long eyes,
And a feeling like I've been killed.
I wake to my Legos,
And say it's time to build.
Red, blue, yellow, green,
All of them are good.
Thoughts of building a war,
And a feeling that I should.
All around me,
Lego people are.
And then I had a thought,
That I should make them a car.
And so I set to work,
Building lots of stuff.
Building with Legos may be fun,
But it's also very rough.
And so I finally stop,
In the middle of the night.
And a feeling like,
I've used my whole day right.
Samuel Vellequette, Grade 5
Douglas Road Elementary School, MI

Woods
Silent
Nice
Beautiful
Green
I love the woods
My woods.
Charles McDonald, Grade 4
Mentone Elementary School, IN

On the Mound
On the mound
I look somewhere.
A person throws.
My back is turned…
Thud!
Falling!
Landing
Thud!
People running to me.
Crying!
Coach checking my eyes.
No concussion
Relief!
Josh Denton, Grade 6
Assumption School, MI

Soccer
Running
Passes
He dribbles
He kicks
Bounces off net
Our team gets it
Sprint to the other side
Someone gaining
Must act quickly
Time running out
He kicks the ball
Ball goes in
Victory!
Nic Ragon, Grade 6
Assumption School, MI

My Friends
My friends
Crazy and smart
Funny and nice
And we laugh all the time

My friends
Running and jumping
Screaming and drawing
Funny pictures for us to see

My friends
Karate chop trees, throw parties
And when I'm sad they hug me
Taylor VanDam, Grade 5
North Muskegon Elementary School, MI

The Dawn of Day
As the sun rises
The birds sing out happily
All mankind awakes
Jon Perrault, Grade 6
Holy Name Catholic School, MI

Fall

Leaves and colors, and colors and leaves
Oh how fun fall can be
Jumping in leaves
Go outside and feel the breeze
Stare at the beautiful trees
Leaves and color, and color and leaves

Jackets and clouds, and clouds and jackets
I can't believe we finally get to put on our jackets
Summer has gone and left us all
I can't believe it's fall
Jackets and clouds, and clouds and jackets

Blank faces all over the places
Summer has left us so soon
No more vacations in the afternoon
Hopefully, I'll still be able to see the moon

Sabriyyah Ricketts, Grade 6
Star International Academy, MI

Deep Sea

As I plummet down to the ocean deep
The marine life comes out to play
Sometimes you can hear the fish weep
Night comes fast as it comes day

Blue sea, wonderful colors, all the world wants it
My heart beats with the sound of the sea
Down at the bottom, there is nowhere to sit
At the bottom of the sea, so free, so free

The blue ocean deep so peaceful
Deep water beauty is what I was after
But I found much more, so grateful
Dolphins ring out with their laughter

Oh my deep ocean blue
Come back to me soon

Nathan Smith, Grade 6
St Mary Cathedral School, MI

Snowboard

In my closet I like to keep,
My snowboard that was snow-covered deep.
Back in my memories,
When I zoomed past snowy trees.
Riding the ski lift up the mountain,
I wish I were at the Holiday World fountain.
I tripped and I tumbled,
I gripped and I grumbled.
I coughed and I sneezed,
I gasped and I wheezed.
So in my closet I like to keep,
My snow-covered snowboard that was snow-covered deep.

Jonathon Murphy, Grade 4
Chrisney Elementary School, IN

My Little Sister

My little sister wants to be like me,
It bugs me sometimes can't you see.

She follows, copies and wants what I do,
It is SO annoying when she sleeps with me, too!

It was embarrassing when we use to have to dress the same,
Don't look at me, my mother was to blame.

We have had some good times doing girlie things together,
And I know deep down that I really love her.

So when I'm fed up I try to remember how happy I was,
When my parents said I had a little sister because…

I had prayed for a girl since I already had three yucky brothers,
And I asked God that she would NOT yet be another!

Seena Greiwe, Grade 6
St Bartholomew School, IN

Grandpa Siders

Grandpa Siders is very important to me,
I think about him every minute of the day,
My grandpa used to talk to me about his childhood,
My grandpa helped me decorate for my fairy birthday party
When I was nine,
We watched TV and laughed all the time,
We played board games,
Now he can see me, but I can't see him,
My grandpa showed me a picture of horses,
He gave it to me as a keepsake,
Grandpa Siders is in a wonderful place,
I know he's safe,
He can hear what I'm saying and thinking,
But I can't hear him,
He knows when I'm thinking about him
Grandpa Siders was the best grandpa in the world,
I will never forget grandpa.

Kaylee Siders, Grade 6
Linton-Stockton Elementary School, IN

Prayer

I look up to the Lord at night
And think of words that are just right
And tell him things that give me a fright
He won't care how long that's all right
I try to say things that are polite
But try not to stay up all night
He will know what will happen because of foresight
I will try to remember what I say and not recite
My room is totally black and white
And stare out my window in the moonlight
And whisper to myself goodnight
Until I wake up to the sunlight

Austin Monroe, Grade 6
St John Lutheran School, MI

The Solid Moon

I am a solid round moon
You know me for the deadly dark night
My mother is a shining glowing star
My father is purple round Jupiter
I was born in the great rocks in space
I live in the dark lonely outer space
My best friend is the blue green Earth
Because I like to shine down on the Earth
My enemy is the hot burning sun
Because I don't get to come out at the morning
I fear giant enormous meteor rocks
Because they will hit me
I love shining on the Earth
Because it makes the people sleep tight
I wish I could shine on the whole entire Earth

Ryo Hirose, Grade 4
Dodson Elementary School, MI

The Catch of the Game

Coach puts me in
I'm in the huddle
I hear the play
I realize the play is to me
when I line up, it's silent
I'm waiting for the quarterback to say SET GO
he says it, I do my pattern
he's under pressure, he throws the pig skin to me
I catch it, the crowd is cheering
I'm getting closer and closer to the end zone
when I'm in the touchdown I get excited
the crowd cheers even louder
the whole team congratulated me
we still lost but I don't care
we had a team party

Noah Osburn, Grade 5
Wayne Gray Elementary School, MI

There Is an Angel Above Us*

There is an angel above us that never in her life had she fussed.
There is an angel above us that always keeps a good eye on us.
She passed away a while ago.
We were all sad to see her go.
She is loved and she will be missed.
She always liked to give a big hug and a kiss.
She was our lucky charm.
She would never do us any harm.
She will always be in my heart.
She was always very smart.
Her time with us was a gift.
Although, very swift.
She still lives within us.
And we will always cherish that precious angel above us.

Nicaela Bilder, Grade 6
Owensville Community School, IN
*Dedicated to my aunt Cora, we love and miss you.

Monster Inside Me

Measles, mumps, chickenpox to "cough, cough, cough"
Oh no, "achoo!!!" I'm as sick as a dog.
Oh man, oh man, somebody quick, go get me a trash can!
Call your doctors, your nurses, air force, marines!
I'm turning a brand new shade of green!
I'm growing spikes down my back and horns out my head.
When my mother saw this she almost fell over dead!
Want to know what happens next?
Well you can't! Even I don't know!
It was just a dream. Everything was normal, so it seemed.
Until I heard my mother do an ear-piercing scream.

Zoey Rupp, Grade 4
Concord Ox Bow Elementary School, IN

I Wish

I wish I could be a multibillionaire.
I wish I could be in every major league sport.
I wish I were perfect.
I wish I wouldn't die.

We might dream some of these dreams.
Some may come true, others may not,
But remember, always keep God in your heart.
He doesn't care if you're rich.
He doesn't care if you're perfect.

Zachary Welp, Grade 5
Holy Redeemer School, IN

Because of Me

Here I am,
Standing on the side of the abandoned street,
All alone…by myself,
Seeking assistance,
I should not have let them take her prisoner,
She was my closest companion,
I will never forget her,
Her voice surrounds my miserable body,
She was taken away this morning…
Because of me.

Thaniel Heath, Grade 6
Linton-Stockton Elementary School, IN

Humid Hot Land

Deserts are mostly deserted
They are bright but lonely
They are hot at day and cold at night
Very few animals can survive there
Deserts are like stoves burning your feet
Deserts are like toasters cooking you
Deserts are where the sun shines down the most
Deserts are where sandstorms strike
Where sorrow is
Where no one wants to be

Gary Zhang, Grade 4
Dodson Elementary School, MI

Owl/Mouse

Owl
feathery, small
flying, hooting, landing
forest, park, cheese, crumbs
crawling, hiding, eating
small, cute
Mouse

Bailey Reffeitt, Grade 5
Hendry Park Elementary School, IN

Softball

Softball is so much fun,
You even get to run!
When you hit the ball,
Make sure you don't fall!
You will also get exercise,
After the sun will rise!!

Vanessa Claar, Grade 4
Liberty Elementary School, IN

Winter Days

Crisp, clean air
A fresh sheet of snow on the ground
Sharp, clear icicles hang for dear life
On the roof of my house
Snow days full of joy
Signs of Christmas are in the air

Jolie Foor, Grade 5
Knapp Forest Elementary School, MI

Depression

Depression is a worn brown.
It sounds of nothingness
It tastes of Tabasco sauce
It smells of dank, moth-ridden clothes
It feels as though there is no world,
   only a deep, dark, diabolical void!!!!

Walker Humphrey, Grade 5
East Elementary School, IN

Black

Black is the dark raven in the cold night.
Black is the endless life taking space.
Black is the astonishing solar eclipse.
Black is the cat creeping in the night.
Black is the sigh of death.
Black is a dark color.

Alec Schmidt, Grade 5
Crissman Elementary School, MI

Leaves

Bright and colorful,
falling slowly to the ground,
gold, brown, and crunchy

Emma Durm, Grade 5
Ballard Elementary School, MI

Ode to Jackson

Oh Jackson, you make me laugh when you shake your fuzzy toy in your mouth.
When you take a bath you shake your long body and get me all wet!
When you get out of the bathtub, you rub your head on the floor, and you get the floor wet.
Oh Jackson, you bit me sometimes, you bite me but that's ok.
Then you give me a lick after you bite me.
Oh Jackson, you are my favorite dog!

JoLee Missi, Grade 4
Morgan Elementary School, IN

Oh Chille, Oh Chille

Oh Chille, Oh Chille you make me laugh when you run in your sleep.
Oh Chille, Oh Chille you lick my face when I am sad.
Oh Chille, Oh Chille you love playing ball with me.
Oh Chille, Oh Chille you always try to pop the ball.
Oh Chille, Oh Chille you get scared of the baby chicken that is smaller then your ears.
Oh Chille, Oh Chille I will always love you.

Annabelle Hunt, Grade 4
Morgan Elementary School, IN

Hawaii

I see volcanoes, blue flowing oceans, beautiful lush flowers
I hear the thunderous waves crashing, the whisk of the wind
I feel the sand between my toes, the cool sea water, the wind on my face
I smell the salty waters of the ocean, the wonderful foods, sunscreen
I taste freshly caught shrimp, imperial long fish and all the exotic foods.

Ethan Writt, Grade 6
St Simon the Apostle School, IN

Fear Is Black

It feels like a ghastly pale ghost touching you in the black darkness.
It tastes like trying to swallow when you can't, and you start to choke.
It smells like smoke when you're in a burning red hot fire.
It sounds like an owl's whooo when you're in the terrifying darkness.
It looks like someone is there when no one's really there.

Brock Hamman, Grade 5
East Elementary School, IN

Leaves

Fallen leaves on the ground in colors of red, orange, yellow and brown.
So many leaves that I can't count.
I just hope I can rake them all up!
Jumping in leaves is so much fun, I yell, scream, jump and run.
Fall is the season I love the most, maybe we should have some toast.

Madeline Powers, Grade 5
Black River Public School, MI

Ode to My Bird Kelly #2

Oh Kelly, oh Kelly, you're the miniature Godzilla flying through the room.
Chance tries to run but it is no use.
He taunts her but does not want her
and when she screeches he runs and yells, "It's the battle cry!"
I don't know why she is green she is lean, but not very mean!

Blake Schickel, Grade 4
Morgan Elementary School, IN

My Home

You were there
when I needed a home.
You, with your crayon-covered walls and
your peeling tile floors,
were my sanctuary.

Yes, you did get messy and
a little bit too small,
But you always protected me
through flashing thunder storms
and listened kindly to me
when I complained.

Your groans, creaks,
and whistles still fill my head
I will never, ever forget you,
my home.

Summer Skibbe, Grade 6
Knox Community Middle School, IN

Summer

I love summer,
It's no bummer!

It is so fun
To play in the sun!

When I go to the ocean,
I need lotion.

From my job I could get much money,
On the beach I could meet my honey.

On the beach there is a lot of motion,
Go to the beach, take a notion!

So you see, summer is no bummer,
I love summer!

Whitney Ward, Grade 4
Chrisney Elementary School, IN

Reach

Keep on moving forward
Never gonna stop
Keep on climbing higher
Until you reach the top
Keep moving up
You may trip
You may fall
You can do it
Just stick to it
You'll reach the top
Never gonna stop
To reach the top

Sarah George, Grade 6
Sycamore School, IN

Baby Boy

This little boy
loves big toys.
He is small and cute,
but you can't put him on mute.
He loves you.
You love him too.
So hold him tight
throughout the night.

When he laughs aloud,
you are wowed.
He's just like you
in what you do.
When he grows up,
he'll get a new pup.

He brings you joy
because he's a boy.
He will make a mess,
but he's the best.
So look and see
what he will be.

Katey O'Brien, Grade 5
Assumption School, MI

Cody

His cute eyes glance
From side to side
Ears droop
Tail wags
He doesn't want people to see
He sneaks some food
He sneaks some food
But the carrots look
So yummy
And the cherry cobbler
So juicy
It just doesn't seem right
Not to do it
He sneaks more food
He sneaks some food
Jump
Snag
Land
He really wants some more
But he waits for dessert
If only it was time

Chase Olson, Grade 5
Dodson Elementary School, MI

Spring

The snow is melting
Hot and cool, bright with beauty
Best time of year, spring

Jaron Phillips, Grade 6
DSA - West Langston Hughes Campus, MI

Ode to a Taco

Oh taco you taste so well.
I like you in a soft or hard shell.
Oh taco you are so neat
You taste so good with all that tasty meat.
Oh taco you don't make me wheeze.
I like you with a lot of cheese.
Oh taco you don't grow moss.
You taste good with a little sauce.

Noah Davis, Grade 4
Morgan Elementary School, IN

Fallstone

CRUNCH, go the *leaves* under my feet,
WISP, goes the *wind* in my hair,
Nothing is better than the crisp fall
. . .
Wait! What is that?
Little beady eyes staring
into your soul
or its imagination.

Abigail Davis, Grade 5
East Elementary School, IN

Ode to My Dad

Ode to my dad, you are my best friend.
Ode to my dad, you are good at baseball.
Ode to my dad, it is fun with you.
Ode to my dad, you are funny.
Ode to my dad, you can't shop.
Ode to my dad, you are getting old.
Ode to my dad, you are the best.
Ode to my dad, I love you so much!

Jaden Wingler, Grade 4
Morgan Elementary School, IN

Compliments

Have you ever got a compliment
all crisp and clean and sweet?
Have you ever got a compliment
and think they're very neat?
For if you get a compliment
be sure to return one back.
For if you don't return a compliment
it's something you'll always lack.

Whitney Drenth, Grade 5
Ebenezer Christian School, MI

Flying

What person doesn't want to fly?
You wish, you hope, you cry.
If you want to fly you might need wings.
And many other important things.
But when you finally get to fly.
You will feel like you'll never die.

Sean Hurley, Grade 6
St Simon the Apostle School, IN

High Merit Poems – Grades 4, 5, and 6

The Winning Goal
The whistle blew it was 2 to 2.
I get the puck and do a slap shot.
As fast as a jaguar
And it goes in the net
I am so happy
So is my team
We won the championship
Carl Bach, Grade 6
Assumption School, MI

Brother/Sister
Brother
tall, active
exciting, annoying, running
food, sports, phone, clothes
talking, shopping, boring
lazy, short
Sister
Taylor Helwig, Grade 5
Hendry Park Elementary School, IN

Dogs
What's a dog?
A playful four-legged creature
A chewing monster
Cuddly, furry bodies
Begging, mooching beast
A constant faithful friend
That's a dog!
Scott Cooper, Grade 4
Bailey School, MI

Mickey/Minney
Mickey
mouse, boy
scurrying, acting, laughing
nice, kind, sweet, caring
shopping, baking, gardening
girl, yellow
Minney
Avrie Sauer, Grade 5
Hendry Park Elementary School, IN

Strawberries
Ruby red
Soft with
A little fuzz
Juicy
Right before you
Sink your teeth
Into it.
Marcera Kimble-Key, Grade 4
Hampton Elementary School, MI

If I Were in Charge of the World*
If I were in charge of the world,
I'd cancel my sister, wars, mosquitos and also darkness.
There'd be mega high tech, green technology,
And kids would be the coolest.
You wouldn't have any bedtimes,
You wouldn't have to learn piano.
You wouldn't have to learn any sport,
Or, "Don't take the iPod!"
You wouldn't even have parents.
The latest car in the current year,
Would be a Model T.
All video games would be rated "E"
And a person who sometimes forgot to put his iTouch in his pillowcase,
And sometimes forgot to help his parents,
Would still be allowed to be in charge of the world.
Sai Yerra, Grade 4
Hampton Elementary School, MI
*Patterned after "If I Were in Charge of the World" by Judith Viorst

The Best Breakfast
I am a scrambled egg
You know me for filling up your hungry stomachs at breakfast
My mother is a clucking hen
My father is a plump rooster
I was born in a blue, squishy egg carton
I live in a loud grocery store called Meijer
My best friend is crunchy bacon
Because we lay on a hard, cold plate together
We like to swing on slimy noodles in the refrigerator
My enemy is wide, yelling mouths
Because they might eat me for my delicious taste
I fear gigantic people
Because they crack me open and cook my yolk
I love salt and pepper
Because they layer me in cozy warm blankets
I dream that I will be on the cover of famous *Breakfast Meal* magazine
Sonia Mistry, Grade 4
Dodson Elementary School, MI

Who I Am
I am strong,
After what I have been through I know I have chosen the right road
I am brave,
I know my limits and I am no longer afraid of them
I am me,
Not a mirror of a photo-shopped model
I am a survivor,
Life is a battle and I refuse to give in
I am confident,
I can get pushed but it won't knock me over anymore
I am serene,
I know what happened but why should it stop me?
The past is the past and if it won't happen again why should I worry?
The past has only made me want to break from my shell and show the world who I am
Valerie Kraft, Grade 5
The Orchard School, IN

My Cousin, Brandon
Aboard the boat
Across the sea
Against the Taliban
In Iran

Among the brave
Within the troops
In my heart
Like a brother
Courtney Eytchison, Grade 6
East Elementary School, IN

Taking a Huge Leap
Running!
Jumping!
Galloping with the wind.
Taking a huge leap to
Steal the prize.
Thudding hoof beats,
And a flowing mane.
While riding without a rider,
Now that's a shame!
Kilee Stearns, Grade 5
Hendry Park Elementary School, IN

My Puppy
My puppy likes to play around,
And sometimes she rolls on the ground.
She's as brown as hot cocoa mix,
And she really likes to lick!

In the summer I'll blow some bubbles.
For my puppy this could mean trouble.
She'll then have to jump as high as the sky,
Or at least she'll give it a try.
Erin Helka, Grade 4
St Raphael School, MI

Piraña
Jumping, sloshing, biting
eating, swimming, gnawing,
hiding, chasing, preying
almost there, almost there,
CHOMP!!!
Timothy Pierce, Grade 5
Hendry Park Elementary School, IN

Where I Am From
I am from fruit with whipped cream,
video games, and my family album.
I am from cheezy banitza with V8,
my homemade cookies, and my fun laptop.
I am from my two cats, 13 year old uncle,
and my homemade banana smoothie.
Natalie Nedeltchev, Grade 4
Hampton Elementary School, MI

Gymnastics
The sport of survivors.
Rib busting,
Ankle popping,
Back cracking.
Gymnasts feel the pain.
It hurts a lot, but we can't restrain.
Practicing 18 hours a week,
Getting our skills perfect.
We practice our skills before we compete.
If we've trained hard, we will win the meet.
The taping of your ankles,
The fastening of your grips,
The punching on the springboard,
The blood from your rips.
Every day you will see some of these,
But a gymnast handles it with ease.
Claudia Eder, Grade 5
Holy Redeemer School, IN

Stick It
Heart pounding
Stomach queasy
You're staring
Down at the vault
Finally you take off
Down the endless runway
Your dashing feet
Hit the spring board
With a big
BOOM!
You fly up in the warm air
Your flexible hands the soft vault
You go up in a perfect handstand
Then you hit the blue mat
You stuck your landing
At last it is over
Myranda Clough, Grade 5
Wayne Gray Elementary School, MI

Playful and Crazy Little Creatures
The thick poofy fur
Its big beady eyes
Looking up at me
The tiny, tiny
Pinkish rabbit nose
Sniffing the fresh air
Its small bunny ears
Twitching to every single sound
I set it on the ground
To watch it eat
The blades of grass
Moist from the morning dew
The fluffy mounds of cuteness
Nobody can resist
Tara Beyer, Grade 5
Wayne Gray Elementary School, MI

Two Faced
The beach is a sleepy tiger
Full and round
So tired it makes no sound.

Its fur so shiny
The water so blue
Lapping waves that are a frothy brew.

Its eyes so bright
Just like the sun
Gleaming as it runs.

When it's up
It soundlessly prowls
Then crashing, the rocks growl.

Right now it's peace
But later havoc
As you see, it's very graphic.
Mary Leighton, Grade 6
Mendon Middle/High School, MI

Seasons
Rain is falling,
Birds are singing,
Flowers are blooming,
Spring.

Sun is shining,
Bees are buzzing,
Kids are playing,
Summer.

Leaves are changing,
Rakes are sweeping,
School is starting,
Fall.

Snow is falling,
Icicles forming,
Hot cocoa slurping,
Winter.
Shannon Faulkner, Grade 6
West Middle School, MI

Beautiful Broken Bracelet
I am wary
About wearing
My bracelet, in a lane
I noticed a pane
In my bracelet is rusting
So to you I am trusting
To you I lend,
My bracelet to mend
Madi White, Grade 6
Perry Middle School, MI

High Merit Poems – Grades 4, 5, and 6

Ageamante
Babies
Young, little
Senseless, funny, future
New, here, used, there
Smart, sleepy, past
Old, big
Adults
R. Evan Smith, Grade 6
Perry Middle School, MI

US Navy
U nder the sea sometimes.
S canning the sea for enemies.

N ever back down.
A lways there for you.
V ery awesome
Y ou are safe with them.
Ethan Davis, Grade 5
Morgan Elementary School, IN

Jasmine
J ust loves chewing things
A dorable
S mells bad after coming in from outside
M y only dog
I nteresting
N ever is aggressive
E xcited about everything
Zoe Calderone, Grade 4
Dibble Elementary School, MI

Baseball
Home run
Gratifying, exhilarating,
Awesome wondrous, splendid
Superior, sweet, bad, sour
Exasperating, aggravating,
Lousy, erroneous, mean
Strike out
Eric Harris, Grade 6
Mary Evelyn Castle Elementary School, IN

Within the Deep Blue Water
Ecolo State Park
Through the deep dark and scary woods
To the scarce, lonely, peaceful banks
Above the sand were puffy clouds
Upon the rock fierce waves piercing it
Within the deep water
Oregon
Austin Peters, Grade 6
Knox Community Middle School, IN

As Morning Shines
Morning is a time for waking up,
Also for a fresh coffee cup,
As morning shines.

Morning is time for milking cows,
Also for kittens squeaking meows,
As morning shines.

Morning is for sunlight, a brand new day,
Time for children to go out and play,
As morning shines.

Morning is for you, not only me,
So put on a smile full of glee,
As morning shines.

As morning shines,
For everyone,
New life will bring you so much fun,
As morning shines.
Hannah Pletcher, Grade 6
St Simon the Apostle School, IN

The TV
He sits there on the stand
Waiting for someone to open
His eyes

There he lies
His mind all blank
Until I come

I turn him on
Sometimes he makes me laugh
And sometimes cry

Every time he blinks
A different channel comes on
And the TV watches me laugh and
Play all day

Until it's nighttime he begins to cry
I say "It's all right big guy,
I'll be here tomorrow and good night"
Justin Fisher, Grade 5
North Muskegon Elementary School, MI

Ode to My Dad
Dad, oh Dad, you were funny.
You like to eat honey.
Dad, oh Dad, you were great.
You drove a truck from state to state.
Dad, oh Dad, I love you very much.
You loved me too.
Colton Ray, Grade 5
Morgan Elementary School, IN

Encounter
We both stopped
Heart dropping
Silent
I was near the house
The snake
Next to
The old garage,
Him
Straining hard
To hear
Me
I not breathing
Saying to self
Don't be frightened
With no sound
Next to us
I said to self don't move!
Did it move
Like a deer
He rose from the garage
And slithered off
Jeffrey Conwell, Grade 5
Gobles Elementary School, MI

Derrick Rose
Derrick Rose is the best basketball player
If you search east or west
He's still the best!
He jumps so high!
I wonder if he can touch the sky!

I wish I was a baller
Maybe a little taller
Then I could play ball with Derrick Rose
I would dunk the ball right under his nose
If I was as tall as Derrick Rose!

When Derrick Rose plays defense
And the coach calls for the 2-3 zone
The crowd all moans
Because he is in the zone!

When Derrick Rose steals the ball
The other team feels so small!
He's the league VIP and his team's MVP
He's Derrick Rose!
Eugene Stewart, Grade 4
Thea Bowman Leadership Academy, IN

Homework
Homework is as hard as steel.
It is my greatest fear.
I really wish I were a magician,
So I could make it disappear!
Dylan Graham, Grade 4
St Raphael School, MI

Grandma Greenwood

At my grandma's wonderful house I smelled dark coffee
I saw my loving grandma smile every day
I heard her caring laugh
I wish I could hear that laugh,
I wish I could see that warm smile one more time,
I know she is all right now,
She is not suffering,
She is in Heaven with my shy Uncle Roger
That's where my affectionate grandma longed to be
Grandma always wanted to go to Heaven
She loved beautiful sunrises
She never got to see them after she got sick
She could no longer walk
Now, she gets to see her gentle sunrises every day
I love you, Grandma Greenwood…
Very much

Laura Greenwood, Grade 6
Linton-Stockton Elementary School, IN

Whirling Windstorm

I am a whirling tornado
You know me for my countless dollars in damage
My mother is a trembling, earth shaking earthquake
My father is a 100 mile per hour wall of wind
I was born in the wild winds of storms
I live in the pitch-black sky year round
My best friend is a threatening thunderstorm
Because it produces me
We like to cause lots of chaos and damage
My enemy is clear blue skies
Because it does no harm to things on the ground
I fear not touching the ground
Because I don't cause millions of dollars in damage
I love causing acres of destruction
Because it's so easy to scare the heck out of people
I wish to be a category 5 tornado

Zachary Beadle, Grade 5
Dodson Elementary School, MI

As We Stand

As the old flag sways back and forth
With those red, blue and white stripes

And the many stars
Everything that shows our country and what it is made of

As the soldiers stand and salute in one country
As we stand in another

We say the pledge and pay our own respect
For the ones standing brave

As the soldier stands in the field feeling sorrow and pain
Let's say thank to all of our fellow soldiers

Mayme Davis, Grade 5
Perry Central Elementary School, IN

Sammy

Sammy the wild cat,
Sammy is my cat who likes to run and jump
I love her so much
Sammy is black and white
She has a tail like a squirrel
Sammy the wild cat
She jumps all over the place
And sometimes she hits my face
I love her so much
She sleeps on my brother's bed
or sometimes she will sleep with my dad
Sammy the wild cat
She jumps like she is a frog
She pounces on your shoe strings like a cheetah
I love her so much
My cat is a really good friend
She is always there for me
Sammy the wild cat
I love her so much

Cameron Murphy, Grade 5
Northern Heights Elementary School, IN

Where I'm From

I am from spending time with my family
and playing poker with my grandpa.
I'm from carbon racing, basketball,
and helping my little brother.

I'm from eating freshly cooked bacon,
riding my rip stick
and my right-handed lay-ups.
I'm from snapping the football
for a long pass to the winning touchdown,
and the winning shot at the buzzer,
to the mesmerizing sight of the ball clearing the fence
for the grand slam at the baseball game.

I'm from wrecking my bike at the end of the brick driveway,
and reading the *Sugar Creek Gang* series.
I'm from the knowledge inside my head.
And then some.

Cody Himes, Grade 6
Knox Community Middle School, IN

Fear

The swirling of fear stuck to the side of my mouth,
Floorboards cracked as I stepped over them as if
Somebody else was with me,
Spiders crawled up my spine as the cold wind
Crept under the doors,
I could see dust gatherings and cobwebs
Where the spiders must have lived,
The smell of dampness scrambled through the house,
Fear was all around me as I crept through the haunted house.

Ella Stadler, Grade 6
St Simon the Apostle School, IN

High Merit Poems – Grades 4, 5, and 6

Nature
People don't understand,
so I say you should take a stand,
animals have the same rights,
as humans might,
so let's all be eco friendly,
not just to your pal Fredley!
Animals have feelings like pain, guilt,
loneliness and sorrow,
let's all work together tomorrow!
Why do you abuse those who are innocent?
They never did anything non-decent.
Dog fights, hunting, and animal mills,
if you get caught you'll all get a huge bill.
So let's all stop all of this,
and give all our cute animals a kiss!
Janae Griffin, Grade 6
Galesburg-Augusta Middle School, MI

Home
Home is a cozy place
A place to get comfy
A place to get warm
A place to cuddle with loved ones

Where mom cooks
Where family comes
Where we have some fun
Where we fight with one another

No matter where
No matter how
No matter who
No matter what
Home is a great place
Emma Chrzanowski, Grade 6
St John Lutheran School, MI

Homework
Homework, oh homework,
I don't like you,
You take up my time,
You make me feel blue,

Homework, oh homework,
If you were alive,
You would follow me everywhere,
I wouldn't survive,

Homework, oh homework,
Teachers say you're fun,
But I don't believe them,
I would rather be in the sun.
Adam Saunders, Grade 6
West Middle School, MI

Fall
Wind and leaves, leaves and wind
will winter come again?
leaves on houses and schools
pile of leaves. parents and kids
raking leaves.

Leaves and wind, wind and leaves
will summer come again?
look up at the trees
and see the beautiful colorful leaves

Wind and leaves, leaves and wind
oh boy I love fall
jumping in all the leaves
looking up at all the colorful trees
look down and see the colorful
leaves on the floor. oh I just love fall
Fatima Faraj, Grade 6
Star International Academy, MI

Squishy Fishy
I have a fat orange fishy
His name is Lucky Bubbles
He's very plump and squishy
He always gets himself in trouble

Once, he jumped out of his tank
And landed on the floor
He almost landed on a spiky plank
He would have been no more

I picked him up, and threw him back in
And much to my surprise
He started swimming around again
My gosh! He's still alive!

I'm glad my fish's life was saved
Because he's still here to this day
Claire Sesko, Grade 6
St Mary Cathedral School, MI

The Sun
The sun is light
The sun is bright
The sun is heat
The sun is bigger than my feet
The sun is kind
The sun is blind
The sun is yellow
The sun is mellow
The sun is circle
The sun is purple
The sun is hot
The sun is dot
Angelia Stottlemire, Grade 4
Joan Martin Elementary School, IN

All Throughout
All throughout the mountains,
And down by the sea,
There's a whisper in the air,
A shadow on the breeze,
As the cats all leap among the grass,
And the birds chirp in the tree,
Something's out there waiting,
Stalking silently,
But as the buds are blooming,
And may there be pollen for the bee,
The drift of silent vagueness,
Is soon to quickly flee,
Then all that's left is laughter,
Not a shadow on the breeze,
All throughout the mountains,
And down by the sea.
Isabella Bohren, Grade 6
Westlane Middle School, IN

Mini Golf
Choose the club.
See the determination on my face.
Touch the club to the ground for the win.
Settling,
Calming,
Driving,
Gasping,
The ball goes flying.
It's soaring on the ground.
It's so far away
Like the chance of losing.
 Bounce,
  Bounce,
   And
    HOLE IN ONE!!
Matt Westman, Grade 6
Assumption School, MI

Tennis
Match point,
My heart is beating,
FAST!
My serve,
Nervous,
Shaking,
Scared,
I hit,
The ball flies,
Spins,
It zooms past my opponent,
Like a cheetah,
It was in,
Ace,
I won!
Eliza Solarewicz, Grade 6
Assumption School, MI

Serve It Up!
Time out!
I'm the last server.
We are up by one
Next point we win.
Whistle blows.
I get the ball
Anticipation.
The whistle blows.
I am sweating like a gorilla.
Sweating
  Waiting
    Shaking
      Stepping
        Hitting
Whoom!
The ball goes flying.
The crowd goes wild
We win.
Erin Dood, Grade 6
Assumption School, MI

Sierra
I am Sierra Marshall
You know me for keeping secrets

My mother is beautiful
My father is a hard worker

I was born in Indiana
I live with my dog Isabelle
My best friend is KyLee Kensinger
  Because she is great
  We like to hang out.
My enemy is no one
Because everybody is my friend
I fear bees
Because they hurt
I love Isabelle
Because she is so cuddly
I dream of being famous.
Sierra Marshall, Grade 4
Mentone Elementary School, IN

Mirrors on the Wall
Mirrors line the wall staring at me
Wondering what move I will do next
I ready myself by inhaling
I slide my feet to fourth position
I begin to take long strides
Then my speed quickens
I leap into the air graceful as a swan
Whoosh!
I then land safely on the floor
The mirrors still watch
Seari Hilyard, Grade 6
Wayne Gray Elementary School, MI

Isabella Rose
A miracle took place,
On the fourth of September.
This is a moment,
I'm sure to remember.

With hair so smooth,
And skin so soft,
Every thing's cute,
Even her little cough!

Brown little eyes,
Chubby little thighs,
Very long toes,
And a button nose!

She looks like her dad,
Which makes him glad!
She looks so sweet,
With her chubby cheeks!
Isabella Rose,
My newest cousin!
Abbey Sexton, Grade 6
West Middle School, MI

Inside This Book
Inside this book
Millions of wonders waiting to escape
Into the endless stream in my mind.

Inside this book
A thousand pages willingly wanting me
To read its noble words

Inside this book it's one of a kind
The words
The phrases
The pool of creativity

"When will you open me?"
It weeps to me, how it weeps.
So longingly wanting to run free
It needs to tell me something
But what?

I will find out.
Inside this book. Inside this book.
Ally Mann, Grade 6
Sashabaw Middle School, MI

Pizza
I like pizza. It's my favorite food.
It's as cheesy as the moon.
It puts me in a very good mood
For more pizza every noon.
Gabe Kosta, Grade 4
St Raphael School, MI

Summer
The air is warm,
The Earth is red,
Then comes a storm,
I like to sleep inside my bed.

Playing in the rain,
It is so fun,
The rain is no pain,
So I'll go outside and run.

The sun is bright,
It makes the Earth warm,
And full of light,
The bugs start to swarm.

Full of light, laughter, and fun,
There is something there for everyone!
Gabrielle Dobrzelewski, Grade 6
St Mary Cathedral School, MI

Florida
A fish swimming across the sea
It doesn't matter what is on the sand
My friends swimming along with me
Even though it is unplanned

A turtle egg in a nest
Raccoons try to eat them
Swimming in the ocean at the west
The shell on their back looks like a gem

On the shore the palm trees sway
The weather is always warm
We really want the sun to stay
But it must go down in a storm

Getting to Florida makes me glad
Leaving Florida makes me sad
Keely Curran, Grade 6
St Mary Cathedral School, MI

Soccer
Hoping for another goal
Dad cheering me
I'm so hungry I can eat a fruit bowl
It's a goal, yippee!
Dad cheering me
People stepping in mud that's gooey
It's a goal, yippee
I just missed the goal, phooey
People stepping in mud that's gooey
I'm so hungry I can eat a fruit bowl
I just missed the goal, phooey
Hoping for another goal
Katherine Rogers, Grade 5
Dodson Elementary School, MI

Football
Fun, sporty
sweaty, physical, long
very popular, hard working
tough.
John Lowe, Grade 6
St Simon the Apostle School, IN

Lacrosse
Ball, stick
Running, charging, moving
Sweating, tired, hot, excited
L.A.X.
Lilly Newmann, Grade 4
Crestwood Elementary School, MI

The Frightening Tiger
Ferocious stripes
Roaring in the jungle
Meat eating animals
Mammal
Jade Sabir, Grade 4
Dodson Elementary School, MI

Snowmobile
I snowmobile with my dad.
Even though the weather is bad.
I go fast.
We have a blast!
Kaitlyn Ditmars, Grade 5
Hendry Park Elementary School, IN

Snow
My house has lots of snow.
From my window I watch it blow.
Into big piles I watch it flow.
On the streets the cars go slow.
Dustin Graham, Grade 4
St Raphael School, MI

Candy
Beautiful, nice
helping, caring, working
She loves me tons.
Mom
Kyley J. Robbins, Grade 5
Hendry Park Elementary School, IN

The Test
Difficult, long
Studying, reading, listening
I must not fail
The test!
Payton Blamey, Grade 6
St Simon the Apostle School, IN

Fall Fest!
Ingredients:
Fun
Scary
Screams
Happy
Prizes
Shopping
Rides, freak out, Pharos's Fury, Skater, 1001 Nights…
Music
Games
Yelling
Parking
Money

Mix in a cup of fun, a sprinkle of scary, a dash of screams, 2 cups of happy,
a quarter cup of prizes, a half cup of shopping, a pound of rides,
pound of music, a ton of games, lots of yelling, stirring in some parking and money
and then you've got your Fall Fest.
Dominique Ceckiewicz, Grade 6
West Middle School, MI

What if Time Destroyed All Clocks?
What if time destroyed all clocks?
Nobody could tell what time it is.
You would never be late.
If time destroyed all clocks, you could wait all morning for a suspected person to arrive.
You would not know if they were late or early.
If time destroyed all clocks, all the lazy people
Will not be active, for they
would not know the momentary time.
If time destroyed all clocks, the world will be off balance.
Everybody would be confused.
If time destroyed all clocks, the plants would topple,
For there are no seasons or days.
The trees would grow far too many leaves or far too little.
If time destroyed all clocks
This world would be a devastating place to live.
Confusion might just take over your mind.
If time destroyed all clocks
This would be a horrible place.
Justin Johnson, Grade 4
Dodson Elementary School, MI

Rain and Wind
Rain and wind come and go, as I watch from my window.
Where they go no one will know.
Through the valley past the stream over trees that's what it seems, is that true?
Oh au contraire you see they have a family there.
A mom a dad a brother too, or possibly a sister like me or you.
They run and play and jump and hide,
over stumps and past the sea tide.
On Valentine's Day they say will you be mine.
They are just like me or you,
I am glad you found out what they do.
Grace Namovich, Grade 5
Black River Public School, MI

Baseball
The ball hurtling towards me
The ball smacking the catcher's mitt
"Strike 1!" The umpire yells

The bat, the swing, the hit
The crowds at the edge of their seats
"Great hit son!" My father yells with pride

The run
The dust in my face as I run to home
First, second, third
The dusty, rough slide into home
"Safe"

More screams of "Yeah!"
We won by
My run
Malachi Adcock, Grade 6
Knox Community Middle School, IN

Mrs. Kemp
Mrs. Kemp is fun,
Mrs. Kemp is cool, she loves the sun.

Mrs. Kemp is cool,
Mrs. Kemp loves the pool.

Mrs. Kemp is funny,
Mrs. Kemp is sunny.

Mrs. Kemp is happy,
Mrs. Kemp is snappy.

Mrs. Kemp is dramatic,
Mrs. Kemp is systematic.

Mrs. Kemp is kind,
Mrs. Kemp is a mastermind.
Aleena Crutchfield, Grade 4
Chrisney Elementary School, IN

Someone Secret
Her big brown eyes stare at me
Waiting for me to play
Head turns
Tail wags
Ears perk
Giving me her cute little face
She picks up her toy and swings it at me
Begging me to throw it back
Waiting for me to agree
I pick it up
It goes far
She comes back and begs for one more.
Kendra Getz, Grade 5
Dodson Elementary School, MI

School
I don't like to go to school
'cause it makes me feel uncool
I'd rather be in a pool
than sit and follow all these rules
I wanna go crazy,
but my mind is kinda hazy
I wanna visit Rome
or at least go home
I'd rather break out in song
than be here this long
the bell is about to ring
but I didn't learn anything
today I have detention
but I won't pay any attention
I wanna ditch real bad
but my teachers would get mad
Joe Lechner, Grade 6
St Simon the Apostle School, IN

Falling from Above
You are at the top
Of the world
Your heart is pounding
Faster than a horse
Flying down the track
One foot off
Two feet off
Air ripped from your
Body
You feel like
Your lungs are collapsing
All you see is blue and green
You pull the string
And you are back
Back to the strong
Solid Earth.
Maddie Tenney, Grade 6
Wayne Gray Elementary School, MI

Rules
R ules of height I am not allowed on
O nly waiting, watching
L istening to the "Clink, clink, clink"
L onging to ride, they are
E xperiencing what I must wait for
R ush of the sharp wind slapping my face

C loser and Closer each year
O ver the heads of kids just like me
A lmost there
S eeing them ride
T orture
E ndless waiting
R ules are like a barrier that keeps you out
McKenna Cameron, Grade 6
Sashabaw Middle School, MI

Lost
I am a sinner
Roaming out alone
In the wilderness
No pillow but stone
But when Jesus came
He took my sins away
And now he found me
Heaven is our stay.
David Joe Bontrager, Grade 4
West Hastings School, IN

The Game
On the field
Across he runs
In the end zone
Pass two defenders
Within five feet of the safety
Next to the field goal
Touchdown!
Kyle Diton, Grade 5
Dodson Elementary School, MI

Gymnast
Gymnast
Bendable, flexible,
Shouting, jumping, flipping
You'll watch in awe
Performing, working, dancing,
Unbelievable, dazzling,
Superstar
Devin Murphy, Grade 5
Perry Central Elementary School, IN

Fire
Fire
Hot, orange
Burning, lighting, crackling
Warm, colorful, wet, crystal-like
Freezing, cooling, hailing
Cold, white
Ice
Kage Kiplinger, Grade 5
Perry Central Elementary School, IN

Hot Dog and Burger
Hot Dog,
Long, juicy
Satisfying, filling, heating,
Picnic, ball-game, restaurant, juicy,
Grilling, eating, frying,
High, stacked,
Burger
Scott Boyd, Grade 5
Crissman Elementary School, MI

The Dreamer

I dream of being someone important,
Someone who everyone wants to be,
But I'm not,
I'm no one to everybody,
Just another oak in the grove,
Another breeze made by wind,
In my dreams I'm the tallest oak,
I'm the strongest breeze,
In my dreams I'm the hero,
The helper,
The wanted,
The healer,
Everyone thanks me for what I've done,
What a different matter — reality,
You do something good they murmur, "Thanks,"
They whisper "Yeah right,"
They scream, "I'm fine!"
Life is so complicated,
Dreams are so easy,
You look up and say,
"Why not?"

Breanne Friskney, Grade 6
Northridge Middle School, IN

Pets

Dogs are like fur balls.
I wonder what games they play.
Do you think they would play with a volleyball?
I bet they would play with it all day.
Cats are fun, but they can be lazy.
Kittens are adorable and tiny.
Hyper cats are very crazy.
Some small cats are also very whiney.
Lizards can be yellow and green.
Geckos can be black and brown.
The ones with teeth can be very mean.
In warm weather, you'll see 'em all over town.
Hamsters are like balls of fur.
They run in their hamster wheel.
With all of that fur, I wonder if they say b-r-r-r.
They are so tiny they don't seem real.
I want a new pet.
Which one will I choose?
If it's a girl, I'll name it Juliet.
I hope my parents don't refuse.

Madison Anderson, Grade 4
St. Raphael School, MI

The Beach

I hear the ocean's waves crashing against the shore.
I feel the sand in my hands slip as I reach for more.
The cold water smacks against my legs and I see the ocean blue.
While I look out onto the beach and fall
As I see a tiny grain of sand which looks so small.

Macie Lucia, Grade 6
St Simon the Apostle School, IN

Volleyball

Last shot,
It was up to me.
One serve.

Last two minutes
My left hand holds the ball out.

Hesitate
My heart is beating like a rock.
I want this.
My right arm swings back.
I glance at the score.
20-20

Bam!!
My arm flew forward, sending the ball flying.

Ace!!

Kate Sakoski, Grade 6
Assumption School, MI

Sleep

Sleep is pure blackness
Eyes closing the curtains on the world
Brain shutting down
Sounds so quiet and peaceful
A pin could drop and you could hear it
Everything quiet, you think there's a ghost
Smells like a long day but ready to relax
With the aroma floating in the air
You don't notice because your eyes drift away
The taste of food
Drool going down your pillow
But never getting the taste
Looks like anything you dream
First, complete darkness
Then, into your own cartoon
Sleep feels like nothing, but sleep is good
The feeling when you get up
Makes you ready for the day

Ethan FitzGerald, Grade 6
West Middle School, MI

Two BFF's

Two older sisters
Two summer lovers
Two hilarious jokers
Two glasses wearers
Two fruit lovers
Two veggie lovers
One Phillipino and one Romanian
One older by 12 days and one younger by 12 days
One dark brown hair and one light brown hair
Two Bff's

Tavie Valdez, Grade 4
Hampton Elementary School, MI

Ode to Grandpa
My grandpa was a great man,
He was in the war,
He was funny,
And he was a great grandpa.
He died in 2009,
From smoking and drinking,
But beside that,
He was the best.
He loved and cared,
He as proud of me,
And all his grandchildren.

He made everyone laugh.
He cared about my mom,
And the rest of family.
He's missed from all,
He will always be,
I may have not seen him often.
But the times I did,
That was the best time,
I had ever had.
Alex Heckman, Grade 6
Mendon Middle/High School, MI

The Tiger's Goal
Upon this coal-black
Mountain,
Here I am resting, the tiger.
I am brave,
Strong,
And very kind.
I save the weak,
Destroy the wicked,
And help the meek
Win back their courage.
For I am the tiger
Who is a hero.

I must enter a dreary cave,
Where the deadly dragon
King roams.
He's captured a serpent
And she can't be freed,
Unless he's defeated.
And as a hero,
I must free her.
Kathryn Bannick, Grade 6
Sashabaw Middle School, MI

Bees
Bees are buzy buzzing around.
Bees are buzy all around town.
Buzzing buzzily to get work done.
Aren't you glad that you're not one!
Rose Bielefeld, Grade 6
St Simon the Apostle School, IN

Best Friends
Dear Brynne,
and Vik,
You guys are my friends
there are no what ifs!
When I am hurt
I know you're there,
When I am sad
I know you care!
Purple, pink,
Red, and blue,
I want you to know
I am there for you too!
I love you guys
from head to toe,
I love you guys
and your funky socks that show!
I wrote this poem
for you to see,
how awesome and great
you both can be!
Emily Denny, Grade 6
Jean K Harker Middle School, MI

Nowhere to Run
Walking, walking,
Step by step,
Down the dark hall,
Never ending corridor.
I glance ahead
The light at the far end of the tunnel
I glance behind
At the rows of bricks
I can't turn around
I can't go ahead
But I just keep walking
Nowhere to go, not even back
I glance behind
Something's following
Lurking in the shadows
Can't be heard and can't be seen
Running, running
In the never ending tunnel
I look behind to face the beast
My shadow.
Lauren Hildreth, Grade 6
West Middle School, MI

Racing
R ush as you go down the strip
A bug of nervous
C atching up to people
I n the zone
N o slackers
G et better at it
Dylan Cleveland, Grade 6
Wayne Gray Elementary School, MI

The Sea's Serenity
The ocean
Is a spectacular thing
It crashes and roars and booms
Yet in all this noise
I find serenity
A lull in the din of the waves
Beyond the churning water
Beyond the boisterous, wild winds
And the frothing, flying foam
I see in the waves
A million colors
I see in the water
A million fish
I hear in the winds
A million songs
And I see in the foam
A million horses
With wings of white water
Galloping wildly to shore
Only to be swept back
Into the strange serenity
Of the wildly swirling sea.
Rebekah Hoffer, Grade 6
Mary Evelyn Castle Elementary School, IN

Bulldogs
Their scrunched up face
All their drool
Their drool is sticky
When they lick you
You see a bulldog run to you
You see them flop when they come to you
Bulldogs lick you
Bulldogs love you
Bulldogs saying, "Hi!"
When they plop on you
Brittany Poe, Grade 5
Heritage Intermediate School, IN

Change
Change is good
Change is bad

Change can make us happy
Change can make us sad

Change is a tornado
Change is an A plus

Change can change
Everyone of us

How has change
Changed you?
Molly Graham, Grade 4
Bright Elementary School, IN

Ocean's Song
The crash of the waves rolling ashore
Opening a door of cool breeze
Spraying a mist by the bay
It's hard to resist I say

The ocean's song I stand and embrace it
I trace the beauty of its melody
It is overpowering to be heard
It reminds me of the singing of a beautiful bird

My feet searching in the sand
Continuously tapping to the beat of ocean's symphony
Only water's true heart determines what it will be
So I can see what it has in store for me

Aubree Lankford, Grade 6
Fort Branch Community School, IN

Nature's Breath
The lightest breeze sweeps through a meadow
No pleasant breeze today, it's hot!
Leaves rustle in the wind
Snow gets blown off the ground

A nice scent of rosemary coming from my garden
The smell of hamburgers wafts through the open kitchen window
The smell of warm apple cider dances in front of my nose
Crisp, cold air fills my nostrils as I step outside

Spring is a happy time of year
Kids run and play in summer
The leaves change to beautiful colors in fall
Get ready for many snowball fights in winter!

Dana Pierangeli, Grade 5
Knapp Forest Elementary School, MI

Under the Ocean
Under the deep blue water,
The seaweed sways in the current,
The fish swim in schools,
A treasure chest lies abandoned on the ocean floor.

Under the sun's bright rays penetrating the water,
The dolphins leap above the flowing tide,
The sharks circle a group of fish,
A shipwreck gets covered in algae.

Under the reflection of the water,
Great big whales swim gracefully through the sea,
Otters dive down to the sandy ocean floor to get seashells,
The Titanic rots under the great big iceberg.

Jayna Lenders, Grade 6
West Middle School, MI

What do you do for others?
What do you do to serve others?
Do you pick up trash,
Or help someone across the street?
Do you play with little ones,
Or share your treats?

What do you do to help others?
Do you give encouraging words,
Or be the shoulder to cry on?
Do you help during tough times,
Or hug them when a loved one is gone?
Do you laugh and play with each other,
Or help them find the area of a hexagon?

What do you do for others?
When they feel weak,
Do you make them strong?
When they have trouble,
Do you help them with a sense of right or wrong?
When they feel lonely,
Do you ring the bell, "ding-dong?"

What do *you* do for others?

Jessica Chen, Grade 6
Clague Middle School, MI

Pond Dog
Sadie, my mom and dad's dog
The dog who not only hates mailmen
Sadie hates all uniforms
As a pup, she devoured our Longaberger baskets
She chewed off the yellow paint in my bathroom

Sadie, who licked my face
Long ago when I used my crib
While I tried to nap for a while
She swam in the dirty smelly pond all summer
Then one day she vanished,

At fifteen, that's not good
My mom and I looked everywhere.
We found her at the neighbor's pond
Trying to swim
She got stuck in the gooey mud

Sadie whimpered in horrible pain at her back legs
Sadie dragged her hind legs the rest of that long week
She was in so much pain
So that Thursday…we had to put her down
Sadie, my mom and dad's dog

Rylee Hollingsworth, Grade 6
Linton-Stockton Elementary School, IN

Candy
Smells like super yummy chocolate
Tastes like super tasty birthday cake
Feels as smooth and creamy as a Twinkie
Looks as round as a small rock
Sounds like the air moving through the sky
Nevaeh Roark, Grade 4
Dibble Elementary School, MI

Animals
A ngry alligators attacking
B ig bats batting
C ute cats crawling
D igging dogs dig
E very elephant exercising.
Jacob McFate, Grade 4
Dibble Elementary School, MI

Chess
C oncentration
H ard
E xciting
S killed
S trategy
Ben Reising, Grade 5
Holy Redeemer School, IN

Ice Cream
Ice cream
Is cold and sweet.
It makes me smile and feel good.
My body shivers like a quake.
So good!
Mavery Brush, Grade 5
Staunton Elementary School, IN

Snowy Toes
With my barefooted toes
I step in the snow
I'm up to my ears
With these blizzard-y fears
Surely winter will go!
Mallory Brooks, Grade 6
St Simon the Apostle School, IN

The Earth
Humans
Giving, generous
Wishing they could rescue the planet
Recycling to save the world
Mammals
Ben Griffith, Grade 5
Dodson Elementary School, MI

Blue
Blue is like the sound of a blue-winged bird flapping its wings in the warm summer air.
Blue is like the smell of a freshly baked blueberry pie.
Blue is like the taste of a cup of tea with glue food coloring.
Blue is like the feel of my bed at night.
Nolan Wilson, Grade 4
Morgan Elementary School, IN

Halloween Black
Halloween black is like the sound of a bat flying through the air
Halloween black is like the smell of a burnt pumpkin pie
Halloween black is like the taste of a black licorice from trick-or-treating
Halloween black is like the feel of a fuzzy black cat on Halloween night
Jill Jacobi, Grade 5
Morgan Elementary School, IN

Brown
Brown is like the sound of a crayon coloring on a piece of paper.
Brown is like the smell of the warm tasty cookies in the oven.
Brown is like the taste of the tasty ice-cream that I eat on a hot summer day.
Brown is like the feel of the warm cozy blanket that I sleep with.
Cameron Voyles, Grade 4
Morgan Elementary School, IN

Fall Brown
Fall brown is like the sound of kids yelling trick-or-treat.
Fall brown is like the smell of the crisp fall air.
Fall brown is like the taste of a cold drink of "Coca-Cola."
Fall brown is like the feel of dead leaves crumbling in my hand on a fall day.
Hannah Dailey, Grade 5
Morgan Elementary School, IN

How Does It Feel?
Knowing that at that very moment you have accomplished something great,
It feels as if at that very moment you are floating on a puffy cloud,
Oh, how superb it feels to receive one of these,
How does it feel to receive an "A?"
Kyle Yust, Grade 6
St Simon the Apostle School, IN

Yellow
Yellow is like the sound of a beautiful trumpet playing in a band.
Yellow is like the smell of freshly cut lemons.
Yellow is like the taste of a nice glass of cold lemonade on a hot summer day.
Yellow is like the feel of a soft yellow blanket.
Wade Hockersmith, Grade 4
Morgan Elementary School, IN

Soccer
S occer is the greatest sport
O ur team is excellent.
C an you score a goal?
C an you win a championship?
E veryone plays his finest.
R un to the ball as quick as you can.
C.J. Pollock, Grade 4
Concord Ox Bow Elementary School, IN

Inside Joy
Inside joy,
There are miles of snow,
Like a blanket of diamonds.
Inside joy,
There are lights twinkling everywhere,
Like bright stars in the night sky.
Max Barnaby, Grade 5
Dodson Elementary School, MI

State Champions
41-42 we're down. Mid-Michigan Magic in the lead.
Coach is screaming, "Foul! Foul! Get a foul!"
We foul.
Ball gets passed in.
Defending like madwomen
We succeed! A steal!
Fast break.
Shaking
Shivering
Sweating
Shot is made on a foul!
The foul shot goes *SWISH*.
44-42 us!
We won.
The crowd goes wild.
North Court Netters AAU number one in the state

Libby O'Brien, Grade 6
Assumption School, MI

Basketball
I see the other angry players
All sweaty and tired
I see the different colors of the worn out jerseys
I hear the excited crowd chanting out team's name
Addison, Addison, Addison, Addison, Addison
The squeaking of the broken in shoes hits my eardrum
I hear the orange ball making its way towards me
I smell the B.O. of the tired players
The smell of the buttery popcorn reaches my nose
I smash into my opponent when I set my hard pick
Everyone leaning in, watching closely
I have the ball
Three seconds on the clock
It gets quiet
I shoot
We win.

Paige Wollet, Grade 6
Wayne Gray Elementary School, MI

Baseball
Baseball is fun
I like it because I get to run
I like to play all day
Especially at Chesapeake Bay
I hit the ball far
It goes all the way to mars
I'll always use a wood bat
I like to wear a baseball cap
I always bring my mitt
While other kids throw a fit
I like when I hit the ball and get to go home
Then I get to take a bath in the foam
The ball smashes through a car
Into the car of Mrs. Mares.

Michael Van Pelt, Grade 6
Eagle Creek Academy, MI

Colors of the Earth
Green is the seaweed that grows down deep.
Black is the sky as it starts to sleep.

Orange is the sun as it starts to rise.
Purple is the mountain with its glorious size.

Blue is the color of the wide open sky.
White is an eagle as it starts to fly.

Green is a forest big and wide.
Gray is a glacier with all its pride.

Yellow is a desert, crisp and dry.
White are the stars way up high.

What a world!

Caleb Swanson, Grade 6
Manistique Middle & High School, MI

Sports
Basketball is my favorite sport
it comes with skill and fun
Volleyball comes in second
because we have to run.
You know the suicides and all that crazy stuff,
but once you get to know it you won't want to stop.
My third sport I don't know a lot about
this one surely comes with skill,
My third one is tennis,
but like I said before,
I don't know very well.
My fourth one is soccer
which I play with my friends a lot.
It probably comes before three
I know a little more about it,
but that doesn't bother me.

Korie McCrea, Grade 6
St John the Evangelist School, IN

A Reverse World
If we lived in a reverse world, would the earth never spin?
Would the best thing be to lose and the worst thing to win?
Would a tortoise go fast and a hare go slow?
Would no mean yes and yes mean no?
Would day be night and night be day?
Would spring be in December and winter in May?
Would a dog meow and a cat bark?
Would you mark a wrong answer with a check mark?
Would it be bad to do good and good to do bad?
Would an extreme smile show you're very sad?
Would right be on the left and left on the right?
Would a principal tell you it's okay to argue and fight?
I don't know how a reverse world would be,
But I hope it's something I'll never see!

Maria Trimborn, Grade 5
Holy Redeemer School, IN

A Celebration of Poets – Great Lakes Grades 4-12 Spring 2011

Escape to Sunlight
The sun was so bright
I had to escape her soon
It shines on the sea
Clare LaLonde, Grade 6
Holy Name School, MI

The Howler
As the night grows dark,
he lets his voice flow in darkness.
And now others hear him.
Josie Williams, Grade 5
Ballard Elementary School, MI

Apple
Sweet red yummy fruit
Shiny smooth hard stem
Sticky on your face
Drew Hulse, Grade 4
Riverside Elementary School, MI

Frog
Green and yellow frog
hopping along a log and
ate a big black fly
Jaina Adams, Grade 5
Hendry Park Elementary School, IN

Breeze
The wind is whistling.
Makes a figure in the mist,
Then it blows away.
Stephanie LaFoille, Grade 6
Manistique Middle & High School, MI

Winter
White glistening snow,
everything smells fresh and cold,
let's go have some fun.
Jack Knoll, Grade 5
Ballard Elementary School, MI

Spring
Winter is all gone
so put your mittens away,
take out your raincoat.
Alma Vazquez, Grade 5
Ballard Elementary School, MI

Leaves
Trees are going bald
So many colorful leaves
Lots of raking now
Elliot Wallace, Grade 5
Ballard Elementary School, MI

Sisters*
Sisters
Sisters
Sisters

Older sisters
Younger sisters
Goofy caring lovable sisters
Brainy beautiful skinny sisters
Those are just a few.
Simple-minded sisters
Butterball sisters
Loving boyfriend-dating sisters
Clumsy hurtful nerdy sisters
Occupied sisters too.
Bragging sisters
Scheming sisters
Don't forget faithful sisters
Last of all, best of all I love my sister!
Emily Kimball, Grade 4
Bailey School, MI
*Patterned after "Beans, Beans, Beans" by Lucia & James L. Hymes

Dads*
Dads
Dads
Dads

Short dads
Giant dads
Serious hardworking dads
Snoring sleeping lazy dads
Those are just a few.
Smart dads
Funny dads
Can't stop talking dads
Monster truck loving dads
Famous dads too!
Friendly dads
Wrestling dads
Don't forget sad dads
Last of all, best of all I love my dad!
Logan Dunne, Grade 4
Bailey School, MI
*Patterned after "Beans, Beans, Beans" by Lucia & James L. Hymes

Smart
I'm talking smart!
I'm talking mega-minded!
I'm talking flippant!
I'm talking witty, opposite of bone head!
I'm talking stylish, sharp, shrewd!
I'm talking intelligent, worldly-wise, clever, bright!
I'm talking learned, A+ on every test, knowing all the answers, sensible, GENIUS!
I'm talking smart!
Maya Smith, Grade 4
Hampton Elementary School, MI

High Merit Poems – Grades 4, 5, and 6

Spring in the Desert
The dry dirt beneath my feet crackles every time I step, I pick up the parched soil and let it run between my fingers. Wind gusts blow by me as if racing to the mountains. The pleasant scent of blooming cactus flowers comfort me. The pure spring air is like no other in the world, and I let out a sigh of relief, knowing I am at peace in the desert.

Lindsay Janssen, Grade 6
St. Simon the Apostle School, IN

Dog
Dog
Cute, adorable
Amazing, running, catching
Nice, beautiful, caring, cool
Laying, sitting, purring
Perfect fur
Cat

Alexis Louden, Grade 5
Sunman Dearborn Intermediate School, IN

Sports
Football
Fun, tough
Tackling, hitting, sacking
Touchdowns, field goals, baskets, free throws
Shooting, passing, dribbling
Cool, hard
Basketball

Logan Hubert, Grade 5
Perry Central Elementary School, IN

Where I Am From
I am from a poor land where there is barely any food.
I am from a place where swords and weapons are heard all the time.
I am from an active place with ferocious animals.
I am from a place where people were forced to France.
I am from where there is war 24/7 nonstop.
I am from where their is volcanos blasting ashes and lava.
I am from a very hot and sunny place.

Onephefus Hudson, Grade 4
Hampton Elementary School, MI

The Great Mountains of Glacier National Park
National park
During the light, blue weather
Along the yellow flower covered grass
On the meadow, at the sunny rolling top on the hill
Above the rocky, brown scenery
Underneath the dusty, rocky bottom
Montana

Katie Rietow, Grade 6
Knox Community Middle School, IN

Fair Life
Absent from the greed epidemic,
They who abide the bogus aphorism,
struggle to live the burden.
Intolerant humans' embellish on the fair life,
Disregarding the compulsion the fair life needs.
They are
Anguished
By the
Megalomania,
Maniacal
Accession
Of the humans,
Though, fair life still fights to prevail
Standing tall, brushing the moon, fair life.

Running and rousing the oceans,
Stomping steadily over forests,
Many humans are thriving, their lives barely timed.
Meandering far and wide, doing as they wish. Walking earthquakes

Try cessation, look fair life in the eye, apologize

You are Mother Nature too,
You can be fair life new.

Mitchell Page, Grade 6
Sashabaw Middle School, MI

Where to Go?
There are adults in the world that are losing their jobs.
Trying to find another job but suffering.
Wondering where they should go live.

People on the streets are
trying to find people to help them
They sit there and say nothing
inside their heads they say, "Help me! I am so confused!"

They sit there and sigh
and they have a bucket for money
and ask for money.

Some people give money
and others walk right by.

When they have enough money
they will get a place to live.

They have children that can't go to school.

Our family can tell how lucky we are.

Danielle Wilson, Grade 4
Dodson Elementary School, MI

Page 217

Silent Hunter
As the silent hunter sneaks through the night
It gets ready to pounce
It jumps!
The mouse goes down without a squeak
The hunter is victorious!
Whereas this hunter sounds great
it is actually quite small
It is a cat…small in size but brave at heart.

Dylan Bowman, Grade 6
Panther Elementary School, MI

An Ode to Dad
Oh Dad, Oh Dad you never frown.
Oh Dad, Oh Dad you don't wear a night gown.
Oh Dad, Oh Dad you like to play pass,
Oh Dad, Oh Dad you like to drive fast.
Oh Dad, Oh Dad you like to play Wii with me.
Oh Dad, Oh Dad you lose your keys sometimes.
Oh Dad, Oh Dad you are rooty.
Oh Dad, Oh Dad you like Call Of Duty.

Steven Tindall, Grade 5
Morgan Elementary School, IN

The Halloween Dream
Halloween has spoken,
and the ghosts have been freed,
watch out for vampires all on Dracula Street…
watch out for your children for they will be eaten…
all by the mayor of Halloween town…
could all of this happen in one day?
do not be frighten or deceived…
for all that it was is Rosie's Halloween day dream!!!!

Nesrine Charara, Grade 6
Star International Academy, MI

The Leprechaun
One day Bob was running through the forest
When he saw something small and green.
Wow! It was a leprechaun.
He said, "I'll give you three wishes,
But you better be wise."
"I want to be a little leprechaun." Bob said.
Seconds later with a poof he looked up and saw a mountain.
He quickly realized it was a pebble, and he was a *little* leprechaun.

Lindsi Mackensen, Grade 6
St John Lutheran School, MI

Green
Green is the color of a frog on a lily pad being blown across a pond.
Green is the color of pine trees being chopped down for Christmas.
Green is the color of seaweed waving in the ocean water.
Green is the color of grass blowing in the cool summer breeze.
Green is the color of my classmate's shirts on St. Patrick's Day.
Green is a color all around you!

Jessica Czapla, Grade 5
Crissman Elementary School, MI

Ode to My Pet Snail
Oh Fredward you were so slimy
Oh Fredward you had such a small shell
Oh Fredward you are lost somewhere in my house.
Oh Fredward you had no fur
Oh Fredward you were the best
Oh Fredward I hope you are still alive
Oh Fredward if you are still alive just know
I love you!

Jessica McComas, Grade 4
Morgan Elementary School, IN

The Beach
A wave breaks and crashes against the shore
White foam settles on the bare surface
All the noise fades as I look upon a never ending ocean
In the distance, two birds dive down and skim the water's surface
The sea breeze gently brushes against my face
For one moment I am alone; in peace
There is no other place like it
No…there is nothing like the beach.

Alexa Christenson, Grade 6
St Simon the Apostle School, IN

Never Land
A place of mystery lay ahead,
That shall be the land of Never Land,
Kids having endless fun,
Laughing and not being shunned,
As the wind skims across my face,
The smell of fresh air fills the space,
Then I taste the water that lay in the clouds,
And I think of my homeland being so confident and proud.

Katie Perry, Grade 6
St Simon the Apostle School, IN

The Race of a Lifetime
I am at the speedway.
I can smell the exhaust from the cars' motors.
I can still taste the hot dog I just ate.
I can see the bright, gleaming cars lining up at the finish line.
I can feel the vibration of the cars on the seats.

I can hear the roar of the cars' engines.
This is definitely the race of a lifetime.

Nicholas Montgomery, Grade 6
St Simon the Apostle School, IN

The Scared Puppy
She walked alone in the street.
Until she noticed her feet,
They were bruised and broken,
She could barely have spoken.
But when she saw the light and the girl in front of her,
She stopped and wagged her tail and went home with her forever.

Mallory Grant, Grade 6
St Simon the Apostle School, IN

The Plants in the Forest
Bushes grow berries,
Trees are very long and thin,
While the grass is short.
Will Hagenow, Grade 6
St Simon the Apostle School, IN

Heaven and Hell
The Ying and the Yang,
The heads and tails of the coin,
The Heaven and Hell.
Jack Lockrem, Grade 6
St Simon the Apostle School, IN

Apples
They're ripe and they're red
They're mellow and they're yellow
Taste one and you'll see.
Bernadette Hughbanks, Grade 6
St Simon the Apostle School, IN

Snow
I see snow outside
I want to go play in it
Then I make snowballs
Daniel Scotto, Grade 6
St Simon the Apostle School, IN

Fish
Fish are very cool.
Fish like to swim in a tank.
Fish are fun to watch.
Chris Freeman, Grade 4
Crestwood Elementary School, MI

Cade, Sam, and Ben
Cade, Sam, and Ben are friends
Cade, Sam, Ben are best of friends
Cade, Sam, Ben are fun.
Cade Baumgardner, Grade 4
Crestwood Elementary School, MI

Dance Class
Warm up at the barre
Ballet and Jazz is what I do
Hear the music play
Kristina Clover, Grade 6
Mio AuSable Middle/High School, MI

Softball
Running the bases!
Ball sliding past the fielders…
Softball is my sport!
Tallyn P. Book, Grade 5
Hendry Park Elementary School, IN

Best Friend
We've been through so much these past years.
We've had moments with laughter, and moments with tears.
You stood by me, through every step of the way.
And along our journey, we grew stronger each day.
When times were tough, you guided me through.
Without your help, I wouldn't know what to do.
But my dear friend;
It just keeps getting hard, and the pain only grew.
I wish you could help, but there's nothing you could do.
My tears keep on falling, and even I can't dry them away.
It seems as if my world where meant to be under dark clouds of gray.
I wish things were different, and these bad feelings were gone.
But I don't think I could do this, I just can't hold on.
And my dear friend;
This may be hard for you, and difficult to understand.
But if you ever need me, next to you is where I'll stand.
Just know that I do love you, and we'll never part.
When the time comes when you feel weak, just look deep inside your heart.
Also my friend, when you miss me, look to the stars above.
And that's when you'll know that you're surrounded with all my love.
Payton Bayliff, Grade 5
Brown Elementary School, IN

Cats*
Cats
Cats
Cats

Black cats
Big cats
Orange little cute cats
Gray big crabby cats
Those are just a few.
Playful cats
Fluffy cats
Ugly hissing fat cats
Cute purring skinny cats
Stray cats too!
Smart cats
Girl cats
Don't forget boy cats
Last of all, best of all I like my cat.
Kimberly Osborne, Grade 4
Bailey School, MI
*Patterned after "Beans, Beans, Beans" by Lucia & James L. Hymes

Music of the Forest
The forest.
It seems almost alive at times, with every rock and tree and flower.
When the wind whispers its song through the trees, the ferns sway from side to side like dancers. *Coo coo, coo coo* sings the dove. The chorus of crickets and frogs join in, uniting all voices as one.
Then, the wind stops.
All is silent once again.
Alyson Yu, Grade 6
Mary Evelyn Castle Elementary School, IN

Life
Life is like a game of chess,
Each move is important,
One usually comes out on top,
A challenge is always great.
Nate Norris, Grade 6
East Elementary School, IN

Penguins
Penguins lay eggs on ice,
When they hatch they feel real nice,
The penguin's fur is very soft,
They sit on icebergs floating aloft.
Elijah Wyatt, Grade 5
Hendry Park Elementary School, IN

Snake
Snake, slimy, green, striped
in black, slithering in the
silence, predator of the
night, and he's not afraid to bite.
Brinston Powell, Grade 5
Hendry Park Elementary School, IN

Deer
Dancing in the meadow
Every single day
Everybody laughing
Running through the field
Jordan Leckie, Grade 5
Perry Central Elementary School, IN

Cupcakes
crumbly, and delicious
warm, and welcoming
tempting
Fancy muffins
Riley Leich, Grade 5
Crissman Elementary School, MI

Sugar Stone
Sugar stone you look so good
Sugar stone you taste so sweet
Sugar stone you smell so fine
Sugar stone you are all mine
Jack Brownley, Grade 4
Dodson Elementary School, MI

Carmel River
Carmel river golden brown
Chocolate trees all around
Purple tulips just like grapes
Carmel River just over Blueberry Mountain.
Tyler Preece, Grade 4
Dodson Elementary School, MI

Dogs*
Dogs
Dogs
Dogs

Tough dogs
Weak dogs
Hefty hairy Newfoundland dogs
Petite elegant Chihuahua dogs
Those are just a few.
Chunky dogs
Scrawny dogs
Huge scary pit-bull dogs
Friendly golden retriever dogs
Snoozing dogs too!
Fast dogs
Ugly dogs
Don't forget playful dogs
Last of all, best of all I like my dog.
Tyler Scripter, Grade 4
Bailey School, MI
Patterned after "Beans, Beans, Beans" by Lucia & James L. Hymes

Cities*
Cities
Cities
Cities

Enormous cities
Puny cities
Loud crowded warm cities
Quiet open cold cities
Those are just a few.
Hustling cities
Tranquil cities
Stormy hail frozen cities
Sunny clear-sky cities
Historic cities too.
Futuristic cities
Gleaming cities
Don't forget dull cities
Last of all, best of all, I like my city!
Adrian Potok, Grade 4
Bailey School, MI
Patterned after "Beans, Beans, Beans" by Lucia & James L. Hymes

A World of White
As I look outside to see a land I don't recognize.
It seems as if the world is covered in a white blanket of snow.

Not spring with rainstorms that go CRASH!
Not summer nor fall.

Why it seems as if the world is like a cookie that has been frosted thickly.
What a crazy thing to think as I sit there by the fire.
Mae Hartsig, Grade 4
Justus Gage Elementary School, MI

The Swaying Saxophone
The astounding music
I play and hear
My notes explode
Through the air
I sing A-D-E-F-E-A
Over and over
My musician's air fills me
With great joy
The smooth air…
Revives me
From a deep coma
The music…
My music…
Jaelyn Walker, Grade 6
Linton-Stockton Elementary School, IN

My Mom
A wesome
B est
C ool
D ancing, mom
E xciting
F un
G reat
H uggable
I ncredible
J ackie
K ind
L ovable
M y mom
N ever aggressive
O h so nice
P erfect
Q uiet
R eliable
S o pretty
T alkative
U sually long hair
V ery comforting
W onderful
X cellent
Y oung
Z oomy
Natalie Pierce, Grade 5
Morgan Elementary School, IN

Grandparents
G rand
R eally great
A lways there for me
N ot bad
D oes good things
P uts family first
A lways makes me happy
R emarkable
E asy to make me smile
N ot mean
T ells me funny jokes
S uper
Trevor Haub, Grade 5
Morgan Elementary School, IN

Justin Bieber
Justin Bieber's eyes are as blue as the ocean.
He sings with a lot of emotion.
When he sing "Somebody to Love"
It sounds just like heaven above.
Hayley Shupert, Grade 4
St Raphael School, MI

Sunlight
Sunlight shines through the clouds
giving light to the home of many crowds.

Sunlight always makes us smile,
and our smiles always go for many miles.

Because everyone around us is cheery,
not even one soul is dreary.

Thank you Lord for the clouds and light,
and for making all of our lives so bright.
Abby Dood, Grade 5
Assumption School, MI

Ode to Sen
Oh Sen, oh Sen you are the best
Oh Sen, oh Sen you play with me every day
Oh Sen, oh Sen you are so cute
Oh Sen, oh Sen you are so playful
Oh Sen, oh Sen you can be lazy
Oh Sen, oh Sen I love you the most
Oh Sen, oh Sen you are my boxer
Oh Sen, oh Sen you are my soft pillow
Oh Sen, oh Sen you are my dog to share
Oh Sen, oh Sen you are so sweet
Oh Sen, oh Sen that is my dog Sen
Hailie Alcorn, Grade 5
Morgan Elementary School, IN

Twinkling Lights
Gorgeous twinkling
Lights there are
Quick sparks
Of tender joy
Like
Delicate snowflakes
Each one unique
In their own way
Inside
Gorgeous twinkling
Lights
Alexandra Wallman, Grade 5
Dodson Elementary School, MI

A Field of Flowers
One day I took a walk
Along the fields of flowers,
Oh they were so beautiful,
They remind me of God's powers!

They were yellow, pink, and red
I could smell their fragrance sweet.
So I picked some to take home,
In a vase they looked so neat.
Janelle Renae Hochstetler, Grade 4
West Hastings School, IN

The Big Undefeat
16-17 we were down,
Everyone on the court and in the stands
Holding their breath,
Then our point guard gets the ball,
I set a screen,
Then our point goes to the basket,
She shoots,
She scores,
We win 18-17,
Now we are 4-0,
We are undefeated!
Taylor Benoit, Grade 6
Assumption School, MI

Disaster
I woke up to a rumble
A big crash
A swirling sound
The sky was dark
It was green
It was scary
Then the wall moved
It started to crack
I ran downstairs
I watch my house go by
There was just a ripped up ground
Jacob Baca, Grade 4
Joan Martin Elementary School, IN

It's So Much Fun!
I can't believe it, I won!
It was so much fun!
In PE I had to run!
I came in number one!
I thought to myself, here I come!
That was surprisingly fun!
I am so glad I won!
Now the race is done,
I had so much fun!
An award I won.
The race was so much fun!
Kaitlin Sanders, Grade 4
Chrisney Elementary School, IN

Best Day!
I saw the beautiful lake
the water touched my toes
it tickled inside
I jumped and made a splash
I thought I was in heaven
the cool water was great
I couldn't leave
when I had to I was sad
it was quiet as a sleeping mouse
Kayla Rutan, Grade 5
Addison Middle School, MI

Justin Bieber
Justin Bieber is as hot as cookies out of the oven.
His songs I'm really lovin'.
He also gets treated like a king.
"Never Say Never" is my favorite song for him to sing.
Jenna Linden, Grade 4
St Raphael School, MI

Justin Bieber
Justin Bieber is as hot as the sun.
His eyes are brown and clear.
I can't believe how many awards he's won!
When he sings "Pray," it is my favorite to hear.
Kendall Meadows, Grade 4
St. Raphael School, MI

Snow
As she dances and twirls
Her snowy white patterned shawl
Flies and flitters in the wind

Snow

From all her twirling
She is dizzy now
So she wobbles around

Snow

She attempts to twirl once more
But collapses to the ground to rest
From the day's show

Snow

She is not only
A dancer
But a magician

Snow

So to end her performance
She winks and says, "Goodbye"
And disappears

Never to come back again
Emma Berends, Grade 5
North Muskegon Elementary School, MI

Football
Football
leather, hard
running, throwing, kicking
love football, it rocks
Pig skin
Dylan Jacob Gallagher, Grade 5
Hendry Park Elementary School, IN

Belle and Me
She is unduly smart
But she doesn't act it

She can be ornery
But doesn't know it

She hates to sleep
But always does it

She breaks thing
But doesn't mean to

She makes me mad
But doesn't try to

She aims to please
And often does it

She makes me sleep
And loves to do it

She like to play
Dawn to dusk

She makes me smile
Most of the time

We love each other
And we know it
Thomas D. Shaw, Grade 6
Knox Community Middle School, IN

Dance of Autumn
Every year fall comes, and the dance begins
Fall leaves
Amber, orange, yellow, brown
Fluttering around like small ballerinas
This is the dance of autumn
Birds singing
For the beautiful dance
All of nature is dancing
This is the dance of autumn
Long, yellow grasses
Wait for this time to come
When they can waltz in the meadows
This is the dance of autumn
Tall trees
Towering over the forest
Swaying to the music of the animals
This is the dance of autumn
Rushing winds
Playfully nipping at your cheeks
Swirling and twirling around this place
This is the dance of autumn
Sydney Lintol, Grade 5
Eagle Creek Academy, MI

High Merit Poems – Grades 4, 5, and 6

In the House
In the house there's lots to do
Ironing, sewing, patching too
Helping mother with all chores
In the house and out of doors

Sweeping floors and mopping too
Those are the things we all should do
Baking cakes and cookies too
These are things we like to do
Kayla Diane Wagler, Grade 4
South Bogard School, IN

Springtime
In the springtime
The birds all sing
And the roses make
Sweet smelling rings

The farmers work
Out in the field
While the birds sing
And their nests build
Loren Lee Wagler, Grade 4
Green Acres School, IN

Horseback Riding
Out of the tack room
Onto the horse
Into the arena
Over the jump
Around the barrels
Near the judges
Off the animal
On the platform
Gold medal!
Emma Mastny, Grade 5
Dodson Elementary School, MI

Stealth
Stealth
Predator, quiet
Stalking, clawing, fighting
Running into silent moonlight
Wolves
Ryan Elliott, Grade 4
Bailey School, MI

Grand Canyon
Through the huge rocky canyon
Beside the bolder-sized rocks
In the weighted down canoe
Over the speeding rapids
Near rocky, yet sandy beaches
Arizona
Jacob Trapp, Grade 6
Knox Community Middle School, IN

Me
Good thinker
Worrier
Risk taker
Bug killer
TV watcher
Junk food eater
Game player
Soccer player
Good swimmer
Good reader
Dog lover
Cat lover
Pig hater
Good listener
And a lover
Mahmoud Mohammad, Grade 6
Star International Academy, MI

Cupcakes!
Cupcakes, cupcakes, cupcakes!
They're really, really yummy!
Bake, bake, bake! They're fun to make!
They go into your little tummy!
They're really, really yummy!
They taste so great!
They go into your little tummy!
If I eat too many I get a tummy ache!
They taste so great!
They go into your little tummy!
If I eat too many I get a tummy ache!
They taste so great!
Bake, bake, bake! They're fun to make
If I eat too many I get a tummy ache!
Cupcakes, cupcakes, cupcakes!
Brene't White, Grade 5
Dodson Elementary School, MI

Swimmy
Swimming in the water
Waiting to be played with
Big eyes looking through the tank
Shiny, sparkly scales
Every morning he wakes up
Swimming up high
To wait for the delicious food
Playing and sharing with other friends
Shiny, sparkly scales
Gray and silver colors
Swimming in the water
Waiting to be fed again
Shiny, sparkly scales
Swimming back and forth
Waving fins around and around
Karen Pham, Grade 5
Dodson Elementary School, MI

Winning Point
One, two, three,
Engarde!
I take a deep breath,
I take one step,
Then another.
Hoping to get this last point.
"Okay,"
My mind thinks,
"One, two, three, LUNGE!"
My arm extends
And I touch her.
Thoughts are running,
Through my mind like a sprinter,
But most of all,
I won the match!
Maddie Ripple, Grade 6
Assumption School, MI

Forest Morning
I look out my window,
On this morning so fine,
I see a young doe in the shining moonlight,
Then comes another,
To warn in fright,
They leave together,
Then comes sunlight,
And the fresh smell of pine,
And the chirping of birds,
Awaits my ears,
There's prancing deer,
And a glistening lake,
Where fish jump,
And leave frogs in their wake,
Urging me to join them.
Abigail Conner, Grade 5
Weiss Elementary School, MI

The Sun Days
It is the sun that hugs you warmly
during the day
It is the sun that says good
morning darling
It is the sun that tucks you in
at night while it's going down
It is the sun that tells me hello
when I'm down

The sun dries up the land after
a long night of rain
The sun makes beautiful rainbows
after scary thunder
The sun shines bright to show
me God's delight
Presley Johnson, Grade 6
Fort Branch Community School, IN

Leaves
Brown, gold, and crunchy,
they fall on the ground gently,
they sway like bubbles.
Elizabeth Clark, Grade 5
Ballard Elementary School, MI

Frog
It is green, slimy, it hops.
It is small, smooth, mushy. It is sticky, moist
It lives in the tropics.
Cole Swihart, Grade 4
Riverside Elementary School, MI

War
Standing in Iraq,
getting shot at by people,
calling for support.
Anthony Duvendack, Grade 5
Hendry Park Elementary School, IN

Cute Frog
Big frog eyes bulge out
a frog is on a tree branch
a little frog sits
Melaina Bradley, Grade 4
Dibble Elementary School, MI

Forest
Birds nesting in trees
Wind blowing through the pine trees
Butterflies flying
Justin Bratton, Grade 5
Crissman Elementary School, MI

The Sky
I don't see the sun,
But I can still see the light.
How's it possible?
Paulina Estrada, Grade 6
Mary Evelyn Castle Elementary School, IN

The Waterfall
Falling, dropping down
The waterfall drops down far
While animals drink
Sam Boyle, Grade 6
St Simon the Apostle School, IN

The Sun Set!
Over the tall trees
Where the sun begins to set
I see the colors!
Jarrett Kelly, Grade 6
St. Simon the Apostle School, IN

States*
States
States
States

Gigantic states
Tiny states
Long shrimpy eastern states
Amazing wide western states
Those are just a few.
Snowy states
Island states
Huge freezing Arctic states
Old midwestern movie states
Rainy states too.
Sandy states
Crowded states
Don't forget my state
Last of all, best of all I like southern states!
Logan Riley, Grade 4
Bailey School, MI
Patterned after "Beans, Beans, Beans" by Lucia & James L. Hymes

Babies*
Babies
Babies
Babies

Drooling babies
Angry babies
Screaming upset crying babies
Sleeping warm tired babies
Those are just a few.
Cuddly babies
Laughing babies
Smiling toothless cute babies
Walking tipping falling babies
Bald babies too!
Babbling babies
Speechless babies
Don't forget crawling babies
Last of all, best of all I like all babies.
Brittany Carr, Grade 4
Bailey School, MI
Patterned after "Beans, Beans, Beans" by Lucia & James L. Hymes

What I Found in My Desk*
A great white shark, a half eaten fish.
A Ichtyosdurus eating a fish, an owl with a mouse in its mouth.
A male lion eating a wildebeest.
A very very very long snake.
A black widow making a web, a bull shark.

And one more thing, I must confess, a note from Mrs. Freels saying CLEAN THIS DESK!
Zac Lowder, Grade 4
Hampton Elementary School, MI
Patterned after "What I Found in My Desk" by Bruce Lansky

Colorful Me

I am not just black.
Neither is anyone else in the world.
It doesn't matter what color you are on the outside but what color you are on the inside.
I mean like your personality, your courage.
Just because you look like you are nice on the outside doesn't mean you are nice on the inside.

You shouldn't be a person who is afraid of your own shadow.
You should let your colors show.
Like the Fourth of July, you should not be shy.
Just be who you are
You're an original!
You cannot be replaced.

Makayla Booker, Grade 4
Thea Bowman Leadership Academy, IN

Paris, France

The Eiffel Tower touches the starry night, showing every restaurant with every glowing light, they shine and shine on crystal waterways
It's dark but hundreds of stars in sight, the city turns on its beautiful glows of light
People babbling back and forth enjoying the music play, all night, here and there water splashes in the air
How many songs will she play?
How does her beauty make her feel?
How long will she be?
I feel relaxed and quite enjoyed, I'm loving, I'm curious and never cold
Beauty lies within its heart
Beauty lies within its heart
Beauty lies within its heart

Nadine Achkar, Grade 6
Star International Academy, MI

The Smoky Mountains

The lovely view as we walk through the woods
　The smell of nature through the whistling wind
　　The flow of the cold creek against the smooth rocks makes it hard to believe that we got angry
　　over little things, this takes your stress away

The soft snow against the mountain turning half of it white and the other half fall colored trees.

Is it the yellow trees that make the sky so blue or the blue sky that makes the trees so yellow?
　I don't know, all I know is that I love the Smoky Mountains.

Arianna Ray, Grade 5
University Elementary School, IN

Words

Words are powerful even though they are small and easy to make or say.
they can help people move on after a hard time or help them get through a hard time.
In a way words are like actions. One small act can change someone's life.
A few small words can hurt people badly.
Words and actions have a ripple effect even when we don't want them to.
So that's why we must be careful with words. How we use them, how we want them to be used.
And we must remember one detail that is too important to be overlooked,
Words are powerful.

Sara White, Grade 6
Christ the King School, IN

The Encounter
I was sitting there
waiting, when I saw him.

A large brown mass
moving slow.
He didn't know I was there.

He was in my view.
Then all that I did
was drew the string.

He then saw me
without a doubt,
with the crack of the string.

The arrow was off
and so was he.

Then he stopped,
turned to me and then was
off again.
Riley Doman, Grade 5
Gobles Elementary School, MI

Hockey
The air is so crisp,
When I take my first stride.
Everything falls out of my mind,
As I lose control of time.
My skates are tied tight,
My stick is so light.
The puck glides over the ice,
As I keep pushing forward.
The cheer of the crowd,
Will not ruin my focus.
The wind in my face,
For the puck I race.
My helmet wobbles,
As I skate full throttle.
I feel a rush,
Going through my body.
My pulse goes wild,
As my teammates get riled.
This is my game,
My life,
This is hockey.
Michael Tucker, Grade 6
West Middle School, MI

God's Blanket
Life is a blanket, woven by God.
Each little thread tenderly placed.
Each a treasure, as important as any other.
If one disappears, all would unravel.
Margaret Henige, Grade 6
Our Lady Queen of Martyrs School, MI

In a Pickle
I'm in a pickle,
I can't think of a rhyme.
I want to write a poem,
but there's simply not enough time.
I sit and think and ponder,
but my imagination seems to wander.
I look around from here to there,
Ideas appear to be everywhere.
How can I choose just one?
Being in a pickle is no fun!
Atara Kresch, Grade 4
Akiva Hebrew Day School, MI

Prisoner
I hang by a rusty chain,
Every day I am beaten without mercy,
Every day I am punched without pity,
Every day I am kicked without sympathy,
But still I hang here
Like a prisoner of the world…
Ripped…old…thrown out,
Into the cold hard world,
Forever,
Never to return…
Levi Fulford, Grade 6
Linton-Stockton Elementary School, IN

Chimpanzee
C urious apes
H ighly intelligent ape of Africa
I t grows up to five feet tall
M anlike looks
P erform in circuses
A nimal has manlike hands
N ever ending fun
Z oo animals
E nter circuses
E ats insects at times
Cole Bailey, Grade 6
Perry Middle School, MI

Love Is Like Chocolate
Love is like chocolate
When it's there you're happy
When it's gone you're sad
When it's dark you're amazed
When it's light you're relaxed
And every day you go open that cupboard
And put the first one in your mouth,
And close your eyes
And swoop into a new beautiful world.
Oliwia Pisko, Grade 6
Eagle Creek Academy, MI

Leaving…Good-bye
Saying good-bye…So long
Packing all my cherished treasures
Leaving…abandoning
Everything I know,
All the memories
Hopefully…they are not forgotten,
Mom and Dad saying, "You will be ok."
If it is going to be ok…
Why am I crying hopelessly?
Saying good-bye tearfully
To my gentle friends and frightened family,
Saying good-bye is the worst part
Good-bye…
Saying good-bye…So long.
Paige Corbett, Grade 6
Linton-Stockton Elementary School, IN

Because of You, Here I Am
Because you always sing to me,
I will always have a song to sing.

Since you always let me preach,
I will always preach the word of God.

Whenever I see your smiling face,
It will always make my heart shine.

Because you never give up on me,
I will never give up in life.

Mom, because you made me who I am,
I will always love you, no matter what.
Vivian Uta, Grade 6
Berrien Springs Middle School, MI

Springtime
I like Springtime best of all
That is when we play softball.
And run in the blazing sun
That is all very fun

When all the birds are singing
The children are swinging
Go riding around the track
Around the field and back

When it feels like there's not breeze
Mom makes ice cream to freeze
It makes us all nice and cool
And we go to bed full
Michelle Diane Swartzentruber, Grade 6
Green Acres School, IN

A Special Kind of Love

For a teacher,
There is a special kind of love.

I spend time with my teachers.
They give me a yearning for learning.

For a teacher,
There is a special kind of love.

At the end of every year there
Is a time when we must part.

We are itching to get home and yell,
"School's out! Woohoo!"

But deep down in our hearts of hearts,
We say, "No! Don't leave!
I love you in a special way.
Just for my teachers of past days."

So I give them a hug and say,
"Goodbye! Have a great summer!
Leaving you is really a bummer!
Maybe our paths will cross someday! Goodbye!
I love you in a special way."

For a teacher,
There is a special kind of love.

Bailey Miles, Grade 5
Pendleton Elementary/Intermediate School, IN

Tricks

Shouts
from down the hall
"He hit me!" and "She called me a name!"
the thumping down the stairs
as the twins ride the laundry basket
and then the sudden crash

It's a Trick
coming around the table
and leaving without stains everywhere
spaghetti and meatballs thrown into the air
as the baby squeals and laughs

Playtime comes
and instantly somebody is getting whacked in the head
or poked in the eye
…back to the screaming again
playing tug-a-war with each other
and the twins toss and tumble

I will never see the end of the messes
ever again…until I quit babysitting

Raymi King, Grade 6
Knox Community Middle School, IN

The Game

The swish of the net, the squeak of the shoes
She tips the ball, the crowd roars
A missed shot, a symphony of boos
The first shot arcs and soars

The players run up and down the court
The concession stand is running out
It's already half time, the game seems too short
I think a high school recruiter's here to scout

Twenty-five seconds left in the fourth quarter
We're down 23-22 and I have four fouls
The Prime Time supporters think the game's over
My coach looks like he could growl

I drive to the basket with power,
Get fouled, hit them both and the game is ours!

Gabby Schultz, Grade 6
St Mary Cathedral School, MI

I Will Always Remember That Day!

It was a very fine day,
Until the terrible news,
I never thought it would happen,
I'd never bothered to think we would move.
I'd never see her again,
Her beautiful sandy hair,
Her smell of cotton candy,
Never thought it was possible,
To separate our friendship,
She was like a sister,
A sister that never told a lie,
Who always forgave me.
Why do I have to say goodbye?
Now that I moved away,
There is nothing else to say,
She will always be my friend!
And I'll always remember that day!

Victoire Bon-Mardion, Grade 6
St Bartholomew School, IN

My Brother

My brother screams and hollers
My brother is a bother
He loves to be loud
When he is really proud
He marches around the room patting his drum
Boom
When he causes all this racket
It is impossible to get him quiet
He sounds like a cat
Getting hit with a big bat
He makes a huge riot
I wish he'd get quiet

Brooke Hurd, Grade 4
Joan Martin Elementary School, IN

Love Blue

The lake, washing in the wind
the sun, shining on its water
the wave, rushing in, hitting the nearby rocks.

The sky that never ends,
the summer rush calmed.

Your lips in the winter,
your eyes in the spring.

The quick burst of relaxation, hope.
Cooling in the summer, warmth in the winter.

The blueberries when ripe,
the icy, sugary drink at fairs.

The bridesmaid dress,
baby-shower gift baskets.

The taste of friendship,
the smell of sparkling heaven.

A jump in a pool with a friend's hand in yours,
a bike ride toward the moon.

Happiness lives in blue,
a new fresh day.

It's life, earth, 73 percent, oceans,

Love Blue.

Hannah Schweitzer, Grade 6
Clague Middle School, MI

My Favorite Color

Blue, the color of the crazy cookie monster
Biting into creamy chocolate cookies
Blue, my enormous stuffed dolphin
Sitting helplessly and lonely on my bed

Blue, the mysterious eyes of a stranger,
Eerily staring at me…
Blue, the dazzling sky above that lurks and watches
My every move

Blue, the sweet cotton candy
Melting in my mouth
Blue the elegant blue jay
Lightly sitting on a rough branch

Blue, the color of the American flag
Waving proudly

Blue, my favorite color

Casey Lifford, Grade 6
Linton-Stockton Elementary School, IN

What Is in Tears?

What is in tears?
Sorrow, sadness
Gloom, dejection
Drops of fright waiting to disappear
Do you feel regretful?
Or brokenhearted or hurt
In tears there is a sprinkle of despair
And crushed happiness
Have you ever felt joyful and delightful when you were crying?

Lauren Wood, Grade 5
Dodson Elementary School, MI

Snow

Snow is a white fluffy blanket
Covering the earth in many layers
Burying plants and trees
Instead of pillows.
The sun lifting the blanket every spring
And tucking plants in every winter.
Snow is demons making the Earth rich in joyful fun.
Snow is the creation chamber of all wintertime fun.

Rubin Williams, Grade 5
Dodson Elementary School, MI

Cat

There is a cat,
pouncing, jumping, sneaking.
That is a cat,
as fast as lightning.
That is a cat,
razor sharp claws.
There is a cat,
pouncing, jumping, sneaking.

Ian Beaudoin, Grade 6
Lake Linden-Hubbell Elementary School, MI

Fall

In the fall, cornstalks grow.
Cider mills open.
People start to make leaf piles, and jump in them.
Fall makes the temperatures drop.
Farmers put out scarecrows, to scare away the crows.
Families buy donuts, apples, and pumpkin pie.
Be sure to go on hay rides, and run through a hay maze.
Fall comes so quickly, so get ready for the very cold days.

Paul Pavliscak, Grade 5
Eagle Creek Academy, MI

Football

Hike the ball, drop back quarterback
You can run, throw, or get sacked
You can tackle, you can block, you can get a strip
Catch the ball, kick the ball, get a hit
It's never a bore when you score

Kevin Flood, Grade 6
St. Simon the Apostle School, IN

A Baby Baboon
I wish I were
a baby baboon
in a zoo with other baboons
dancing for people passing by
gracefully

Luke Drye, Grade 5
Pendleton Elementary/Intermediate School, IN

Brothers
Brothers
Mean and grumpy
Beating, punching, kicking
Hurt, pain, mad, frustrated
Baby brothers

Gabriel Eckstein, Grade 5
Sunman Dearborn Intermediate School, IN

Fatty Catty
There was a cat that was fat
He rested on a welcome mat
The cat could not get out of bed
He could not fit in the shed
The welcome mat is where he sat

Spencer Ravage, Grade 5
Pendleton Elementary/Intermediate School, IN

School
These be
Three of the best things
Eating a tasty lunch
Having a playful recess
and riding home on a bus.

Aaron Candiano, Grade 5
Pendleton Elementary/Intermediate School, IN

White Shark
I wish I were
a malicious Great White Shark
waiting and hiding in the murky shallows
thrashing and annihilating my prey with vengeance
idly

Matthew Vetor, Grade 6
Pendleton Elementary/Intermediate School, IN

Ode to My Rascal
Ode to my Rascal you are so small.
Your name is Rascal. You are black and white.
You're not old to me and when we play
Sometimes you bite but you're still nice.
Rascal your eyes are blue. Rascal I still love you.

Alyssa Deneen, Grade 4
Morgan Elementary School, IN

Raspberries
Raspberries are
red luscious tiny little fruits
You can find them nice and tasty during summer
growing in the fields
to give you a delicious taste in your mouth

Gabriella Burke, Grade 5
Crissman Elementary School, MI

Purple
Purple is my cozy sweat shirt on a cold night.
Purple is the sweet tangy taste of a grape Jolly Rancher.
Purple is my veins running through my body.
Purple is our beta fish snipe his colors shine in the light.
Purple is the marker that Mrs. Schmitt uses to instruct us.

Noah Paraventi, Grade 5
Crissman Elementary School, MI

Three Wonderful Things
These be
Three wonderful things
butterflies in the spring
birds singing in the trees
a cool summer breeze

Haylie Stephenson, Grade 5
Pendleton Elementary/Intermediate School, IN

Sam
There once was a student named Sam
Who gleefully ate lots of ham.
He ate it too quick
And then he got sick.
And now no more ham for Sam.

Sam Hubert, Grade 5
Sunman Dearborn Intermediate School, IN

Do You See It?
Many things seem like optical illusions
twistings, turning, funny confusions
things you think you see but really don't
things you want to see but really won't
falling, flying, mystical delusions.

Christina Magers, Grade 5
Pendleton Elementary/Intermediate School, IN

The Puppy
The puppy
I walk on the sidewalk.
People think I'm so cute.
The leash falls from her hands.
And she yells, "Oh, shoot!"

Kaitlyn Zillick, Grade 5
Sunman Dearborn Intermediate School, IN

Friendship
As friendship grows through the years,
It's like a garden that grows,
Like a seed that becomes a tree.
Will it die young
Or last forever?

Friendship is the most important thing of all.

Makenzie Nash, Grade 6
Sherman Middle School, MI

My Week
A sprinkle of sewing
A dash of dance
A teaspoon of typing
A hint of homework
A spoonful of school
Mix thoroughly, and bake in oven for 10 minutes at 360 degrees
And you'll get my week

Lauren Colone, Grade 6
West Middle School, MI

Insulin
I nsulin
N eed it to survive
S ugar level reducer
U navailable in a type 1 diabetic pancreas
L ife saver for diabetics
I ncredible wonder for the human body
N ot a cure for diabetes

Jacob Dessellier, Grade 6
Lake Linden-Hubbell Elementary School, MI

Deserts
Deserts are so hot below, so humid and so tropical,
with no water to even flow. Thunderstorms are rare,
though sandstorms are fair. The sand under my hot
feet blazes in the sun's strong heat. I look in all places in search
of an oasis, to get a nutritious, delicious snack of some sort.
The outrageous, orange sunset sets to tell me to stop my quest.
The temperatures drop so I stop to rest and hope for the best

Nicole Cerar, Grade 6
St Simon the Apostle School, IN

Little, Furry Face
I like little monkeys
Picking bugs off their tiny backs
They're brown, brown as tree bark
Mini monkeys muddle together, get warm
Short monkeys sipping water from a leaf
Their mini eyes staring at bright yellow bananas
Small hands hanging from tree branches

Bianca Rodriguez, Grade 5
Wayne Gray Elementary School, MI

Having a Friend
Elegant, soft, black dog,
How I loved it when you tickled my fingers
With your wet, cold, saliva tongue.

You never left my side,
Through all the weather or my moods
I am grateful to have a friend,
As lovable and huggable as you.

I always would laugh when you made your
Teeth chatter, but I never knew it was making
Your life shatter.
Dad took you to a vet, but he didn't come
Back with you.

I came home to find you not there,
Dad said you were someplace happier, in
The heavens of midair. He said you had a tumor
In your lungs, what a dog you were
To stay so strong.

Elegant, soft, black dog,
I will see to it, that I will see you again.
Until then, your body lays silently, in South Bend.

Faith A. Rowe, Grade 6
Knox Community Middle School, IN

Dad
I remember
when you were beside me,
outside working
You taught me how to drive
a lawnmower with a trailer on it.

My daring dad you were
Even knowing you were sick
you still worked hard.
Put a towel under
the lawnmower then
you asked, me
where the towel was.
I forgot, so did you.
Then we moved the lawnmower
and we found the towel;
we laughed.

I was in the truck with you
when you were going to Chicago Hospital
November 6, 2005, you died on your birthday
I miss you, I love you
Dad

Olivia Doty, Grade 6
Knox Community Middle School, IN

High Merit Poems – Grades 4, 5, and 6

The Adored Color
Purple…
The sour taste of
Smooth grapes in my mouth
Purple…
It calls to me with
A thundering voice
Purple…
The colorful rainbow
After a terrible storm
Purple…
The morning sunrise
Appears majestic
Purple…
It comforts me with
Its silky touch
Purple…
The color of
Wildflowers in a vast field
Purple…
Hanna Camden, Grade 6
Linton-Stockton Elementary School, IN

Around the House
Round the house we've lots to do,
And I bake some cookies too,
I also like to bake a cake,
There is always something to make.

I often have to sweep the floor,
Wipe fingerprints off the door,
I always have to wash the clothes,
And my dear brothers dig big holes.

In the garden we pull the weeds.
And we plant some funny seeds.
I always have to mow the yard.
Usually I get so very tired.

When it's time to can things to eat,
I always like to can meat,
I wash the windows sparkling clean.
I always have to make them gleam.
Jennifer Renae Knepp, Grade 4
South Bogard School, IN

Dogs
Dogs are loving,
Dogs are kind,

Dogs have a mind.

Dogs are smart,
Dogs are stinky,
Dogs rock.
Caitlin Sheahan, Grade 4
Dodson Elementary School, MI

Walking By
As we look
Out the window,
We see a person
Walking by.
We know
That it's not
Normal
For it
Is midnight.
We know
It's not
An animal
For those
are way too small.
I guess
this will be
a mystery
that we
have not yet
solved.
Emily Ball, Grade 4
James R Watson Elementary School, IN

My Dog
He stares up at me
His little black eyes
Makes me sorry
To leave him alone
In his cramped cage
While we go to school
As I put him in
And I shut the door
I become caught
In his sad stare
He makes me give him
A piece of ham
He does it with his eyes
A voice from the hall
Shouts to me
I'm going to be late
I grab my things
I slip out the door
Goodbye Leo
I'll see you when I come home
Olivia Allam, Grade 5
Dodson Elementary School, MI

My Cat
My cat is as white as snow,
And the way she eats, she can really grow.
She is so very nice
Can you believe she's afraid of mice?
She likes to run around,
And play with balls on the ground.
Deanna Leighton, Grade 4
St Raphael School, MI

The Hit
"Coach, coach!
I've only got one hit this season,
Let John do it.
He's got on base every time this season."

"No," coach said.
"I want you to do it."

"Ok" I said.
Up to the plate.
First pitch…
Second pitch…
Strike two,
A bully said, "We lost. He stinks!"

That really made me mad.
3rd pitch…CRACK
The ball was like a jet passing the fence.
A home run we won the game 7-6
Chad Wildman, Grade 6
Assumption School, MI

A Mistreated Book
I'm opened
Closed
Read
Ripped
Torn
Tossed into a box
I wait
I'm opened
Read again
Left outside
Water logged
I tumble
Into a river
And gently carried
To the bottom
Of a pond
My journey
Ends
Here
Lucas Veldboom, Grade 6
Ebenezer Christian School, MI

Knicky
The moment I saw his long body
His short legs and low body
Seeing him run with his floppy ears
Seeing him beg with his cute face
Waiting for a drop of food
Seeing his tail wag crazy when
He meets someone he loves
I knew that he was mine.
Zachary Murry, Grade 5
Dodson Elementary School, MI

My Room

My room is red.
My room is yellow.
It is my cave of chaos
in which I bloom.
U.S.C. adorns the walls,
with Mark Sanchez at the head of them all.
My room, my arsenal of airsoft and paintball.
Inside I work to rebuild them all.
Tape, screwdrivers, parts of gun,
make for many, many hours of fun.
Loud sounds of Ozzy Osbourne,
and Guns N' Roses fill the house,
as I play my electric guitar
and perfect my craft.
My room is awesome,
full of surprises.
I never know
what to expect.
I enter my special haven
my own...
sanctuary.

Triston Perry, Grade 6
St Bartholomew School, IN

Sleep My Little One

Gently sleep, my sweet child
You will be strong like your father
You must avenge him with all your might
You must fight in war as he did
The moment he died
My heart fell apart
It broke like a piece of chocolate
I never knew he was that important
In my life
But, now I know you don't know what you have
Until the moment it disappears
Because when the army told me he passed away
I went out of whack, so now you see
You are my last hope little one
It is your duty to do as he did
You must keep the rest of this family together
Your father was a hero in my heart
So you must do your best.... please!
This attempt is to try and comfort you
Be brave and free!
Be what he would be!

Basel Hassan, Grade 6
Star International Academy, MI

Velociraptors

Velociraptors could jump high off the ground.
A lot of skeletons have been found.
It was as swift as a race car.
And it could run very far.

Anthony Crisologo, Grade 4
St Raphael School, MI

Ode to My Dog

Kado, oh Kado, I miss you.
You are the best dog I've ever had.
Kado, oh Kado, you loved to play tug-of-war.
Of course, you always won.
Kado, oh Kado, you are always my baby puppy.
I love you Kado.

Kylee M. Shepard, Grade 5
Morgan Elementary School, IN

Ode to Sunshine

Oh sunshine, oh sunshine, you are my best friend.
You cheer me up when I lose a friend.
Oh sunshine, oh sunshine, you stick up for me.
When someone says something to me.
Oh sunshine, oh sunshine, you're older than me.
But I don't care, you're like a sister to me.

McKenzie Dobson, Grade 5
Morgan Elementary School, IN

I Am Small

I am small
Everyone I know is small
I live in an attic or anywhere else in the world
I am so small because I am a fly and that is all
True until..."beep beep beep"
My alarm goes off

Jadyn Huffman, Grade 5
Heritage Intermediate School, IN

Sorrow

Sorrow knows when to darken your mood
When to vanquish joy from your very soul
When to darken your happiness
Sorrow is like a disease vanishing your happy cells
Sorrow knows when to sweep away joy like dirt
Devours every last bit of light in your body

Renell Hansen, Grade 5
Dodson Elementary School, MI

The Friends of the USA

Air Force...the guardians of the air
Air Force...the bold pilots with skill
Air Force...the airplanes that aid the Rangers
Air Force...demanding parents leave their families
Air Force...the branch that keeps us safe
Air Force...the guardians of the air

Devon Hill, Grade 6
Linton-Stockton Middle School, IN

Ode to My Dog Bandet

Oh Bandet, Oh Bandet, why did you run away.
Bandet, Bandet, I miss you soo.
Bandet, Bandet, I found you one time.
Bandet, Bandet, I wonder where you are.

Heather Martin, Grade 4
Morgan Elementary School, IN

The Christmas Flames

Click, light, roar it rises up.
"Thank you for bringing me to life!"
Then it runs away
Leaving nothing but ash behind it.
As you put more wood
On the trail it leaves,
It comes back.
You blow on it to make it bigger
It starts dancing
Back and forth, up and down.
And then it stopped just stopped.
So, there was nothing to burn and all was ash,
It stopped dancing and it was gone.
That wonderful magical…

Fire.

Samantha Kersman, Grade 5
North Muskegon Elementary School, MI

Encounter

We both looked
Deep in to each others eyes
His dark blood red, mine sky blue,

I was frightened
As I looked at his snow white fangs,

I listened to my heart pump faster and faster
Questions racing through my mind,

The vampire cocked his head
And gave me an evil looking smirk,

He loosened his stance
And ran into the deep black night
I have not seen him since.

Lauren Gettys, Grade 6
Gobles Elementary School, MI

Mexico

Mexico is my home.
It is where my parents were born.
I was also born there.
Mexico is awesome.

All my cousins live in Mexico.
When we came to Indiana, I had to leave them.
But I still hear from them every once in a while.
Mexico is my home.

Mexico is a hot place.
Mexico is my beginning.
Mexico is full of memories.
Mexico is an album of memories one after the other.

Pedro Sanchez, Grade 6
St Bartholomew School, IN

The Nightmare

Haiti, the poor little ones growing up
Without their parents' tender love
Haiti, parents sadly realizing that their kids are gone forever
Haiti, people replaying the nightmare
Over and over

Haiti, people having little amounts of
Fresh food and clear water
Haiti, people wondering why did they deserve it
Doctors, rescue workers, and volunteers
Going to Haiti to offer help

Haiti, the little ones
Living with one leg or a broke arm
Haiti, the one thing that is on my mind
No matter what

Madison Robbins, Grade 6
Linton-Stockton Elementary School, IN

I Am a Football

I am the sharp, pointy, brown, pigskin football
You know me for throwing me at afternoon recess
My mother is the texture of football skin
My father is the grip of my football skin
I was born in a loud and giant football factory
I live in a cardboard box
My best friend is the fast throwing baseball
Because we like to be in the air
We like to be catched by joyful kids
My enemy is the hard, dirty, green ground
Because if kids don't catch me, I fall to the ground and get hurt
I fear the black and white soccer ball
Because people think the soccer ball is better than me
I love to get out of my box and be in my new home
Because I like to explore all the other balls kids have
I wish that every kid could buy one of me

Haris Niazi, Grade 4
Dodson Elementary School, MI

In the Future

In the future
A giant computer room
Scientists…
Wearing lab coats…steel-rimmed spectacles
Scampering across the room
Typing strange words
Lights…blinking everywhere
Computers overheating
Bright…immense
The air-conditioning on full blast
Feels like the top of a mountain
Monitors pack one wall…
The computers watch you
Be careful…be careful

Luke Wilson, Grade 6
Linton-Stockton Elementary School, IN

Goodbye

All of my dreams have been destroyed
Wasting my life on what I can't have
I don't know what I need to do
But I do realize what I want
Nothing ever seemed more important than you
When you left I was depressed
Regaining happiness in what I lack
Crying so much it kills me inside
I've never felt like this before
So many emotions fill my head
Life feels like it's already over
The times with you I'll never forget
This is just too hard to handle
I can't stand when you're not around
You're off somewhere that I don't know
I don't think I can hang on any longer
You were ripped away from me
Faster than I can blink my eye
It hurts to know that you're gone now
It's really too late to say goodbye

Rikki Weaver, Grade 6
Linton-Stockton Elementary School, IN

Michigan

Michigan is the place to be
You can bring your family
You should come for many reasons
Like the four seasons
In the winter the temperature can get really low
You can go in the snow or
You can visit the auto show
In the spring you can see the leaves bud or
When it rains splash around in the mud
The grass starts to turn green
What an awesome scene
In the summer you can take a ride in a boat
You barely have to wear a coat
In the fall the trees start to look bare
Right before the Halloween scare
So don't miss out on my state
It is the one with the mitten shape
Surrounded by Great Lakes
Please come visit my state
It is really great

Griffin Benson, Grade 6
Seneca Middle School, MI

Nothing Left

No more tears, rain, only desert
None in us, all to be blind
Clouded eyes, can't see
Morning is coming, no hope for us
Will morning come fast or slow, but there's none
Nothing to be done, nothing to come…

Bryson Stevens, Grade 6
Woodrow Wilson Middle School, IN

Blue

Blue is cool, awesome, and great
Blue is the taste of blueberries, water, oceans,
    and smells like cotton candy
Blue makes me feel cold
Blue is the sound of the wind and a small breeze
Blue is calm, fresh, and cold
Skies are blue
My jeans are also blue
Blue is minty

Ben Hogan, Grade 5
North Muskegon Elementary School, MI

Color

Pink is the color of tulips that just have bloomed.
Black is the color of the scary word doom.
Orange is the color of the sun when it sets.
Green is the color of the money I just bet.
Blue is the color of the ocean that animals share.
Bright green is the color of the bright, new picked pear.
Yellow is the frosting on my birthday cake.
Brown is the color of the slithering snake.
What are colors to you?

Meghan Mans, Grade 6
West Middle School, MI

Sparkling Snow

Fluffy, soft, white snow.
Glamorously sparkling silver and white snow.
Attractive in northern locations.
Shivering, wild winds carry snow swiftly off the ground.
A wonderful match for snow pants and boots.
Terrific for building snowmen, forts and snow sculptures.
A mismatch if you like warmer weather conditions.
Enemy for snow shovelers.
Don't forget it is not a long lasting toy.

Nicholas Hughes, Grade 4
Dodson Elementary School, MI

Fall

All of the different color leaves
Umbrella is what we are under on Halloween
Time to go Trick or Treating
Use pumpkins to carve faces
Many ciders to try
New fresh made turkey on Thanksgiving

Michael Van Pelt, Grade 6
Eagle Creek Academy, MI

Loneliness

Loneliness is the color purple,
It sounds like a baby crying in the dark, cold night,
It tastes like the begrimed dirt on Earth,
And feels like a baby fox without a mother,
It smells like the mud on your shoes.

Magnolia Harshman, Grade 5
East Elementary School, IN

Books

They can be
sad or funny

Books
can tell
your feelings

Books
they can
be big
or small

Books
can have
10 pages
or 20,000

Books
can tell
the future

Books
are cool
so read
a book!!!

Leah Lenius, Grade 5
North Muskegon Elementary School, MI

My Dream Place

Wind
Hushed
Leaves
Colored
Water
Deathlike

Swish, splash, swoosh
The waves go up the side of the
Boat

I wait on a boat.
In the middle
Of nowhere.
With all my worries…gone
Waiting for rescue

Beautiful view
Sun setting
Pink, red, orange
The orange is walking across
The ocean blue
Everything is so
Serene

Allison Clark, Grade 6
Sashabaw Middle School, MI

I Am a Monster Truck

I am a monster truck
You know me for my tallness
My mother is a limo
My father is a semi
I was born in a Ford's car lot
I live in a big garage
My best friend is a Ford
Ranger, XLT
Because we are trucks
We like to have races
My enemy is an axe
Because it can hit me and break me
I fear getting put in a junk yard
Because I can get crushed to bits
I love saving kids from school
because they are my friends
I dream that I could live at
Lexie's house.

April Slone, Grade 4
Mentone Elementary School, IN

The Color of Nature

Green…
The wet leaf holding a single raindrop
Running down the waxy structure
Green…
The sweet smell
Running through your body
Giving you nonstop chills
Green…
The bittersweet taste
Tickling your tongue
Green…
The feel of the soothing aloe
Stinging your sunburn
Green…
The light humming whistle
Forcing your eardrums to rattle
Green…
The color of nature.

Camryn Huffman, Grade 6
Linton-Stockton Elementary School, IN

Chameleon

Strange lizard
Slowly creeping
Along a twig

Chameleon

Changing color
In the blink of an eye
Snatching up prey with its tongue
He is now a lonely leaf

Mitchell Moulton, Grade 5
North Muskegon Elementary School, MI

Springtime

Spring is the best time of the year
No more winter winds will blow
The earth gets warm beneath the sun
And some things peep through the snow.

You can help to hoe the garden
Those plants are all very straight
You can make it so very fun
But to hoe some people do hate.

When the vegetables all get ripe
Oh, what a feast it will be
Watermelons would be super
But we have none as you see.

Baby animals are so cute
Even if they cannot talk
They are still so fun to watch
It looks so cute when they walk.

Susan Knepp, Grade 5
Green Acres School, IN

What's the Color?

This color is a forest in the summer,
Or the beautiful color of a Hummer.
The seasoning in a warm yellow soup,
A plant house not a chicken coop.

"Don't pick that yet it's not ripe!"
It's the color of money not a wipe.
A plant or a fruit with good taste,
The color of my room or mint paste.

This color can be a drink.
It can also be mold in a sink!
A hopper that's in the grass,
My pocket dictionary that's got mass.

This color is made by two,
These colors being yellow and blue.
So, I ask you now, what is this color?
Why, this color is green!

Katie Munoz, Grade 5
Staunton Elementary School, IN

My Rose Bush

Over the patio,
through the yard,
on the grass,
beneath the open sky,
to the old gate,
under a leafy branch,
at the rosebush
I sit thinking.

Jaelyn Himes, Grade 5
Northern Heights Elementary School, IN

Michael Jordan
Michael Jordan
White, red
Ducking, swishing, shooting
Soared through the air
MJ
Alex David, Grade 5
Hendry Park Elementary School, IN

Summer
Summer is the best time of the year,
You can play all you want with no fear,
No more school,
That is so cool,
For it is summer so stand up and cheer!
Taylor Osborn, Grade 6
St Simon the Apostle School, IN

Cookie
Cookie
warm, yummy
dunking, eating, enjoying
I love hot cookies
Chocolate chip
Kylie Bowen, Grade 5
Hendry Park Elementary School, IN

Basketball
Basketball
Black, orange
Dribble, shoot, swoosh
Basketball is *very* fun!
Sport
Tyler Steffel, Grade 5
Hendry Park Elementary School, IN

Colors
Colors
Vivid, brilliant
Glowing, sparkling, fading
Orange fiery crimson sunsets
Rainbows
Dakota Estel, Grade 4
Bailey School, MI

Shoes
Shoes
flip flop, boots
walking, running, jumping
there are so many
Shoes
Lydia Martin, Grade 5
Hendry Park Elementary School, IN

What Is Purple???
Purple is my sister's contacts as she cleans them monthly
My Lego's are purple as I build a purple mansion
Grapes that aren't shriveled up yet are purple.

As I walk I hear purple on carpet I can hear purple
I can hear purple when I listen for birds chirping outside my bedroom window
When I wash the soap off my hands.

When I see old people watching TV I can smell purple
I smell purple when my mom's lilacs bud on the first day of spring.

As I rub against my smooth hair I feel purple
I feel purple when I take charge at home
When I lay down in bed with my silky blanket I feel purple.

When I visit Mackinac Island, it makes me feel purple
As I play basketball and the ball goes through the hoop I feel purple
When confetti falls on me I feel purple.

Purple is the Mall of America as my hands are loaded with bags
Purple is a dolphin fin as I hold it at Discovery Cove.

A castle with a king and queen roaming around is a purple place
When the wind goes through my hair on a roller-coaster I'm a purple place
I'm in a purple place as I enter a little girl's bedroom.

When I put purple pop in my mouth I can taste purple
As my mom fills up the car with gasoline I taste purple. Purple is Mellow.
Christa Keys, Grade 6
Lewiston Elementary Middle School, MI

Never Born
Have you ever just wondered what life would be like if you were never born
Your family could have died — a baby wouldn't cry
A dog will never groan — even a friend will never have a telephone
The world would end — chickens take over — you'll never find a 4 leaf clover
You would never call your old dog Rover — and the moon will never turn over
Trees wouldn't grow — they would never ever, ever invent a gardening hoe
The oceans would dry out — dogs wouldn't have snouts
Pizza wouldn't have cheese — no one would say please
Everyone is quiet — while the cats make a riot
And the cats are now queens and everything
There would be no pork — no pig at all spiders — all they do is crawl
Robbers roam freely — while innocents are locked up
You would never know the time — cause they haven't invented clocks
You would never have a friend — all sidewalks are dead ends
Bees will bite — and bunnies don't have mites…people do
No one would have shoes — there is no theater show
There's only stop and never go — question marks are on people's heads
They wouldn't have rubber bands or beds — they world would die out
Don't you see? Washington never made history
Have you ever just wondered what life would be if you were never born
Your life would be torn
Kelsey Chizum, Grade 5
Heritage Intermediate School, IN

High Merit Poems – Grades 4, 5, and 6

Snow
Twisting, turning,
Falling, floating,
What a sight.
Dancing, descending,
Spiraling, swirling,
What a sight.
Glistening as the flakes fall to the ground,
They shimmer and shine as the day passes by.
What a sight.
Blanketing the Earth,
In a white, sparkling sheet.
What a sight.
Snow, delicate snow,
Awaiting spring.

Natalie Rosenquist, Grade 6
West Middle School, MI

Summertime
Summertime is time for fun,
Summertime is time to run.
You are supposed to have fun in the sun,
You are supposed to jump, skip, play, and run.
Take a vacation,
Have a celebration!
Go home and go to bed,
Read a book you've never read!
Have a water fight,
It will be fun, I know I'm right!
Summertime can't be boring,
So, why don't you go exploring?
Hurry up and jump in a pool,
Because before you know it you're back in school.

Summer Skelton, Grade 4
Chrisney Elementary School, IN

Mutt and Jeff
When the puppies were young,
their eyes were shut; they did not sniff around.
They had no tiny teeth and only stump tails
coming out of shiny fur
They had tiny bodies, but they had a big heads.

When they were older
Their eyes were open peering around;
they sniffed wherever they could.
Their tough teeth like to chew on things, and
they still have stump tails. Their bodies got just the right size
to hold their heads up.

These puppies were Boston Terriers

Alex Fisher, Grade 6
Knox Community Middle School, IN

Missing You
Blue
I think of you
All alone in the war
Without you, blue is a bore, a
Hue

Sierra Stellhorn, Grade 6
Pendleton Elementary/Intermediate School, IN

Summer
The hot sun is beating down on me
I can hear the children play in the pool until they get cold
I look at the warm views outside of my window
Playing outside with friends with water gun fights
Hoping summer will last forever

Justin Byers, Grade 5
Dodson Elementary School, MI

Dog
Dog
Cute, sweet
Eating, playing, fetching
Laughing, fun time, excited
Fun

Emma Schneider, Grade 5
Sunman Dearborn Intermediate School, IN

Green
Green is like the sound of whistling grass in the summer.
Green is like the smell of freshly cut grass.
Green is like the taste of sour apple Jolly Ranchers.
Green is like the feel of a warm, cozy, fuzzy blanket
    when you sit in front of a warm fire in the winter.

Waylon Dicus, Grade 5
Morgan Elementary School, IN

The Sleepy Werewolf
There once was a werewolf named Fred
who didn't want to get out of bed
to howl at the moon
he wanted to sleep way past noon
and everyone thought he was dead.

Aubree Lanman, Grade 6
Pendleton Elementary/Intermediate School, IN

Blue
Blue is like the sound of waves crashing against the seashore.
Blue is like the smell of fresh, sweet blueberry pie.
Blue is like the taste of a sour mountain berry sucker.
Blue is like the feel of a warm, soft, fuzzy electric blanket
    cuddling you when you're cold.

Brooklynn Dooley, Grade 5
Morgan Elementary School, IN

Maggie

My dog Maggie is cute and small
Even though she thinks she is a great Dane large and tall

She will always be there for me
Or the whole family

She has the cutest face
And an unusual pace

When she runs she waddles
When she walks she dwadles

When she chases the cat
It will run and hide under a hat

She feels no danger
Even when there is a stranger

John Kutschman, Grade 6
St John Lutheran School, MI

Candy

Candy candy
Sweet and chewy
Sometimes hard
Or maybe gooey
My parents say it's bad for me
But I just have to disagree
Something that is so good and yummy
Has to be really good for me
My parents think I'm crazy
They say I'm getting lazy
But I think they're the crazies
They say my habit is getting worse
They say I'll be as fat as the universe
Eating candy is staring to hurt
I don't think I've ever felt worse
I'm sorry I don't think I can rhyme another verse
I think I've eaten all the candy in the universe

Ryan Jennings, Grade 5
Heritage Intermediate School, IN

Soccer

Soccer is my favorite game to play
In the game I like to score
No matter what time of day
Which leaves the fans wanting more

I kick the ball as hard as I can
It screams through the air as it knocks people down
Into the stands it hits the fans
The queen of soccer I shall be crowned

I'm the only lefty on the team
But it still feels the same
It's more exciting than it seems
Kicking the ball every game

Even though I'm put to the test
I always seem to do my best

Anna Zaremba, Grade 6
St Mary Cathedral School, MI

Night Time Visitors

I look out of my window on a cold, dark night,
Oh, I can't believe what a wondrous sight.
Your spaceship has a speechless sound,
Your capsule shape looks so round.

I wonder do you come from Mars,
Or some other distant stars.
I have fallen under your magical spell,
Never being able to tell.

Your distant lights starts to move,
There is so much to prove.
You cause lots of suspicion,
But I have no hesitation.

Don't let my dreams burn,
Please, Please, Please return.

Jamie Crosby, Grade 6
West Middle School, MI

Music

Music is always there
Rain or shine it's by my side
Nothing can compare
It's always on my mind
Rain or shine it's by my side
I'm always happy
It's always on my mind
Sometimes it makes me feel like I need a nappy
I'm always happy
Nothing can compare
Sometimes it makes me feel like I need a nappy
Music is always there

Abigail Tucker, Grade 5
Dodson Elementary School, MI

Friends

Friends can come in every shape or size,
Friends can be very smart and wise.
It's always nice to know that a friend is there,
To support you and show they care.

You can be there for your friends too,
If they want to talk to you.
Help your friend when she feels sad,
Always make up when you are mad.

Good friends can last your whole life through,
If you're good to them, they'll be good to you!

Aviva Levi, Grade 4
Akiva Hebrew Day School, MI

Haley

Haley, a little, funny, baby girl.
Only one year old. With
red, swiftly moving, luscious
hair. My little baby cousin.
My little sweetheart. Pebbles!

Tyler Hollis, Grade 5
Northern Heights Elementary School, IN

Book

A book is a planet
many adventures await in both
you always want to see a new one
fun waits in both
both can be forgotten

Nicholas Borninski, Grade 4
Dodson Elementary School, MI

My Dragonfly

My little dragonfly,
He can fly so high,
And when you say boom,
He'll go zoom,
Then you will have to say bye.

Kyra Lovett, Grade 5
Gobles Elementary School, MI

Ricky

R icky my grandpa.
I wish he was still here.
C ry cry with all my tears.
K yle loves him with all my heart.
Y ou can love him too.

Kyle Hoppenrath, Grade 4
Liberty Elementary School, IN

My Precious Prince

Prince is
Most loving cat
I have ever owned.
I love him with all my heart.
Always!

Valerie Deakins, Grade 5
Staunton Elementary School, IN

Panda

Plump, fat
Eat, sleep, drink
Cute, cuddly, friendly, soft
Bear

Julia Van Luven, Grade 4
Crestwood Elementary School, MI

Last Words

The sound of Poppie's voice in the morning
When I stay overnight, him breathing
I leave the next day, hugs and kisses goodbye
"I love you" are the last words he said to me, ever

November 9, 2009, is the date I will never forget
November 11, 2009 was the day of his funeral
I was even sadder because I wasn't at his funeral
I was in the hospital waiting to get dismissed

I got out of the hospital November 11th, scared
I still remember all the days we fished together
Poppie laughing, me laughing, and my grandpa laughing
The rest of my family and I cleaned out his room

We saved all of his favorite things
Special things…
Pictures of him
We kept them in a trunk, safe from all harm

Before he died, he told my dad that he loved me
I was the only great-grandchild who will remember fishing with him
I will never forget the last thing he said to me…
I love you

Emily Wright, Grade 6
Linton-Stockton Elementary School, IN

Summertime

Summertime is the warmth outside
The bees buzzing around the daisies
The cool water in the pool
The green grass all around
Children happily laughing and screaming as they are chased around with water balloons
The night bug humming
The birds chirping
The smell of barbecuing chicken
Everyone having a good time on their summer vacation

Katerina Klomp, Grade 6
St John Lutheran School, MI

Where I Am From

I am from busy, crowded streets.
I am from the most known city in the world.
I am from pushing and shoving to get where you want.
I am from a beautiful city and kids playing together.
I am from everyone telling me I could be my sister's twin if she was my age,
    and people asking me which one I am in the pictures.
I am from delicious, fancy and good tasting food.
I am from no pets allowed in restaurants and hotels.
I am from trains everywhere and kids likely to get lost if they don't follow their parents.
I am from big fountains you can swim in!
I am from a sweet-smelling bakery.
I am from where a lot of girls like to jump rope outside apartment buildings.
I am from a wonderful place called France!

Sarah Bel Hassan, Grade 4
Hampton Elementary School, MI

Where I Am From

I am from a big, peaceful, sky-blue house in Pakistan that would be protected by a chocolatey-brown dog.
I am from a family with many pets; a black cat named Night,
10 goldfish and 25 birds that were very colorful, black, brown, blue, gold and red.
I am from a culture that is very colorful and calming to our eyes
because we wear clothes that are all different kinds of colors, fancy, filled with silver and gold sparkles.
I am from a culture and a family that is kind, hardworking and thoughtful.
I am from a country that is filled with freedom and kindness, America.
I am from a family that works together and helps each other and cares about me and will always love me.

Haadiya Najam, Grade 4
Hampton Elementary School, MI

Love Bites or Can Be the Most Wonderful Thing

Love is lust and just takes a loyal heart to fall into such luscious romance, but love bites when you fall for the wrong lad.
Then after he has had his fun and is finished with you, you feel lackadaisical and all that lad can give is a laconic reply to your sadness "I'm sorry but there's someone else."
Now you feel like have a lacuna in your heart.
The next day you are in language arts your best friend notices your lack of interest and spirit so he asks you what's wrong you tell him how your man dumped you after his basketball game.
Then he asks you out to the valentines dance you accept.
That night after the dance you realize he is your one your, only true love.

McKenna Hammond, Grade 6
Martin Middle/High School, MI

U.S.A.

America looks like white, tiny snowflake laying on the ground.
I see green grass full of flowers and different colors of leaves on the ground flying through my shoes.
It feels like a calm wind going through my body, the yellow, hot sun heating my body
and white, little cold balls of snow landing on my shoes.
America tastes like sweet, greasy hamburgers, well-done, roasted marshmallows and sweet, blue cotton candy.
America smells like the flowers blooming, trees blossoming with new leaves and the sweet cherries growing.
America sounds like a thousand birds singing in the sun.
America is my home.

Daniel Cota Avila, Grade 4
Hampton Elementary School, MI

Ode to Glasses

Glasses, oh glasses, you are something I wear on my face.
Glasses, oh glasses, you are something I have to clean once a day.
Glasses, oh glasses, you are something we have to buy.
Glasses, oh glasses, I have to make sure you don't break.
Glasses, oh glasses, you drive me crazy sometimes when you are on my face.
Glasses, oh glasses, you might drive me crazy but you help me to see so ou are my favorite glasses.
Glasses, oh glasses, you are pretty, you are a pretty purplish-blue color, you are the best glasses I have ever had.

Caitlin Hendrich, Grade 5
Morgan Elementary School, IN

Sports

S uperiorly awesome and challenging
P lay lots of fun games
O pponents that are challenging help you get better
R ewards aren't the most important part of a game; playing the best you can is all that matters
T ournaments are always the most exciting, but sometimes there can be lots of pressure
S tamina is one of the most important traits to have in sports

Austin Flinn, Grade 6
St. Simon the Apostle School, IN

High Merit Poems – Grades 4, 5, and 6

Watchers of the Night
Ice cold eyes watching you in the night
sucking the braveness away.
Their open mouths prepared to scare away
the intruders with their loud booming voice.
Hearts made of stone and as black as
the darkest night. Their mysterious designs
all swirly and never-ending.

The Toltec statues of Mexico are
the night watchers of the village.

Jacky Magdici, Grade 6
Knox Community Middle School, IN

What's in Tears?
What's in tears?
Moist vicious despair
Ravished hopes and dreams
Hopeless obscured happiness
A salt and water collision
Worried feelings
Drops of melancholy
My swirling emotions squabbling for attention
Joyous enchanted hope

Nia Reed, Grade 5
Dodson Elementary School, MI

The Cloud
The cloud I see
drifts by me.
The cloud I see drifts by me happily.
The cloud I see drifts by me happily.
I watch as it moved across the sky.
The cloud I see drifts by me happily.
I watch as it moves across the sky
with the sun shining, high in the
light blue sky.

Alexia Cline, Grade 6
Lake Linden-Hubbell Elementary School, MI

Ode to Grandpa
Ode to Grandpa I love you so.
Ode to Grandpa me and Grandma miss you.
Ode to Grandpa why did you die so young?
Ode to Grandpa you were 58.
Ode to Grandpa I love you and miss you
Ode to Grandpa you were special and you still are!!!

David Hardin, Grade 4
Morgan Elementary School, IN

The Cat
Creeping through the darkness, unwilling to confess,
At who really stole it; we can only guess!
Whoever took that cookie was a sneaky little one.
I'm willing to guess; it was the cat.

Jordan Falk, Grade 5
Rockford Christian School, MI

Free Throw
Three seconds left.
32-30.
Down by two.
The clock ticked
Three
Two
One.
Last chance to make both free throws.
The player stood
Concentrated
Hoped to make it.
With determination in his eye, he shot.
His heart was beating like a race horse.
Everyone was screaming and cheering.
The ball sat
Wiggled
And wobbled on the rim.
Sadness swept through the stands like a tornado.
We had lost to our arch-rival.

Kirsten Brinkmeier, Grade 6
Assumption School, MI

Little Cousins
From small to bigger
from blond to strawberry blond.
The girls were sweet and innocent,
but now they're rude and bossy.

I remember when as babies the kids were teething and laughing,
but now they're loosing teeth and complaining.
Or when they toppled and wobbled,
but now they're walking and running.

I used to hear the pitter patter,
of their little feet,
but now I hear the angry stomping,
of their devilish fleet.

I look back at the memories,
gifts from my little cousins.
But I also look ahead,
on the many memories yet to come.

Joshua Joseph, Grade 6
Knox Community Middle School, IN

Shadow
A shadow knows how to mimic
It vanishes in the dark
And a shadow breaks in upon the land at day
A shadow knows how to irritate its master
They frolic with the sun and its master
Shadows are like devoted dogs
Shadows are like a clever fox
Very whimsical

Richard Ding, Grade 5
Dodson Elementary School, MI

Where I'm From

I am from pastures with mud pies,
with grassy hills from riding horses,
to bringing
cows around to the big red barn.

I am from playing at mamaw and papaws
smelling homemade banana bread, riding for wheelers,
and while
listening to birds chirp the most relaxing songs,
chewing spirit gum.

I am from getting called to the house
by "Bub."
And staring at the sparkling blue
ocean colored sky!!

Darvin Patrick, Grade 6
Knox Community Middle School, IN

Romance

I am romantic love
You know me for bringing peace to the world
My mother is happiness
My father is joy
I was born inside a heart
I live in the soul
My best friend is a heartwarming song
Because it helps me bring people together
My enemies are sorrow and hate
Because they bring sorrow and anger to the world
I fear angry people
Because it causes me to have a feeling of disgust
I love happy people
Because they make romance come true
I wish to wash away hate!

Tala Hussini, Grade 5
Dodson Elementary School, MI

Goodbye Winter! Hello Spring!

Goodbye winter!
Goodbye slipping on ice and breaking my back.
Goodbye layers of clothes on me making me fall down.
Goodbye snow falling from the black night sky.
Goodbye going down the McClumpha Hill and going fast.
Goodbye all of the snowball fights and getting it in the face.
Goodbye jumping on the snow and not getting hurt where I hit it.

Hello spring!
Hello all of my black t-shirts.
Hello the sun blazing on my skin.
Hello no snow to block my face when I'm running.
Hello the nice grass everywhere I look.
Hello the blood sucking mosquitoes sucking my blood.
Hello the nice warm air that hits my skin.

Austin Martin, Grade 5
Dodson Elementary School, MI

Goodbye Winter

Goodbye winter!
Goodbye freezing my tail off
Goodbye awesome snow forts
Goodbye putting on snow pants, boots and other snow gear
Goodbye sledding fun down the hills with my friends
Goodbye shoveling snow with my dad
Goodbye snowball fights that I play with my friends

Hello spring!
Hello trampoline that I can jump on
Hello annoying bees that sting me
Hello my b-day that will be coming soon
Hello running in my sandals
Hello staying up late
Hello to the spring flowers

Ben Lukasiewicz, Grade 5
Dodson Elementary School, MI

Allen Iverson

This six foot beast has already released
Driven' down the lane
Causin' you pain

From three's to two's
From swish to bank
This slim quick warrior has you in the tank

You can yell, you can scream
You can curse his name
But all your gonna do is earn him fame

You can't stop him
Don't even try
One step on the court and he'll make you cry

Matt Manner, Grade 6
Mary Evelyn Castle Elementary School, IN

I Am

I am a shiny soup spoon
You know me for slurping up delicious Italian soup
My mother is the salad fork
My father is the dinner knife
I was born in a clean silverware factory
I live in a family's section of their neat kitchen drawer
My best friend is the bowl
Because I take huge dives in the bowl
My enemy is the rusty dishwasher
Because I hate being twirled and whirled around
I fear children's sweaty hands
Because I hate being all smiley
I love when I get polished and scrubbed
Because I feel gorgeous
I dream of being the shiniest spoon on Earth

Meera Patel, Grade 4
Dodson Elementary School, MI

High Merit Poems – Grades 4, 5, and 6

Spirits

The laugh is cold — the laugh is shrill;
an odious cackle
It seems to come out of nowhere

And then you see it: a ghostly shape materialize
but not abate
You shake your head and rub your eyes,
but this is real — this is true
What's standing right in front of you;
both twisted visage and evil laugh

So run away and don't come back,
for if you do then you shall hear
the laughter of the spirits

Isaiah Zuercher, Grade 5
Heritage Intermediate School, IN

Responsibility

R espect to others
E verlasting amazing ideas to save the world
S ponsoring good teamwork and thoughtfulness.
P ouring with good excitement.
O ver going bad things
N ever leaving the world.
S urprising how good it feels to be responsible.
I s the best way for a kid to prove to an adult that they can do it.
B est thing the world has.
I ridescent colors of happiness
L ivable
I ndestructible
T he best missing homework solution
Y ears of people that have proved that they used responsibility.

Brittin Bailey, Grade 6
Perry Middle School, MI

I Gave You a Lemon

I gave you a lemon, but you took a lime,
I gave you a second, but you took more time,
I gave you ice cream, but you took cake,
I gave you real, but you took fake.

I gave you a lemon, but you took a lime,
I gave you a dollar, but you took a dime,
I gave you a spark, but you took a fire,
I gave you a car, but you took a tire.

I gave you a lemon, but you took a lime,
I gave you a riddle, but you took a rhyme,
I gave you an enemy, but you took a friend,
I gave you a beginning, but you took an end.

Rachel Warner, Grade 6
Sherman Middle School, MI

Reading

When I read a book I…
Run through an open meadow.
I swim in the deep blue sea.
I fly through the night blue sky.
I dance on the moon.
I play cards with Dolley Madison.
When I read I travel to another world, all when I read a book.

Kate Amin, Grade 6
West Middle School, MI

Raiders

P atrolling the high seas when a call from above…
I see a ship!
R un up the flag!
A ttack the enemy and sink their ship.
T reasure for the crew
E xecute prisoners and
S ail away

Keegan MacDonell, Grade 6
St Simon the Apostle School, IN

Letters

L et us all sit down to relax and hold a pen
E xecuting with our hands in nonstop grammar
T aking the time to sit and think
T alking about life and about each other
E xpressing ourselves in old-fashioned notes
R esponding in a different way than text
S igning our name on a masterpiece

Maggie Kassenbrock, Grade 6
St Simon the Apostle School, IN

Summer

S un is shining bright
U r shoulders start to turn red
M om reminds me to put on sun screen
M y mother runs to the water and makes a splash
E veryone is in the big, cool water
R ight now is the times I cherish

Nikkie Bemis, Grade 5
Perry Central Elementary School, IN

Light

Once in our world, Earth was filled with a warm bright light,
then darkness found its way inside us.
We created a war and fought over what was left of the light,
therefore creating more darkness.
But a select few people saw that they still had light.
Because within the deepest darkness, light remains.

Michael Splan, Grade 5
Thomas M Cooley School, MI

Volleyball
Volleyball
Bump, set, spike, score
Teammates, cheering, having fun
Volleyball is a great sport to play
Best sport!
Kaitlyn Crowe, Grade 6
Saint Simon the Apostle School, IN

My Dog
Jericho
Play, drink
Licking, running, fetching
He is the best
Dog
Noah Schoenherr, Grade 5
Hendry Park Elementary School, IN

The Happy Day
The sun shined down on our city.
The children were laughing and playing.
None of the dogs were barking,
Then, it was quiet.
Everyone was happy.
Hailee Danks, Grade 6
St Simon the Apostle School, IN

Cryin' Ryan
There was a boy named Ryan,
He always dreamed of flyin'
He rode a train
Instead of a plane,
And then he started cryin'.
Andrew Brennan, Grade 6
St Simon the Apostle School, IN

Chihuahua
Chihuahua
Spunky, soft
Jumping, barking, snuggling
Makes me happy
Golden friend
Claudia Williams, Grade 5
Perry Central Elementary School, IN

Dad
Dad
Strong, wise
Working, fighting, surviving
He is a good provider
Warrior
Adam Cavasos, Grade 6
DSA - West Langston Hughes Campus, MI

Grandma Pat
Grandma Pat, I will never forget your scent
You smelled like cinnamon and apples

Grandma Pat, I will never forget how you hugged me
When you hugged me, you were so warm and you made me feel loved

Grandma Pat, without you, I probably wouldn't know how to be kind
If you wouldn't have been around, I probably wouldn't have any friends

Grandma Pat, I miss your loving music we listened to
I miss the times we used to go caroling on Christmas Eve

Grandma Pat, I miss your personality and your brown eyes
I miss your gentle kindness and your stories

Grandma Pat, I miss the times we played out in the sun
I miss the times we spent together during the summer

Grandma Pat, I miss making apple pies with you
I miss getting fluffy white dough all over the place with you

Grandma Pat, I miss your velvety-red chair you owned
I miss the times you sang me songs in that chair

But the thing I miss the most is...you
I love you, Grandma
Taylor Floradis, Grade 6
Linton-Stockton Elementary School, IN

My Time Has Come
I will be a butterfly, all I got to do is try
I'll spread my wings and fly
I'll be purple, and green...I'll be green and purple
I'll be a helper of God
Satan won't enter when I'm around, the world will be so sound
Temptation will be no more; all our troubles will be gone
I'm a butterfly, get ready...I'm coming

My time has come
Those that follow can see me now, will they follow, will they run
My beauty is rare my wings are strong, strong enough to take me there
When I turn I see, yes those that see do follow
Now I will take them there

I turn to see the followers I have now
Their heads they are turning, turning the other direction
A trace of daisy pollen on my wings, my colors begin to change
I begin to glow like a lightning bug...Ah yes, those that follow are turning
We can continue on

We are there, we are here
Those that follow they run, those that follow descend...
Onto the cradle of alyssum and lilies, the nectar is indescribable
Their time has come, change anticipated, success fulfilled, my further task awaits...
Hadley Martin, Grade 6
Milltown Elementary School, IN

High Merit Poems – Grades 4, 5, and 6

Rascal Is Your Name
Running through the grass
Getting away from me
Stumbling with your short legs
Stopping to eat grass for a break

Running through the maze of legos
That I built for you in an hour
Playing hide-and-seek in the house
Giving yourself away

Afraid of the dark and monsters
me there to comfort you
Eating buttery popcorn
Watching a scary movie

Having fun
Best of friends
From when you were a baby
I raised you

Eaten by my brother's stupid dog
You will be forever missed
Buried under your favorite oak tree
My poor guinea pig
Nathan Trujillo, Grade 6
Knox Community Middle School, IN

I Am a Cloud
Float, float, float
I am a cloud
As water pours in me

I see children playing
I see dogs laying
Float, float, float

I go higher and higher
Nothing to see
As water pours in me

Everything back in sight
I see farmers plowing
Float, float, float

"Oh no" not again
I scream as I reach higher
As water pours in me

Finally low again
I release my water
Float, float, float
As water pours in me
Logan Bachelder, Grade 5
Northern Heights Elementary School, IN

The Cold World
She saw a future, it was very nice
Her mom's heart was as cold as ice
She ran away into the dark, dark night
She saw a light, but it wasn't very bright
It was miles to sleep
The forest was very deep
And she could not find her way out
Soon she didn't pay attention
So she slipped and fell in a spout
A small cold iceberg pushed against her leg
She yelled for help, but no breath to beg
She drowned in the cold
She wrinkles as if she's old
Falling in with no hope
The only thing that she can do is cope
Her mom's missing her baby
But wondering why
But the only thing she can really do is cry
A miss, no kiss
Her mom could only say goodbye
Not telling the truth, so in the bed she'll lie.
Dejamaree D. Davis, Grade 6
DSA - West Langston Hughes Campus, MI

Buzzer Beater
My teammate gets the rebound.
Sprinting
Fast as a cheetah down court
Teammate throws the ball.
　Ball in my hand
　2 seconds
　　Dribble,
　　　Dribble,
　　　　I shoot a 3.
　　　　　1 second,
Down by 2
　Desperately
　　Hoping,
　　　Hoping,
　　　　Hoping it will go in.
　　　Buzzer sounds.
Ball in the air
　Clanks off the backboard.
　Hits the rim
　Goes in
　　We win
Aaron Hall, Grade 6
Assumption School, MI

Pigs
Cuddly, stinky,
Snorts, rolls, eats,
Cute, smelly, loud, muddy,
Piglet
Alyssa Hedstrom, Grade 4
Crestwood Elementary School, MI

My Great-Grandma Rose
She is dead
I'm alive

She was funny
So am I

She *loved* kids and babies
I *love* babies and animals

She loved to cook so much
I *love* to cook all the time

She loved me even though
She did not know me
I love her even if
I just saw a picture of her
Presleigh Anderzak, Grade 5
Dodson Elementary School, MI

Frustration
Frustration…
people constantly anger you,
life is never simple
Friends…
who you thought were trustful
never really were
Rumors…
viciously spread
were never pure of heart
No one…
really wants to talk to you
Frustration…
runs through my emotional mind
My hopeless life…
is now forever gone
Frustration
Drew Moronez, Grade 6
Linton-Stockton Elementary School, IN

Walking in the Trails
Getting tacked up
With all my friends
Wind blowing in our faces
While walking on the trails
Giggling things over and over again
Starting to trot
Hearing birds chirping and horses neighing
Stopping at the creek
To let the horses get a drink
The horses pulling at the reins
Off again on the trip
Starting to gallop
Until we hit the road
Time with friends is everlasting!
Montana Rose, Grade 5
Addison Middle School, MI

My Favorite Thing

I get butterflies in my stomach,
when I'm up on the block.
I hear the whistle blow,
then I shoot off
and I let the water cradle me

The coach announces
that we'll be swimming free.
I clear my mind of everything except
1,2,3 breathe 1,2,3 breathe.
I feel so free, calm, and relaxed,
there's nowhere else I'd rather be at that moment.

I get extremely nervous,
when it's my turn to swim.
"Down and back, that's all it is,"
I tell myself.
After I'm in the water,
I'm not at all nervous.
It's the waiting, nervousness, and anxiety I hate.

I always go home feeling incredible,
and I can't wait until the next meet.

Noelle Heise, Grade 6
Knox Community Middle School, IN

Seasons I'm Alone

In spring me and my Dad break out my mitt
that has done me well for so
many years awaiting the ball
to snap in my glove for
the first catch of the year

In summer the ball zooms by me
as I'm running dashing to get the ball
I toss the ball to the pitcher
as the batter is sliding,
The Umpire calls "YOU'RE OUT"

In fall the seasons over tossing
the ball for the last time
of the season before
my trusty mitt goes in my
room until next year

In winter my mind is racing
as my glove is counting the days
and months before its spring again
to feel the pop in my glove,
but for now a mitt can only dream

Hunter Fletcher, Grade 6
Knox Community Middle School, IN

The Yellow River

In winter
the river freezes
it feels the children skating on it,
parents sit on the bank and watch
the water moves slowly under the ice

In spring
the ice melts away
the river's water level goes up,
you can hardly tell the sandy island is there —
fish have yet to arrive

In summer
water level goes down
you can see the sandy island again
people fish on the banks
while others swim in the river

In fall
leaves and slender twigs fall into the river
the water is starting to get cold
fish have left until next year
then it starts all over again

Katlin Fletcher, Grade 6
Knox Community Middle School, IN

Harley

Harley, where have you gone?
I have wondered for years
You interest me to know.
Where have you gone and why?

Why couldn't you stay with our family.
We knew you loved to go outside
But not for running away.

We always thought you were calm and relaxed,
But, we could've been wrong
I wanted to thank you
For being my cat for a while.

I hope some day to know where you have gone
I liked the way you wanted to be petted.
You would always curl up on us,
And plead and beg for someone to scratch your ears.

You were so white with black and brown patches,
I have actually named some cats after you
So give me a meow — any cat sound,
And let me know where you are.

Tara Conley, Grade 6
Knox Community Middle School, IN

I Know Halloween Is Over
I know Halloween is over
but I am going to make it last forever!
The yummy candy is still here
And I am going to make it last all year!
Candy in my lunch,
I like a bunch
I love to munch,
on my candy that makes a crunch.
I love the feeling of the
Poppers popping in my mouth
Chocolate melting right on my tongue
The crunch of a Kit Kat
And all the chewing of all my flavors of gum
Yum yum yum in my tum tum tum
I know Halloween is over
But, I am going to make it last forever!
The yummy candy is still here
And I am going to make it last all year!
Alexis Hess, Grade 6
West Middle School, MI

The Shell
One day I found a shell
And it ruined my day
I hate that little shell
That's all I have to say

That shell broke my TV
Tore off my pet bird's beak
It ruined all my stairs
And now all of them squeak

Stupid selfish shell
You're the monster under my bed
You're like a rabid dog
You're messing with my head!

One day I found a shell
And it ruined my day
I hate that little shell That's all I have to say
Tyra Edwards, Grade 6
Mary Evelyn Castle Elementary School, IN

School Is Cool
Go to school,
School is actually cool.
Don't think your grades are low, bad, or crazy,
If that's true you are lazy.
Don't turn school down,
Come back into town.
Kids are pouring in and out,
Just like a waterspout.
Go to school, it is awesome,
Then, your mind will blossom.
Steven Blair, Grade 4
Chrisney Elementary School, IN

Paris
The Eiffel Tower is narrowing
with its immense steel pillars
people are crowded with their fancy looks
The pale light was
bouncing off the pillars
with a shining light
I can hear the crowd of fancy people and cars
the sound of wind rushing in my ears
I also hear the unknown language that I don't
know the Paris language
how many people are around?
did anybody get up there yet?
would it ever get bigger?
how old is it?
I felt the loving and
surprised
awe in my heart
crowded
crowded
crowded
Rasha Tiba, Grade 6
Star International Academy, MI

Perfectionism
I'm a perfectionist,
in so many ways,
so maybe I'll be an artist.
Paint the everlasting sky
and make my dreams my life,
if only I was an artist.

Perhaps I'll have an education,
reading, writing, advanced in all,
but that is because I'm smart.

Through the years, I'll learn to look through,
many,
many,
different views.
I'll make varied philosophy, on why people do the things they do.

But most of all,
I'll change slowly,
Into another me.
Lauren Asam, Grade 5
Miller Elementary School, MI

Ode to Chile
Oh Chile, oh Chile you are always chewing,
and you're always doing something.
Oh Chile, oh Chile you are so cute,
but sometimes I wish I could put you on mute.
Oh Chile, oh Chile you are a chinchilla,
but sometimes you think you're bigger than Godzilla.
Shelby Kondovski, Grade 5
Morgan Elementary School, IN

Where I'm From

I am from
Delicious churros on Easter morning covered in powdered sugar almost like a donut.
I am from
A caring and loving mom that's by my side at every tough situation.
I am from
A brave uncle that served for our state but passed away July 7, 2003.
I am from
Winning the state championship and throwing off our gear because we were number one in the state.
I am from
Getting hit with a pitch but still getting up and making it to the all-star game and making the winning play.
I am from
Our beautiful dog, Peanut, with shining fur, half pug, half Chihuahua.
I am from
The sticky cinnamon roll from McDonald's every year on my birthday.
I am from
Waking up to a glamorous room in Hawaii looking out the window at a great view of the ocean.
I am from
A supportive dad encouraging me to work harder and be positive.
I am from
Riding every ride at Cedar Point multiple of times with my family.
From, Joe

Joe Fontana, Grade 6
West Middle School, MI

Regular Week Cupcake

Ingredients
3 Cups of friends
5 Cups of crazy things
2 Teaspoons of disappointment
1 Teaspoon of mean words from bullies
1 Cup of wild music
6 Teaspoons of rude siblings
2 Teaspoons of love and happiness
1 Cherry of joy

Directions
Mix the 6 teaspoons of rude siblings, 2 teaspoons of disappointment, and 1 teaspoon of mean words from bullies in a small bowl. Mix that until it is liquidy. Transfer that into a cupcake pan. Preheat that at 120° F then bake it for 7 days straight. Then for the frosting, mix the 3 cups of friends, 5 cups of crazy things, and 1 cup of wild music together. Mix slowly until it's light and fluffy. Spread the frosting across the top of the cupcake. Then sprinkle the 2 teaspoons of love and happiness on top. Finally put the cherry of joy on top. You have just made a regular week cupcake.

Jordan Schamp, Grade 6
West Middle School, MI

Where I Am From

I am from climbing in a window to our computer room whenever my sister accidentally locked the door.
I am from a playground my brother, my sister and I found and named Duck Playground because there was a huge duck on the roof.
I am from my dad working hard and my mom teaching us math, and my English teacher Emily (I got my name from her!)
I am from getting under the table with my sister and putting a blanket over and stopping them from falling with books so we could
    hide from my brother.
I am from sharing an old car with my big family.
I am from a small country, but BIG with my BIG family's love watching over us.
I am from Seoul, South Korea!

Emily Choi, Grade 4
Hampton Elementary School, MI

High Merit Poems – Grades 4, 5, and 6

Life
Sometimes life is running,
running full speed down the hill.
Not seeing any details,
never even standing still.

Sometimes life is pacing,
walking, walking, back and forth.
You keep searching, you keep looking,
for that one small open door.

Sometimes life's a big ball,
spinning, bouncing all around.
Friendship, happiness, schoolwork, too,
so far most important can't be found.

Sometimes life is frustrating,
bad grades and fighting.
People stab you in the back,
it can be very frightening.

Sometimes life is terrible,
sometimes life is great.
But you should cherish every moment,
before it is too late.
Julia Salloum, Grade 6
West Middle School, MI

When Spring Is here
When Spring is here we go to play.
We will go barefoot if we may.
When I go out I see the flowers.
That's why I like the springtime hours.

There's work to be done we all know.
Windows clean, and grass to mow,
Dishes to wash, floors to sweep,
Wash the clothes, thrown in a heap.

Birds are singing their cheery song,
We clean the house all day long.
The buds are all on the trees.
That's what draws the many bees.

It rains a lot it makes things grow.
Out in the garden row after row
The vegetables are growing tall
We will harvest them in the Fall

We go fishing at the brook
To catch a turtle on our hook
Thank God for the blessings of Spring
And all the wonders it does bring.
Annetta Kay Wagler, Grade 5
Green Acres School, IN

My Little Brother
M ean
Y esterday fun

L ittle
I t's time to bug me
T alks a lot
T -r-o-u-b-l-e
L ame
E xtraordinary at crazy

B ad boy
R idiculous
O h is he bad
T errifying
H orrible
E asy to scare
R eally bad
Patrick Galligan, Grade 4
Morgan Elementary School, IN

Navy Sailors
The sailors move the ship west
That way seems best

The battleship rattles
It's been through many battles

Now the sailor crew
Sails the deep blue

They will fight
On that ship tonight

On the tip
The captain peers off the ship

The captain yells "what do you see?"
"Nothing but the deep blue sea."
Jonathan Nalezyty, Grade 6
St John Lutheran School, MI

Siblings!
We fight with each other
We yell at the other
We kick because we are mad
We scream for no reason
We complain about EVERYTHING
I annoy them, they annoy me
I get ignored, so do they
But…
I stick up for them when they need it
I sometimes love them
I am grateful for them
And that's just how siblings are!
Genna Clarke, Grade 6
St John Lutheran School, MI

Monsters
Monsters creep around at night
Oh its such a fright
I wonder what they will do
Maybe they will say boo!
Will he smile?
Will he stay for a while?
Will he be big?
Or as small as a twig?
Will his name be Larry?
But either way monsters are scary!
Britney Carnagie, Grade 6
St John Lutheran School, MI

My Special Pet
Her fin splashes
Waiting for her food
Eye wobbles
Color changes
Crazy eyes stare at me
Waiting for me to feed her
Giggles when I make a face
Sighs when I leave
She is my pal
Splash! Splash!
Emma Bowman, Grade 5
Dodson Elementary School, MI

Ode to My Daddy
Dad oh dad you were my hero.
I wish you were here.
You hugged me.
I poked you.
You know you'll always be my dad.
When I die I will visit you
In white fluffy clouds.
Daddy I will love you no matter what.
I love you dad.
You are my all.
Shelby Ray, Grade 4
Morgan Elementary School, IN

My Life Is a River
My life is a river
I like the gentle bends
I like the smooth waters
They bring me peace and joy
I don't like the rocks
They are like struggles in my life
I enjoy the nice and peaceful waters
Having ups and downs
Twists and turns
Trying to smooth them out.
Ghazaleh Akbarian, Grade 6
Star International Academy, MI

Colorful Winter
Winter is white
Like snow falling down on me
A snow day because of a blizzard
And building a round tall snowman
Winter is scarlet red
Like a crackling warm fire
A Christmas poinsettia
And fuzzy warm gloves on a cold winter day
Winter is turquoise blue
Like a frozen pond to go ice skating on
A scarf to keep a child warm
And a robin's egg laying on the ground
Isabel Anderson, Grade 4
Dodson Elementary School, MI

The Cat
That little girl
Had a little pearl
She was called Jan
And her brother was Dan
She owned a cat
That was so fat
That it had no fun
So it sat in a bun
He was called Rick
And he had a crazy lick
It was a sin
That he had a fin
Ian Smith, Grade 6
St John Lutheran School, MI

Cold Winter Months
Cold and snowy
White and gray
Trying to stay warm
People sledding, people laughing
Snowmen everywhere
Happy and cold, crystals floating
In the air.
Sick people in care
Cold, frozen ponds and lakes,
Where people love to skate.
Animals in caves and holes hibernating,
Waiting for spring.
Victoria Deakins, Grade 5
Staunton Elementary School, IN

Evette
E very day loving
V ery happy
E very way helpful
T he mom of my world
T he mom that loves
E .J. for short!!!!!
Elissa Rodgers, Grade 6
Perry Middle School, MI

Horses
Horses like running.
Saddle sliding off its back,
bolted right past us.
Darbi Brumbaugh, Grade 5
Hendry Park Elementary School, IN

Index

Abate, Sara 115
Abbott, Sydney 148
Abriani, Emily 165
Achkar, Nadine 225
Adams, Alan 173
Adams, Emily 168
Adams, Jaina 216
Adams, Julia 160
Adcock, Malachi 210
Aguirre, Cristina 74
Akbarian, Ghazaleh 249
Al-Ibrahimy, Batoul 32
Alcorn, Hailie 221
Aldelahmawi, Sara 167
Alderman, Carly 174
Aldridge, Ian 166
Algee, Alex 145
Allam, Olivia 231
Allen, Kayla 156
Allen, Megan 60
Allison, Carley 159
Alosachie, Michelle 55
Alugaili, Rhenna 97
Alva, Arianna 179
Alway, Serena 146
Amin, Kate 243
Ammerman, Samantha 67
Amor, Amber 195
Anderson, Alaina 96
Anderson, Isabel 250
Anderson, Jeffrey 71
Anderson, Katie 91
Anderson, Madison 211
Anderson, Reily 194
Anderson, Savannah 11
Anderzak, Presleigh 245
Andrews, Beau 158
Andrews, Claire 48
Andrews, Stephen 136
Ang, Sara 184
Angeles, Jose-Luis 172
Annee, Alexis 127
Applin, Bryan 13
Arnold, Casey 193
Arnold, Chelsey 188
Asam, Lauren 247
Ash, Dorian 57
Ash, Sarah 134
Ashworth, Hannah 90
Atkins, Libby 166
Attkisson, Johnathon 141

Atwell, Emma 35
Austin, Abby 120
Azmanova, Victoria 52
Baca, Jacob 221
Bach, Carl 203
Bachelder, Logan 245
Bailey, Brittin 243
Bailey, Cole 226
Baker, Adela 77
Baker, Briana 181
Baker, Shelbi 16
Baker, Sierra 43
Baker, Tarez 86
Bales, Zack 97
Ball, Emily 231
Bancroft, Isaac 115
Bannick, Kathryn 212
Banooni, Daniel 101
Barnaby, Max 214
Barnes, Corianne 194
Baron, Spenser 73
Barth, Rebecca 36
Bartholomew, Dakota 89
Bartz, Lindsey 30
Bastin, John 11
Bates, Connor 195
Baumgardner, Cade 219
Bayless, Jonathan 134
Bayliff, Payton 219
Bays, Elizabeth 86
Beadle, Zachary 206
Beaudoin, Ian 228
Becharas, Maria 141
Beck, Lenah 162
Beddow, Kevin 172
Bednarski, Beverly 103
Bedwell, Christian 195
Begley, Joná 53
Bel Hassan, Sarah 239
Belcher, Bradley 121
Bell, Lyric 152
Bemis, Nikkie 243
Bender, Katelyn 198
Bennett, Ashley 101
Benoit, Morgan 68
Benoit, Taylor 221
Bensen, Kristen 160
Benson, Griffin 234
Bentley, Travis 35
Benton, Sylvan 68
Berends, Emma 222

Berger, Brooke 161
Bergman, Alyssa 167
Bernath, Garrett 181
Bernauer, Drake 164
Berro, Aliya 91
Berry, Shelby 78
Berryhill, Wilson 161
Beydoun, Zeinab 161
Beyer, Andrew 159
Beyer, Kyle 138
Beyer, Tara 204
Bhatia, Kunal 197
Bhatti, Hasif 183
Bickel, Cody 117
Bielefeld, Rose 212
Bierlein, Elizabeth 127
Bilder, Nicaela 200
Bivens, Shanise 83
Blair, Steven 247
Blamey, Payton 209
Blevins, Chelsie 11
Blewitt, Mary 148
Blocker, Katie 131
Bloom, Rebecca 143
Blust, Brian 191
Bohren, Isabella 207
Bolen, Ashley 97
Boller, Kaytlin 89
Bolles, Drew 95
Bon-Mardion, Victoire 227
Bond, DeAnna 47
Bonkowski, Charlie 114
Bontrager, David Joe 210
Booe, Madison 70
Book, Tallyn P. 219
Booker, Cortney 195
Booker, Makayla 225
Booms, Danielle 123
Booth, Emily 140
Borkin, Lindsay 20
Borninski, Nicholas 239
Bournias, Nina 121
Bowen, Kylie 236
Bower, Ashley 57
Bowman, Dylan 218
Bowman, Emma 249
Boyd, Scott 210
Boyle, Sam 224
Bradley, Melaina 224
Bratton, Justin 224
Braun, Skyler 96

Breen, Danielle 23
Brennan, Andrew 244
Bressler, Jennifer 162
Brich, Taylor 84
Briggs, Dalton 112
Brinkman, Macy 184
Brinkmeier, Kirsten 241
Brinksneader, Dakota 164
Brinn, Kara 39
Brittingham, Troy 36
Brockway, Nicole 153
Broerman, Daniel 109
Brooks, Mallory 214
Brothers, Allison 145
Brown, Brittany 189
Brown, Jade 138
Brown, Maegan 129
Brown, Mariah 193
Browne, Hailey 124
Brownley, Jack 220
Brumbaugh, Darbi 250
Brunet, Jonathan 139
Brusdahl, Kaila 155
Brush, Jared 71
Brush, Mavery 214
Buckley, Rachel 105
Buczkowski, Leanne 37
Buhl, Libby 113
Burczak, Forest 30
Burk, Taylor 31
Burkardt, Kyle 29
Burke, Gabriella 229
Burkhart, Jake 190
Burns, Matthew 136
Buskard, Marissa 22
Bustamante, Maria 184
Butler, Asia 128
Butterworth, Kassie 105
Buursma, Thomas J. 177
Byers, Justin 237
Byrd, Brittney 113
Caballero, Zoey 79
Calderone, Zoe 205
Caldwell, Kristen 170
Caldwell, Taylor 112
Calso, Jonathan 65
Camden, Hanna 231
Cameron, McKenna 210
Campbell, Christine 189
Campbell, Jillian 172
Candiano, Aaron 229

Cardoza, Juan 145	Colone, Lauren 230	Davis, Jaxon 189	Downs, Ellianna Monroe.. 174
Carey, Amelia 191	Colston, Emily 112	Davis, Mayme 206	Downs, Susan 35
Carie, Lexie 104	Conley, Tara 246	Davis, Noah 202	Doyle, Katie 57
Carmona, Victoria 101	Conley, Tonya 163	Davis, Whitney 77	Drenth, Megan 96
Carnagie, Britney 249	Conner, Abigail 223	Dazel, Brittany 26	Drenth, Whitney 202
Carpenter, Jake 60	Connop, Melissa 124	De La Rosa, Jordan 109	Drogt, Marie 148
Carr, Brittany 224	Conwell, Jeffrey 205	de Leon, Tessa 79	Drye, Luke 229
Carter, Leah 69	Cook, Kristyn 144	De Ruby, Ethan 88	Drylie, Nicole 173
Caserio, Jacqueline 72	Cooper, Scott 203	Deakins, Valerie 239	Dudek, Miranda 88
Cashero, Madison 175	Corbett, Paige 226	Deakins, Victoria 250	Dunford, Amy 187
Castaneda, Jose 84	Cornelius, Deanna 83	Deal, Alena 75	Dunn, Catherine 124
Castner, Kyle 133	Corravo, Andrew 167	DeFord, Haley 117	Dunne, Logan 216
Causey, Kenneth 21	Correa, Jacob 189	Dehn, Chelsea 54	Dunscomb, Jalen 163
Cavasos, Adam 244	Correa, Javier 81	DeLong, Brittany 120	Durkee, Katherine 36
Ceckiewicz, Dominique 209	Costantini, Gino 152	DeMarco, Michelle 45	Durm, Emma 201
Celis, Adriana 131	Cota Avila, Daniel 240	DeMarco, Olivia 146	Duvendack, Anthony 224
Cerar, Nicole 230	Coultas, Megan 169	DeMink, Kylie 34	Duyen Do, Tammy 26
Cerda, Cris 114	Counter, Brandon 108	Deneen, Alyssa 229	Dyer, Katy 64
Chacon, Zaida 182	Cowan, Nathan 30	Dennis, Alex 62	Earl, Cheyenne 130
Chandler, Katelynn 140	Cowell, Brittney 12	Dennis, Donovan 14	Eckstein, Gabriel 229
Charara, Nesrine 218	Cowen, Quin 191	Denny, Emily 212	Eckstein, Kaitlyn Kay 115
Chaturvedi, Kavya 159	Coy, Westley 23	Denton, Josh 198	Eder, Claudia 204
Chaturvedi, Nikhil 25	Crawley, Kristin 99	Deogun, Dylan 128	Edick, Josie 182
Chen, Jessica 213	Creed, Hunter 96	DePorre, Patrick 92	Edmonds, Catherine 90
Chen, Sasha 102	Crisologo, Anthony 232	DeRosia, Tyler 156	Edwards, Haley Ann 88
Chennault, Courtney 82	Crockom, Brock 72	Dessellier, Jacob 230	Edwards, Tyra 247
Childress, Russell 17	Crosby, Jamie 238	Devernay, Kelley 169	El-zein, Jamila 195
Childs, Megan 64	Crosby, Meghan Mary 41	Devlin, Libby 43	Elam, Sarah 120
Chipman, Andrea 163	Cross, Katie 196	DeVore, Mabel 177	Elinski, Mark 84
Chizum, Kelsey 236	Crowe, Kaitlyn 244	DeWald, Rachel 19	Ellert, Susan 96
Choi, Emily 248	Crowell, Celeste 10	DeWald, Tyler 21	Elliott, Maddie 181
Christensen, Caleb 160	Cruickshank, Katie 172	Diaz, Tally 74	Elliott, Rachel 167
Christenson, Alexa 218	Crummett, Autumn 135	Dicus, Waylon 237	Elliott, Ryan 223
Christenson, Catherine 171	Crutchfield, Aleena 210	Dietz, Brandon 134	Escamilla, Monserrat 39
Chrzanowski, Brian 64	Cuc, Dylan 110	Diller, Kyle 102	Espinoza, Erika 49
Chrzanowski, Emma 207	Cundiff, Liz 51	Ding, Richard 241	Esquivel, Austin 72
Claar, Vanessa 201	Curley, Marty 107	Ditmars, Kaitlyn 209	Estel, Dakota 236
Clair, Jillian 65	Curran, Keely 208	Diton, Kyle 210	Estelle, Clayton 189
Clark, Allison 235	Curtis, Joshua 127	Dixon, Lonell 173	Estrada, Paulina 224
Clark, Elizabeth 224	Curtis, Valerie 63	Dobrzelewski, Gabrielle 208	Eveler, Owen 193
Clarke, Genna 249	Czapla, Jessica 218	Dobson, McKenzie 232	Exford, Keondra 165
Cleeter, Shelby 100	Dagger, Jason 43	Doctoroff, Nicole 63	Eytchison, Courtney 204
Clemons, Elizabeth 159	Dail, Alyssa 63	Dodson, Christian 193	Ezzeddine, Nesreen 137
Cleveland, Dylan 212	Dailey, Hannah 214	Doerr, Bryan 140	Fairbotham, Nate 41
Cline, Alexia 241	Danks, Hailee 244	Dolmage, Lauren 107	Falk, Jordan 241
Clock, Serena 87	Dare, Riley 136	Doman, Riley 226	Faraj, Fatima 207
Clough, Myranda 204	Dashiell, Molly 76	Donahue, Alexis 165	Farquhar, Bodhi 64
Clover, Kristina 219	Daunhauer, Lucas 171	Donarski, Erik 10	Faulkner, Ashley 142
Clute, Michaela 36	Davenport, Madyson 148	Dood, Abby 221	Faulkner, Shannon 204
Cobb, Emily 197	Davey, Joe 79	Dood, Erin 208	Faurote, Abby 170
Cobb, Jimmy 183	David, Alex 236	Dooley, Brooklynn 237	Feeler, Dexter L. 159
Cockrell, Anna 92	Davidson, Kaitlyn 113	Dorado, Maria 121	Fellows, Emma 147
Coleman, Blaire 150	DaViera, Andrea 37	Dosch, Colleen 150	Fenwick, Hannah 135
Colinco, Alexa Gail 153	Davis, Abigail 202	Dotson, Katie Leigh 149	Fernandez, Marina 69
Collins, Cierra 155	Davis, Connor 169	Doty, Olivia 230	Finger, Cheyanne 93
Collins, Erin 135	Davis, Dejamaree D. 245	Douglas, Bryce 179	Firestine, Taylor 52
Collins, John 193	Davis, Ethan 205	Douma, Natalie 50	Fisher, Alex 237

Index

Fisher, Emily 98
Fisher, Justin 205
Fistrovich, Alessandra 118
FitzGerald, Ethan 211
Fletcher, Hunter 246
Fletcher, Katlin 246
Flewelling, Kayla 107
Flinn, Austin 240
Flinn, Katelyn 156
Flood, Kevin 228
Floradis, Taylor 244
Flynn, Jaycie 19
Fodera, Matthew 129
Foersch, Paul 69
Foerster, Andrea 111
Fogg, Samantha 87
Fontana, Joe 248
Fontana, Sam 106
Foor, Jolie 201
Foote, Tina 50
Forbes, Haley 126
Forston, Bailey 139
Fortner, Jake 35
Fouchia, Dana 11
Fowler, Natalie 148
Fox, Devon 31
Fox, Jazlyn 144
Franc, Joey 100
Franklin, Dana 155
Fraser, Justin 108
Freeman, Chris 219
French, Sandra 180
Friskney, Breanne 211
Frizzell, Kalyn 146
Frost, Lily 172
Fulford, Levi 226
Fuller, Tristan 150
Funk, Corey 169
Furgerson, Nicole 17
Furst, Trevor 104
Gabriel, Erin 81
Galaske, Michaela 155
Galford, Aislyn 145
Gallagher, Drew 140
Gallagher, Dylan Jacob 222
Galligan, Patrick 249
Galvez, Yesenia 103
Garberick, Alex 112
Garcia, Araceli 34
Gardner, Elaina 28
Gardner, Tamika 79
Gardner-Brown, Cydney 175
Garrett, Kyna 45
Gassert, Kaitlin 29
Gelfius, Luke 72
Gentner, Danielle 30
George, Calvin 116

George, Sarah 202
Gerken, Kendall 192
Gestwicki, David 167
Gettys, Lauren 233
Getz, Kendra 210
Ghena, Emily 136
Ghisolf-Astacio, Daniel 155
Gilan, Eden 182
Gillette, Brad 131
Glaza, Samantha 67
Goedde, Lucas 45
Going, E.C. 117
Gonyea, Seth 12
Gonzalez, Christina 192
Gonzalez, Talisa 79
Gorczewicz, Tyler 80
Gordon, Keimon 181
Gordon, Matthew 174
Gordon, Meghan 168
Gorney, Brenden 163
Gosselin, Melani 76
Goszkowicz, Grace 185
Gould, Megan 98
Gourley, Lyndsey 118
Graber, Daniel Hernan 188
Graber, Viola 120
Graber, Wilma Arlene 86
Graham, Dustin 209
Graham, Dylan 205
Graham, Molly 212
Grant, Mallory 218
Grassley, Colleen 47
Grazia, Tyler 82
Green, George 176
Green, Josh 62
Green, Sarah 27
Greene, Kaytlen 100
Greenwood, James 44
Greenwood, Laura 206
Gregory, Christopher 176
Greiwe, Seena 199
Greyson, Grant 138
Grieze, Katie 129
Griffin, Janae 207
Griffith, Ben 214
Griffith, Elizabeth 173
Grimes, Harley 57
Grimmett III, Anthony 33
Gross, Casey 88
Grougan, Morgan 104
Grove, Mariah 118
Gubanche Jr., Nathan 13
Guo, Lucy 20
Gupta, Rhea 186
Gushwa-Williams, A.J. 95
Hagen, Benjamin 75
Hagenow, Will 219

Haines, Haley 127
Hall, Aaron 245
Hall, Jacob 77
Hall, Kipton 77
Hall, Meghan 119
Halls, Alexis 189
Hamilton, Christopher 76
Hamilton, Ramey 100
Hamilton, Tre'Veona 19
Hamka, Yasmine 173
Hamman, Brock 201
Hammond, McKenna 240
Hampton, Brendan 192
Hanebutt, Sara 194
Hanks, Morgan 24
Hannah, Jacob 155
Hansen, Renell 232
Hanson, Madi 117
Harabedian, Aaron 92
Harbin, Elizabeth 194
Hardin, David 241
Harding, Grayson 90
Hardy, Mickella 115
Harford, Ivy 160
Harman, Karla 52
Harper, Drew 197
Harris, Eric 205
Harris, Peter 76
Harris, Trea 93
Harrison, Chelsea 70
Harshman, Magnolia 234
Hart, Alexandra 64
Hart, Kelsey 119
Harthorn, Brandon 101
Hartnagel, Augustino 139
Hartsig, Mae 220
Hasik, Sarah C. 166
Haske, Paige 82
Hassan, Basel 232
Haub, Trevor 221
Hawkins, Brandi 31
Hayden, Christina 184
Hayes, Glendin 165
Haynes, Nicholas 105
Hazergian, Mikaela 196
Heath, Thaniel 200
Heckman, Alex 212
Hedstrom, Alyssa 245
Heilman, Clarissa 130
Heim, Tyler 102
Heins, Brenna 192
Heise, Kailey 105
Heise, Noelle 246
Helka, Erin 204
Helwig, Taylor 203
Hemmelgarn, Lucy 102
Hendon, Jeremy 95

Hendrich, Caitlin 240
Hendzel, Sara 131
Henige, Margaret 226
Henrickson, Marisa 81
Hensley, Logan 73
Hentkowski, Shane 42
Herd, Nicholas 24
Herr, Kaylee 73
Hess, Alexis 247
Higbee, Marley 124
Higgins, Kaylin 61
Hightower, Nia 74
Hilbert, Nathan 91
Hildebrand, Taylor 46
Hildreth, Lauren 212
Hill, Devon 232
Hilyard, Seari 208
Himes, Cody 206
Himes, Jaelyn 235
Hincka, Korynn 107
Hinton, Hallie 185
Hirose, Ryo 200
Hirschman, Kendall 72
Hiser-Smith, Farrah 166
Hoban, Isa 180
Hochstetler, Janelle Renae 221
Hochstetler, Lanae 66
Hockersmith, Wade 214
Hodge, Cameron 171
Hodges, Kayla 145
Hoehn, Ella 197
Hoffer, Rebekah 212
Hogan, Ben 234
Holbrook, Maggie 171
Hollingsworth, Rylee 213
Hollis, Tyler 239
Holmes, Jessica 103
Holmlund, Morgan 187
Holt, Eric 146
Homsy, Matthew 146
Hooker, Damon 183
Hopkins, Parker 171
Hopkins, Whitney 149
Hoppenrath, Kyle 239
Hopple, John 94
Horak, Anna 155
Hormann, Hannah 21
Horn, Autumn 133
Hornick, Catherine 41
Hoskins, Meghan 54
Hottell, Abigail 159
Houston, Angelic 23
Howell, Victoria 56
Howitt, Tristen 138
Hubbard, Sydnee 49
Hubert, Logan 217
Hubert, Sam 229

Hudson, Demetrius 29	Jordan, Shamel 105	Knepp, Leah Renae 168	Le Mire, Alisha 44
Hudson, Onephefus 217	Jorgenson, Mason 67	Knepp, Marilyn Rose........... 96	Leady, Joshua 123
Huff, Elijah........................ 143	Joseff, Ben 170	Knepp, Mary Viola............. 150	Learman, Victoria 100
Huff, Tayler 187	Joseph, Joshua................... 241	Knepp, Matthew 86	Leatherman, Erin 184
Huffman, Camryn.............. 235	Julian, Paige L.................... 160	Knepp, Myron Lee 158	LeBert, Austin 178
Huffman, Jadyn.................. 232	Julien, Savannah 129	Knepp, Rosetta Jean 170	Lechner, Joe 210
Hughbanks, Bernadette 219	Justice, Gabriela 108	Knepp, Susan 235	Leckie, Jordan 220
Hughes, Marina 167	Kahle, Anna......................... 74	Knepp, Teresa Joanne 168	Lee, Daehyun 60
Hughes, Nicholas 234	Kaledas, Michael 178	Knoll, Jack 216	Lee, Jenna 183
Huitt Wray, Mandy 56	Kalinowski, Michael 86	Knutson, Sara 55	Lee, Marcus 129
Hukerikar, Aditi................. 168	Kanaski, Nicholas 76	Koch, Johny 88	Lee, Nathan 159
Hulse, Drew 216	Kane, Aaron 12	Koger, Briana 42	Leich, Riley........................ 220
Hulsmeyer, Sarah................ 56	Kang, Da-in 161	Kolenda, Bailey 149	Leighton, Deanna 231
Humphrey, Walker 201	Kassem, Amal 195	Komorowski, Cassidy 110	Leighton, Mary.................. 204
Humphrey-Phillips, Isabel 101	Kassenbrock, Maggie 243	Kondovski, Shelby............. 247	Lemieux, David 77
Hunt, Annabelle 201	Katt, Eli 183	Korelitz, Zoe 159	Lemke, Jaimie 175
Hunt, Cory.......................... 25	Katulski, Hailey................... 66	Koss, Haley 161	LeMond, Ali 93
Hunt, Sara 53	Kauffman, Kevin 198	Kosta, Gabe 208	Lenders, Jayna................... 213
Hupp, Taylor 113	Kelly, Jarrett...................... 224	Kozyrski, Jack 179	Lenius, Leah 235
Hurd, Brooke..................... 227	Kelly, Nicholas 80	Kraemer, Keelin 66	Lenz, Amber 178
Hurley, Sean 202	Kemp, Katie........................ 40	Kraft, Valerie 203	Lenz, Raechel 45
Huser, Samantha 80	Kempf, Taylor 164	Kresch, Atara 226	Leo, Julianna 196
Hussini, Tala 242	Kennedy, Devin 179	Krzewski, Cameron 66	Lester, Cassandra 167
Iott, Mary 34	Kennedy, Vickie 93	Kucera, Kennith 22	Levi, Aviva........................ 238
Irish, Brittney 28	Kerber, Daniel 191	Kulkarni, Sanjana 177	Levin, Joe............................ 37
Irving, Dejah Monet............ 79	Kerckhove, Dustin.............. 155	Kuntz, Camden 166	Lewis, EJ............................. 48
Iser, Kayla......................... 107	Kerrigan, Jessica 118	Kutschman, John............... 238	Li, Sophia 14
Jackson Jr., Stephen 106	Kersman, Samantha........... 233	La Foe, Sarah 111	Liepert, Lucas...................... 90
Jackson, Jr., Jason................ 43	Kettler, Kandace 138	LaBine, Taylor 66	Lifford, Casey 228
Jacobi, Jill 214	Keys, Christa..................... 236	LaFave, Michelle 139	Light, Hannah 196
Jacobs, Jasmine 169	Khreizat, Ivana 172	Lafi, Maryam 17	Lilley, Garrett 189
Jacobson, Sarah 160	Kight, Cameron 169	LaFoille, Stephanie 216	Linden, Jenna.................... 222
Jagger, Alissa 194	Killey, Margo 100	LaFreniere Jr., Brian 55	Lindsey, Rachel 81
Jain, Ankur 93	Killingsworth, Jade............ 140	Lakshmi, Sudarshana......... 182	Lintol, Sydney 222
Jajjo, Jonathan 169	Kilmer, Madi...................... 170	LaLonde, Clare 216	Lisak, Brianna 41
Jamesen, Christian............. 156	Kimball, Emily 216	Lamar, Nathan 162	Lloyd, Sarah 171
Janssen, Lindsay................ 217	Kimble-Key, Marcera........ 203	Lambert, Ethan 113	Lockrem, Jack 219
Jasper, Larry 78	Kimmel, Kaitlynn 137	LaMoreaux, Susan 28	Lockwood, Susan 43
Jaworski, Tiffany 156	King, Jimmy 116	Lamour, Andrew................. 38	Lodewyk, Amber 57
Jayatilake, Janith 125	King, MacKenzie 60	Lane, Marissa 99	Lofman, Sami 179
Jeffrey, Gabrielle................. 35	King, Raymi 227	Lang, Zoe........................... 111	Logan, Jonathan 112
Jenkins, Hannah Kay 55	Kinney, Taylor 188	Lange, Tyler........................ 92	Logsdon, Bryce.................. 164
Jenkins, Joey...................... 144	Kiplinger, Kage.................. 210	Lange, Vittoria................... 179	Lohe, Kaitlyn..................... 184
Jenkins, Keyla.................... 116	Kirkpatrick, Grace............. 131	Lanham, Madison 75	Long, Christian 147
Jenkins, Roy Benjamin 153	Kirkpatrick, Ross............... 195	Lanham, Meg 123	Lopez, Lauren 92
Jenkins, Sydney 18	Kirshenbaum, Jaron 124	Lankford, Aubree 213	Lorenzen, Katherine 108
Jennings, Ryan................... 238	Kitchen, Natasha................. 14	Lankford, Holly 97	Lori, Jalynn 179
Jensen, Cory 18	Kivela, Tyler...................... 153	Lanman, Aubree 237	Louden, Alexis 217
Jesuit, Lucas 191	Klaybor, MaryKatherine...... 80	Lannan, Mikayla 167	Loudermilk, Brittney 138
Jewell, Kortny 46	Klecha, Kirby...................... 54	Large, Lauren 97	Love, Kharii........................ 22
Jinkins, Tamar 92	Kleist, Kassidee 184	Lasher, Brooke 183	Love, Samantha 179
Johansen, Makayla 156	Klemczak, Gavin 171	Lasley, Evan 177	Lovejoy, Teresa 27
Johnson, Justin................... 209	Kline, Taylor...................... 133	Lauer, Tori 137	Lovell, Amanda 22
Johnson, Presley 223	Klomp, Katerina................ 239	LaVelle, Sam 162	Lovett, Kyra 239
Johnson Jr., Keigel............. 196	Kloss, Seth 101	Lawrence, Katelynn 176	Lowder, Zac 224
Jonca, Rieley 162	Knepp, Anthony Steven 158	Lawson, Wyatt 134	Lowe, John......................... 209
Jones, Desean 25	Knepp, Jennifer Renae 231	Lax, Trey............................ 136	Lucas, Deisy........................ 92

Index

Name	Page	Name	Page	Name	Page	Name	Page
Lucia, Macie	211	McCain, Kyle	195	Moore, Brianna	122	Norris, Nate	220
Luck, Jake	117	McCall, Erika	53	Moore, Liz	96	Norskov, Hannah	173
Lukasiewicz, Ben	242	McCarren, R.J.	86	Moore, Mary	170	Norton, Kaitlin	56
Luton, Deanna	71	McCauley, Daniel	154	Moore-Horton, Glynnat	88	Nusawardhana, Alexandra	190
Ly, Lucie	102	McClain, Taylor	162	Morgan, Marissa	41	Nye, Katelyn	103
Lyon, Stephen	152	McComas, Jessica	218	Moronez, Drew	245	O'Brien, Katey	202
Lyons, Jordan	32	McCombie, Cassandra	187	Morrison, Courtney	99	O'Brien, Kelly	178
Lysher, Alyssa	109	McCorkle, Madison	196	Moubadder, Marwa	170	O'Brien, Libby	215
MacDonell, Keegan	243	McCormick, Amanda	70	Moulton, Mitchell	235	O'Brien, Patrick	81
Mace, Dakota	55	McCrea, Korie	215	Mount, Hannah	119	O'Bryant, Victoria	162
Mack, Mikala	112	McDaniel, Jordan	136	Moyer, Cody	145	O'Donohue, Nick	170
Mackensen, Lindsi	218	McDonald, Charles	198	Muehlbrandt, Hannah	176	O'Hanlon, Michaela	156
MacLean, Annie	180	McDonald, Jaelan	21	Muhlada, Marley	178	Oakley, Kenzie	128
Maddox, Chance	136	McElfresh, Trenton	172	Muir, Brandon	88	Oley, Derrick	105
Magdici, Jacky	241	McFate, Jacob	214	Mulinaro, Maddie	91	Olson, Avery	164
Magers, Christina	229	McGerty, Laurel	137	Mulka, Tracy	37	Olson, Chase	202
Maguire, Julia	171	McGraw, Caroline	108	Munoz, Katie	235	Olson, Kellee	57
Majchrzak, Gavin	168	McLachlan, Rebecca	38	Munroe, Jessica	116	Olson, Payton	182
Mallard, Kristin	156	McLouth, Nathan	173	Munsell, Sarah	61	Orr, Taylor	99
Mallett, Timya	191	McNeece, Shoshona	98	Murphy, Cameron	206	Osborn, Garrett	97
Malouin, Maya	193	McWilliams, Quinlan	39	Murphy, Devin	210	Osborn, Taylor	236
Mangal, Ankita	42	Meadows, Kendall	222	Murphy, Jonathon	199	Osborne, Jacob M.	83
Mangold, Adam	10	Medilo, Kenneth	45	Murry, Zachary	231	Osborne, Kimberly	219
Mann, Ally	208	Melnyk, Zoe	72	Musson, Darth	109	Osburn, Noah	200
Manner, Matt	242	Mendes, Kyle	166	Musson, Emily	106	Osment, Caitlin	23
Mans, Madelyn	131	Menzock, Serenity	77	Myers, Maegen	94	Oswalt, Elizabeth	125
Mans, Meghan	234	Mercurio, Anthony	51	Nagda, Maharshi	78	Otley, Nat	85
Manthey, Andrew	140	Merritt, Ella	65	Najam, Haadiya	240	Owens, Donielle	23
Mantz, Kendra	48	Mervine, Hannah	162	Najem, Alec	165	Owens, Kate	130
Marchand, Joshua	134	Messner, Charlotte	98	Nalezyty, Clare	181	Paalksnyte, Ugne	51
Mark, Rachel	123	Meyers, Ashley	64	Nalezyty, Jonathan	249	Pace, Alexandra	90
Markules, Chris	160	Mickey, Alexandra	37	Naman, Tessa	92	Packer, Madison	171
Marples, Samantha	186	Migliore, Claire	128	Namovich, Grace	209	Paea, Joel	67
Marsh, Zach	117	Miles, Bailey	227	Nash, Makenzie	230	Page, Jared	46
Marshall, Allison	175	Milinsky, Ariel	28	Natividad, Camille	89	Page, Mitchell	217
Marshall, Sierra	208	Miller, April	37	Nedeau, Corinne	168	Palazzolo, Alyssa	54
Martin, Austin	242	Miller, Erin	173	Nedeltchev, Natalie	204	Paraventi, Noah	229
Martin, Cameron	20	Miller, Ethan	94	Neel, Bethany	141	Park, Kaitlin	73
Martin, Emily	139	Miller, Haley	187	Neff, Kendra	63	Parker, Jonathon	48
Martin, Hadley	244	Miller, Karlin	195	Nehls, Breanna	68	Parker, Olivia	160
Martin, Heather	232	Miller, Kimberly	26	Nellis, Holly	50	Parker, Samantha	133
Martin, Kathryn	99	Miller, Ruby	141	Nelson, Christie	20	Parkey, Genevieve	67
Martin, Lydia	236	Millick, Madison	170	Nelson, Kody	170	Patel, Meera	242
Martin, Mattee	127	Milliman, Noel	144	Neu, AJ	142	Patel, Neel	169
Martinez, Brianna	96	Minanov, Nikolas	98	Newkirk, Jessica	86	Patin, Cam	162
Mason, Danni	52	Miner, Rachael	23	Newmann, Lilly	209	Paton, Adrienne	84
Mast, Torrie	107	Minkkinen, Amanda	119	Newton, Ariel Sabrina	118	Patrick, Darvin	242
Masterson, Samantha	176	Misiak, Brandon	86	Newton, Sarah	72	Patrick, Emma	175
Mastny, Emma	223	Missi, JoLee	201	Ngugi, Joy	151	Patrick, Zella Mae	105
Matney, Caitlin	144	Mistry, Sonia	203	Nguyen, Christina	14	Patterson, Annie	84
Matthes, Allison	187	Mohammad, Mahmoud	223	Nguyen, Selena	98	Patton, Haley	82
Matthys, Sydney	68	Monahan-McLearon, Shane	109	Niazi, Haris	233	Paul, Andrea	40
Maurer, Allison	67	Monroe, Austin	199	Nicholl, Brendan	171	Paulino, Danata	143
Mayfield, Catherine	168	Monroe, Garrett	127	Nichols, Madeleine	88	Paulson, Garrett	138
McArthur, Kaitlin	69	Montgomery, Faith	132	Nichols, Naomi	85	Paulson, Samantha	186
McAtee, Katie	70	Montgomery, Nicholas	218	Nieto, John	100	Pavelko, Jada	189
McAvoy, Kelly	108			Nixon, Erica	156	Pavliscak, Paul	228

Pearce, Jared 61	Preece, Tyler 220	Ripple, Maddie 223	Sanchez, Pedro 233
Peavey, Tyler 57	Price, Julia 68	Rippy, Justin 167	Sanchez Montalvo, Ana 169
Pelland, Brennon 169	Price, Taylor 154	Risner, Quintin 192	Sanders, Adam 188
Pena, Constancia 87	Prince, Ashley 174	Ristau, Breana 85	Sanders, Kaitlin 221
Pena, Joe 164	Printz, Alexandria 101	Ritchings, Camille 90	Sanders, Samantha 30
Pequignot, Josh 165	Prinz, Autumn 32	Ritter, Cameron 102	Sanders, Samantha 144
Pérez, Xan 156	Pugliese, Carly 95	Rivard, Sarah 95	Santos, Austin 113
Perrault, Jon 198	Pulter, Matthew 47	Roark, Nevaeh 214	Sarkisian, Emily 110
Perry, Katie 218	Purcell, Sierra 147	Roark, Terissa 192	Sauer, Avrie 203
Perry, Triston 232	Quartey, Sharon 133	Robbins, Kyley J. 209	Saunders, Adam 207
Persinger, Seth 128	Quick, Mikayla 53	Robbins, Madison 233	Saunders, Courtney 101
Peters, Austin 205	Rabbers, Gabe 162	Roberts, Abigail 159	Sawdey, Katie 170
Peterson, Jessica 151	Rachwal, Shelby 111	Roberts, Amber 36	Schabel, Madeline 105
Petrovich, Jon 65	Rafferty, Grant 154	Roberts, Claire 135	Schaefer, Elizabeth 186
Petry, Jasmine 130	Ragon, Nic. 198	Roberts, Elizabeth 22	Schaffer, Abigail 196
Pham, Karen 223	Raheem, Vali 191	Roberts, Hannah 161	Schamp, Jordan 248
Pham, Lauren 185	Ramesh, Shreeya 169	Robinson, Kristie 46	Scheel, Andy 110
Phillips, Jaron 202	Ramey, Taylor 109	Robinson, Paige 152	Scheer, Noah 75
Phillips, Sabrina 191	Ramsey, Clarissa 87	Robles, Alexis 60	Schenten, Lindsey 42
Pier, Dustie 146	Ransom, Haley 78	Robotham, Ellis 18	Schickel, Blake 201
Pierangeli, Dana 213	Rardin, Taylor 185	Roddy, Chance 178	Schilling, Megan 117
Pierce, Mersadies 102	Rasmussen, Tony 61	Rode, Hannes 53	Schipp, Livvy 110
Pierce, Natalie 221	Ravage, Spencer 229	Rodgers, Elissa 250	Schizas, Marlena 54
Pierce, Timothy 204	Ravi, Ananya 78	Rodriguez, Bianca 230	Schmidt, Alec 201
Pierce, Will 134	Ray, Arianna 225	Roe, Madelyn 197	Schneider, Emma 237
Piljac, Kayla 79	Ray, Colton 205	Roedel, Olivia 143	Schneider, Randy 16
Pisko, Oliwia 226	Ray, Shelby 249	Roese, Rachelle 136	Schoenherr, Noah 244
Pleiman, Olivia 106	Rayl, Katelyn 15	Rogers, Anthony 91	Schoettle, Tyler 91
Pletcher, Hannah 205	Raymer, Evan 173	Rogers, Katherine 208	Schultz, Gabby 227
Plummer, Cassandra 185	Rearden, Mikayla 76	Rohlfs, Ella 126	Schultz, Tatum 75
Podolsky, Neela 90	Reckelhoff, Amelia 49	Rokita, Drew 168	Schurman, Rachel 137
Poe, Brittany 212	Redd, William 141	Romel, Lauren 87	Schwark, Julia 158
Pohle, Jaden 159	Redman, John 49	Romel, Lyndsey 84	Schwartz, Connor 112
Polito, Anthony 41	Reed, Audrey 191	Romig, Tia 63	Schweitzer, Hannah 228
Pollock, Ayelet 170	Reed, Nia 241	Ronto, Brittany 122	Scott, Bailey 119
Pollock, C.J. 214	Reed, Samantha 137	Root, Journey 39	Scott, James 80
Polonis, Samantha 42	Reetz, Mallory 105	Root, Travis 40	Scott, Jonika 116
Pond, Kilie 74	Reeves, Mikey 151	Rose, Montana 245	Scott, Morgan 69
Ponik, Lindsay 10	Reffeitt, Bailey 201	Rosenquist, Natalie 237	Scotto, Daniel 219
Popa, Alexander 186	Regalado, Anita 44	Ross, Alexa 141	Scripter, Tyler 220
Popa, Bryce 67	Reichstetter, Caitlyn 69	Rowe, Faith A. 230	Sebo, Courtney 38
Pope, Marquise 17	Reilly, Conor 114	Ruban, Ivette 141	Seewald, Brenden 160
Porile, Alicia 123	Reinhardt, Sydney 168	Rucker, Devan 10	Sellers, Braden 44
Porter, Chrystal 114	Reinke, Justin 189	Rupp, Zoey 200	Semans, Kennedee 62
Porter, Sara 120	Reising, Ben 214	Rushlow, Skylor 70	Sesko, Claire 207
Porter, Solei 181	Reiter, Brooke 154	Rutan, Kayla 221	Sexton, Abbey 208
Posada, Paige 165	Rhode, Emilee 62	Ryan, Brandon 191	Shadley, Ashley 139
Potok, Adrian 220	Rhodes, Alexus 102	Rydzinski, Danniele 130	Shadowen, Hanna 130
Potter, Jasmine 64	Rhodes, Mikyla 164	Rynearson, Leah 76	Shahnazary, Victoria 176
Powell, Brinston 220	Rhodes, Sian 189	Sabir, Jade 209	Shammas, Austin 161
Powell, Evan 166	Ricca, Taylor 13	Sachdeva, Shiva 140	Shannon, Caleb 181
Powers, Kaitlyn 123	Richardson, Aarionna 47	Sage, Molly 123	Sharpe, Austin 74
Powers, Madeline 201	Richter, Mary 79	Saint-Phard, Emmanuel .. 128	Sharpe, Travis 69
Prabhu, Prince 90	Ricketts, Sabriyyah 199	Sakoski, Kate 211	Shaver, Savannah 137
Pradhan, Sanjna 196	Rieke, MaKayla 61	Sall, Caitlin 98	Shavers, Joelle 187
Prakash, Praveen 161	Rietow, Katie 217	Salloum, Julia 249	Shaw, Alex 175
Pratte, Savannah 175	Riley, Logan 224	Salois, Kirsten 111	Shaw, Thomas D. 222

Index

Sheahan, Caitlin 231
Sheesley, Rhianna 84
Shepard, Kylee M. 232
Sherman, Danielle 153
Sherman, Wyatt 75
Sherrill, Kelsea 162
Shi, Jerald 49
Shidler, Samantha 193
Shipley-Snider, Jaiden 171
Shipp, Sara Kate 120
Shively, Brooke 181
Shtjefhilaj, Ornela 196
Shupert, Hayley 221
Siders, Kaylee 199
Silk, Lyric 97
Silva, Brianna 48
Silva, Elena 164
Silva, Jenifer 38
Silva, Matheus 139
Simmons, Daniel 68
Sims, Ky'la 87
Sinigos, Eleni 42
Skaggs, Travis 110
Skelton, Summer 237
Skibbe, Summer 202
Skornicka, Anne 80
Skorup, Jakelyn 187
Skwirsk, Jacob 184
Slaughter, Uniqua 54
Slaughterback, Jacob 182
Slavin, Nora 25
Slone, April 235
Smalley, Cortney 25
Smeltzer, Katy 104
Smiley, Drew 79
Smiley, Joie 167
Smith, Halle 66
Smith, Ian 250
Smith, Madison 103
Smith, Maya 216
Smith, Nathan 199
Smith, R. Evan 205
Smith, Taya 125
Snuske, Caryn 14
Snyder, Alexandria 83
Snyder, Kelci 51
Sobh, Ali 160
Solarewicz, Eliza 207
Sollars, Colin 146
Soper, Maddisson 174
Sowle, Allison 75
Spica, George 71
Spicer, Sara 169
Splan, Michael 243
Spray, Luke 95
Squillante, Joyce 24
St. Peters, Dominic 123

Stadler, Ella 206
Stafford, Megan 68
Stafford, Megan 121
Stalboerger, Brett 173
Staltari, Anna 164
Stansbury, Isaac 101
Stearns, Kilee 204
Stedman, Rachael 71
Steel, Brooke 98
Steel, Lauren 84
Steffel, Tyler 236
Steffen, David 121
Stegehuis, Angelica 33
Stellhorn, Sierra 237
Stenzel, Olivia 47
Stephens, Brady 133
Stephenson, Haylie 229
Stevens, Bryson 234
Steward, Kristina 117
Steward, Miranda 94
Stewart, Eugene 205
Stickley, Alex 46
Stine, Clayton 172
Stoll, Dwayne Amos 158
Stottlemire, Angelia 207
Stradford, Kayla 114
Strantz, Brandon 27
Streicher, Kayla 65
Strobel, Will 166
Strycker, Madelyn 149
Sturtevant, Jake 170
Styma, Maria 148
Styma, Sarah 10
Suggs, Angelo 135
Suida, Abbey 68
Sullivan, Emily 177
Summers, Kaleb 119
Sundelius, Trevor 50
Suresh, Raagini 29
Surugeon, Leigh 106
Sutherby, Kyle 162
Sutter, Maia 23
Swanson, Caleb 215
Swartz, Mason 16
Swartzentruber,
    Michelle Diane 226
Swihart, Cole 224
Taleb, Zaynah 193
Tam, Olivia 18
Tanana, Kassie 159
Tang, Aoxue 11
Taphouse, Dakota 40
Tatoris, Danielle 60
Taylor, De'Qjuan 15
Taylor, Elliot 62
Taylor, Mesay 114
Taylor, Symantha 95

Tellis, Chris 14
Tenney, Maddie 210
Testa, Joseph 83
Theobald, Nathaniel 29
Thieman, Holly 20
Thompson, Desmund 174
Thompson, Leah 98
Thompson, Michael 164
Tiba, Rasha 247
Tiede, Erinn 15
Tindall, Steven 218
Tippmann, Greg 149
Tippmann, Sierra 138
Tirado, Anthony 73
Tobin, Brian 172
Tokarz, Jennifer 26
Toliver, Haley 35
Torres, Nadia 24
Torsky, Nick 194
Tosh, Taylor 136
Touma, Ethan 197
Townsend, Rebekah 128
Trapp, Jacob 223
Traver, Tabby 158
Trent, Millie 89
Trimborn, Maria 215
Trosper, Macie 108
Trujillo, Nathan 245
Trulock, Megan 178
Tubicsak, Mayghan 187
Tucker, Abigail 238
Tucker, Michael 226
Tuckerman, Lydia Kay 169
Tudor, Meghan 82
Turon, Maya 73
Umana, Daniella 112
Underhill, Jaron 189
Unland, Wendy 167
Upshaw, Khalil 122
Uta, Vivian 226
Valdez, Bethany 171
Valdez, Tavie 211
Van Eck, Chloe 195
Van Luven, Julia 239
Van Nostrand, Emma 27
Van Pelt, Michael 215
Van Pelt, Michael 234
VanDam, Taylor 198
Vandermeer, Matt 34
VanderZwaag, Chelsea 25
VanNoort, Andrew 195
VanVolkenburg, Haley 198
Vargas, Alexis 62
Vargas, Olivia 107
Varghese, Christina 159
Vaughn, Tony 80
Vazquez, Alma 216

Veenstra, Amanda 137
Vega, Felicia 82
Veldboom, Lucas 231
Vellequette, Samuel 198
Vetor, Matthew 229
Vierkant, Stephanie 16
Vitez, Mitchell 34
Voyles, Cameron 214
Wabich, Megan 29
Wagler, Annetta Kay 249
Wagler, Bethany Sue 188
Wagler, Carol 90
Wagler, Christopher 70
Wagler, Glenda Jean 188
Wagler, Jonathan Dale 86
Wagler, Kayla Diane 223
Wagler, Loren Lee 223
Wagler, Natheniel 96
Wagler, Rachel Diane 158
Wagler, Stanley Eugene ... 158
Wagler, Travis Devon 130
Wagner, Brett 156
Wagner, Shianne 99
Wahr, Nathan 176
Wainscott, Alina 159
Wait, Alexis 43
Walker, Jaelyn 221
Walker, III, Richard A. 166
Wallace, Elliot 216
Wallman, Alexandra 221
Walters, Rebekah 149
Walton, Allie 164
Wanner, Josie 149
Ward, Whitney 202
Wargel, Shelby 158
Warner, Gabby 146
Warner, Lauren 198
Warner, Rachel 243
Wartella, Emily 47
Warvszewski, Justin 76
Washington, Riaunah 22
Wathen, Tanner 152
Watson, Cameron 187
Watts, Lucy E. 160
Watts, Tristen 141
Weaver, Jennifer 164
Weaver, Rikki 234
Weidner, Casey 83
Weiss, Haylee 112
Weisweaver, Tyler 126
Wells, Cayla 21
Wells, Jessica Lynn 147
Welp, Zachary 200
Wenning, Bailey 158
Wenz, Jacob 196
Wenzell, Carly 186
Wertman, Keith 188

Wesley, Jessica A. 52
Wesley, Laura E. 149
West, Hayley 116
Westgerdes, Emily 120
Westman, Jake 166
Westman, Matt 207
Weyer, Kendra 184
Whitaker, Riley 188
White, Alexa 16
White, Brene't 223
White, Madi 204
White, Sara 225
Whitman, Jobe 178
Widduck, Christian 132
Wilcox, Ashley 56
Wilding, Sydney 132
Wildman, Chad 231
Wiley, Scott 11
Wilks, Alexis 103
Williams, Autumn 187
Williams, Claudia 244
Williams, Destiny 81
Williams, John 45
Williams, Josie 216
Williams, Kiara 189
Williams, Laura 51
Williams, Paige 161
Williams, Rubin 228
Wilmes, Adam 44
Wilson, Christina Nicole 40
Wilson, Danielle 217
Wilson, Luke 233
Wilson, Nolan 214
Wingler, Jaden 202
Wink, Nicole 93
Winquest-La Ponsie,
  Alexis 163
Wise, Ben 70
Wise, Emma 178
Wisniewski, Maren 61
Wittmer, Christina Leann . 171
Wittmer, Hannah 153
Witzerman, Matthew 165
Wolford, Hunter 190
Wollet, Paige 215
Woo, David 72
Wood, Emily 177
Wood, Lauren 228
Woodard, Nina 142
Woolsey, Kaleigh 104
Woolwine, Nicole 94
Wright, Brittany 33
Wright, Emily 239
Writt, Ethan 201
Wrobleski, Billie 64
Wyatt, Elijah 220
Wyzlic, Makenzie 128

Yahl, William 163
Yarbrough, Kayla 16
Yeager, Alyssa 57
Yeager, Megan 135
Yee, Megan 40
Yerra, Sai 203
Yingling, Morgan 182
Yocum, Everly 178
Yoder, Christopher Dean ... 188
Yoder, Jeremy 191
Yoo, Jin 165
Yoon, Grace 152
Yost, Shareece 106
Young, Sydney 170
Yu, Alyson 219
Yun, Christopher 94
Yust, Kyle 214
Zaborney, John 156
Zaremba, Anna 238
Zhang, Ellen 129
Zhang, Gary 200
Zhu, Xinlei 147
Ziebarth, Kaylin 30
Zillick, Kaitlyn 229
Zimmerman, Carlee 12
Zimmerman, Kelsy 76
Zoller, Alisa 87
Zuercher, Isaiah 243